T0339435

Trust in Epistemology

Trust is fundamental to epistemology. It features as theoretical bedrock in a broad cross-section of areas, including social epistemology, the epistemology of self-trust, feminist epistemology, and the philosophy of science. Yet epistemology has seen little systematic conversation with the rich literature on trust itself. This volume aims to promote and shape this conversation. It encourages epistemologists of all stripes to dig deeper into the fundamental epistemic roles played by trust, and it encourages philosophers of trust to explore the epistemological upshots and applications of their theories. The contributors explore such issues as the risks and necessity of trusting others for information, the value of doing so as opposed to relying on oneself, the mechanisms underlying trust's strange ability to deliver knowledge, whether depending on others for information is compatible with epistemic responsibility, whether self-trust is an intellectual virtue, and the intimate relationship between epistemic trust and social power.

This volume, in Routledge's new series on trust research, will be a vital resource to academics and students not just of epistemology and trust but also of moral psychology, political philosophy, the philosophy of science, and feminist philosophy—and to anyone else wanting to understand our vital yet vulnerable-making capacity to trust others and ourselves for information in a complex world.

Katherine Dormandy is an assistant professor of philosophy at the Institute for Christian Philosophy and the Digital Science Center, University of Innsbruck, and works on epistemology, the philosophy of trust, and the philosophy of religion.

Routledge Studies in Trust Research

Series Editors:
Rosalind Searle and Ann-Marie Nienaber

Trust in Epistemology

Edited by Katherine Dormandy

Routledge
Taylor & Francis Group

NEW YORK AND LONDON

First published 2020
by Routledge
605 Third Avenue, New York, NY 10017

and by Routledge
2 Park Square, Milton Park, Abingdon, Oxon, OX14 4RN

First issued in paperback 2021

Routledge is an imprint of the Taylor & Francis Group, an informa business

Library of Congress Cataloging-in-Publication Data
A catalog record for this book has been requested

ISBN 13: 978-1-03-208871-6 (pbk)
ISBN 13: 978-1-138-57003-0 (hbk)

Typeset in Sabon
by Apex CoVantage, LLC

Contents

SECTION 3
Trust and Epistemic Responsibility

SECTION 4
The Vulnerabilities of Trust

Acknowledgments

This volume arose from the conference "Philosophical Dimensions of Trust" held at the Institute for Christian Philosophy at the University of Innsbruck in December 2016. I'd like to thank all of the conference participants, as well as those who helped put it together, including Monika Datterl, Susannah Haas, Federica Malfatti, and Ksenia Scharr. Thanks for discussion and input on this book go to Sandy Goldberg, Christoph Jäger, and Jesper Kallestrup, as well as many who anonymously reviewed individual chapters. Thanks to Mary Del Plato, Eswari Maruthu, and the rest of the team at Routledge, including the editors of the Routledge Studies in Trust Research, Rosalind Searle and Ann-Marie Nienaber. I would also like to thank the Austrian Science Fund (FWF) for generously funding both the conference and the work on this book. Thanks finally to Michael Dormandy for his encouragement and support throughout this project.

—Katherine Dormandy, University of Innsbruck,
April 2019

1 Introduction

An Overview of Trust and Some Key Epistemological Applications

Katherine Dormandy

Trust in other people and ourselves is fundamental to accomplishing our aims. These include epistemic aims, such as the acquisition of knowledge, evidence, or understanding; the cultivation of intellectual virtue; and the overcoming of epistemic injustice. There are copious philosophical literatures on both trust and epistemology, yet scholars from each are only beginning to draw on the other. Much conversation is still needed, and this volume aims to promote and shape it.

The authors focus on the role that trust plays in epistemology. This is called for because, with some exceptions to be discussed later, it is not uncommon for epistemologists to regard trust as simply part of the philosophical wallpaper: as a precondition for testimonial knowledge (when directed toward others) and for rationality (when directed toward oneself), but of limited interest in its own right.

A précis of the contributions can be found in Section 3. Before that, to facilitate the conversation between the philosophies of trust and knowledge, I give an overview of the trust literature and then of six central issues concerning epistemic trust. The survey of trust in Section 1 zeroes in on the kinds of expectations that trust involves (1.1), trust's characteristic psychology (1.2), and what makes trust rational (1.3). The discussion of epistemic trust focuses on its role in testimony (2.1), the epistemic goods that we trust for (2.2), the significance of epistemic *trust* in contrast to reliance (2.3), what makes epistemic trust rational (2.4), and epistemic self-trust (2.5 and 2.6).

1. Theories of Trust

We can trust objects, such as shelves or software, as well as persons. My topic here is trust in persons. Accounts are too varied to systematize neatly, so I will list some salient features on the basis of which they may be grouped.

One feature that I will mention only to set aside concerns how many relata the trust relation has: three, two, or even one. With three-place trust, one person trusts another for some end, such as to be driven to the airport. With two-place trust, one person has a trusting attitude toward another even if there is no particular end for which he trusts her. And with one-place trust, he is simply a trusting person: he goes through life with a high degree of "basal security" (Jones 2004). There is ample room for research into two- and one-place trust,[1] but three-place will be the focus of this introduction. One reason is that epistemic trust certainly involves three-place trust, namely for certain epistemic goods (see Section 2.1), and this holds regardless of whether three-place trust is basic or can be understood in terms of a lesser-place trust.

Three-place trust essentially involves the truster's *relying* on the trustee for something; this amounts roughly to working into his plans the supposition that she will do what he is relying on her for (Holton 1994, 68).

Beyond this common view that (three-place) trust entails reliance, there is widespread disagreement about what else it involves. I will look at three areas of debate.

1.1. Predictive and Normative Expectations

In a trust relationship, the truster is commonly taken to have certain expectations, either predictive or normative, toward the trustee. A *predictive* expectation is an expectation *that* someone will do something—for example, that the trustee will do what you are trusting her for. A *normative* expectation is an expectation *of* someone to do something—for example, the expectation *of* the trustee to come through. Predictive and normative expectations can come apart: one partner expects *that* the other will wash the dishes (because he usually washes them when she has worked late) without expecting *of* him that he'll do it (it may, strictly speaking, be her turn). And she can expect *of* him that he will wash them (it is his turn tonight) but not expect *that* he will do so (because he often forgets).

One way to group accounts of trust is by the types of expectation that they posit. There are four views. One says that predictive expectations alone are constitutive of trust; I'll call this the *mere-predictive account* (Dasgupta 1988; Hardin 1993; Coleman 1990, chapter 5). Another says that trust is constituted by predictive and normative expectations; we may call this the *combined account* (Baier 1986, 1991; Nickel 2007; McMyler 2011; Cogley 2012; Keren 2014, this volume). The third, which I'll call the *mere-normative* account, says that only normative expectations are constitutive (Holton 1994; Becker 1996; Jones 1996, 2004; Hinchman 2005; Faulkner 2007; Darwall 2017). There is conceptual space for a fourth account, on which trust does not necessarily come with any expectations at all, being characterized instead, for example, in terms of the psychological profiles discussed in Section 1.2, or on which there is no single account of trust (Simpson 2012). But this section limits discussion to the three accounts on which trust comes with expectations of one form or another. In considering how each type of expectation may feature in trust, we will see some plusses and minuses of each account.

Let's look first at predictive expectations. Accounts positing them differ over how strong the predictive expectations need to be; two alternative requirements have developed. What I'll call a *strong* predictive-expectations requirement says that the truster must *believe* that the trustee will come through (Hieronymi 2008; Keren 2014, this volume; McMyler 2011). What I'll call a *weak* requirement says, more generally, that he may harbor any kind of positive expectation, ranging from belief to a probability assignment just above one-half (Hardin 1993; Hawley 2014a).[2]

The strong predictive-expectations requirement is motivated by the following sort of case (Hieronymi 2008, 218): you accept your friend's invitation to dinner, but are subsequently invited to a clashing event. Unbeknownst to you, your friend learns of the conflict. As a result, he does not believe that you will make good on your dinner commitment, so when you turn up he expresses pleased surprise. Hieronymi argues that you have cause to be dismayed at his response, on the grounds that his disbelief displays a lack of trust in you.

Against the view that trust involves strong predictive expectations, however, is the observation that trust is voluntary, whereas beliefs are not (Holton 1994): a person can choose to trustingly rely on someone even if his confidence that she will come through amounts to less than full-on belief. Indeed, trust can be "therapeutic" (Horsburgh 1960, 346; Faulkner 2007, 886): you might trust someone simply for the sake of encouraging her to grow in trustworthiness, even if you do not believe that she will come through. The classic example is of a father, aiming to cultivate trustworthiness in his teenage daughter; he goes away for the weekend, trusting her not to trash the house even though his confidence that she won't is too low to constitute belief (Jones 2004, 5). These observations support the claim that if trust requires predictive expectations, the requirement is weak rather than strong.

The mere-predictive view of trust might posit either a strong or a weak requirement; what it insists on is that trust is constituted by predictive expectations alone, not normative ones. With this view, most commonly held in the social sciences, trusting someone is simply a matter of incorporating her anticipated actions into your plans. This view is argued to be insufficient to capture full-fledged trust (Baier 1986; Holton 1994; Nickel 2007; Ruokonen 2013; Kallestrup, this volume). The criticism is that making plans on the basis of a person's predicted behavior, by itself, is not trust, but mere *reliance*. To see what this distinction amounts to, consider the oft-cited example of Kant, whose habits were allegedly so regular that his neighbors could set their clocks to the time at which he left his house each day. Kant's neighbors could *rely* on him to be punctual, but they cannot be said to have *trusted* him for this. They would have no cause to feel betrayed, for example, should he have overslept one day (Baier 1986, 234). Yet trust legitimates such reactive attitudes: it is appropriate for the truster to feel grateful if the trustee comes through and to feel betrayed or let down if she does not (see Dormandy, this volume chapter 10, and Hinchman 2017 for discussions of betrayal).[3] Trust, unlike mere reliance, comes with norms that make reactive attitudes appropriate.

A closer look reveals that trust comes with other norms too. One is that the trustee ought to clearly signal her acceptance of trust (Jones 2017) and do her reasonable best to come through for the truster. Another is that the truster ought not micromanage the trustee's efforts (Baier 1991, 117). A third is that both parties ought to represent their intentions toward each other authentically (Frost-Arnold 2014a). None of these norms applies in the case of Kant's neighbors timing their clocks to his movements. The difference is that Kant and his neighbors are not engaged in a cooperative relationship, so their actions swing free from obligation or responsiveness to each other. In a trust relationship, by contrast, each party must take the other into account, at least with respect to accomplishing the end being trusted for (Greco, this volume, discusses the relationship between cooperation and trust).

This due consideration of the other party that characterizes trust over mere reliance can be understood in terms of *care* (Baier 1986, 1991; Becker 1996; Jones 1996; Cogley 2012; Hinchman 2017; Grasswick 2018). It is not that one party is expected to *feel caring* toward the other, but rather that the actions normatively expected in trust are actions characteristic of care. Each party grants the other a measure of discretion as to how to best care for him: the truster leaves it to the trustee to determine when and how to come through, and the trustee exercises discernment in how best to come through for the truster in his context. For example, if your neighbor trusts you to water his plants while he is away, then he leaves it to you to decide how to fit this activity into your day. As for you, you might fulfill his trust by doing something beyond just watering his plants: for example, in the surprising event that you also discover his tap running, you turn it off. His explicit trust in you is for the plants, but there is an area of discretion surrounding this task that may sometimes extend to other things (Baier 1986; Hinchman 2017). The norms of trust, in summary, preside over a cooperative relationship of care.

If trust, as opposed to mere reliance, comes with special norms, then it surely constitutively involves normative expectations, whether or not it also involves predictive ones. If this is so, the mere-predictive account is mistaken. It may capture one phenomenon that we sometimes call "trust," but it misses the normatively rich sort just described. The philosophical literature tends to reserve the term "trust" for the latter phenomenon. On this picture, the expectations of trust are characterized either by the combined account or the mere-normative one; as for the mere-predictive account, this is thought to describe mere reliance. I will follow this usage here.

But which of the two normative accounts is preferable? The only difference between them concerns whether they think that trust involves only normative expectations or predictive ones too. To adjudicate between them, let's look more closely at the role of predictive expectations in trust. Recall that there are two alternative predictive-expectations requirements—strong and weak—and that if trust includes one of them, it is arguably the weak one, since trust seems compatible with greater doubt than full-fledged belief permits. However, it bears asking whether trust can withstand greater doubt still: perhaps it does not require any (positive) predictive expectations at all. This would suggest a mere-normative account over a combined one. Let's consider what such an account might look like.

A mere-normative account might be mild or extreme. A *mild* version says that although trust does not require *positive* predictive expectations, it is incompatible with negative ones. That is, you can count as trusting someone even if you suspend judgment about whether she will come through, but not if you think her *unlikely* to. I won't linger on this view here, because I want to explore the extreme form of the mere-normative account. This version says that trust *is* compatible with negative predictive expectations—that is, with the expectation that the trustee will let one down.

One might be tempted to reject this suggestion on conceptual grounds. The thought would be that the idea of trusting someone whom you think is more likely than not to fail you is incoherent. After all, isn't the whole point of trust to obtain what you are trusting for? It is difficult to engage with this objection without simply trading intuitions. But let me spell out a scenario in which trust—or what I will provisionally call trust—is compatible with negative predictive expectations. It is a situation in which the point is *not* to obtain what the person is trusting for, but some extrinsic end.

The example I have in mind is therapeutic trust. Recall the father trusting his teenage daughter with the house for the weekend: we may imagine that his primary aim is not to preserve his house in one piece, but to cultivate trustworthiness in his daughter. And this is compatible with thinking her more likely than not to trash the house. He presumably *hopes* that she will take good care of the house, but he may judge that even if she trashes it, the exercise will still cultivate trustworthiness in the long run (say, through her processing her emotions of feeling sorry). Indeed, the father might judge that there is no more effective way to teach his daughter trustworthiness and that the risk to the house is therefore worth it. So the extreme version of the mere-normative account cannot so easily be rejected on the grounds that the point of trust is just to achieve what you are trusting for.

The objector might simply deny that the father *trusts* his daughter, as opposed to simply acting as if he does (Keren 2014, 2610–11). In cases of real trust, one might say, the purpose *is* to achieve what you are trusting for, and here you cannot count as trusting if you have a negative predictive expectation that the trustee will deliver. In response, we may envision another scenario that calls this stark conceptual claim into question: it is one in which you *can* trust—or do what I'll provisionally call trusting—even if your sole aim *is* to obtain the thing that you are trusting for. This may happen if there is unfortunately no more effective way to obtain it. If I am dangling from a cliff, I might trust my bitterest enemy to hoist me up, knowing that the only alternative is plummeting to certain death. I may think it more probable than not that she will let me fall, but I may desperately trust her in the blind hope that she will be responsive either to my plight or at least to what is normatively expected of her. And this cannot be chalked up to mere reliance as long as there are norms in place and my attitude (albeit without much hope) presupposes them.

So the extreme version of the mere-normative view cannot be so easily dismissed (and thus nor, presumably, can the mild one). But determining whether the two cases I have described are conceptually admissible examples of trust would take us too far afield.

A final question remains: What is the source of the norms of trust relationships? One possibility is that they are moral, so that doing right by someone in a trust relationship is a way of *doing right* (Baier 1986; Holton 1994; Nickel 2007; Faulkner 2011; McMyler 2011; Frost-Arnold 2013; Hinchman 2017; Darwall 2017). The idea is not simply that the actions performed in trust relationships are answerable to morality in general—for every action is so answerable, including those not involving trust. It is rather that trust relationships come with special moral norms of their own. Consider an example: it is a general moral truth that if I steal your cake, I have done something wrong. However, if you *trust* me not to steal it and I accept your trust, then if I steal it anyway, I have committed an additional moral infraction above and beyond stealing: I have betrayed your trust.[4]

Against the moral view stands the observation that some instances of trust and trustworthiness—such as between members of a mafia—are patently *immoral* and that some instances of betrayal—say, to prevent a crime—are good (Baier 1986; Mullin 2005; Jones 2017). Jones (2017) rejects the moral view (as does Becker 1996), arguing that trust, though constrained by moral norms, has an intrinsic, non-moral, normativity of its own. Mafia partners, in Jones's view, can instantiate good trust even as the actions that this involves are wrong. However, the observation that trust relationships can be immoral and betrayal good does not compel us to Jones's view.[5] One could hold that the norms of trust are *pro tanto*, so that the goodness of upholding them in a given situation can be outweighed by other moral norms.[6]

In summary, there is widespread agreement that trust, as opposed to mere reliance, comes with normative expectations, but there is disagreement over what sorts of norms are at issue and over the necessity of positive predictive expectations.

1.2. *The Psychology of Trust*

Beyond predictive or normative expectations, there are other psychological features that many think are constitutive of trust. A second division among accounts concerns these. The views tend to focus on the psychology of the truster, but we can infer from them a corresponding psychology of the trustee. More specifically, we can infer a corresponding psychology of a trustee *who accepts the trust*. It is possible to be a trustee, in the sense of being trusted by someone, yet to not accept his trust: you might be unaware that he is trusting you, or have signalled unwillingness to do what he needs. The accounts to be discussed here concern trustees who do accept the trust. Note finally that accepting trust does not entail *being trustworthy*, so discussions like those of Daukas (2006), Jones (2012b), and Simpson (2013) that explore trustworthiness cannot automatically be imported into a discussion of the psychology characteristic of a trustee.

There are roughly three types of account of the psychology of trusting and accepting trust.[7] On the first, the truster relies on the trustee to be motivated to come through for him, where he takes this motivation of the trustee's to be self-interest (Coleman 1990, chapter 5; Hardin 1993). The corresponding account of accepting trust would thus say that it is self-interest that motivates the trustee to come through.

The self-interest account is standardly paired with one of the two views on which trust involves predictive expectations,[8] but there is no entailment between a self-interest view and a predictive-expectations view. You can rely on someone to come through out of self-interest, without expecting that she will be competent to do so (you might, for instance, be in the unfortunate situation, described in Section 1.1, of lacking better options), and you can predict that someone will come through without relying on her self-interest (you may rely, for instance, on her goodwill; see later).

However, the self-interest account *does* seem to entail that trust does *not* come with normative expectations (Ruokonen 2013; Kallestrup, this volume). Why? Because it is hard to see how a relationship defined in terms of self-interest and reliance on self-interest could *also* be answerable to the special moral norms of trust. For example, in such a relationship, it does not seem legitimate for the truster to expect *of* the trustee that she perform any actions that would not serve the latter's interests—after all, this is not part of the terms of their cooperation; so failing to come through cannot legitimately be met with feelings of betrayal. Consider the signing of a real estate contract: when seller and buyer show up and sign, gratitude is less appropriate than relief, and a buyer who pulls out at the last minute might legitimately cause annoyance, but not feelings of betrayal. When self-interest is (and is accepted as) the motivating factor in a relationship, what we have is not trust, but mere reliance.

One might think that there is a version of the self-interest view that leaves room for the special moral normativity of trust. On the "encapsulated-interest" view, the truster relies on the trustee to adopt his interests as her own (Hardin 1993). A trustee can adopt a truster's interests for unselfish reasons, such as because she cares about him—and relationships of care *are* governed by special moral norms. So it would seem that the encapsulated-interest account can characterize trust, in the richly normative sense, over and above reliance. But this conclusion is too quick. On the encapsulated-interest view, if special moral norms enter into a case of trust, they do so not as part of the trust itself. Instead, they are smuggled in by whatever aspect of the relationship, extrinsic to the trust, motivates the trustee to adopt the truster's interests in the first place. If she is motivated by her care for him, then the special normativity comes from the care; but if she is motivated by self-interest, it remains unclear, in the encapsulated-interest view, where the special moral normativity of trust might come from. As long as trust itself is characterized only in terms of self-interest, it lacks the normativity that would make it anything more than reliance. The self-interest view, then, is more appropriately called a view of mere reliance.

The second account of the psychology of trust also turns on the truster's ascribing a certain motive to the trustee. But this motive, unlike self-interest, is other-directed. Views differ over what this other-directed motive is. Some say that it is goodwill toward the truster or toward some shared project (Baier 1986, 1991; Jones 1996; Becker 1996),[9] and others say that it is the trustee's awareness that the truster is depending on her (Hinchman 2005; Faulkner 2007; Jones 2004; McMyler 2011; Ruokonen 2013). Still others say that the trustee is motivated by moral uprightness (McLeod 2000). We may infer a corresponding account of accepting trust, on which the trustee has the requisite other-directed motive.

How does the other-directed account of trust's psychology square with accounts of its expectations? The other-directed account does not entail, and is not entailed by, the claim that trust involves *predictive* expectations. Again, you can take a trustee to be motivated to come through for you without thinking that she will (she may be incompetent), and you can think that she will come through for you without thinking that her reason for doing so is other-directed. A parallel point holds for normative expectations. The other-directed account does not entail that trust has any normative expectations: ascribing or having goodwill does not entail the existence of norms that mandate or legitimate certain sorts of behavior. Nor do normative accounts of trust's expectations entail an other-directed view of its motives: it might be legitimate to expect of someone that she do something even if she does not happen to be motivated by some other-directed concern to do it. That said, some other-directed views of trust's psychology add a mere-normative account of its expectations (Becker 1996; Jones 2004; Hinchman 2005; Faulkner 2007; Darwall 2017), and others add a combined account of its expectations (Baier 1986, 1991; McMyler 2011; Cogley 2012).

Motives feature prominently in explaining people's behavior, so motive-based accounts have the advantage of explaining why the trustee would accept the burden of trust to begin with. But one problem with such accounts is that they have trouble supplying a corresponding account of *distrust* (Hawley 2014b). The key to this argument is that the theoretical tools that feature in your account of trust should also be able to account for distrust, yet the tools of the motive-based account cannot do this.

Hawley argues this by listing and rejecting some ways in which motive-based accounts might construe distrust (I'll limit this discussion to her arguments for accounts in which the motive is other-directed). Such an account might say, first, that distrusting someone is simply a matter of not trusting her—that is, of declining to ascribe to her an other-directed motive (and hence declining to rely on her on account of such an ascription). But this is not sufficient for distrust (Hawley *ibid.*). For example, most of us do not rely on our colleagues to buy us champagne, the reason being that we do not ascribe them an other-directed motive to do so. Yet this does not mean that we *distrust* our colleagues vis-à-vis the provision of champagne; rather, we neither trust nor distrust them. Second, an other-directed motive account might suggest that distrust is a matter of ascribing *negative* other-directed motives to the trustee, such as ill will. But such an ascription is not necessary for distrust: a putative trustee might bear you no ill will whatsoever (she may, for instance, just be interested in enriching herself), yet you might still distrust her (*ibid.*, 6). Finally, an other-directed motive account might suggest that distrust is a matter of ascribing negative motives, if not toward the (putative) truster himself, then toward the prospect of his obtaining the thing that he would trust for. But this is not sufficient for distrust: someone may be motivated to thwart your aims without meriting your distrust. For example, she may, in a perfectly honorable manner, be running a campaign for your political opponent (*ibid.*). Here too, you neither trust nor distrust her vis-à-vis your aim of getting elected.

The proponent of the motive-based view might respond by denying that distrust must be accounted for by the same mechanisms used to account for trust: although an account that does so may be more theoretically elegant, there is little empirical reason to think that the world will conform to our aesthetic preferences.

This suggestion has bite if no means can be found to account for trust and distrust simultaneously. But Hawley argues that there is such an account. This brings us to the third view of the psychology of trust: the *commitment* or *obligation* account (respectively Hawley 2014b; Nickel 2007).[10] Here, the truster ascribes to the trustee not a specific motive, but rather a commitment or an obligation to do what she is trusted to do. This commitment is compatible with various motives, other-directed or self-directed.[11] Trusting someone, then, includes both thinking that she is committed (or obligated) to coming through and relying on her to do so, and distrusting her is thinking that she is committed (or obligated) to coming through, yet *declining* to rely on her. From this psychology of the truster we may infer that someone who accepts trust is committed to coming through.[12]

Note that thinking that someone is committed to doing something is different from expecting that she will do it, so the commitment account does not entail that trust comes with predictive expectations. Nor does the claim that trust involves predictive expectations entail that the truster ascribes a commitment to the trustee (he may think that she will come through for reasons independent of a commitment). What about normative accounts of the truster's expectations? The commitment view does entail that the truster has normative expectations of the trustee. The reason is that commitment only makes sense against the backdrop of norms governing the keeping of commitments. A normative account of trust's expectations, however, does not entail the commitment account, since you can expect *of* a person that she come through for you, and rely on her to do so, without thinking that she is committed to doing it.

I have discussed two groupings of accounts of what trust is: one in terms of the sort of expectations it involves, and the other focusing on its psychology; I'll now turn to what makes trust rational.

1.3. Rational Trust

The third grouping of accounts of trust centers on how to construe its rationality. One thing that is plausibly involved in rational trust is evidence. Yet trust and evidence are often contrasted, with trust portrayed as constitutively opposed or unresponsive to evidence (Baker 1987, 1; Hardwig 1991, 693; Jones 1996, 15; Becker 1996; Faulkner 2007, 876; Hieronymi 2008, 222; McGeer 2008, 240; Grasswick, this volume). How does the idea that trust can be rational, and that rational trust involves evidence, fit with the supposed contrast between evidence and trust? The key lies in seeing what makes actions in general rational and how sometimes even rational actions can go beyond one's evidence. We will then see how these considerations apply to the actions of reliance involved in trust.

What makes an action rational is that it is the best means available to the agent, at least as far as he can tell on the basis of his evidence, for achieving an end that he values. We may construe evidence broadly, as including any reason for belief, including experiential reasons and intellectual seemings. Evidence helps an agent determine how the world is and thus shape his actions accordingly: it tells him which actions are the best means available, all things considered, to achieving his valued end. To see what makes trust rational, then, we must look at the different sorts of end that it can promote and at the role that evidence plays in cases where rational trust goes beyond it.

One end that trust might promote is simply that of obtaining what the truster is trusting for: a lift from the airport, emotional safety in a relationship, and so forth. In many such cases, trust is rational simply when the truster has sufficient evidence that the trustee will deliver and that there is no better way to achieve this aim. But not in all cases: as we saw in Section 1.1, trust can sometimes be rational even when the truster *lacks* sufficient evidence that the trustee will come through.[13] This can happen when the thing that he is trusting her for is worth a risk and there is no better way to obtain it (think of my enemy pulling me up from the cliff edge). Here, the evidence that will make his trust rational pertains primarily to whether trusting her is the best way to attain the end in question (including the costs of the risk), even if it is merely the best of an assortment of bad ways.[14] On the specific matter of whether the trustee will come through, the trust here goes beyond the truster's evidence—yet his trust, because it fits his evidence on these other matters, is still rational.

Another sort of end that trust might promote, as we saw in Section 1.1, is extrinsic to the trust itself: it is something other than the objective for which the truster is trusting. Recall our example of the father therapeutically trusting his teenage daughter not to trash the house while he is away.[15] Here, the evidence needed to rationalize the father's trust need not primarily concern whether his daughter will keep the house in one piece, but—more importantly—the value of teaching her trustworthiness and whether leaving her with the house (whether or not she takes good care of it) is the best way available to him to do so, even if it is the best of a bad lot.

These considerations point to the falsehood of what we may call the *narrow evidential constraint*.[16] This constraint says that trusting someone to do something is only rational if your total evidence on balance supports the belief that she will do it (Hardin 1993; Coleman 1990, chapter 5). "Belief" here may be understood, in the terms given in Section 1.1, as a strong, as opposed to a weak, predictive expectation. The narrow evidential constraint is surely true in some cases, such as when you cannot afford a risk, or when there may be better options for achieving your end than trusting (Simpson 2017). But as a general constraint on rational trust, the narrow evidential constraint is false (Frost-Arnold 2014b; Simpson *ibid.*). It is too narrow in two respects. First, as we have seen, the evidence that rationalizes trust concerns more than whether the trustee will come through, and second, trust is made rational not just by the truster's evidence but also by his value of the end that he seeks to promote.

We may summarize this observation as what I'll call the *broad evidential constraint*. This says that trusting someone to do something is only rational if it is sensitive to (i) the values that you assign to particular outcomes and (ii) the balance of your total evidence, not just about whether the trustee will come through but also about the likelihood that particular actions will yield particular outcomes. The broad evidential constraint brings the two apparently conflicting ideas into harmony: that trust is made rational by evidence, but that trust—even when rational—often exceeds evidence, at least about whether the trustee will come through.

I have left many issues out of this brief overview of trust. One is the question of whether there is a unified account of trust at all or whether it is a pluralistic phenomenon (Simpson 2012; Kappel 2014); we have already seen that two competing phenomena are sometimes called "trust," and I have followed the literature in calling one "trust" and the other "mere reliance." Another important topic is what makes for *trustworthiness* (Jones 2012b; Simpson 2013; Daukas 2006) and whether this is a virtue. Yet another is what betrayal of trust amounts to (see Hinchman 2017 and Dormandy, this volume), and another is what value lies in trusting others as opposed to relying on oneself (see Simpson's and Fricker's contributions to this volume). These issues must remain undiscussed here in the interest of turning to the way in which trust features in epistemic contexts.

2. Epistemic Trust

Epistemic trust is trust for epistemic goods, such as knowledge or recognition as a knower (see Section 2.2). Our gateway to a discussion of epistemic trust will be a topic in which it features heavily: the justification of beliefs formed on testimony. Examining this context for epistemic trust will help us isolate some of its general features, including two types of epistemic good that we may trust other people for (Section 2.2) and the characteristics that make it *trust* instead of mere reliance (Section 2.3). I'll then discuss what makes epistemic trust rational (Section 2.4). I will end with a discussion of the extent to which these aspects of epistemic trust in others apply to epistemic trust in oneself (Sections 2.5 and 2.6).

2.1. Epistemic Trust in Testimony

Testimony occurs when one person, a speaker, tells something to another, a hearer.[17] In testifying, the speaker gives the hearer the option of believing what she says on the basis of the fact that she tells it to him. Some have resisted the idea that belief in testimony can ever be epistemically beneficial (in this volume, see Simpson's discussion of Locke and Keren's discussion of revisionism), but contemporary epistemologists largely agree that belief in testimony, done right, is an important source of knowledge.

But much debate concerns what believing rightly on testimony amounts to—how the hearer's belief, should he take up the speaker's offer, can be justified or constitute knowledge. This concern arises because the hearer's evidence, if he has any, pertains not to the domain under discussion, but rather to the speaker (E. Fricker 2006). After all, if the hearer had enough evidence about the domain, he could justifiably form the belief on his own. Most views of testimonial justification agree that the hearer in a testimonial scenario trusts the speaker, but they differ over what relevance this fact has to the hearer's justification; so I will look at some views of testimony through the lens of the role that they assign to trust (but see Greco, this volume, for a more detailed taxonomy of views).

To make matters more tractable, I will limit discussion to what Hinchman has called "consummated" testimonial exchanges (2005, 567)—that is, those in which the hearer *believes the speaker*. These are exchanges in which the speaker purports to be trustworthy (i.e., sincere and competent) and the hearer believes what she says because he takes her at face value.[18] The question for theories of testimonial justification, then, is what justifies the hearer in *believing the speaker*? And our question in this section is what role the various theories of testimonial justification assign to epistemic trust.

One view, *reductionism*, says that what justifies the hearer's belief is the balance of his total evidence[19] about how likely the speaker is to speak truly (E. Fricker 1994, 1995; Lyons 1997; Lipton 1998; Adler 2002). This includes anything that may be relevant to her trustworthiness, most saliently any empirical evidence that he may have about her and speakers relevantly like her. If the speaker and hearer have a relationship of trust, then this fact gets thrown in with the rest of the hearer's evidence, typically raising the probability that she will speak truly. But if they have no such relationship, then the hearer simply takes account of whatever other evidence he has, such as the fact that the speaker is competent or that her interest in this case lies in speaking truly. According to reductionism, then, facts about trust do not play any special justificatory role other than being one consideration among others that contribute to the hearer's total evidence about the speaker's likelihood of speaking truly.[20]

Reductionism is so-called because it claims that testimonial justification can be understood reductively in terms of the familiar sort of justification made available by evidence. *Anti-reductionism*, by contrast, says that there is something special about the testimonial act that delivers justification in a way that bypasses the need for the hearer to appeal to his total evidence. On this view, there is only one type of situation in which a hearer's total evidence is relevant: when that evidence includes defeaters—that is, evidence indicating that the speaker will not in this case speak truly.

Versions of anti-reductionism differ over what it is about testimony that enables this bypassing of the hearer's total evidence. I will group these views according to the role that they assign to trust. What I will call *classic anti-reductionism* says that hearers have a special entitlement to believe a speaker. On some views, this entitlement is simply *a priori* (Ross 1986; Coady 1992; Burge 1993; Webb 1993). On others, it derives from the reliability of testimony or the social practices within which it occurs (Goldman 1999, 126–30; Goldberg 2010; Kappel 2014), or from the proper functioning of a cognitive mechanism for uptaking testimony (Plantinga 1993). Trust, on classic anti-reductionism, is simply the state that the hearer is in when he believes the speaker. It does not play a significant role in justifying the hearer's belief.

Another form of anti-reductionism is what I'll call *perceptual anti-reductionism* (M. Fricker 2007). Here, the epistemically unique aspect of the testimonial exchange is the hearer's perceptual experience of the speaker testifying. This perception either portrays the speaker as possessing properties that inspire the hearer's trust or delivers a holistic impression of her *as trustworthy*. This perceptual experience, a tiny subset of the hearer's total evidence, is all the evidence that he needs, though Fricker adds the virtue-theoretic proviso that this perception must be produced by the hearer's epistemic virtues. Perceptual anti-reductionism has two alternative roles for trust. First, the hearer's perception of the speaker under a trustworthy guise may *cause* him to trust and thus believe her. Second, the hearer may happen to trust the speaker already, in which case his trust itself helps cause his perception of the speaker as trustworthy. In the first case, the hearer's trust is a consequence of his perception, so it has no independent justificatory role; in the second, his trust helps bring about his perceptual evidence and thus plays an indirect justificatory role. The epistemic role of trust on perceptual anti-reductionism, then, depends on whether the hearer antecedently trusts the speaker.

A final anti-reductionist view, whose proponents give it various names but which I'll follow Hinchman (2012) in calling the *assurance view*, gives trust the most significant justificatory role.[21] Here, trust brings about the hearer's testimonial justification *directly*. It can do this because, on the assurance view, it has epistemic significance in its own right.

There are three versions of the assurance view. The first two say that the trust at issue is the *hearer's trust in the speaker*. Of these views, one is *internalist*, saying that the fact that the hearer trusts the speaker is itself evidence[22] that the speaker is trustworthy, and this evidence is what justifies the hearer's belief. This version of the assurance view resembles reductionism in its internalist appeal to evidence alone. Yet unlike reductionism, it does not consider facts about trust just one sort of evidence among many. On the contrary, the internalist version of the assurance view says that the fact that the hearer trusts the speaker *makes any other evidence epistemically unnecessary*, indeed inappropriate. Why? Because if the hearer were to consider additional evidence, this would, by definition, destroy the very trust that makes testimony justificatory (Faulkner 2011; McMyler 2011; Zagzebski 2012; Keren 2014; see also Section 2.4). For trust, on this view, is incompatible with considering one's evidence concerning whether the trustee will come through. According to the internalist assurance view, then, the hearer can bring about his own justification simply by trusting the speaker.

The second version of the assurance view criticizes this move, on the grounds that it licenses a vicious bootstrapping (Hinchman 2012). But it maintains the idea that the hearer's trust in the speaker plays a direct justificatory role. It says that the hearer's trust, instead of providing the hearer with *evidence* that the speaker will testify knowledgeably, simply *causes* her to do so, or at least causes it to be likely that she will. Why? Because trusting someone sets in gear a response on her part to meet you in your dependence. This version of the assurance view, then, is *externalist*, positing a reliable process—trusting the speaker—that tends, when conditions are right, to elicit knowledgeable testimony (Hinchman 2012; cf. McGeer 2008).

The first two versions of the assurance view, internalism and externalism, have in common that the *hearer's trust in the speaker* is what plays the direct justificatory role. A third version of the assurance view is possible, on which the epistemically relevant trust is *the speaker's trust in the hearer*. The idea is that the speaker, in testifying, puts her epistemic reputation on the line: she entrusts it to the hearer, giving him leverage over it should she fail to testify knowledgeably; in this case, he will think less of her and perhaps bring others to do so as well. The speaker's epistemic reputation, then, is like a driver's license offered as collateral for an audio-tour headset: entrusted to the hearer, this serves as a guarantee that she will not let down the trust that he, in turn, has invested in her for knowledge.[23] On this third version of the assurance view, then, the speaker's trust in the hearer directly justifies the hearer's belief on her testimony.

In summary, the prevailing views of testimonial justification all feature trust, but they do so in different ways. Reductionism says that trust can be one among many things that supplies evidence about the speaker's trustworthiness. Classic anti-reductionism construes trust as a background condition without any significant theoretical role; perceptual anti-reductionism says that the hearer's trust can play an indirect justificatory role; and the assurance view ascribes trust, on some accounts the hearer's and on others the speaker's, a direct justificatory role. Greco and McCraw, in their respective contributions to this volume, expand this discussion by arguing that there is a commonality across all cases of testimonial justification, whatever account you endorse. Greco argues that this commonality is the fact that trust is an essential constituent, and McCraw argues that it arises from the fact that the hearer exercises the virtue of proper epistemic trust.

The epistemology of testimony, with the exception of the third version of the assurance view, is concerned primarily with the hearer's trust in the speaker (a concern that Kallestrup, this volume, extends to *group* hearers and speakers). In order to achieve a more complete understanding of epistemic trust, we must redress this imbalance by contrasting it with the trust that a speaker exhibits in a hearer. The next section discusses both forms of epistemic trust.

2.2. *Epistemic Goods That We Trust For: Representational and Recognitional*

To understand epistemic trust, we must understand the epistemic goods that we trust for. In the case of testimony, there are two types of epistemic good: one that the hearer trusts the speaker for and another that the speaker trusts the hearer for.

When we think of trust for epistemic goods, it is the former that standardly comes to mind: goods for which the hearer trusts the speaker, such as knowledge, evidence, or true beliefs. Grasswick (this volume) adds *inquiry*, which someone else can do on one's behalf. I'll call these *representational* epistemic goods, for they either produce, or are aimed at producing, cognitive states that represent reality well. In trusting a speaker for representational goods, a hearer makes himself vulnerable (to practical mishaps, false belief, and the like) should she inquire irresponsibly or be dishonest and thus testify falsely, unfoundedly, or unreliably; and he does so in the context of norms that hold the speaker responsible for her words and license the hearer to feel betrayed should she fail him.

Epistemic trust is typically defined *just as* trust for representational goods (e.g. McCraw, this volume; Keren, this volume). But speakers characteristically trust hearers too, for another kind of epistemic good that I'll call *recognitional*. To see this, consider that testifying is a way of claiming epistemic status as a knower of what you testify, standardly trusting the hearer to recognize you as having that status. Epistemic recognition comes in various forms. One way of according a speaker recognition is by believing her. Another is by giving her appropriate credit as the source of the information, granting her the final say in how her words are to be interpreted, and keeping confidence if she requests it.

A speaker who trusts a hearer for epistemic recognition thereby makes herself vulnerable (Dormandy, this volume). Should she deserve recognition and the hearer decline to accord it, she may be subject to epistemic harm (M. Fricker 2007; Dotson 2011; Peet 2017). For example, not receiving the epistemic recognition that she deserves may negatively affect her epistemic self-trust (see Section 2.6 and Mikkola, this volume), and if this happens in front of third parties, it may damage her social standing as an epistemic agent. The speaker may shy away from sharing knowledge in the future, which will in turn cut her off from leaving her mark on the community's store of knowledge and will isolate her from discourse that might otherwise help her refine her own knowledge.

These harms may result from a speaker's receiving *less* epistemic recognition from hearers than she deserves. But some speakers—think of celebrities or authority figures—receive *more*, and this, too, can be epistemically harmful. For example, undeserved epistemic recognition can "spoil" a speaker, desensitizing her to her epistemic shortcomings and thus hampering her epistemic development in the long term (Medina 2013). She might place too much trust in her own reasoning or ignore her intellectual debts to others; even if she is competent in her domain, she may develop the bad intellectual habit of testifying too often, crowding out equally or more deserving speakers (Frost-Arnold 2014a).

Recognition is an epistemic good in its own right. We have just seen why this is so for speakers who merit it. But according deserving speakers epistemic recognition is also epistemically good for the hearer. Not only does this put him in a position to acquire testimonial knowledge and other representational goods from speakers, but recognition of deserving speakers *as* deserving is a form of epistemic success.

In summary, there are at least two kinds of epistemic good for which trust may be extended: representational goods, for which a hearer may trust a speaker, and recognitional goods, for which a speaker may trust a hearer.

Let's look more closely at epistemic trust, bearing in mind that it can be trust either for representational or recognitional goods.

2.3. *Epistemic Trust: More Than Mere Reliance*

We have been discussing how hearers and speakers can trust each other for epistemic goods. But they might also merely rely on each other. This occurs when one or both parties doubt that the other will abide by the norms of trust or have the requisite other-directed attitude. A hearer merely relies on a speaker for the truth (for example) if he thinks that, given the chance, she would lie or testify carelessly and that it is pure self-interest that keeps her from doing so. The speaker may, for instance, be acting as a witness in a criminal investigation for the sake of reducing her own sentence. Similarly, a speaker can merely rely on a hearer for epistemic recognition if, for example, she thinks that he does not want to accord it. In this case, she may testify because she has little choice—she may, for instance, have been subpoenaed to testify before a jury that she knows is biased against her.

Given that the exchange of epistemic goods can be powered by trust or mere reliance, we may ask which of these is standard or at least more prevalent. There is reason to think that trust, rather than mere reliance, is the norm (see Grasswick, this volume, and Keren, this volume, endnote 6). For epistemic contexts standardly legitimate reactive attitudes.

A hearer may (and arguably should) feel betrayed if a speaker lies or fails to do diligence to her evidence, and the speaker may (and should) feel similarly if a hearer, for no reason, accords her less credibility than she deserves. This is certainly true of ongoing epistemic relationships (Grasswick, this volume); but even in the relationally pared-down case of a local stranger directing a tourist to the train station, it is appropriate for the tourist to feel grateful for good directions and betrayed by bad ones, and for the local to be offended if the tourist, for no apparent reason, disbelieves her.

One might think that science is an exception—that it is not trust, but mere reliance, that governs the exchange of epistemic goods. Because scientists attach such value to perceived epistemic prowess, it is surely naïve to expect that the norms of trust, let alone other-directed motives, will be enough to keep them epistemically on the straight and narrow. Indeed, is this not precisely why science comes with such stringent professional norms, which sanction shoddy data gathering or the usurping of credit due to others? These norms, and the sanctions that accompany them, aim to ensure that it is in scientists' self-interest to be epistemically reliable collaborators.

Yet closer inspection points to trust, not mere reliance, as the epistemic motor of science. One reason is that a culpable failure to come through in science licenses reactive attitudes: falsified data and the usurpation of credit are not just annoying but personally offensive. Such reactions would not be legitimate in relationships of mere reliance. A second reason is that the norms of science are arguably inadequate to deter epistemic betrayal; the prevalence of trust explains why science can function in spite of this. When it comes to the exchange of representational goods (e.g., knowledge or evidence), Hardwig (1991) argues that professional norms are inadequate to deter dishonesty on the part of speakers, such as the falsification of data, because the chances of getting caught are slim, since science is too fragmented for experts in one field to check up on the experts in another on whom they depend. Yet scientists continue to depend on each other for knowledge. And when it comes to the exchange of recognitional goods, Frost-Arnold (2013) argues that the professional norms of science are inadequate to deter hearers from maliciously declining to give epistemic recognition to deserving speakers, as when senior scientists usurp credit for the results achieved by their junior colleagues. Yet scientists do depend on each other for due credit. If Hardwig's and Frost-Arnold's arguments are on target, it would seem that a large dose of *trust*, as opposed to mere reliance, is needed. What scientists depend on in colleagues from other fields, and what junior scientists seek and often find in senior colleagues, are personal commitment, other-directed motives, and moral sensibilities (Hardwig *ibid.*, Frost-Arnold *ibid.*). And if science, which due to its professionalism is among the least "touchy-feely" of domains, is marked by epistemic trust rather than mere reliance, then all the more so will other sorts of more casual epistemic relationship be.

If we take seriously the idea that the exchange of epistemic goods is standardly powered by trust instead of mere reliance, then another aspect of epistemic trust becomes apparent. Trust, as we saw, comes with norms governing a cooperative relationship of care between persons; this means that we can expect epistemic trust relationships to involve a species of *epistemic* care (Hinchman 2012; Grasswick 2018 and this volume). What does epistemic care look like in the case of the two types of epistemic good?

When it comes to the hearer's trust in the speaker for representational goods, Hinchman (2012, 2017) and Grasswick (2018 and this volume) give an answer. Hinchman notes that people's needs, including their epistemic ones, differ from one context to another. Accordingly, he argues, a hearer trusts a speaker for more than just knowledge; he trusts her for knowledge *tailored to his specific epistemic needs*. Hinchman gives the example of a hearer with a nut allergy who asks about the contents of a snack bowl (*ibid.*): for this hearer, much more hangs on whether the bowl contains nuts than it would for a hearer without such an allergy. Fulfilling this hearer's trust requires a speaker to bear in mind the dire consequences that false information would have for him and thus to hold herself to especially high evidential standards. Another example, not discussed by Hinchman, is that of our tourist asking for directions to the train station. If there are road closures, this hearer has different needs than he would if he asked for directions when the roads were open. A local speaker, advising him, should bear the closures in mind. While she is at it, she does well to envision how he might not notice the turnoff, which is easy to miss (it is landmarked by a red postbox). And she should *not* send him on an indirect route via the café that she owns. Cases like this show that what hearers trust speakers for is not just information in the abstract, but epistemic care in the form of information tailored to their needs. This fact is all the more evident in cases of the sort that Grasswick discusses (2018 and this volume), in which we are not trusting someone to give us knowledge, but to carry out inquiry on a topic about which we may never, ourselves, come to know, such as medicine or national security, but that is nonetheless important to us.

A parallel point applies to trust for recognitional goods. The speaker, in trusting the hearer for these, trusts him too for a kind of epistemic care suited to her context. This includes trusting him to accord her neither too little nor too much credibility, to bear in mind any practical consequences that she might face should her testimony be leaked, to triangulate her need to be heard with that of others whom she does not wish to inadvertently speak over, to understand her testimony well enough to represent it accurately to third parties (and ask follow-up questions otherwise), to competently determine which third parties can be told and which cannot, and so forth. The contextual factors that delineate a speaker's epistemic needs are legion, and a hearer who accepts her trust must be alive to them.

In summary, taking seriously the fact that epistemic trust is *trust* instead of mere reliance helps us see that what we epistemically trust others for is epistemic care: not just information or recognition, but these goods tailored to our epistemic needs in our contexts.

Having looked at some descriptive features of epistemic trust, I will now return to the question of its normativity.

2.4. Rational Epistemic Trust

Epistemic trust, like trust in general, can be rational or irrational. Consider first a speaker's trust in a hearer for epistemic recognition. This trust is rational in the same way that trust in general is rational: that is, just in case it is the best available means to achieve whatever aim the speaker has in mind in trusting the hearer with her words. This end might simply be to obtain recognition, but it might also be something else, such as furthering her message at all costs, or teaching the hearer to accord epistemic recognition appropriately. Thus, if trust in general, as I argued in Section 1.3, is subject to the broad evidential constraint, then so is trust for epistemic recognition. That is, a speaker's trust in a hearer for recognition is rational only if the speaker takes into account (i) the values that she assigns to particular outcomes of trusting as opposed to not trusting and (ii) the balance of her total evidence: about whether the hearer will, in fact, accord her recognition, but also about whether trusting him is the best available way to achieve her valued outcomes (including any costs incurred by the trust itself).

Matters are more complicated when the rationality in question is that of a hearer trusting a speaker, where what he trusts her for are representational goods such as knowledge or evidence. In this case, there are two kinds of rationality to consider. One is the decision-theoretic rationality that I have been discussing so far. Here, the rationality of the hearer's trust depends, in the familiar way, on (i) the value that he assigns to the outcome of trusting as opposed to not trusting the speaker and (ii) the balance of his total evidence about whether trusting the speaker is the best way to achieve his valued outcomes.

When it comes to decision-theoretic rationality, the hearer trusting the speaker for representational goods might have a variety of aims, nonepistemic or epistemic. First, the hearer's aim might not be epistemic. It might instead be to achieve some other end that believing the speaker would further. This might, for instance, be to avoid conflict with the speaker or, if she is testifying optimistically that he will recover from an illness, to further his prospects for doing so by believing her. In such cases it could be rational, in the decision-theoretic sense, to trust the speaker even if his total evidence does not favor her trustworthiness (at least, as long as he can bring himself to believe her despite insufficient evidence).

Second, the hearer's aim may be epistemic: to obtain the representational good for which he is considering trusting the speaker (e.g., knowledge, evidence, the truth). If his total evidence indicates that she is trustworthy and that no alternative means would secure his aim more effectively, then it is straightforwardly rational to trust her for it. But what if the hearer's total evidence does not indicate that the speaker is trustworthy? He might still, in some circumstances, be rational in trusting her in the current, decision-theoretic, sense. For example, suppose that he values the prospect of forming a true belief more than he disvalues the prospect of forming a false one or none at all, and suppose that there is no better way available to form a true belief than to trust this speaker. (His friend may claim to be innocent of a crime that she is accused of, and he wants to believe truly—but places greater value on a true belief that she is innocent than on a false belief that she is guilty, since the latter would ruin their friendship.) In this case, it could be decision-theoretically rational to form the belief—betting, so to speak, on its truth.

In summary, the first form of rational trust for representational goods is strictly decision-theoretic, depending (among other things) on the hearer's aims in trusting.

There are some sorts of epistemic aim, however, that mere decision-theoretic rationality cannot achieve for the hearer. We saw that this sort of rationality can help him form true beliefs in certain circumstances. But if his aim is to obtain something more normatively laden, such as knowledge or evidence, this sort of rationality is not enough. For even if he wound up forming a true belief, it would not count as knowledge *unless it were also epistemically rational*—that is, unless it were appropriately related to something like evidence, a virtuous epistemic character, or the like. Epistemic rationality, the second type of rationality governing trust for representational goods, we have seen already; I have been calling it *epistemic justification* (Section 2.1).[24]

On the face of it, epistemic justification looks like decision-theoretic rationality, just applied to cases in which the agent aims for the truth. But this conclusion is too quick. First, a belief can be decision-theoretically rational with respect to this aim and yet fail to be epistemically justified. A case in point is the friend scenario earlier, in which the hearer's evidence does not support the trustworthiness of his friend about her innocence, but other considerations, such as the value he places on believing truly compared to the possibility of believing falsely, make it rational to trust her anyway.[25] Second, a belief can be *irrational* in the decision-theoretic sense noted earlier and yet epistemically justified. For example, a person may aim to keep himself in the dark about the truth of some proposition, such as the end of a film that he has not yet seen—but if his friend inadvertently reveals it to him, he would be epistemically unjustified not to believe it, even though doing so goes against his aim (Kelly 2003). So, when it comes to epistemic justification, a person's values play a smaller role than they do in determining decision-theoretic rationality.[26] Epistemic justification is an *epistemic* good, whether or not any particular agent desires it or any other end it might promote.

Epistemic justification, then, differs from decision-theoretic rationality: it is not subject to the broad evidential constraint. For this constraint, as we saw in Section 1.3, takes on board not just an agent's total evidence about whether the trustee will come through but also the truster's values and the likelihood that trusting (as opposed to doing something else) will lead to his desired outcome. Yet the latter two considerations, the truster's values and aims, do not factor in epistemic justification, at least not as saliently (see endnote 26). The only factor that is a candidate for relevance to epistemic justification is the first: the hearer's total evidence about whether the speaker will come through. But this is just the narrow evidential constraint. Recall that I rejected this constraint as being too narrow to apply to rational trust in general—but perhaps this makes it just the constraint to apply to epistemic justification. In the context of epistemic justification, the narrow evidential constraint becomes the claim that trusting a speaker for knowledge (or the truth, etc.) is justified only if your total evidence on balance supports the belief that she is trustworthy.[27]

We have seen this claim before (Section 2.1): it is reductionism about testimonial justification. The various forms of anti-reductionism, by contrast, deny that a hearer is only justified in believing the speaker when his total evidence supports her trustworthiness. And some forms of the assurance view's version of anti-reductionism, as we saw, go as far as to say that the hearer should *not* employ any evidence beyond the speaker's testimony itself. Epistemically rational hearer trust, then, is a controversial matter—but whatever it amounts to, it presents a different kind of rationality than the decision-theoretic sort.

I'll finish this section with a brief discussion of the extreme claim propounded by versions of the assurance view, that epistemically justified testimonial belief involves *not* making recourse to any evidence beyond the testimony itself. What would recommend this view? One answer is that the speaker, being better situated than the hearer with respect to the truth, is likely to base her belief on better evidence than he is—and that for this reason the hearer would do well to disregard his other evidence (Keren 2007, 2014, this volume; cf. Zagzebski 2012; Constantin and Grundmann, forthcoming). Another answer is that the norms of the trust relationship are excellent guarantors of the speaker's trustworthiness—and that a hearer who seeks additional evidence violates them, thus risking this relationship (Faulkner 2007; Moran 2005; Hinchman 2012; McMyler 2011).

The assurance view is surely on to something in claiming that the trust relationship itself is epistemically significant. But it must still address why it is so significant as to upstage appeals to additional evidence, especially if such evidence happens to be easily available (or even possessed by the hearer already). That is, we need a response to the main argument supporting the narrow evidential constraint for epistemically justified testimonial belief. This argument is that a hearer's total evidence about the speaker is likelier to provide a more complete, and thus more accurate, sampling of reality than the small subset constituted by the fact of her testimony (Dormandy 2018). The answer that Keren provides (this volume) is that the hearer's trust in the speaker enables him to base his belief vicariously on *her* evidence, which is likely to be better than his. Whether this idea pans out depends on whether one person can really be said to base his belief not just on the say-so, but on the evidence (to which he himself may have no access) of another person.

In summary, epistemic trust for recognitional goods is subject to the norms of decision-theoretic rationality just like trust in general. Epistemic trust for representational goods is subject to this kind of rationality in certain cases, but is more properly governed by *epistemic* rationality (or epistemic justification), which swings freer from many of the agent's own aims and values. Whether the narrow evidential constraint applies to it, however, is controversial.

2.5. Epistemic Self-Trust as Rationally Necessary

It is not just other people in whom we invest epistemic trust—it is also ourselves. Epistemic self-trust is of great intrinsic value (Fricker, this volume). More than this, it is arguably a causal and rational precondition for all of our epistemic endeavors. A body of literature has developed that aims to show why this is so. This section sketches three prominent views of trusting oneself for representational goods, and Section 2.6 considers whether epistemic self-trust is also possible for recognitional ones.

Each argument for the rational necessity of epistemic self-trust works from a different construal of epistemic (as opposed to decision-theoretic) rationality. On Foley's view (2001), to be epistemically rational is to be able to defend yourself against epistemic criticism. His view might be thought to cast us all as irrational, for there is an important epistemic critique, launched by philosophers such as Descartes and Locke, against which we seem unable to defend ourselves: the fact that we cannot noncircularly prove the reliability of our cognitive faculties. For the belief that they are reliable relies on the assumption that they were reliable in bringing us to hold that very belief. But Foley responds that we can count as rational on his view, namely by exercising epistemic self-trust. He grants that this "leap of intellectual faith," as he styles it (*ibid.*, 19–20), is our only option—but he insists nonetheless that it is a rational one. More than this, he insists that self-trust is rational *precisely because* we have no alternative. The idea seems to be that what is rational must, on pain of violating the maxim that *ought implies can*, be located within the range of things that we are able to do. Since all that we are able to do is exercise epistemic self-trust, it is rational to do so.

The first response is that it is not obvious that we can do nothing other than exercise epistemic self-trust. There are two ways in which declining to trust yourself for knowledge and other representational goods seems possible. First, it seems possible to decline to rely on yourself for knowledge and related representational goods, at least in isolated cases when you can muddle along without a belief in a particular matter—though Foley is right that a global failure to rely on yourself would be paralyzing. Second, even in the cases where you must rely on yourself, this reliance need not amount to trust. For you might lack the requisite other-directed attitudes (such as goodwill or commitment) toward yourself, and you might not normatively expect yourself to have them. This is arguably not an epistemically healthy way to be, but it is possible. And if this is so, then self-trust is not rational simply because it is the only option. At best, self-reliance on a global scale, whether or not this also amounts to self-trust, is the only option—so at best it is this, not self-trust, that Foley shows to be rational.

Another worry is that Foley's claim that self-trust (or self-reliance) is by default rational might rationalize a dogmatic adherence to whatever our faculties deliver, for better or worse. Foley resists this consequence by arguing that, even though trusting (or relying on) himself is all that an agent can do, some ways of doing this are epistemically preferable to others. We should not, for example, rely on each individual faculty by default, but should use our other faculties to critically reflect on it. Even though doing this requires trusting those other faculties, we can test them in turn against each other and against the first faculty. Epistemic self-trust (or self-reliance), then, is rational in Foley's view because we can do no other—but only when combined with critical self-reflection.

Foley views epistemic self-trust negatively, as a fallback position given our lack of a noncircular proof of cognitive reliability. This attitude makes sense if rationality, as he claims, is a matter of defense against epistemic criticism: a noncircular proof would make for a stronger defense. But two other views, Lehrer's (1997) and Zagzebski's (2012), do not see the lack of such a proof as an epistemic liability. For they locate epistemic rationality in coherence, and on coherence views, proofs *just are* circular. Where Lehrer's and Zagzebski's views part ways is in how they construe coherence and thus rational epistemic self-trust.

On Lehrer's view (1997), epistemic rationality—or "reasonableness," as he calls it—amounts to coherence among a person's beliefs. This means that two beliefs can epistemically support each other, either directly or by supporting intermediary beliefs. (Opposed to a coherentist view of epistemic support is a foundationalist view, in which epistemic support only goes one way.) What holds a coherent belief system together, on Lehrer's view, is epistemic self-trust. More specifically, what holds it together is the agent's acceptance of Lehrer's "keystone premise:" that she is trustworthy concerning the beliefs that she accepts. What makes acceptance of the keystone premise rational? Like any self-respecting coherentist, Lehrer argues for it circularly—indeed, with two (circular) arguments. The first says that the keystone premise, a fortiori, implies the further claim that the agent is epistemically trustworthy in accepting the keystone premise itself. This further claim, in turn, makes her acceptance of the keystone premise rational—because it is rational to accept propositions with respect to which you are trustworthy. Lehrer's second argument says that the keystone premise supports everything else that the agent believes and that a subset of those things, in turn, supports the keystone premise. In this way epistemic self-trust is rationally necessary, but also epistemically justified.

A similar dogmatism worry arises for Lehrer's view as for Foley's. The keystone premise does not exclude the agent's taking herself to be *infallibly* trustworthy in the beliefs that she accepts, but this would by her lights lend infallible support to the keystone premise (Cohen 1999). Lehrer might respond by claiming that the other beliefs that the agent accepts do *not* support the infallibility version of the keystone premise, preventing her from being rational in accepting it. But this response only holds for agents whose other beliefs are like this. In principle, an agent could accept only beliefs that support her own infallibility (*ibid.*) and come out justified in Lehrer's view in so doing.

Whereas Lehrer locates rationality in the coherence among an agent's beliefs, Zagzebski (2012) takes this notion to apply to a broader whole that also includes his affective states and willings. Being epistemically rational, she says, amounts to conscientiously eliminating any cognitive dissonances that there may be among all of these aspects of oneself. Epistemic self-trust emerges on her view as the most effective means of doing so: a person should examine his cognitive, affective, and volitional states and resolve dissonances in favor of whichever he trusts the most. One might worry, however, that there are some cognitive dissonances that not even self-trust can resolve, such as those in which his self-trust itself conflicts with some other state that delivers reasons against trusting oneself. For example, an agent might think that skeptical worries about his ability to know rationally undermines the self-trust that he exercises in forming perceptual beliefs. How, on Zagzebski's view, can self-trust overcome this obstacle to coherence? Her answer is that epistemic self-trust always rationally wins out, even over cognitive states that yield reasons to question it. Why? Because we naturally trust *our self-trust itself* more deeply than any of our other states (*ibid.*, 45). So on Zagzebski's view, epistemic self-trust is rationally mandated for creatures like us—or at least for those of us who do invest greater trust in our self-trust itself than in other states. (This leaves open the possibility that there are people for whom self-trust is *not* rational, namely those of whom this empirical claim is false.) Zagzebski's position, like the other two, might seem to legitimate an uncritical dogmatism. Her response is similar to Foley's: she mandates that self-trust be exercised conscientiously.

Yet it is not clear that appeals to internalist epistemic abilities like conscientiousness or the capacity for self-criticism can play the rationally legitimating role that Zagzebski and Foley claim for them. As Mikkola (this volume) shows, human cognition is subject to many adverse influences at the implicit level that make many of us prone to overestimate or underestimate our cognitive status and abilities. She argues that these factors can sabotage the abilities of certain people—for example, the marginalized in society who are targets of negative epistemic stereotypes—in their attempts to exercise conscientious epistemic self-trust, because they will be overly cautious or self-critical. She argues that epistemically beneficial self-trust cannot be promoted by prescribing individual measures such as conscientiousness, but requires social education that aims to uproot these pernicious biases.

The views discussed in this section aim to establish the rational necessity of epistemic self-trust. What epistemic trust *is*, however, gets less discussion. The next section turns to this question.

2.6. *Epistemic Self-Trust Is More Than Reliance*

The three views just discussed differ about how and why epistemic self-trust is rationally necessary, but they share an assumption about what it is. Epistemic self-trust, they seem to agree, is not trust as such, but mere reliance. To see this reading, note that the attitude that the authors have in mind is not directed at *oneself*, but rather at one's "opinions and faculties" (Foley 2001). Zagzebski (2012) for her part says, "I trust my epistemic faculties to get me to the truth. Trusting myself in this sense is like trusting my car" (36 cf. E. Fricker 2016, 154, who says explicitly that epistemic self-trust is a matter of [mere] reliance on one's faculties).[28] Yet opinions, faculties, and cars are things, not persons, even though they belong to and are steered by persons. As such they can be relied on, but are not proper objects of trust in the morally normative sense at issue here. The importance of this point must not be underestimated. If epistemic self-trust is no more than reliance, then it is a fundamentally different sort of thing than (most of) our epistemic trust in others.[29]

One clue that there may be more to epistemic self-trust, however, comes from Zagzebski herself. She makes a point of characterizing a self as being "conscious of itself" and "the inner world of a person" (29), neither of which applies to a person's faculties or opinions taken on their own. This rich talk of selves leads us to suspect that Zagzebski, in later comparing the object of our self-trust to a car, sells self-trust short even by her own lights. There is a similar incongruence in Hinchman (2012).

As we saw earlier, he takes epistemic trust to be trust for "a distinctively epistemic species of care" (80) that can only arise in a personal relationship. Yet in discussing how trust "is realized intrapersonally" (77), he says that "you rely on your epistemic faculties" (*ibid.*). Faculties, however, cannot care for you—so it would seem that epistemic self-trust on Hinchman's view cannot be a type of trust, as opposed to mere reliance, after all.[30]

The deflationary view on which epistemic self-trust is mere reliance on one's faculties should be rejected. Although we do rely on our faculties, we also extend epistemic trust to ourselves *qua* persons—and this claim gives a better account of how we secure epistemic goods. Before arguing this, it is worth establishing that trust in onself is a psychological possibility—that is, that a person can direct the normative expectations and psychological attitudes characteristic of interpersonal trust toward herself and that she can accept her own self-trust accordingly.[31]

To see this, consider normative expectations. We can let ourselves down, a situation that normatively licenses reactive attitudes such as disappointment in ourselves. And we can and sometimes should be grateful to ourselves: although we do not tend to speak this way, teachers of self-coaching will be quick to assure us that it is a coherent sentiment and will encourage us to thank ourselves or pat ourselves on the back for a job well done. And they may explicitly encourage us to hold ourselves to high expectations on the grounds that "you know you can do it"—where the second "you" refers to the addressee, not (just) his faculties. So we do seem to have, and respond to, normative expectations of ourselves that look very much like those accompanying trust. As for the relationship-responsive attitudes, a person can have goodwill toward herself, can respond to her own needs, and can be committed to living up to her own expectations. To trust herself, she must simply rely on herself to respond to these attitudes.

But granting that trust in oneself is a live possibility, why think that it is this, rather than mere self-reliance, that secures us epistemic goods? There are two questions here. One is why think, when a person *relies* on himself for epistemic ends, that this reliance is in fact on his self and not just his faculties? The second is: supposing that the object of his reliance is his self as opposed to his faculties, why think that, in the epistemic case, this self-reliance has the additional features that make for self-trust? I'll answer each question for self-trust for representational epistemic goods, then turn to recognitional ones.

So consider representational goods, such as knowledge, true beliefs, evidence, and inquiry. In answer to the first question (i.e., why think that it is a person's self that he relies on for these, not just his faculties): although a person does rely on his faculties for these goods, he himself occupies his faculties' "control center." It is he who determines how and when to rely on them and who is thus epistemically responsible for much of their output. This means that he does not rely only on his faculties, but also on *himself* to manage them responsibly. Indeed, some go as far as to make epistemic responsibility—and thus reliance on oneself to exercise it—a necessary condition for representational goods such as knowledge (Code 1987; Montmarquet 1993; Zagzebski 1996; McCraw, this volume). Foley and Zagzebski come close to agreeing. Recall that both, in response to the objection that their views of epistemic self-trust seem to license dogmatism, appeal to epistemic responsibility, alternatively called critical self-reflection or conscientiousness, as the antidote. Yet epistemic responsibility presupposes reliance on oneself, *qua* person, to exercise it. Reliance on one's faculties is not enough.

Let's turn to the second question, why this reliance on oneself for representational goods is best construed as *trust* in oneself. The answer is that self-trust is more epistemically effective than mere self-reliance. For the person in a trust relationship with herself has more factors in place that promote epistemic success than the person who merely relies on herself. One factor is the internal psychological arrangement characteristic of trust: the self-truster holds herself to normative expectations, including to not let herself down epistemically, and she is inclined to respond positively to her own epistemic needs. The (mere) self-relier, by contrast, relies on herself to do what she would do irrespective of considering her own needs—an arrangement apt to be subject to the impulses of the moment and inimical to cultivating virtuous epistemic habits.

A second factor favoring the success of the self-truster is this. Trusting someone signals that you construe her as trustworthy: as someone who will respond to your normative expectations, who will have a positive attitude toward you or your needs, and who will competently come through for you. And people tend, all else equal, to unconsciously conform their self-concept, and thus their behavior, to the way in which others construe them (Hinchman 2012; Alfano 2012, chap. 5; D'Cruz 2019). Merely relying on a person, by contrast, signals just that you construe her as someone who will behave in the usual predictable ways, irrespective of her relationship to you. This gives her no positive vision to conform to, and possibly even a negative one. If trust, as opposed to mere reliance, can exert this sort of psychological influence from one person to another, it is apt to do so all the more forcefully within the psyche of a single person. These two factors put in place by trust, over and above mere reliance, make the self-truster likelier to enjoy epistemic success than the (mere) self-relier. So not only do we rely on ourselves rather than just our faculties, but this reliance, when epistemically effective, has the marks of *trust* in oneself.[32]

Let's turn to recognitional epistemic goods, to which a similar line of thought applies: self-trust for these cannot adequately be construed as mere reliance. Taking our two questions in order: first, why is the reliance at issue reliance on oneself and not just on one's faculties? The reason here is ontological: epistemic recognition is not the kind of thing that a mere object can accord. Second, why is our self-reliance for recognitional goods best construed as self-*trust* as opposed to mere self-reliance? The answer is that although one *could* merely rely on oneself for epistemic recognition, trusting oneself is more effective at securing it. Just as with representational epistemic goods, in the case of self-trust for recognitional ones, psychological factors are in place that promote the appropriate ascriptions of epistemic recognition to oneself, whereas these factors are not in place in the case of (mere) self-reliance.

To see this, note that according oneself appropriate epistemic recognition is not always easy; it often requires virtues such as courage, honesty, and discernment (Tanesini, this volume). It involves (for example) sticking up for what you know when you come under pressure to self-censor, yet being unafraid to admit when you do not know; it involves insisting on the epistemic credit you deserve when others belittle you or try to usurp it; it involves ceding the floor to others who are equally epistemically deserving but less influential than you are; it involves believing the conclusions that you draw on the basis of good reasoning, yet declining to believe conclusions that you draw for poor reasons; and so forth. These activities are not for the faint-hearted, but require courage, honesty, and discernment.

The self-truster is in a better position to exercise these virtues than the (mere) self-relier, for reasons we have seen. First, the self-truster relates to himself a person, with the accompanying normative expectations and counting on himself to meet his own needs. That is, he holds himself to normative expectations to accord himself appropriate epistemic recognition, and he counts on himself to be responsive to his own need for such recognition. Someone whom you treat as a person—including yourself—is apt to be moved by the norms and the personal attitudes to do things in the context of the relationship that he might not do otherwise. The mere self-relier, by contrast, lacks this internal arrangement with himself, relying only on what he would do anyway. Second, the self-truster, *in* trusting himself for epistemic recognition, thereby signals that he construes himself as trustworthy for it, thus encouraging himself to act in a trustworthy manner by according it in appropriate measure. The mere self-relier, by contrast, lacks this positive vision. So epistemic trust, for recognitional no less than representational goods, is best made sense of as a form of self-trust, as opposed to reliance either on one's faculties or (mere) reliance on oneself.

Section 2 has looked at epistemic trust in others through the lens of testimony and applied some of the resulting insights to the case of epistemic trust in oneself. I do not pretend to have exhausted the epistemic phenomena in which trust plays a role. And I have limited this discussion to trust between (or within) individuals, though an important area for continued research is the way in which epistemic trust, both for recognitional and representational goods, features between groups (see Kallestrup's contribution in this volume) and epistemic communities (Grasswick 2018). But I hope that this exploration of epistemic trust through the lens of testimony and self-trust has lain some groundwork for future discussion. The contributions to this volume aim to advance many of them, and I turn to them now.

3. Chapter Overview

3.1. *The Value of Trust in Others and in Oneself*

In "Locke on Trust," Thomas W. Simpson discusses the value of trust, starting with an apparent puzzle in the work of John Locke and finishing with his own alternative view. On the one hand, Locke's political philosophy places a high positive value on trust. On the other hand, in Locke's epistemology, trust is presented as the ultimate epistemic sin. The key to resolving this apparent disunity in Locke's views, Simpson argues, is to recognize that Locke thinks that the only possible value that trust can have is instrumental. This means that, in the case of political trust, trust is valuable because it sets up norms according to which the state is responsible to its citizens. In the case of epistemic trust, by contrast, Locke sees only disvalue, because he takes it merely to discourage individuals from thinking autonomously. So Locke's view is coherent given the premise that the only value to trust is instrumental. But Simpson rejects this premise, arguing that trust has great *intrinsic* value, whether in politics or epistemology.

Value is also the focus of Elizabeth Fricker's "Epistemic and Practical Dependence and the Value of Skills or: Satnavs, Good or Bad?" In counterpoint to Simpson, who explores the noninstrumental value of epistemic and practical trust, Fricker focuses on the noninstrumental value of *not needing to trust others*. Fricker acknowledges that there is great positive value in trusting others for knowledge and other things, but she explores the idea that there is noninstrumental value in being skilled to know and do things for ourselves. What things, and under what circumstances? Fricker argues that, of metaphysical necessity, each one of us has reason to acquire a certain set of skills, the exercising of which will bring him pleasure. She then argues that there is noninstrumental value in having some skills (as opposed to being entirely unskilled), which derives from the fact that, given the sorts of beings we are and the sort of world we inhabit, we derive self-respect from having skills. Finally—and most controversially—Fricker argues that there is a specific set of core skills that every person, given the sorts of beings we are and the sort of world we inhabit, has reason to acquire. Taken together, Simpson's and Fricker's chapters yield a complementary picture of the noninstrumental value both of trusting others and of having the skills on the basis of which to trust oneself.

3.2. *Trust in Testimony*

We move from the value of trust across epistemic and nonepistemic domains to a discussion of its specifically epistemic value in Greco's chapter, "The Role of Trust in Testimonial Knowledge." Against the idea that interpersonal trust cannot be epistemically interesting in its own right because, unlike such notions as evidence and reliability, it does not help constitute epistemic aims, Greco argues that *trust is essential to testimonial knowledge.* He offers two arguments, both of which depend on the premise that testimonial knowledge is transmitted knowledge. But Greco then argues that the transmission of knowledge essentially involves joint agency—which in turn essentially involves interpersonal trust. Along the way Greco casts new light on social-epistemological categories, distinguishing two forms of reductionism (source reductionism and transmission reductionism) and situating so-called "trust theories" of testimonial justification, such as the assurance view, within this framework. His chapter yields a new, finer-grained way to think about the epistemic value of trust, and through this about epistemic value in general.

In "Trust, Preemption and Knowledge," Arnon Keren also discusses trust in testimonial knowledge. Whereas Greco focuses on the necessity of epistemic trust for testimonial knowledge, Keren aims to give an account of epistemic trust itself. He claims that trust is a matter of declining to take precautions against the trustee's failing to come through and that this amounts in the epistemic case to declining to rely on evidence for the testified proposition, instead relying solely on the testifier. But if this is so, how can trust play a positive epistemic role, rather than a negative one? The key, Keren argues, lies in recognizing that trust is *preemptive*: Trusting someone entails believing that she is trustworthy, and this belief *preempts* any other evidence about whether she is trustworthy. In other words, this belief gives the agent a good reason to desist from relying on any evidence other than the trustee's word. But if trust is preemptive, how is it compatible with epistemic responsibility, which seems to involve relying on your own evidence? Because, Keren claims, preempting your own evidence in favor of the testifier's say-so enables your belief to be supported by *her* evidence—which, we may assume, is superior to your own. Far from abandoning epistemic responsibility, then, epistemic trust on the preemptive account gives you justificatory access to a swathe of evidence that you would not otherwise have had.

The contributions thus far focus on epistemic trust between individuals, but Jesper Kallestrup extends the discussion to epistemic trust between groups. In "Groups, Trust and Testimony," he argues that if groups can have knowledge and can testify in ways that cannot be understood reductively in terms of the knowledge or testimony of their individual members, then groups can also engage in relations of epistemic trust. He offers some considerations supporting the antecedent, that groups can irreducibly engage in these epistemic activities. But he notes that one might resist the consequent, that groups can engage in relations of epistemic trust, on the grounds that trust—given its normative and affective dimension—seems the kind of attitude that only individuals can enjoy. But Kallestrup appeals to a variety of cases to argue that, because groups can enter into testimonial relations of trust over and above any such relations between their individual members, group trust is equally irreducible to trust between individuals. Kallestrup's chapter synthesizes two cutting-edge conversations: one on group epistemic attitudes and another on the role of trust in testimonial knowledge.

3.3. Epistemic Trust and Epistemic Responsibility

So there is an apparent tension between trust and evidence (highlighted, for example, in the contributions by Simpson and Keren); yet trust also has an important epistemic role to play (as all of the contributions have emphasized). These two observations make it relevant to ask how trust can be *epistemically responsible*. For epistemic responsibility includes, among other things, responsibility to one's evidence. Heidi Grasswick, in "Reconciling Epistemic Trust and Responsibility," aims to do just that. Grasswick sets up a broad-lens framework. She distinguishes two types of epistemic trust, trust in testimony (the kind discussed in the contributions so far) and trust in inquiry, which involves trusting others to research and safeguard important knowledge even if they do not wind up testifying it. And she focuses not mainly on responsibly trusting a testifier for a one-off belief, but rather on the responsible development of epistemic-trust relationships that extend over time. This framework enables her to pinpoint three layers of epistemic responsibility that make for "healthy" relationships of epistemic trust: responsibility toward the evidence we have at a given time, responsibility in developing and maintaining communities of epistemic trust, and responsibility in critically evaluating the epistemic norms in play in our communities, for example by listening to the epistemically marginalized who are not served well by them.

In "Proper Epistemic Trust as a Responsibilist Virtue," Benjamin McCraw also seeks to elucidate the relationship between epistemic trust and epistemic responsibility—here, by construing proper epistemic trust itself as a responsibilist epistemic virtue. He develops an account of epistemic trust and then, drawing on contemporary psychology and Linda Zagzebski's account of epistemic virtue, presents an account of what makes it proper. McCraw argues for the existence of this virtue on the basis of its theoretical fruits. First, it fills a theoretical space between the epistemic vices of suspiciousness and gullibility. Second, it fits neatly into two different types of virtue theory: proper epistemic trust contributes to the epistemic good life, and the paradigmatically rational or virtuous epistemic agent will be motivated to display it. An important feature of proper epistemic trust is its context-sensitivity. McCraw draws on this to argue, third, that his account successfully arbitrates a number of epistemological debates, including about low-grade knowledge, reductionism vs. anti-reductionism in the epistemology of testimony, and the rational response to peer disagreement. Far from conflicting with epistemic responsibility, epistemic trust—at least when proper—instantiates it.

Whereas the discussions thus far have centered mainly on epistemic trust in others, Alessandra Tanesini, in "Virtuous and Vicious Intellectual Self-Trust," turns her attention to epistemic *self*-trust. She construes this as a set of dispositions to rely on one's faculties (so, as a form of what I have called "mere reliance"), together with positive epistemic feelings and confidence in one's willpower. Tanesini distinguishes one epistemically beneficial form of epistemic self-trust, confident optimism, and three pathological ones: arrogant, timid, and servile self-trust. Drawing extensively on psychological research, she argues that each form of epistemic self-trust arises from a corresponding form of self-esteem. Confident optimism has its roots in healthy self-esteem, which frees the agent to be motivated in her inquiry by the prospect of achieving epistemic aims. Arrogant, timid, and servile self-trust derive from warped forms of self-esteem that focus the agent not on epistemic goods, but rather on her own vulnerability. Confident optimism about one's faculties, then, turns out to be epistemically virtuous, whereas the three pathological forms of self-trust turn out to be epistemically vicious. What Tanesini gives us is a psychologically robust account of epistemic self-trust within the framework of epistemic virtue responsibilism.

3.4. *The Vulnerabilities of Trust*

One running theme of the contributions thus far is that trust incurs vulnerability (Simpson, Fricker, Keren); another is that our relationships of trust are deeply embedded in social structures (Grasswick, Kallestrup). Katherine Dormandy's contribution explores some ramifications of both ideas for epistemic trust in others; Mari Mikkola's does so for epistemic self-trust.

In "Exploiting Epistemic Trust," Dormandy looks at vulnerabilities arising in relationships of epistemic trust in others, specifically in testimony. She starts with a discussion of how trust in general can be exploited; a key observation is that trust incurs vulnerabilities not just for the party doing the trusting but also for the trustee (after all, trust can be burdensome), so either party can exploit the other. She applies these considerations to epistemic trust specifically in testimonial relationships. There, we standardly think of a hearer trusting a speaker. But we miss an important aspect of this relationship unless we consider too that the speaker standardly trusts the hearer, for example for epistemic recognition. Given this mutual trust, and given that both trustees and trusters can exploit each other, we have four possibilities for exploitation in epistemic-trust relationships: a speaker exploiting a hearer (i) by accepting the hearer's trust or (ii) by imposing her trust on him, and a hearer exploiting a speaker (iii) by accepting the speaker's trust or (iv) by imposing his trust on her. One result is that you do not need to *betray* someone to exploit her—you can exploit her just as easily by doing what she trusts you for. Through exploring these four forms of exploitation, Dormandy seeks to better understand interpersonal epistemic trust itself, as well as its embeddedness in social power structures.

In "Self-Trust and Discriminatory Speech," Mari Mikkola also considers the interplay between social power and trust, focusing on epistemic self-trust. Discriminatory speech (as opposed to hate speech) is legally protected on the grounds that, even if false, it can at least be argued against. But Mikkola argues that, contrary to this common view, discriminatory speech *weakens* the ability of its targets to argue against it, because it damages their epistemic self-trust. Drawing on the recently burgeoning literature about the cognitive role of social stereotypes, Mikkola singles out three types of effect—implicit bias, stereotype threat, and striking generics—that operate at a less than fully conscious level and are exacerbated by discriminatory speech. She argues that, because of the operation of these mechanisms, such speech bypasses rational thought and directly inhibits the targets' ability to trust themselves epistemically. Epistemic self-trust, then, is a fragile phenomenon that is vulnerable to the social structures and norms that yield our social stereotypes. Rather than ban discriminatory speech, however, Mikkola advocates education to counter the pernicious stereotypes themselves.

There is much more to say about trust in epistemology than the chapters of this volume can say. Each makes a significant contribution to the ongoing conversation, but I encourage readers not to simply take my word for it.

Notes

1. See Jones (2004), Becker (1996), Faulkner (2015), Domenicucci and Holton (2017).
2. Proponents of both requirements, however, tend to exclude the possibility that trust is compatible with certainty that the trustee will come through.
3. Holton (1994) defines trust in terms of a disposition to form reactive attitudes, but McLeod (2000, 474) and Hawley (2014b, 8) argue that this account is insufficient.
4. Some go as far as to say that the very concepts of trust and trustworthiness are moral; i.e., that merely predicating them of something implies that that thing is good (McLeod 2000; Stern 2017; Ruokonen 2013). Similarly, that the concept of betrayal is bad, implying that anything on which it is predicated is bad.

5. Jones herself argues indirectly by criticizing Scanlon's (2003) moral view of the norms of trust. See also Hinchman (2017), who argues that the norms of trust are not necessarily moral.
6. Thanks to Arnon Keren. This is arguably the view of (Baier 1986).
7. One view that does not fit neatly into this division is that of Pettit (1995), in which the truster ascribes both goodwill and self-interest to the trustee. Another is that of Kappel (2014), in which trust is a disposition to rely on someone.
8. So either the mere-predictive account or the combined account (see Section 1.1).
9. I take it that Baier (e.g. 1986) is often misread as saying that the goodwill ascribed to the trustee be directed toward the truster himself (e.g., Holton 1994, p. 65), which gives rise to various counterexamples. As Mullin points out, however (2005, 317), this is too narrow a reading.
10. Hawley (ibid.) argues that commitment is a better notion for an account of trust than obligation.
11. Other views posit commitments and a specific motive on the part of the trustee (Hinchman 2005; Faulkner 2011; McMyler 2011).
12. Views positing a commitment on the part of the trustee might differ over what she is committed to. She might be committed to some person (standardly but not necessarily the truster; Hawley 2014b) or simply to the norms of trust (Mullin 2005; Hinchman 2005; Faulkner 2011).
13. In cases like this and the one considered in the following paragraph, accounts on which predictive expectations are essential to trust will be committed to saying that, if the evidence causes one's predictive expectation to drop below a certain level of confidence, the action is no longer one performed in trust.
14. Some argue that the fact that you trust someone is relevant evidence, because your trust can encourage her to come through (McGeer 2008; Faulkner 2007; Pettit 1995; Hinchman 2012).
15. Frost-Arnold (2014b) discusses two other types of extrinsic ends for which one might trust.
16. Simpson (2017), who introduces it, just calls it the "evidential constraint."
17. I am using the terms *speaker* and *hearer* as synonyms for the precise but more unwieldy terms *teller* and *audience*. For simplicity I will adopt the convention of calling the speaker "she" and the hearer "he."
18. Not every case in which the hearer believes what the speaker says, even if he believes it because she says it, counts as consummated. For example, the hearer may think that the speaker intends to lie but that, whenever she intends this, a cognitive quirk ensures that she in fact tells the truth. In such cases, the hearer believes what the speaker says because she testifies it, but he does not take her at face value by believing her: it is not a consummated testimonial exchange.
19. This is not the standard characterization of reductionism, which usually specifies that the evidence is inductive or inferential; characterizing it as a total-evidence view maintains neutrality between these possibilities while leaving open other types of evidence too.
20. This also holds for Lackey's "dualism" (2006), which adds a reliability condition to reductionism.
21. Faulkner (2011) and McMyler (2011) resist the label "anti-reductionism," but they construe it more narrowly than I do, as something logically in between reductionism and anti-reductionism. On my broader usage, anti-reductionism is just the denial of reductionism.
22. Proponents of the assurance view use the term "evidence" more narrowly than I do. On their view, this term is reserved for any reasons for belief other

than the one supplied by the hearer's trust in the speaker. On my broader usage, this reason too counts as evidence.

23. This possible version of the assurance view is similar to that of Moran (2005), who argues that the speaker's testimony functions as a guarantee, or assurance, to the hearer. Moran, however, does not focus on either party's trust in the other. Yet doing so, I suggest, would enable him to counter an important objection to his view. The objection comes from Faulkner (2007), who argues that the hearer, on Moran's view, has no way to know whether the speaker's guarantee is deceitful. If Moran were to understand the speaker's guarantee in terms of her entrusting him with the collateral good of her epistemic reputation, this would supply the hearer with a reason to believe that she is being sincere and doing her best to testify competently.

24. Some authors keep these notions distinct, but for simplicity I will use them interchangeably.

25. That said, some argue that beliefs can be epistemically justified in some cases even when evidence does not support them, as long as the evidence does not actively speak against them (e.g. James 1921). But I would argue that this view conflates epistemic justification with decision-theoretic rationality.

26. This is not to say that the agent's aims play *no* role in determining what is epistemically rational. For agents themselves have a measure of control over the evidence that they are exposed to. And some argue that it is up to an agent whether to adopt an epistemically risky policy (forming more beliefs even if some might turn out false) or an epistemically cautious one (forming fewer beliefs in order to avoid falsehoods at all costs) (James 1921).

27. This need not entail that the hearer must explicitly hold the belief that the speaker is trustworthy.

28. Lehrer does not specify the object of self-trust one way or another, but reliance on one's faculties suffices for his argumentative purposes.

29. Tanesini (this volume) is one of the few who discuss this matter explicitly. She does not claim wholesale that epistemic self-trust is a matter of mere reliance. Rather, epistemic self-trust is a complex state involving mere reliance on one's faculties, on the one hand, and trust in the normative sense in one's own *will*, on the other.

30. Jones (2012a), by contrast, seems more sympathetic to a view of epistemic self-trust as directed at oneself *qua* person, rather than simply at one's faculties, speaking of epistemic self-trust as a normatively rich phenomenon.

31. Govier (1993, 106–09) makes a similar argument for nonepistemic trust in oneself.

32. McCraw (this volume) goes as far as to argue that epistemic self-trust is an epistemic character virtue.

References

Adler, Jonathan. 2002. *Belief's Own Ethics*. Cambridge, MA: MIT Press.

Alfano, Mark. 2012. "Expanding the Situationist Challenge to Responsibilist Virtue Epistemology." *Philosophical Quarterly* 62(247): 223–49.

Baier, Annette. 1986. "Trust and Antitrust." *Ethics* 96(2): 231–60.

———. 1991. "Trust and Its Vulnerabilities, and Sustaining Trust." In *Tanner Lectures on Human Values*, vol. 13, 107–74. Salt Lake City: University of Utah Press.

Baker, Judith. 1987. "Trust and Rationality." *Pacific Philosophical Quarterly* 68: 1–13.

Becker, Lawrence C. 1996. "Trust as Noncognitive Security about Motives." *Ethics* 107(1): 43–61.

Burge, Tyler. 1993. "Content Preservation." *The Philosophical Review* 102(4): 457–88.

Coady, Cecil Anthony John. 1992. *Testimony: A Philosophical Study.* Oxford: Clarendon.

Code, Lorraine. 1987. *Epistemic Responsibility.* Hanover, NH: University Press of New England and Brown University Press.

Cogley, Zac. 2012. "Trust and the Trickster Problem." *Analytic Philosophy* 53(1): 30–47.

Cohen, Stewart. 1999. "Review: Lehrer on Coherence and Self-Trust." *Philosophy and Phenomenological Research* 59(4): 1043–48.

Coleman, James. 1990. *Foundations of Social Theory.* Cambridge, MA: Harvard University Press.

Constantin, Jan, and Thomas Grundmann. Forthcoming. "Epistemic Authority: Preemption through Source Sensitive Defeat." *Synthese.*

Darwall, Stephen. 2017. "Trust as a Second-Personal Attitude of the Heart." In *The Philosophy of Trust,* edited by Paul Faulkner and Thomas Simpson, 35–50. Oxford: Oxford University Press.

Dasgupta, Partha. 1988. "Trust as a Commodity." In *Trust: Making and Breaking Cooperative Relations,* edited by Diego Gambetta, 49–72. Oxford: Basil Blackwell.

Daukas, Nancy. 2006. "Epistemic Trust and Social Location." *Episteme* 3(1–2): 109–24.

D'Cruz, Jason. 2019. "Humble Trust." *Philosophical Studies* 176(4): 933–53.

Domenicucci, Jacopo, and Richard Holton. 2017. "Trust as a Two-Place Relation." In *The Philosophy of Trust,* edited by Paul Faulkner and Thomas Simpson, 149–60. Oxford: Oxford University Press.

Dormandy, Katherine. 2018. "Epistemic Authority: Preemption or Proper Basing?" *Erkenntnis* 83(4): 773–91.

Dotson, Kristie. 2011. "Tracking Epistemic Violence, Tracking Practices of Silencing." *Hypatia* 26(2): 236–57.

Faulkner, Paul. 2007. "On Telling and Trusting." *Mind* 116(464): 875–902.

———. 2011. *Knowledge on Trust.* Oxford: Oxford University Press.

———. 2015. "The Attitude of Trust Is Basic." *Analysis* 75(3): 424–29.

Foley, Richard. 2001. *Intellectual Trust in Oneself and Others.* Cambridge: Cambridge University Press.

Fricker, Elizabeth. 1994. "Against Gullibility." In *Knowing from Words,* edited by Bimal K. Matilal and A. Chakrabarti, 125–61. Dordrecht: Springer.

———. 1995. "Telling and Trusting: Reductionism and Anti-Reductionism in the Epistemology of Testimony." *Mind* 104(414): 393–411.

———. 2006. "Second-Hand Knowledge." *Philosophy and Phenomenological Research* LXXIII(3): 592–618.

———. 2016. "Doing (Better) What Comes Naturally: Zagzebski on Rationality and Epistemic Self-Trust." *Episteme,* 1–16.

Fricker, Miranda. 2007. *Epistemic Injustice: Power and the Ethics of Knowing.* Oxford: Oxford University Press.

Frost-Arnold, Karen. 2013. "Moral Trust and Scientific Collaboration." *Studies in History and Philosophy of Science Part A* 44(3): 301–10.

———. 2014a. "Imposters, Tricksters, and Trustworthiness as an Epistemic Virtue." *Hypatia* 29(4): 790–807.

———. 2014b. "The Cognitive Attitude of Rational Trust." *Synthese* 191(9): 1957–74.

Goldberg, Sanford. 2010. *Relying on Others*. Oxford: Oxford University Press.

Goldman, Alvin. 1999. *Knowledge in a Social World*. Oxford: Oxford University Press.

Govier, Trudy. 1993. "Self-Trust, Autonomy, and Self-Esteem." *Hypatia* 8(1): 99–120.

Grasswick, Heidi. 2018. "Understanding Epistemic Trust Injustices and Their Harms." *Royal Institute of Philosophy Supplement* 84: 69–91.

Hardin, Russell. 1993. "The Street-Level Epistemology of Trust." *Politics and Society* 21(4): 505–29.

Hardwig, John. 1991. "The Role of Trust in Knowledge." *Journal of Philosophy* 88(12): 693–708.

Hawley, Katherine. 2014a. "Partiality and Prejudice in Trusting." *Synthese* 191: 2029–45.

———. 2014b. "Trust, Distrust and Commitment." *Noûs* 48(1): 1–20.

Hieronymi, Pamela. 2008. "The Reasons of Trust." *Australasian Journal of Philosophy* 86(2): 213–36.

Hinchman, Edward. 2005. "Telling as Inviting to Trust." *Philosophy and Phenomenological Research* 70(3): 562–87.

———. 2012. "Can Trust Itself Ground a Reason to Believe the Trusted?" *Abstracta* 6(Special Issue VI): 47–83.

———. 2017. "On the Risks of Resting Assured: An Assurance Theory of Trust." In *The Philosophy of Trust*, edited by Paul Faulkner and Thomas Simpson, 51–69. Oxford: Oxford University Press.

Holton, Richard. 1994. "Deciding to Trust, Coming to Believe." *Australasian Journal of Philosophy* 72(1): 63–76.

Horsburgh, Howard John Neate. 1960. "The Ethics of Trust." *The Philosophical Quarterly* 10(41): 343–54.

James, William. 1921. *The Will to Believe, Human Immortality, and Other Essays in Popular Philosophy*. London: Longmans, Green, and Co.

Jones, Karen. 1996. "Trust as an Affective Attitude." *Ethics* 107(1): 4–25.

———. 2004. "Trust and Terror." In *Moral Psychology: Feminist Ethics and Social Theory*, edited by Peggy DesAutels and Margaret Urban Walker, 3–18. Lanham, MD: Rowman and Littlefield.

———. 2012a. "The Politics of Intellectual Self-Trust." *Social Epistemology* 26(2): 237–51.

———. 2012b. "Trustworthiness." *Ethics* 123(October): 61–85.

———. 2017. " 'But I Was Counting on You!' " In *The Philosophy of Trust*, edited by Paul Faulkner and Thomas Simpson, 90–108. Oxford: Oxford University Press.

Kappel, Klemens. 2014. "Believing on Trust." *Synthese* 191(9): 2009–28.

Kelly, Thomas. 2003. "Epistemic Rationality as Instrumental Rationality: A Critique." *Philosophy and Phenomenological Research* LXVI(3): 612–40.

Keren, Arnon. 2007. "Epistemic Authority, Testimony and the Transmission of Knowledge." *Episteme*, 368–81.

———. 2014. "Trust and Belief: A Preemptive Reasons Account." *Synthese* 191(12): 2593–615.

Lackey, Jennifer. 2006. "It Takes Two to Tango: Beyond Reductionism and Non-Reductionism in the Epistemology of Testimony." In *The Epistemology of Testimony*, edited by Jennifer Lackey and Ernest Sosa, 160–91. Oxford: Oxford University Press.

Lehrer, Keith. 1997. *Self-Trust: A Study of Reason, Knowledge, and Autonomy.* Oxford: Oxford University Press.

Lipton, Peter. 1998. "The Epistemology of Testimony." *Studies in History and Philosophy of Science* 29: 1–31.

Lyons, Jack. 1997. "Testimony, Induction and Folk Psychology." *Australasian Journal of Philosophy* 75: 163–78.

McGeer, Victoria. 2008. "Trust, Hope and Empowerment." *Australasian Journal of Philosophy* 86(2): 237–54.

McLeod, Carolyn. 2000. "Our Attitude Towards the Motivation of Those We Trust." *Southern Journal of Philosophy* 38(3): 465–79.

McMyler, Benjamin. 2011. *Testimony, Trust, and Authority.* Oxford: Oxford University Press.

Medina, José. 2013. *The Epistemology of Resistance: Gender and Racial Oppression, Epistemic Injustice, and the Social Imagination.* Oxford: Oxford University Press.

Montmarquet, James. 1993. *Epistemic Virtue and Doxastic Responsibility.* Lanham, MD: Rowman and Littlefield.

Moran, Richard. 2005. "Getting Told and Being Believed." *Philosophers' Imprint* 5(5): 1–29.

Mullin, Amy. 2005. "Trust, Social Norms, and Motherhood." *Journal of Social Philosophy* 36(3): 316–30.

Nickel, Philip J. 2007. "Trust and Obligation-Ascription." *Ethical Theory and Moral Practice* 10(3): 309–19.

Peet, Andrew. 2017. "Epistemic Injustice in Utterance Interpretation." *Synthese* 194(9): 3421–43.

Pettit, Philip. 1995. "The Cunning of Trust." *Philosophy and Public Affairs* 24(3): 202–25.

Plantinga, Alvin. 1993. *Warrant and Proper Function.* Oxford: Oxford University Press.

Ross, Angus. 1986. "Why Do We Believe What We Are Told?" *Ratio* 28(1): 69–88.

Ruokonen, Floora. 2013. "Trust, Trustworthiness, and Responsbility." In *Trust: Analytic and Applied Perspectives*, edited by Pekka Makela and Cynthia Townley, 1–14. Amsterdam and New York: Rodopi.

Scanlon, Thomas M. 2003. "Promises and Contracts." In *The Difficulty of Tolerance*, edited by Thomas M. Scanlon, 234–69. Cambridge: Cambridge University Press.

Simpson, Thomas W. 2012. "What Is Trust?" *Pacific Philosophical Quarterly* 93(4): 550–69.

———. 2013. "Trustworthiness and Moral Character." *Ethical Theory and Moral Practice* 16(3): 543–57.

———. 2017. "Trust and Evidence." In *The Philosophy of Trust*, edited by Paul Faulkner and Thomas Simpson, 177–94. Oxford: Oxford University Press.

Stern, Robert. 2017. " 'Trust Is Basic': Løgstrup on the Priority of Trust." In *The Philosophy of Trust*, edited by Paul Faulkner and Thomas Simpson, 272–93. Oxford: Oxford University Press.

Webb, Mark Owen. 1993. "Why I Know about as Much as You: A Reply to Hardwig." *The Journal of Philosophy* 90(5): 260–70.

Zagzebski, Linda. 1996. *Virtues of the Mind*. Oxford: Oxford University Press.

———. 2012. *Epistemic Authority: A Theory of Trust, Authority, and Autonomy in Belief*. Oxford: Oxford University Press.

Section 1

The Value of Trust and Self-Trust

2   Locke on Trust

Thomas W. Simpson

1. Introduction

Trust is philosophically interesting because of its hybrid nature in at least the following two ways. First, it is an attitude that seems rationally responsive both to practical and to theoretical reasons. To trust someone is to respect them, and to distrust is to slight. As it is embedded in and constitutive of valuable interpersonal relationships, I have practical reasons to trust. But trust is vindicated when I have trusted the trustworthy and not trusted the untrustworthy, and it is theoretical reason that seeks to discriminate between these. This is unusual, because most attitudes are either cognitive, responding to theoretical reasons only, like belief, or noncognitive, responding to practical reasons only, like intention, affection or desire. Moreover, these may conflict. There are times when there are theoretical reasons to take someone to be untrustworthy and practical reasons nonetheless to trust someone, and this can lead to practical dilemmas. Richard Holton gives the example of putting an ex-con on the shopping till who has a track record of theft but will be unable to reintegrate into society unless someone gives him a chance (1994). How should we make sense of these conflicting intuitions?

Second, I may trust others both for the truth of what they say, in testimony, and that they will fulfill their commitments, paradigmatically in promises. The same attitude plays a role in reasoning about both what to believe and what to do, and a central one at that, given how social our theoretical and practical lives are. If it is the same attitude in both cases, the presumption must be that it is justified by the same set of conditions. Moreover, the goods that trust can make available are determined by those justification conditions. The same set of justificatory conditions, if met, yield the same goods in both practical and epistemic contexts. So, is there a unified account that explains when trust is justified, and what its value is, for both epistemic and practical contexts?

This chapter focuses on these ways that trust is hybrid by examining the roles that trust plays in John Locke's thought. Trust has an important role in Locke's politics and epistemology, but its valence is opposite in the two domains, and in the key works of the *Two Treatises of Government* and the *Essay Concerning Human Understanding* in particular. In Locke's politics, trust is basically viewed positively. It is the central category for describing the proper relationship between the people and the government: the latter exercises a "fiduciary power" or "fiduciary trust" on behalf of the former (*Two Treatises*, II §§149, 156). Although it can be betrayed and is revocable, trust is the key condition for legitimacy. Things are otherwise in his epistemology, where trust is basically viewed negatively. In some strikingly dismissive passages in the *Essay*, Locke identifies believing on the basis of trust as an extremely vicious epistemic practice. His objection is not to pathologies of trust, such as gullibility. It is to trust itself.

Prima facie, this is puzzling. Why should the same attitude be viewed as of such markedly different worth in the two contexts? The first task of this chapter is thus exegetical and interpretative: to outline what Locke's view of trust was in both his politics and epistemology and to ask whether it is consistent. I argue that, contrary to initial impressions, his view is consistent. The attention and role he gives to trust in both works does not reflect any special interest that Locke had in trust. Rather, it reflects and is explained by Locke's deep commitment to individual freedom. This thesis is controversial, given that some scholars have taken the task of securing trust to be the priority of Locke's philosophy. In important prior work on this topic, John Dunn has remarked that:

> [Locke's] moral and political thinking as a whole (and in my view the central burden of his philosophical thinking in its entirety) was directed towards an understanding of the rationality and moral propriety of human trust. . . . [T]he synthesis of trust (the creation and sustaining of trust) remains, and will always remain, an indispensable human contrivance for coping with the freedom of other men.
>
> (1984, 280–1, 299)

Having spent too much time thinking about the topic, I tend to see trust under every rock. Yet this seems to me to get things backwards. Dunn is correct that the synthesis of trust is necessary for coping with others' freedom. But it is the latter which Locke was primarily concerned to understand and to defend. The unifying thread of his thought is the basic status of the "natural liberty" of individuals, both epistemic and practical. Trust is invoked where it is necessary or desirable to preserve this or castigated where it threatens it, and not otherwise.

The second task of the chapter is to evaluate, in a preliminary way, Locke's view of trust. Though I am indebted to historians of intellectual thought, such as Dunn and John Yolton, who have traced out the controversies and debates that Locke was intervening in, my present goal is to evaluate Locke's view of trust on its own merits. This is the principal reason for my interest in Locke's view of trust: I think it expresses an evaluation of trust that both has relatively wide appeal and is dissatisfactory. I suggest that, although his proposals for politics and practical reasoning are, in fact, consistent, both are ultimately deficient. They fail to recognize that trust is valuable to us not merely for what it enables but for what it contributes to our lives as such—a value that casts doubt on the priority of individuals' natural freedom.

2. Trust in the *Two Treatises*

The target of the *First Treatise* is Robert Filmer's claim that absolutist monarchy is the basis of the right to rule. The *Second Treatise*, accordingly, must show that governments are legitimate only if the executive is subject to law and the reach of the law is constrained. Both conditions are required if citizens are not to be subject to absolute, arbitrary power: law prevents rule from being arbitrary, and limits on the kinds of laws that can be passed prevent rule from being absolute. Legitimate government requires more than structural constraints, however. It also requires justification of why governments rule—in Locke's terms, a statement of the "end" of government. Locke's account of legitimacy thus explains the end and the limits of civil government in terms of trust. It also explains the end and the limits of its component parts, namely the executive and legislature, in terms of trust.

Start with the purpose of government. In the state of nature people have rights to the preservation of their lives and their property. The "Fundamental Law of Nature" is that the lives and property of all members of society should be preserved as much as possible (II §§16, 135, 159, 183; this Fundamental Law remains in force under the state).[1] A consequence of individuals' rights to the preservation of their lives and property is that, in the state of nature, each is entitled to enforce his or her property rights through punishment, prevention and taking reparation (II §§6–11). "Property rights" is Locke's shorthand for rights to the security of one's person as well as goods (II §173). But this leads to the errors that private judgment tends to: in judging their own cases, "ill nature, passion and revenge" lead to excessive force. To avoid this problem, people transfer their power to punish to the magistrate, who enforces property rights on their behalf (II §13). The powers of making and enforcing laws, of waging war, of raising taxes, the willingness to submit to an authority, which people are naturally free from—"all this for the preservation of the property of all the members of that society, as far as is possible" (II §88; also §222). As the preservation of property is the justification for civil power, so that is the purpose which the state must act for. Government holds its powers in trust to serve this purpose. Trust also sets limits on what the government may do: it may not act in ways that violate these rights. "These are the *bounds* which the trust that is put in them by society, and the law of God and nature, have set" (II §142).

The component parts of the state, like the state as a whole, also hold their powers on trust. Locke's concern is principally with the legislature and the executive. Each has specific responsibilities that, when fulfilled, help to protect property. The legislature is constrained to govern only by publicly proclaimed, universal laws, which are designed for the good of the people; it must not raise taxes without the consent of the people's representatives; and it cannot transfer the power to make law to another body (II §142).[2] The "supreame executor" holds his powers in a "double trust," as having a part in both making and executing the law (II §222). The executive is also responsible for foreign policy (the "federative power"; II §148), assembling the legislature, regulating the way in which the people are represented in the legislature, and exercising discretionary powers through the prerogative (II §§155–8, 161).

What is the nature of the trust that, according to Locke, exists between a legitimate government and the people it rules? The majority of contributions to the contemporary debate about the nature of trust identify the attitude as involving some kind of moral expectation on the part of the truster, where this involves taking the trusted to be under a moral obligation or commitment to fulfill that which they are trusted to do. There are different ways of parsing what this expectation consists of, as either holding a moral claim against the trusted oneself or believing that the trusted takes himself to be under such a claim (e.g. Holton 1994; Lähno 2001; McGeer 2008; Faulkner 2011; Hawley 2014a). An implication of these accounts is that if someone betrays one's trust, one's appropriate affective response is resentment or anger. A minority of contributions eschew any notion of moral commitment. These include accounts on which the motivation to be trustworthy is derived from the trusted's self-interest only, such as Hardin (2002), or on which the attitude of trust is solely a predictive bet or gamble on how others will act in the future, and as such is unconcerned by the possible motives of the trusted, such as Dasgupta (1988), Coleman (1990) and Sztompka (1999). In contrast to accounts based on moral commitment, it is an implication of these nonmoral accounts that the appropriate affective response by the truster, if she is let down by the trusted, is disappointment only. Anger is appropriate when I have a claim against another that is denied or violated. When I lack such a claim, although I may be disappointed in others by the way they have acted, or disappointed in myself that my judgment has proven inaccurate, I nonetheless lack the standing to accuse them of wrong.

Locke's view of trust in the *Second Treatise* clearly anticipates the majority view that trust involves a moral expectation. This is entailed by the central claim of his project, that political power is held by the state only on the basis of first-order natural rights to property and second-order natural rights to enforce those rights, with the rights to enforcement delegated by individuals to the state. This anticipation is implied more specifically by Locke's lengthy descriptions of how that trust may be breached. If the state tries to take away and destroy property, contrary to the Fundamental Law, or the executive tries to establish an arbitrary rule, this is to "betray the liberties of their country." With a deliberate air of paradox, he argues that in breaching trust, the state becomes a rebel, because rebels oppose rightful authority with mere force (II §222, 226). Both of these descriptions of how the government may breach trust— betrayal and rebellion—are morally freighted modes of evaluation. They are the basis of allegations of wrong-doing if trust is breached and indicate that the complainant has standing to accuse the wrongdoer of violating her rights.

That moral commitment underpins practical trust, for Locke, shows that his account of its political role is essentially positive. It reflects a positive judgment of another person that one takes her to be responsive to moral reasons, and to such a degree that one is able to rely on that responsiveness. In taking that person's commitment to be sufficient to motivate her to be reliable, and in coming to rely on her merely because of that commitment, so I expressively communicate my good judgment of her character. That good judgment can be illustrated by contrasting trust with different ways that other people can be induced to act in a way that one can rely on. Consider deception or threats. In contrast to deception or threats, trust is both publicly avowable and communicates respect. Deception can be a stable basis for inducing another person to be cooperative, but it works only if the deception is hidden. If the person relying on another says, "I am relying on you because I have managed to deceive you into doing what I want," the basis for reliance breaks down. Not so with trust. Unlike deception, threats are publicly avowable and may still provide a way to induce someone to act in a way that can be relied upon. Indeed, the threat needs to be publicly avowed, at least to the person threatened, in order to work. But threats expressively communicate disrespect; they show that one does not regard the person threatened as having the moral standing or the mental capacity to need reasons for action other than those derived from pure prudence. There is a longstanding worry that incentives, which are central to nonmoral accounts of trust, have the same semiotic significance as threats, in at least some contexts (Grant 2011). Locke could have said political power was a necessary evil, to be restricted to the greatest extent possible, because it is merely an exercise in threatening people. But he did not say that. He said that political power was a "right of making laws" (II §3), which is exercised on trust. Because it is based on trust, the relationship between government and governed is one that is publicly avowed and expressively communicates respect from the latter to the former.

Locke's account of political trust also commits him regarding what Karen Jones calls the "justification conditions of trust" (1996, 4). A deep intuition about trust is that it is seemingly resistant to counter-evidence. Suppose you are friends with someone, so trust him, and yet hear reports that he has behaved badly. Your trust may lead you to be hesitant about believing those reports, even though you would be unhesitant if they were about someone else you do not trust (Baker 1987, Jones 1996, Stroud 2006, McGeer 2008). This is an instance of the puzzle posed by the hybrid nature of trust noted in the opening paragraph, namely that it seems to respond to both practical and theoretical reasons in ways that can lead to practical dilemmas (Hawley 2014b seeks to dissolve this puzzle). Different ways to resolve this tension are at the heart of the debate as to whether trust is a cognitive attitude—constituted by or entailing a belief, with that belief having as propositional content the trustworthiness of the trusted—or noncognitive, such as an emotion, or judgment for the purposes of practical reasoning, or something else.

Locke's view of political trust does not take a stand on the cognitive/noncognitive debate, but it is committal on the closely proximate question of the relation between trust and evidence. In a metaphor, does trust follow the evidence, or in some sense does it go beyond it? Given the assumption that belief follows the evidence, with evidence construed in a suitably general way, cognitive accounts usually imply that one's trust should be evidentially constrained; that is, it should be proportioned to the evidence for the other's trustworthiness. Conversely, part of the motivation for noncognitivist accounts is the attempt to make sense of the idea that trust can appropriately go beyond the evidence. Noncognitive accounts divide here. Most build in a defeasibility condition, which allows that trust may be appropriate when there is a lack of positive evidence for trustworthiness, but is inappropriate when the evidence that someone is untrustworthy is sufficiently strong (e.g. Holton 1994, 71). Some, however, eschew the defeasibility condition. On these, trust is always a matter of going beyond the evidence. If you decide to rely on someone else because of the evidence for that person's trustworthiness, then, whatever else you may be doing, you are not trusting (e.g. Swinburne 1981, Adams 1984, Hurka 2001, 108; arguably Lagerspetz 1998).

On Locke's account, and at a minimum, political trust has a defeasibility condition; it is possible that it is also evidentially constrained so that it is proportioned to evidence for trustworthiness. But at a minimum, political trust should be revoked when there is evidence of untrustworthiness: that is, when there is evidence that the state has or will betray the trust placed in it. When citizens see that political power is not being exercised in accordance with the ends that justify it—when leaders try to take away or destroy property, establish an absolute or arbitrary power, corrupt the people's representatives or the process of election—they are no longer under a duty to obey the state's mandates.

> [O]ne cannot but see, that he, who has once attempted any such thing as this, cannot any longer be trusted. . . . [If the people] universally have a perswasion, grounded upon manifest evidence, that

designs are carrying on against their liberties, and the general course and tendency of things cannot but give them strong suspicions of the evil intention of the governors, who is to be blamed for it?

(II §§222, 230)

The principle that emerges is that if the people have evidence that the king or legislature intends mischief, then this licenses resistance (II §§239, 149). Although there may be a relation of trust between the people and the government, this does not entail or imply any "leap of faith" on the part of the people.

Locke thought that most of the time, no harm would come from this permission to resist the state when there is evidence of untrustworthiness. The obvious criticism is that his work is an anarchist's charter, and he must reply to it. Such a right to resistance entitles everyone to withhold their compliance when they individually judge that the state is not acting properly. Indeed, Locke is explicit that this right is held not only by the people acting collectively but also by each person acting individually— "Every one is at the disposure of his own will" (II §212). Moreover, this right to resistance reintroduces the problem that the state was supposed to solve, namely the infelicities that arise when individuals use private judgment to enforce their rights. Locke replies that people are sluggish and averse to change. In his view, the danger is not that trust would be rescinded when doing so was inappropriate, but that trust would continue to be extended when it ought to be rescinded. So, it is more likely that people will tolerate illegitimate governments than that they will resist legitimate ones (II §223, 230). Further, in Locke's view, the practically pressing question is when trust should be revoked, not the conditions under which it should be established. This is because trust is assumed to exist *de facto*, because leaders emerge through an organic process whereby people use "their natural freedom, to set up him, whom they judged the ablest, and most likely, to rule well over them" (II §105. Locke "does not help us to understand quite how, or quite when, the trust relationships between the people and their government is brought into being"; Laslett 1988, 116).

In sum, Locke's picture of political trust is that suggested by the Russian proverb, "Trust, but verify." His account is inconsistent with noncognitive accounts that lack a defeasibility condition. If not in contradiction, it is at least in tension even with those noncognitive accounts that do have a defeasibility condition. Though such a condition captures the need to prevent gullibility and exploitation, noncognitive accounts generally are motivated in part by a need to explain why monitoring is in tension with trust. Locke has no such qualms. The role he ascribes to political trust is consistent with the view that trust is often evidentially constrained—to reiterate, that there are some contexts where trust is appropriate only given sufficient evidence for trustworthiness, and that one of the contexts where this evidentialist constraint applies is in high-stakes practical cases, such as politics. I give systematic reasons for favoring this view elsewhere (Simpson 2017). Nonetheless, though subject to rationality constraints, trust remains an essentially positive description of the moral relation between the citizen and the state. Trust is an appropriate way to describe the relationship between citizen and state only if the moral commitment involved in the relationship is doing some kind of work, as I have argued that it indeed is.[3]

3. Trust in the *Essay*

In contrast to practical contexts, Locke views the role of trust in epistemology extremely negatively. It is not that there are good and bad ways of trusting others in epistemic contexts. Rather, trusting others is itself an epistemic vice. This can be inferred from the contexts in which he writes explicitly about trust, and I shall argue that even though trust is not mentioned in his account of testimony, it is also implied there. The importance of this theme should not be overstated. Locke's attack on epistemic trust is not central to the project of the *Essay* in the way that political trust is central to the project of the *Two Treatises*: no chapter is devoted to discussing it; it does not recur as frequently as in the *Two Treatises*, for instance, and when he uses the term it is usually in the context of making a point about something else. But, nonetheless, the disapprobation of epistemic trust in the *Essay* is both consistent and striking. Moreover, it seems to me it is the *Essay*'s central project that generates the view that epistemic trust is worthy of contempt.

The position in the text of the first mention of trust supports my claim that this negative construal is implied by the *Essay*'s central project. The Epistle to the Reader sets out the purpose of the book. Needless to say, as the title indicates, the subject of his treatise is "the understanding"—the faculty of the soul that searches after truth, the pursuit of which gives pleasure and delight in the same way that hawking does, but yields a richer prize. The second and third paragraphs of that Epistle then make the connection. Locke sets out a principle that enquiry must be individual in a sense that needs elucidation. "The understanding, like the eye, *judging of objects, only by its own sight*, cannot but be pleased with what it discovers" (italics added). It is not that the process of enquiry must be individual, although the presumption is that it largely will be. Rather, the discovery of truth is essentially individual: people must learn for themselves, letting "loose their own thoughts, and follow[ing] them in writing." Because of this principle, that the understanding must judge of objects by itself, so:

> he who has raised himself above the alms-basket, and not content
> to live lazily on scraps of begg'd opinions, sets his own thoughts on

work, to find and follow truth . . . 'Tis to [the reader's thoughts], if they are thy own, that I refer my self: But if they are taken upon trust from others, 'tis no great matter what they are, they not following truth, but some meaner consideration; and 'tis not worth while to be concerned, what he says or thinks, who says or thinks only as he is directed by another. If thou judgest for thy self, I know thou wilt judge candidly.

(*Epistle to the Reader*)

Right at the center of Locke's epistemological project is this principle, that enquiry and learning must be individual. Not only so, but this is a duty that one is under; in the terms of contemporary epistemology, which Locke is no small part of the founding of, it is part of the ethics of belief. As one of the section headings has it and which, according to Dunn, his mature philosophy centers on, "Men must think and know for themselves" (I.IV §23; Dunn 1984, 285). It is a consequence of this principle that one ought not trust others; if you do so, you are not following truth, which is what the understanding ought to do, but some "meaner consideration." It is an abdication of epistemic responsibility to trust others and, to anticipate the discussion of testimony later, it fails to yield knowledge.

This condemnation of epistemic trust then recurs through the *Essay*, where Locke's repeated target is the uncritical acceptance of what others currently think. "[T]here cannot be a more dangerous thing to rely on [than] *the opinion of others*" (IV.XV §6; also IV.XX §17). Nicholas Wolterstorff describes the *Essay* as "an unrelenting attack on tradition. Tradition is up against the wall" (1996, 151). Its starting point, occupying Book I and central to its empiricism, is a battery of arguments intended to show that nothing can be known or understood that is not experienced or demonstrated *a priori*. Humans are not born assenting to a set of propositions, either practical or theoretical; there are no "truths imprinted on the soul" either at birth or which we become aware of when we come of age (I.II §5). Locke thinks the claim that there are innate principles leads to widespread falsehood and error on its own accord. "[I]f it be the privilege of innate principles, to be received on their own authority, without examination, I know not what may not be believed" (I.III §27). But he is particularly exercised by the danger that, under the guise of so-called innate principles, people are induced to accept existing opinions credulously. Innate principles become a pseudo-justification for gullibility. Locke saw this in the epistemic practice of those around him and viewed it as pernicious.

[I]t was of no small advantage to those who affected to be masters and teachers, to make this the principles of *principles*, that principles must not be questioned. For having once established this tenet, that there are innate principles, it put their followers upon a necessity of receiving some doctrines as such; which was to take them off from the use of their own reason and judgment, and put them upon believing and taking them upon trust, without farther examination: in which posture of blind credulity, they might be more easily governed.

(I.IV §24)

The aim of controverting credulity, by which enquirers renege on their obligation to seek the truth out for themselves, does not itself require that innate principles be denied; their denial is part and parcel of his empiricism. But it is undeniably useful for this larger project, of controverting credulity, that innate principles should be rejected. Moreover, the fact that, by his lights, innate principles do not exist gives Locke secure grounds for weighing in strongly on those who suppose themselves to be doing so.

He does so in forceful terms. With the destructive work of Book I complete, Locke weighs in on epistemic trust. When we examine humanity, there are few who do not "take upon trust" some revered propositions and so expose their own "ignorance, laziness, education, or precipitancy" (I.III §24). He reaffirms the duty to seek truth for oneself, which trust is an abrogation of:

> Ideas and notions are no more born with us, than arts and sciences. . . . [S]ome (and those the most) taking things upon trust, misemploy their power of assent, by lazily enslaving their minds, to the dictates and dominion of others, in doctrines, which is their duty carefully to examine, and not blindly, with an implicit faith, to swallow.
>
> (I.IV §22)

Not only is trust an abdication of epistemic responsibility, it also leaves the truster worse off than if she had sought to discover the truth for herself. This is because of the doxastic states that trust yields rather than personal enquiry. Trust yields mere belief and opinion; personal enquiry yields knowledge and comprehension. Anticipating the account of testimony in Book IV, someone who merely "takes it upon trust" from someone else that the sum of three angles of a triangle equals two right angles merely has a "probable opinion," whereas someone who follows the proof has knowledge of its truth (I.IV §22). Further:

> The floating of other men's opinions in our brains makes not one jot the more knowing, though they happen to be true. What in them was science, is in us but opiniatrety, whilst we give up our assent only to reverend names, and do not, as they did employ our own reason to understand those truths, which gave them reputation. . . . In the sciences, every one has so much, as he really knows and comprehends:

what he believes only, and takes upon trust, are but shreads; which however well in the whole piece, make no considerable addition to his stock, who gathers them. Such borrowed wealth, like fairy-money, though it were gold in the hand from which he received it, will be but leaves and dust when it comes to use.

(I.IV §23)

These passages are the longest treatments of trust in the *Essay*. Locke then returns to the main points that they make—that trust is an abdication of epistemic duty, that pseudo-justifications can conceal illicit credulity, and that trust cannot yield knowledge—in discussing abuses of memory and the practice of enquiry.

The abuse of memory, according to Locke, is a "cause of great obstinacy in errour and mistake." People stick to their past judgments, being unwilling to revise them, even when confronted by counter-arguments or contrary opinions. "Men hold their opinions with the greatest stiffness." But Locke diagnoses the problem here as not one to do with memory. The problem is that people pretend to remember a past conclusion as being well supported by reasons, though they forget what those reasons are, when in fact the opinion was adopted on poor grounds in the first case. "The fault is not that they rely on their memories, for what they have before well judged; but because they judged before they had well examined" (IV.XVI §3). Locke accordingly pleads for an irenic attitude in circumstances of disagreement. In the best case, the person whom I confront with a counter-argument to his view may be "one that examines before he assents." In that situation I should give him "leave, at his leisure" to reconsider the matter; that is to say, I should expect him to agree with me only on the basis of reasons that he is persuaded by. In the worst case, he may "be one who takes his opinions on trust," in which situation "how can we imagine that he should renounce those tenets, which time and custom have so settled in his mind, that he thinks them self-evident, and of an unquestionable certainty." In either situation, I should not expect another person to take *my* judgment as determinative. That would be for him to

embrace [our opinion] with a blind resignation to an authority, which the understanding of man acknowledges not. For however it may often mistake, it can own no other guide but reason, nor blindly submit to the will and dictates of another.

(IV.XVI §4)

The consequence is that we should "do well to commiserate our mutual ignorance." In this "fleeting state of action and blindness," we are forced to believe "without knowledge," and so I should generally worry more about getting my own opinions right than expecting others to conform to what I believe. In this short discussion, Locke again affirms these three contentions: that trust is an abdication of epistemic duty, which does not yield knowledge, and that a pseudo-justification (in this case, "I remember having good grounds for . . .") can conceal illicit credulity.

The same points recur in his discussion of how people can wrongly give assent, with religious propositions a particular point of concern. Sometimes no proofs are available, and sometimes people are not capable of understanding those proofs that are available; this is particularly true of "the greatest part of mankind, who are given up to labour" (IV. XX §2). But there is another category of person who has proofs available and can understand them but just cannot be bothered to "though they have riches and leisure enough." Some of these are distracted by other sources of pleasure or the drudgery of business. Some avoid it "out of fear, that an impartial enquiry would not favour those opinions, which best suit their prejudices, lives and designs, [so] content themselves without examination, to take upon trust, what they find convenient, and in fashion." This illicit credulity is particularly blameworthy. "[M]ethinks they have a low opinion of their souls . . . what a shame and confusion it is, to the greatest contemners of knowledge, to be found ignorant in things they are concerned to know." Men of "lower condition who surpass them in knowledge" will lead that gentleman who is "certainly the most subjected, the most enslaved, [because so] in his understanding" (IV.XX §6). Knowledge is available here, but trust is inappropriate and yields mere opinion. And a failure to pursue enquiry with any diligence breaches one's epistemic duty.

With trust consistently condemned by Locke in epistemic contexts, the obvious question that must be considered is how he accounts for testimony—the practice of believing propositions on the basis of someone else's say-so. Testimony, surely, is an instance of trust, and yet it is so deeply a part of our normal epistemic lives that to repudiate it would be a form of skepticism. And indeed, Locke is not skeptical about testimony. He values it highly as a way of learning about matters of fact which are consistent with our experience and of historical events.

> That there is such a city in Italy as Rome: that about 1700 years ago, there lived in it a man, called Julius Caesar; that he was a General, and that he won a battle against another called Pompey. This, though in the nature of the thing, there be nothing for, nor against it, yet, being related by historians of credit, and contradicted by no one writer, a man cannot avoid believing it, and can as little doubt of it, as he does of the being and actions of his own acquaintance, whereof he himself is a witness.
>
> (IV.XVI §8; also IV.XVI §11)

Testimony is also possible for propositions that may be demonstrated, such as that the sum of the angles of a triangle is equal to two right angles or that God exists (IV.XV §1, also I.IV §22). Nonetheless, although he is not skeptical about testimony, Locke does not himself use the word "trust" to describe testimony-based beliefs. Although there is a sense of the word on which any hearer's acceptance of a speaker's testimony is a kind of trust, it may not be just an accident that he does not use the term. For one, doing so would be in tension with the significant evidence earlier that he thinks that epistemic trust is a pathology. For another, given his conception of how testimony rationally ought to work, it is arguable that there is a deeper incongruity between his conception of testimony and paradigmatic kinds of trust.

Locke's challenge is to make sense of how one can rationally respond to a speaker's testimony in such a way that it is consistent with his mandate to search out the truth for oneself, in accordance with one's own understanding. On a pre-theoretical understanding of how testimony works, a speaker tells you something, thereby giving her word. In believing her, a hearer thereby comes to know what she said. In the old locution, it is belief on the basis of authority. Being a person who gave and learned from testimony, Locke was, of course, familiar with this, and he shows this in a nice *tu quoque* challenge to Filmer in the *First Treatise* (I §51). Nonetheless, in his official account in the *Essay* of how testimony ought to work, Locke rejected this understanding that belief could be based on authority. On his account, a hearer adopts some doxastic stance towards some proposition, on the basis of testimony, after evaluating its probability. "*[T]he mind, if it will proceed rationally, ought to examine all the grounds of probability* . . . and upon a due balancing the whole, reject, or receive it, with a more or less firm assent, proportionably to the preponderancy of the greater grounds of probability on one side or the other" (IV.XV §5). That Locke's account of rational testimonial acceptance is probabilistic in structure, not just in name, is shown by the grounds he gives which a hearer ought to take account of in weighing what someone says. They are the conformity of the proposition to our own experience; the number, integrity, competence, intentions and consistency of the witnesses; and contrary testimony (IV.XV §4). Locke's fourth "wrong measure of probability," namely authority, further shows that his account is intended to deny the prior understanding of how testimony works. The "*giving up our assent to the common received opinions*" is the gravest source of error and ignorance; "there is not an opinion so absurd, which a man may not receive upon this ground" (IV.XX §17; also *Essays on the Law of Nature*, 1954, 129).

Locke is not a reductionist in the exact way of understanding the term. That is, he does not think that belief based on testimony is simply a species of inductive inference, thereby "reducing" the warrant for testimonially based beliefs to that which is identical for inductive beliefs. As Alexander George has observed, Locke affirms that there are "two foundations of credibility, *viz*. common observation in like cases, and particular testimonies in that particular instance" (IV.XVI §9,; George 2016, 16). The innovation and achievement in Hume's reductionism were to find a way to render testimony and experience commensurable; in effect, Hume found a way to compare apples with apples in the cases where testimony and experience conflict. In contrast, were he a reductionist about testimony, Locke would not have affirmed that there were "two" foundations of credibility; Hume's position rules out that possibility.

Nonetheless, Locke's account of testimony is sympathetic to characteristically reductionist theses. Although he does not directly state whether there is a default entitlement to believe someone's testimony—a characteristic anti-reductionist thesis (e.g. Reid 1785, Coady 1992, Burge 1993)—Locke's discussion of the grounds regarding when one is entitled to believe another, and when not, presumes that this is not the case. More importantly, perhaps, Locke's account of testimony is a paradigm instance of what Ben McMyler has helpfully called *epistemic autonomy*. This is the view that "fully rational agents are always solely epistemically responsible for the justification of their own beliefs" (2011, 6). McMyler's own project is to make sense of how this could be denied. He argues that an audience is entitled to defer epistemic challenges to belief that she has acquired on the basis of testimony back to the speaker. This is what relations of epistemic authority entitle. Others take up the challenge in different ways: Paul Faulkner argues that testimonially acquired belief, when (roughly) the audience fulfills their epistemic duty, enjoys "the extended body of warrant" from the testimonial chain (2011, 22); Sandy Goldberg talks about "extended reliability" (2010). Abstracting from the details, these are all anti-Lockean theses denying epistemic autonomy. Moreover, each of these anti-Lockean accounts may naturally describe their view as a defense of epistemic trust. The epistemic dependence on others is not just a surface-level feature of the account; it is a constitutive and pervasive feature of testimonially based belief. In seeking to eschew such dependence, it is no surprise that Locke eschews the term "trust."

In sum, for Locke, there is no positive role for trust in epistemology. There is a single use of the term "trust" in the *Essay* where the connotations are not strongly condemnatory, and that concerns a practical decision, namely which doctor I should choose to prescribe me some pills (IV. XX §4). It is not that there are good uses of trust and, regrettably, also misuses. Trust itself is the problem. Although I may rely on what others say, I should do so only in specific instances and in such a way that the decision is mine.

4. The Value of Trust

I claimed earlier that it is surprising that Locke ascribes such starkly different values to trust when it occurs in practical and epistemic contexts, respectively. But there are really two questions here. First, why is it that

Locke ascribes such a negative value to trust in epistemic contexts, and positive in practical, such that it describes properly functioning relationships of authority? Second, *is* it surprising? That is, why should there be a unified account that explains the value of trust and when it is justified, for both epistemic and practical contexts? In this concluding section, I argue that the answer to the first, interpretative question helps to illuminate what is at stake in the second question. In identifying why Locke ascribes trust such a different valence in the two contexts, we see why there should be something surprising about the fact that he does. What is at stake is, by implication, one's conception of the well-lived life—and Locke's is impoverished.

The priority of individual freedom explains Locke's different valuations of trust in both epistemology and politics. Taking them in sequence: I argued earlier that the *Essay* is well summarized by one of its section headings, "Men must think and know for themselves," with its converse vice, that one should "blindly submit to the will and dictates of another" in matters of belief. Locke's broadsides against epistemic trust should be understood in this light. Trust stands in the way of the individual making up her own mind epistemically. The same governing priority is evident in Locke's politics. But because trust here helps to protect and enable the individual's natural freedom, rather than to restrict it, it is regarded positively. John Dunn identifies three reasons why trust is the salient way for Locke to describe the proper relation between the citizens and state. First, it reverses who is accountable to whom. Instinctively, the subordinate is accountable to the one in authority. Monarchists in the eighteenth century, whom Filmer spoke for, applied this instinctive assumption to the king–subject relation. In a fiduciary relationship, the one trusted is accountable to the truster. By identifying authorities as trusted by the citizenry, Locke found a subtle way of asserting that the ruler is accountable to, and is to serve, the ruled. (This would have been so paradoxical as to have made no sense to his audience, were Christian theology not to have prepared the ground; cf. Luke 22:27.) Second, trust articulates the claim that entitlement to rule is something that no one is born to, but rather is justified by rights that people delegate to the ruler. There is an external structure of rights that form and constrain the relationship. Third, it expresses the asymmetry of power of the ruler over the ruled, which puts the citizenry in a state of ongoing vulnerability (Dunn 1984, 296).

There are some further reasons why trust is salient for Locke, and it is the final one which is determinative. Fourth, trust captures the unpredictability and open-endedness about the actions that civic authorities may have to undertake, which are still guided by an overarching purpose, namely the public good. For example, the executive is responsible for assembling and dismissing the legislature. It should not be done too often or too infrequently; circumstances and judgment show when it should happen. This is "a case where the uncertainty and variableness of human affairs could not bear a steady fixed rule . . . [so] the best remedy could be found for this defect, was to trust this to the prudence of one who was always to be present, and whose business it was to watch over the public good" (II §156). The same is true for the way that representatives are chosen (II §157–58).

Fifth, and most significantly, trust is revocable. As noted earlier, it should be withdrawn when there is evidence that political power is being used in ways that betray the purpose for which it was given. "[A]ll power given with trust for the attaining an end, being limited by that end, whenever that end is manifestly neglected, or opposed, the trust must necessarily be forfeited." As a result, "there remains still in the people a supreme power to remove or alter the legislative, when they find the legislative act contrary to the trust reposed in them" (II §149). This is the key point for Locke. Identifying trust as a condition of legitimacy gives a clear test for when resistance and revolution becomes appropriate. It is appropriate just when the state betrays the purpose for which trust was bestowed, which according to Locke is the need to protect property rights.

The conclusion of the *Two Treatises* is that it is sometimes lawful to resist the king. As Richard Ashcraft notes, if we would understand Locke's intent, a useful overarching question to ask is why he came to that conclusion (1994, 226). The answer is that people's natural freedom is maintained only if they retain the right to judge whether the powers of the state are being used properly and to act with force to reassert their rights to property when they judge that it is not. So, protecting natural freedom requires justifying the right to revolution. Nor is this right held collectively only. It is held distributively; that is, each individual holds the right to judge for herself whether her trust has been abused. The connection with natural freedom is explicit when trust is first introduced.

> The liberty of man, in society, is to be under no other legislative power, but that established, by consent, in the commonwealth; nor under the dominion of any will, or restraint of any law, but what that legislative shall enact, according to the trust put in it.
>
> (II §22)

So, Locke's differing views on the value of trust are explained by the overarching priority of individual liberty. "We are born free" (II §61). Individuals have the prerogative and responsibility to act and think for themselves. Nicholas Wolterstorff notes this shared emphasis. "In Locke's epistemological thought, as well as his political thought, the sovereign individual occupies center stage" (1996, 151). Locke contests for individuals' freedom in both epistemic and practical contexts, to act in a way unconstrained by others' arbitrary authority, and to believe only the truth, unconstrained by inherited dogma. Trust is an aid to the former and an obstacle to the latter. Accordingly, it is valued positively in his politics, albeit under specified constraints, and it is valued negatively in his epistemology. The valuation reflects simply the effect that trust has, as to whether it promotes freedom.

Once this shared priority is identified, what may seem more of a puzzle is why there should be any presumption in favor of what I have termed a "unified account" of trust. Why suppose that, in both epistemic and practical contexts, there should be a single explanation of why trust is valuable and when it is justified? Given the different effects that trust may have, and the criteria against which those effects may be evaluated, why not just accept that trust may be valuable in some contexts, not in others, and that the conditions which justify it are plural, some relevant on some occasions and not on others? In this line of thought, the desire for a unified account of trust's value is a symptom of a Kant-like aesthetic, in which a taste for order trumps faithfulness to reality, rather than reflecting a genuine intellectual requirement. If a unified account of trust implies that its value is the same in practical and epistemic contexts but the normative facts say otherwise, so much the worse for the presumption that such an account is important.

It seems to me that this misses something important. Locke's valuation of trust is consistent because of the terms by which it is evaluated, namely by its effects. Trust is viewed positively in politics and negatively in epistemology, because (by Locke's lights) it is instrumentally effective in the former but not the latter at enhancing human freedom. Clearly enough, trust can be assessed on instrumental grounds by what it enables in terms of enhancing individual human agency. In military terms, artillery and engineers are "force multipliers." When they support infantry and armor, the latter are greatly more effective. One unit of investment in combat support may increase fighting power by the equivalent of five units of investment in a combat arm. Trust is an "agency multiplier." Trusting well gives an individual far better returns than the same investment of effort in doing the project alone. Locke thinks that this is not the case in epistemic projects, but that it is in our practical projects, and hence values trust accordingly.

It seems to me, however, that this misses out on the larger significance of trust. Trust should not be assessed in instrumental terms only. Its value is not found solely in its agency-multiplying effects. Trust also matters to us because of its interpersonal significance: because of the relationship that it instantiates between truster and trusted or what it says about that relationship. Here are two reasons for thinking so. First, although trust is not always the most instrumentally effective basis for cooperation—threats of violence and shame work pretty well too—it is a generally preferable way. And this is true not only when contrasted with "negative" reasons for cooperation. Cooperation may be based on the offer of extrinsic rewards, such as money, yet people often still prefer to cooperate on the basis of trust. Second, the egoist can recognize the agency-enhancing value of trust. This is a strong indication that something is missing from an account on which trust's value is solely instrumental. Egoism is a pathology in which the social, relational dimensions of a person are malformed. An account is inaccurate if the full value that it ascribes to trust could be endorsed by the egoist. Because Locke values trust only for it what enables, that is true of his account.

In contrast, it seems to me that trust is central to our conception of the normal human life not just for what it enables but for the kinds of relationship that it expresses and constitutes. Trusting relationships are good ones, where both parties are concerned for the other and committed to them. This can be true both in the intimate settings of family and friendship and the wider settings, less affectively freighted but nonetheless vital, of cooperation in pursuit of joint goals or in social contexts where each relies on the other not to renege. Trust is not always normal in a statistical sense: there are contexts where most relationships between people are not trusting. (Think of the social results of the gang warfare for control of the drugs trade in Haiti and Honduras, for instance.) But it is in the original, normative sense of that word: as an achievable part of the flourishing human life.

The presumption in favor of a unified account of trust is indicative of a sense that trust has value as such and not solely for what it enables, significant though that it is. For if trust as such has value—interpersonal value, as I have termed it—then it has that value, regardless of domain. I offered earlier a putative objection to a unified account, which suggested that because trust may have different effects in different contexts, so the conditions that justify it are plural, some relevant on some occasions and not on others. I am generally sympathetic to a pluralist approach to trust (my 2012 paper gives a genealogical account of the concept). The problem with Locke's view of trust is that it is not pluralist enough. In his valuation of trust being driven solely by its effects on human freedom, he fails to see a different basis on which it may be valuable, namely the ways in which trust serves as a positive basis by which people can come together. A unified account does not need to assert a single way in which trust is valuable. An account is unified if it identifies a way in which trust is valuable, which may be realized in both practical and epistemic contexts. The interpersonal value of trust does this.

Nor is it surprising that Locke does not notice the interpersonal value of trust. As noted, the touchstone for Locke's thought is the priority of individual freedom, where this is understood in terms of one person's capacity to decide. In this view, consent is the foundational normative power. As Patrick Deneen has remarked recently, in the liberal anthropology proposed by Hobbes and Locke, humans are "by nature, nonrelational creatures, separate and autonomous. Liberalism begins a project in which the legitimacy of all human relationships—beginning with, but not limited to, political bonds—becomes increasingly dependent on whether those relationships have been chosen" (2018, 32). An implication is that those ways in which I may engage with others, in which my consent is *not* the determining factor in deciding whether this relationship continues, diminish my freedom and are accordingly dis-valuable. Yet trust in its richer, fuller sense of mutual commitment to the other's good entails exactly this vulnerability. So it is no surprise that Locke should value trust solely in terms of its power as an agency multiplier.

That trust has interpersonal value is true, in an uncomplicated way, in practical contexts. It is less transparent for epistemic contexts. At a minimum, epistemic contexts make it plain that it is possible that the instrumental value of trust, and its interpersonal value, may conflict. When I disbelieve my friend's testimony, because she doesn't know what she's talking about, the conflict is made stark. Nonetheless, the possibility that such conflicts exist is itself oblique support for the claim that epistemic trust instantiates some kind of interpersonal value, as well as being evaluable in terms of how truth-conducive it is. The task is to develop a truly social epistemology in which the *relationship* with another person, which is describable in second-person terms, is truth-conducive—and not just the *encounter*, which is describable in third-person terms. I try to articulate how this may be possible rationally elsewhere; doing so is also an attempt to make sense of the first way in which trust is hybrid, as seemingly responsive to both practical and theoretical reasons (Simpson 2018).[4]

Notes

1. Quotations from Locke preserve his spelling and italics, but not the capitals. Where the context is clear, I omit "*Two Treatises*" or "*Essay*" from the citation.
2. Locke would have voted Leave in the UK's 2016 referendum on EU membership, it seems, to repatriate legislative powers that had been unjustly alienated by the executive through treaty.
3. Two further areas of practical reasoning, namely parenting and education, are also exercises of trust for Locke—the first explicitly so (II §59), the latter by implication. The model of education that emerges from *Some Thoughts Concerning Education* is hardly a Rudolf Steiner–style voyage of self-discovery: "children, when little, should look upon their parents as their lords, their absolute governors; and, as such, stand in awe of them" (1690, §41). But the disagreement here is about means, not ends. Locke is clear that the goal of both parenting and education is to equip children to exercise their freedom, when they are adults, through the use of their reason (1690, §41; II §58–59, 63). Parents may not kill their children, e.g., because children are not their parents' property (II §65–66). In describing fatherhood as "a temporary government," the structural affinity is made explicit (II §67. Locke talks of fatherhood primarily to focus his criticism on Filmer and is deliberate in extending the point to mothers, II §64). Parenting and education are different from political power, in that children are not competent to revoke the trust until they reach their majority, when the trust then lapses anyway.
4. It is always risky straying into others' areas of specialization, and I am very grateful to three anonymous reviewers who saved me from some errors in interpretation and who, along with the editor, gave me probing feedback on an earlier draft. As always, mistakes remain mine.

References

Adams, Robert M. 1984. "The Virtue of Faith." *Faith and Philosophy* 1: 3–15.

Ashcraft, Richard. 1994. "Locke's Political Philosophy." In *The Cambridge Companion to Locke*, edited by V. Chappell, 226–51. Cambridge: Cambridge University Press.

Baker, Judith. 1987. "Trust and Rationality." *Pacific Philosophical Quarterly* 68: 1–13.

Burge, Tyler. 1993. "Content Preservation." *Philosophical Review* 102: 457–88.

Coady, C. A. J. 1992. *Testimony: A Philosophical Study*. Oxford: Clarendon Press.

Coleman, James S. 1990. *Foundations of Social Theory*. Cambridge, MA: Belknap Press.

Dasgupta, Partha. 1988. Trust as a Commodity. In *Trust: Making and Breaking Cooperative Relations*, edited by D. Gambetta, 49–72. Oxford: Basil Blackwell.

Deneen, Patrick J. 2018. *Why Liberalism Failed*. New Haven, CT: Yale University Press.

Dunn, John. 1984. "The Concept of 'Trust' in the Politics of John Locke." In *Philosophy in History: Essays on the Historiography of Philosophy*, edited by Richard Rorty, Jerome B. Schneewind, and Quentin Skinner, 279–301. Cambridge: Cambridge University Press.

Faulkner, Paul. 2011. *Knowledge on Trust*. Oxford: Oxford University Press.

George, Alexander. 2016. *The Everlasting Check: Hume on Miracles*. Cambridge, MA: Harvard University Press.

Goldberg, Sanford C. 2010. *Relying on Others: An Essay in Epistemology*. Oxford: Oxford University Press.

Grant, Ruth. 2011. *Strings Attached: Untangling the Ethics of Incentives*. Princeton, NJ: Princeton University Press.

Hardin, Russell. 2002. *Trust and Trustworthiness*. New York: Russell Sage Foundation.

Hawley, Katherine. 2014a. "Trust, Distrust and Commitment." *Noûs* 48: 1–20.

———. 2014b. "Partiality and Prejudice in Trusting." *Synthese* 191: 2029–45.

Holton, Richard. 1994. "Deciding to Trust, Coming to Believe." *Australasian Journal of Philosophy* 72: 63–76.

Hurka, Thomas. 2001. *Virtue, Vice and Value*. Oxford: Oxford University Press.

Jones, Karen. 1996. "Trust as an Affective Attitude." *Ethics* 107: 4–25.

Lagerspetz, Olli. 1998. *Trust: The Tacit Demand*. Dordrecht: Kluwer.

Lähno, Bernd. 2001. "On the Emotional Character of Trust." *Ethical Theory and Moral Practice* 4: 171–89.

Laslett, Peter. 1988. "Introduction." In *Two Treatises of Government*, edited by P. Laslett, 3–126. Cambridge: Cambridge University Press.

Locke, John. 1954. *Essays on the Law of Nature*, edited by W. von Leyden. Oxford: Clarendon Press.

———. 1689 [1975]. *An Essay Concerning Human Understanding*, edited by Peter H. Nidditch. Oxford: Clarendon Press.

———. 1690 [2000]. *Some Thoughts Concerning Education*, edited by John W. Yolton and Jean S. Yolton. Oxford: Clarendon Press.

———. 1698 [1988]. *Two Treatises of Government*, edited by Peter Laslett. Cambridge: Cambridge University Press.

McGeer, Victoria. 2008. "Trust, Hope and Empowerment." *Australasian Journal of Philosophy* 86: 237–54.

McMyler, Benjamin. 2011. *Testimony, Trust, and Authority*. Oxford: Oxford University Press.

Reid, Thomas. 1785 [2002]. *Essays on the Intellectual Powers of Man*, edited by Derek R. Brookes and Knud Haakonssen. Edinburgh: Edinburgh University Press.

Simpson, Thomas. 2012. What Is Trust? *Pacific Philosophical Quarterly* 93(4): 550–69.

———. 2017. "Trust and Evidence." In *The Philosophy of Trust*, edited by Paul Faulkner and Thomas Simpson, 177–94. Oxford: Oxford University Press.

———. 2018. "Trust, Belief, and the Second-Personal." *Australasian Journal of Philosophy* 96: 447–59.

Stroud, Sarah. 2006. "Epistemic Partiality in Friendship." *Ethics* 116: 498–524.

Swinburne, Richard. 1981. *Faith and Reason*. Oxford: Clarendon Press.

Sztompka, Piotr. 1999. *Trust: A Sociological Theory*. Cambridge: Cambridge University Press.

Wolterstorff, Nicholas. 1996. *John Locke and the Ethics of Belief*. Cambridge: Cambridge University Press.

3 Epistemic and Practical Dependence and the Value of Skills or: Satnavs, Good or Bad?

Elizabeth Fricker

1. Our Extensive Epistemic Dependence on Testimony and a Question It Makes Salient

Testimony[1] as a distinctive epistemic source comprises the spoken or written word of a speaker or author, who (actually or apparently) seeks to impart her knowledge to others by means of linguistic assertions aimed at achieving this.[2] Primary testimony consists of face-to-face telling, a personal transaction. Extended testimony includes personal letters and emails, all purportedly factual television and radio programs, similar newspaper and magazine articles and books, and of course nowadays all purportedly factual Internet sources.

In modern societies our epistemic dependence on testimony for what we know and believe is massively extensive. Through reliance on what we learn from others, we gain access to a rich heritage of accumulated theoretical belief, hopefully much of which is knowledge—of history, geography, the sciences, and so forth. True, one may first acquire a belief through testimony but then later acquire nontestimonial evidence for it. Nonetheless, it is obvious that, in the circumstances of modern society, for much of what each person believes they do so only on the basis of testimony; and if their belief is indeed knowledge, this is due to its source in suitable testimony.[3] Moreover there is an oblique dependence on testimony even for beliefs immediately arrived at through one's own perception, when the conceptual background enabling one's perception of some fact involves concepts that gain their identity from their place in a theory one's knowledge of which is mediated by testimony. This is an everyday phenomenon; for instance, to see that someone is using her mobile phone one must possess that concept, and this entails one's grasp of a network of knowledgeable beliefs epistemically dependent on knowledge acquired from others.[4]

So, for each one of us members of an epistemically advanced society with a rich accumulated heritage of knowledge, one's massive epistemic dependence on one's past acceptance of the word of others is a fact of one's epistemic circumstances. The wealth of one's epistemic superabundance is bought at the price of one's huge epistemic dependence on the word of others—one's past and ongoing accepting reliance on testimony, primary and extended.[5]

The reliance of each one of us on others' testimony for one's knowledge is a fact of our modern epistemic predicament, one that there is no going back on—it is not feasible, without giving up on any semblance of a normal modern lifestyle, to prescind from all reliance on knowledge gained from accepting others' testimony. In this chapter I explore a question made salient by this fact. One relies on others for knowledge when they possess epistemic skills that oneself lacks. But although one cannot aspire to acquire all possible epistemic skills oneself, over time one faces choices about which skills to continue to rely on others to exercise on one's behalf and which to set out to acquire oneself.

What holds for epistemic skills holds for skills more generally—practical as well as epistemic. At a given point in time, if another possesses a skill one lacks, one relies on her for its outputs, epistemic or material, in the domain in question. But over time one faces a choice: to continue to rely on the other, or to set out to acquire the skill in question oneself. And so I ask the question: does one have some reason to acquire and exercise skills, practical or epistemic, oneself, where one can, rather than relying on others to exercise them on one's behalf?[6]

One's skill-related reliance may be only indirectly on other persons. This is so when one relies directly on a machine or electronic device designed and manufactured by others who deployed skills and knowledge that oneself lacks. Reliance on devices that one does not know how to construct oneself, nor fully understand how they work, is almost as old as civilization itself. But its extent, and its pace of advance, have become extreme in the last 50 years. With the advent of advanced microchip technology, smart devices are now being designed and marketed that have the capability to substitute for and replace very many highly sophisticated skills that previously have been exclusively the province of intelligent human beings—self-driving cars are but one example. More and more of what were exclusively human skillful activities can be given over to robots and other computer-controlled devices, leaving the humans without any need, as in the past, to develop and exercise the skill in question.

Society should be concerned about this. By concern I do not mean anxiety. But it is important that we ask questions about this radical new development overtaking us, before it is too late to influence and direct its course. This is one central motivation for my question about the value of possessing and sometimes exercising skills. There is also a more specific autobiographical spur to my concern with this issue. My interest in the question I address was in part prompted by arguments with my children about the desirability or otherwise of being able to navigate on a car journey oneself, albeit with the use of a map, rather than relying uncritically on the audible instructions of an electronic "satnav" or GPS device. My instinctive view was that having some understanding of the route of one's journey was of value; that something of what is worthwhile in human life is lost if one abdicates from all pretensions both to grasp the layout of one's environment and the skills to navigate it, and is happy blindly to obey the dictates of an electronic device in achieving arrival at one's intended destination. This chapter explores a broader question whose answer determines whether there is any good philosophical argument to support my initial prejudice. My conclusion is that there is. To see how, and to find out if you agree with me, you must read on. Some more scene setting is needed, before I can address my main question about the value of skills—that is, of possessing and sometimes exercising them.

2. The Nature of Our Epistemic Dependence on Testimony

A recipient of testimony may respond to it epistemically in any of four different ways. She may disregard it epistemically, giving it no credence; she may actively disbelieve it; she may take the fact of the speaker's testimony that P as some evidence for P, but without believing it outright; or she may take the speaker's word for what she states and form the belief that P on her say-so. My concern in this chapter is with this last, canonical response.[7]

A speaker who tells her intended audience that P purports to be expressing her knowledge that P: she presents herself as doing so. The recipient's complementary role in this "Gricean handshake"[8] is to accept the speaker to be indeed doing what she purports, viz. expressing her knowledge with a view to imparting it to her audience, and to form a belief in what she is told on this basis—taking the speaker's word for what she states and forming a belief on her say-so. A recipient who believes what she is told on this basis is committed to accepting that the speaker knows what she states—discovering she does not know it defeats the basis for her belief.[9] A few freak cases apart, she will be epistemically placed to know this only if she is in a position to know that the speaker has this property:

Trus$_{S,P,O}$ Not easily[10] would S tell me that P on this occasion O unless she knew that P.

When one thus takes a speaker's word for what she states, trusting[11] her with respect to her testimony, one has *epistemic dependence* on the speaker for the knowledge one thereby gains. That is to say, first: the recipient comes to know that P in this way only if the speaker, in telling, expressed her knowledge. (See Fricker 2006a, 2015.) Second: the positive status as knowledge of the recipient's belief is partly inherited from the fact that the speaker knew, and hence had suitable evidence for, what she stated.[12] So, in forming a belief through trust in another's testimony, I rely for the status of my belief as knowledge on the relevant epistemic and character virtues of the testifier—her sincerity and competence, which together comprise her trustworthiness (Trus S,P,O) on this occasion. I rely on the speaker to know what she tells me; in doing so, I rely on her abilities correctly to gather, interpret and assess the evidence for what she tells—on her relevant epistemic skills.

3. One's Choices Regarding Remaining Epistemically and Practically Dependent Versus Acquiring New Skills

As we have already acknowledged, this epistemic dependence on others for much of one's knowledge is a practically inevitable feature of modern life—if one attempted to restrict oneself to belief in what one can know without dependence on what one has learned from others, one would know impossibly little. The supposed ideal of the autonomous knower, who takes no one else's word for anything and believes only what she is able to find out for herself, using her own individual cognitive resources, is not a realistic practical possibility. Moreover, this supposed ideal is in reality no such thing: someone who never trusts another person's word shows either an irrational paranoia or a complete lack of a grasp of folk psychology. Everyday knowledge of the world, and of the nature and situation of oneself and other people, shows one's own limited epistemic reach, and the fact that on many matters others are better placed epistemically than oneself and well enough placed to attain knowledge. Hence in many situations it is not merely epistemically permissible to take the word of others, but epistemically mandatory to do so, in some situations to override one's own previous opinion. Refusal to accept another's judgment over one's own in a case where she is evidently better placed to know than oneself shows not laudable epistemic self-direction, but irrational, pig-headed epistemic egoism. (These arguments are developed in more detail in Fricker 2006b.)

So our epistemic dependence on others for much of our knowledge is a fact of modern human life. Trying to eliminate it entirely is both infeasible and would be, in our actual human epistemic and cognitive circumstances, irrational. But although total elimination of one's epistemic dependence on others is not an option, there remain further questions we can and should ask. Here is one: should one seek to minimize one's epistemic dependence on others to the maximum extent feasible? Despite the constraints set by our limited cognitive capacities and our worldly situation, including time constraints, there is much room for choices here. One may have no choice but to trust another's word, on pain of remaining ignorant on a topic, at a given moment in time. But when one considers the progress of one's life, including one's epistemic activities over time, it is clear that major choices confront one. Over time one can take steps to acquire both knowledge and knowledge-gathering skills in a domain of enquiry. I will refer to these as epistemic skills.

A particular epistemic skill, say the ability to identify birds in the wild, will typically consist partly of mastery of a system of propositional knowledge, and partly of cognitive-cum-practical abilities, including perceptual recognitional abilities. Together, this package equips its bearer to acquire new knowledge in fresh circumstances, where someone lacking the package cannot do so. For instance the bird expert can tell what bird just flew overhead or was making its call, while the novice cannot. (This may be through a combination of perceptual recognitional capacity, plus background knowledge of what bird species are likely to be in the area.)

Our bird example illustrates a key pervasive feature: that the gleaning of fresh knowledge through perception is very frequently dependent on background knowledge and training. A microbiologist looking down a microscope at a slide may be able to draw all sorts of conclusions about the sample, whereas someone ignorant of the relevant science would see only some dark wriggly things. A cricketing enthusiast may see the batsman swing at a loose ball and catch an edge and be caught at second slip, where one not familiar with the game will struggle to see anything much at all. This is why, to repeat, epistemic skills most importantly confer the ability to gain fresh knowledge in a situation, where one lacking the skill cannot do so.

Individuals make choices in their lives, and choices are certainly there for them, as to which epistemic skills they are content to rely on others to exercise on their behalf, gaining their knowledge in the domain in question only at second-hand,[13] and which they set out to acquire for themselves, to attain first-hand knowledge. For instance, if I know only enough about cars to be able to drive one, then I am entirely reliant on my mechanic to diagnose a fault, and to tell me what is wrong with my car and what is required to repair it.

There are similar choices to be made as regards which practical skills one is content to allow others to exercise on one's behalf, and which one decides to acquire and exercise for oneself. In fact there is no clear separation between practical and epistemic skills—most skills include elements of both; and epistemic dependence tends to go hand-in-hand with practical dependence. Hence there is no clear separation between the choices to enlarge the domain of one's epistemic and one's practical skills: if I understand nothing of how a car engine works, I will both have to trust my mechanic as to what its fault is and rely on her to repair it for me.[14] Learning more about car engines will enhance my perceptual knowledge-getting skills when I inspect the engine, and is likely to enable me to do at least some simple repairs myself.

4. Some Normative Principles Regarding Skills

One depends epistemically on another when one relies on her to deploy her epistemic skills to obtain knowledge in some domain and then supply it to one, where one lacks the epistemic skills to obtain this knowledge for oneself. One depends practically on another in some domain of activity with a material output when one lacks the practical skills to achieve this output for oneself, and so must rely on her to exercise her practical skills in the domain on one's behalf, to create the output and then provide it to oneself. As already remarked, epistemic and practical dependence are strongly correlated, since they are interconnected: if I know nothing about how a car works, then I am badly placed to diagnose what is wrong with my car, and for the same reason badly placed, even if under some description I know what is wrong with it, to effect the repair myself.

Virtually all skills involve a mixture of the practical and the epistemic in their exercise. We shall say a skill is epistemic when its proprietary output is propositional knowledge,[15] and that it is practical when the proprietary output of its exercise is a material object or outcome—a fully functioning car, or a beautiful mahogany cabinet, or a well-designed building meeting various desiderata, or a perfect sponge cake; for the skill of archery, hitting the target; for the skill of hunting, catching or killing the intended prey. But this differentiation in terms of type of output conceals the fact that the material output of a practical skill requires the deployment of knowledge—both that and how—along the way to achieving it; and for an epistemic skill, although the output is knowledge, in most cases practical skills must be deployed along the way to achieving it. For instance, a microbiologist must be able to collect suitable samples and prepare her slides before she can gain knowledge from observing them under the microscope. Moreover, many skills, if individuated intuitively, have both material outcomes and knowledge as potential proprietary outputs, and as such are practical-cum-epistemic skills. This is true of the complex skill mediating the ability to repair motor vehicles and of the complex skill underlying the ability of an expert cabinet maker.

Is there anything less than fully satisfactory about my situation when I have total epistemic and practical dependence on my mechanic vis-à-vis how things stand with my car and its potential repair? Would it be better for me if I had the epistemic-cum-practical skill to allow me to diagnose the fault and repair the car myself? This question turns on broader ones about the normative status of epistemic and practical dependence, and about the normative prudential value of skills, epistemic and practical. Should one seek to acquire epistemic and practical skills? Should one seek to acquire as many as possible? Which ones should one seek to acquire? Are there certain skills that each one of us has reason to seek to acquire?

In this chapter I make a preliminary foray into addressing these questions that are of urgent importance in our contemporary circumstances. To do so, I formulate some principles regarding skills, and then consider with respect to each whether a plausible case can be made defending it. Here are the principles, which are all variants on the thesis that one has some reason to acquire skills, which I abbreviate to RAS.

Unrestricted-RAS: For any skill (practical and/or epistemic) that one lacks and is able to acquire, each one of us has some reason (pro tanto reason) to acquire and sometimes exercise that skill; where this is not merely instrumental reason.

Certain-RAS: For each one of us, there is a certain set of skills one has or is able to acquire such that one has some reason, for each skill in the set, if one lacks it, to acquire and sometimes exercise it; and if one has it, to maintain and sometimes exercise it; where this is not merely instrumental reason.

Some-RAS: Each one of us has some reason to ensure that one has and sometimes exercises some skills—that one is not entirely skill-less; where this is not merely instrumental reason.

Core-RAS: There is a certain set of broad skill-types such that each one of us has some reason to ensure, if she is able, for every skill-type in the set, that she has and sometimes exercises a skill of that type; where this is not merely instrumental reason.

The reasons in play in these principles are pro tanto reasons, not all-things-considered reasons. In many cases the reason may be very weak, and in very many cases it will be overridden by other cumulatively stronger reasons. But the reason is overridden, not defeated, by these other reasons. It is still there—it just is not strong enough to mandate action all things considered.

The reasons in our principles are normative reasons—reasons *for* acting in a certain way. Following a distinguished leading tradition in contemporary ethics, we say that there is for agent A a normative reason for her to perform an action of a certain kind φ-ing, when φ-ing would have some property that counts in favor of performing it, for agent A.[16] I will assume that properties of φ-ing that count in favor of performing it for A provide a *prudential* normative reason for A to φ. (If there are properties of some actions that provide a moral or perfective reason for A to perform them, they will not be considered in this discussion.) And I will assume, along with a mainstream tradition, that the property of φ-ing that confers such prudential normative reason is that φ-ing would contribute positively to A's well-being—to how well A's life goes *for her*. Well-being or welfare is the central concept in most contemporary theories of what a person has prudential reason to do—her well-being is the good it is rational for her to pursue from the point of view of her self-interest.[17]

So: A has a prudential normative reason to φ just if φ-ing will in some way contribute positively to A's well-being. This principle tells us what needs to be shown, for each of our principles, to establish it: the acquiring of skills as specified in the principle must contribute positively to the agent's well-being.

However, to vindicate our principles, acquiring and exercising skills as specified must not contribute only instrumentally to the agent's well-being, due to further contingent causal consequences of possessing or exercising them; rather, **their possession or exercise must in itself directly contribute to the agent's well-being**. However, I will understand this broadly, so that if possessing or exercising a skill constitutes a necessary background condition for the subject's attaining an adequate level of well-being in her life, this counts as a direct, not instrumental reason to acquire and exercise that skill.

Normative reasons are different from motivating reasons. The latter are just that—reasons that motivate an agent to act and which then explain why she acted. An agent has a motivating reason to act if she has an inclination, a desire, to so act. There can exist a normative reason for A to φ, but A may not be motivated to φ if she is unaware of this reason. However, normative reasons would be of little interest if they did not link to motivation. As Raz observes (Raz 1999, chapter 2), one of the distinctive features of human beings is that we are responsive to reasons: if someone is rational and is aware of a prudential normative reason (PN-reason) for her to φ, then she will have some motivation to φ; though this may be overridden by other stronger reasons or by weakness of will. This places a constraint on what features we can propose as providing PN-reason to φ.

Different theories of well-being provide different accounts of what features of an action provide a PN-reason for A to perform it. The desire-fulfillment theory of well-being ensures that normative reasons and motivating reasons coincide, since it says one has a PN-reason to perform an action just if one desires to do so. But other "objective" theories allow for the two sorts of reasons to come apart. However, to repeat, the proposed PN-reason-providing property of an action, the feature which contributes to well-being, had better be one that tends to motivate when the agent is aware of it, on pain of irrelevance to her plans and actions. In my defense later of the principles, I appeal only to uncontroversial ingredients of well-being that are undeniably motivating as features of prospective actions: pleasure and enjoyment, and happiness.[18]

Though, as just explained, motivating reasons (which category includes all desires) are not ipso facto normative reasons, getting what one wants generally tends to make for an improvement in one's well-being—and so I will assume that, where an agent has the desire to acquire a skill, she has some normative reason to do so.[19] The more difficult task is to show that an agent has some reason to acquire and exercise a skill, even when she lacks any inclination to do so. To say she does is to maintain that she is missing out on some good of human life, something that would contribute to her well-being, if she fails to acquire and exercise the skill—i.e., that exercising the skill would contribute directly to her well-being in a specific way not otherwise available.

The principles speak of one having reason to "acquire and sometimes exercise" a skill. One will have PN-reason to do so if this would contribute to one's well-being. "To acquire a skill" is a success verb, whose success is possession of the skill, which is required for its exercise. So which of these exactly is the bearer of PN-value,[20] the contributor to the agent's well-being—the process of skill acquisition, its upshot skill possession, or the skill's exercise? Typically it will be the skill's exercise rather than mere possession that contributes to the agent's well-being; although in my argument for Some-RAS, I suggest possession in itself contributes to well-being. A significant limitation of my treatment here is that I assume that the process of acquisition in itself has no PN-value: it never contributes to the agent's well-being. This assumption is certainly false, and I make it only as a simplification in a first treatment of complicated issues. Acquiring a skill always takes some effort, in many cases sustained over a long period. There may be instrumental PN-value in qualities of character, such as discipline and perseverance, that are reinforced by such efforts. Alternatively, the efforts and processes of acquisition may themselves be enjoyable, directly or in their concomitant side effects. For instance, someone may have PN-reason to take up watercolor painting because she is lonely and this involves enrolling in classes where she will meet other like-minded people. Such direct benefits and beneficial side effects of the process of skill acquisition are ignored in the present discussion.

A major simplifying assumption behind the formulation of my four principles is that one either has or lacks a given skill, since they do not speak to the issue of improvement of skill level. Thus I ignore the fact that many skills come in degrees—for instance, playing the piano. Taking account of this fact would mean modifying my principles to include this issue: given that I have a skill to some level, do I have some PN-reason to seek to improve my level of skill? I am confident that accommodating the fact that skills come in degrees would complicate my arguments, rather than requiring a different approach.[21] Here, I assume that acquiring a skill means acquiring it to a middling standard of competent performance.

The principles speak of one having "some reason" to acquire a skill. So this reason may be very weak; it may be so weak as to be always overridden by other competing reasons. This is bound to be so in most cases of skills, because finite time and capacities mean one can only acquire a very few of the skills which one has the capacity in principle to acquire—even a skilled multilinguist can only learn a small fraction of all the world's hundreds of different languages. In other cases, the reason may be a very strong one that will be overridden only in exceptional circumstances. Does this latitude mean that the principles are so weak as to be uninteresting? I do not think so. Necessarily, any human will acquire in her lifetime only a tiny fraction of the multitude of skills she in principle has the capacity to acquire. There is a question of principle as to whether she is missing out on something of potential value to her through this lack, some good which, if she possessed it, would contribute distinctively to her well-being. This is the issue my formulation and evaluation of the principles are focused on.

5. Putting Aside Two Instrumental Reasons to Acquire Skills

My interest is in whether there exists some PN-reason for one to acquire and sometimes exercise skills, where this is direct, not merely instrumental reason. In this section I note, only to put aside, two purely instrumental reasons.

When one lacks a certain skill, epistemic or practical, one is reliant on others to exercise that skill and deliver its outputs to one on one's behalf. So one has epistemic or practical dependence on others. And this dependence brings with it risks. For epistemic dependence, there is the ever-present risk of being given inaccurate information, due to incompetence, carelessness, bad luck or malevolent intent, by those one relies on for their expert knowledge. Various routes are open to a layperson to evaluate the credentials and hence the credibility of epistemic experts; one is not entirely helpless and at the mercy of a particular expert (see Goldman 2001, Fricker 2006b). But still, the risks of being fed falsehoods are a powerful instrumental reason to seek to become to some degree expert oneself in a domain where accurate information is important to one's well-being. This purely instrumental reason to acquire epistemic skills oneself is undeniable and is not my present topic.

Similar considerations apply with practical dependence on others. "If you want a job done properly, do it yourself" is an everyday maxim. It is certainly true that doing a job oneself is the only way to avoid the risk of being let down in various ways by others—due to incompetence or just not giving high enough priority to getting it finished by the due date.

We may be let down not by other people, but by the machines they have invented. In our contemporary world of hugely sophisticated electronic technology, our everyday lives are imbued with dependence on its products: our laptops and the Internet services they connect us to, the complicated computer systems that control the various services relating to air travel, that control the banking system, medical data and services—virtually every area of modern economic and social life. We are regularly reminded of the risks incurred by this massive and ubiquitous dependence when we wake to headlines of some disaster caused by the crashing of a computer control system. I think these risks are something we should be more aware of; but these instrumental risks are not my present concern.

This is a good point to note that skill-possession and dependence are not mutually exclusive alternatives. The advent of new devices that replace a previous human skill necessitate a new skill: that of using these very devices. So an instrumental case for acquiring new skills in order to avoid the risks of dependence would not work for such skills that sit on top of our dependence on technology—the skills of using the devices in question.

Instrumental PN-reasons for acquiring skills, to avoid the risks incurred by dependence on others, are not our current topic. We also need to distinguish between the different ideas that exercising skills is somehow noninstrumentally valuable and that incurring dependence on others is somehow noninstrumentally bad. If that were so, that would provide reason to avoid it, either by acquiring the skills in question oneself or by adopting a lifestyle that eschews the many benefits that reliance on others' skills provides—becoming a hermit. In fact there seems no reason to hold that incurring dependence, whether epistemic or practical, on others is noninstrumentally bad. Indeed, many important goods that form part of human well-being arise through our dependence on others in interpersonal and social relationships. Emotional dependence is primary here, but it is natural for this to go with some division of labor and trusting epistemic and practical interdependence in various areas.

A limitation of this chapter is that it takes an individualistic standpoint. Many skills are exercised jointly by a group, and cooperative endeavor involving large research teams is the rule in modern science. A fuller treatment would allow for this. But this fact does not render invalid my question: "is there some PN-reason for an individual to acquire and exercise skills?", so long as some skills are exercised by an individual, not a group.

We are almost ready to give the arguments for my principles. But first, a bit more about skills.

6. Skills and Abilities

Skill is an everyday notion, and there is no need to provide an explicit definition of practical or epistemic skills, necessary and sufficient conditions for being one, to proceed with the argument of this chapter. But it will be useful to make some remarks and a distinction.

We can make a distinction between skills and abilities. Abilities are dispositions. One has the ability to achieve a certain target outcome when this holds: one is very likely (sufficiently so) to succeed in achieving the target outcome when one tries. This condition must be relativized to a suitable range of circumstances, including one's own state. Thus, for example, I have the ability to hit the target in archery practice if I am very likely to do so when I attempt to, so long as I am in the required state—not drunk, or with drops in my eyes that blur my vision, etc.—and conditions are suitable—there is not a hurricane blowing or thick smoke obscuring the target.[22]

Abilities are individuated by what they are the ability to achieve. The achievement is an intended outcome of my action.[23] What then are skills, if not identical with abilities? Skills can be thought of as the mediators of abilities. I am able to hit the target in archery because I am a skilled archer; my skill explains why and how I am able to achieve this success. The same ability can be mediated by substantially different skills, so two people can differ as to the skill-based explanation of their possession of the ability. For instance, one person may be a good cake baker because she meticulously follows the instructions in a good cookbook, weighing out ingredients carefully, setting the oven temperature and following the recipe's timings; another may bake entirely by bottom-up experience-acquired instinct, not even using scales to weigh her ingredients, doing what "feels right" to her. Their overall skill is the same—the skill of cake baking—but its simple component skills are different.

Skills and abilities come in great variety: from whistling and swimming to cake baking and cabinet making; from the skills of a good launderer to those of a research astrophysicist. In one sense any skill, and any ability, has a proprietary intended outcome. But in some cases this is simply engaging in the skilled activity in question, as with whistling and swimming. Swimming and whistling have no proprietary intended outcome except in this trivial sense; they are not substantially teleological skills.[24] Other skills are substantially teleological; they have a proprietary separate material output—for instance, the skill of cake baking has as the end result of its exercise a cake. The skill to bake a cake is mediated by various more specific skills employed in the process—weighing, mixing, stirring, etc. These, however, combine to constitute the overall skill of cake baking.

For present purposes it is important to distinguish these two broad kinds of skill. One kind is substantially teleological; call these means-end skills. Such skills are a necessary means to achieving a desired end. For instance, doing laundry is needed in order to obtain the good of clean clothes. A person normally engages in such means-end skilled activity only when she seeks the end it produces.

Other skills do not have a separate end result; they are skillful activities, the only end involved is the internal one of engaging in the activity itself—such as swimming, whistling, reading Russian poetry or listening appreciatively to a Wagner opera.[25] More complex cases are a mixture of both, for instance climbing to the summit of a mountain or playing a competitive game. The aim of one's climbing trip is to reach the summit, and maybe the best bit of the trip is when one does so; but one's project is to *climb* to the top of the mountain—getting there by road or helicopter would not be the same at all.

Many means-end skilled activities are ones that humans only engage in because they are a necessary means to achieve their end result. They are generally regarded as drudgery, a tedious chore that must be done to get the desired result. Who would spend time washing clothes by hand unless they needed clean clothes and have no access to a washing machine? Skilled activities with no separate end result do not fit the means-end model. There is no reason to engage in them unless either one finds them enjoyable or they serve some further instrumental purpose external to their identity. (One may cultivate the skill of golfing and go on the firm's golfing days, though one dislikes playing golf, in order to network with one's colleagues.)

Armed with this distinction, we will now consider the case for our principles.

7.   A Pleasure-Based Case for Certain-RAS, None for Unrestricted-RAS

As examined in our previous section, some skills, like clothes washing, are the means to an outcome, such as clean clothes, that is the ontologically distinct result of their exercise. One has PN-reason to acquire and exercise such means-end skills when one will benefit from the outcome[26] and has no other means to attain it. But this is instrumental reason, and if this beneficial consequence is the only well-being-enhancing feature of the skill, then one has no reason to acquire and exercise the skill to attain the outcome once a preferable alternative way of obtaining it is available—in our laundry case, a washing machine.

Of course, if in addition one enjoys washing clothes, then the situation is different: one has a PN-reason to engage in clothes washing for its own sake, not merely for its consequences (more of this shortly).

For such means-end skills, if one does not enjoy exercising them and it does not make one happier, then doing so does not contribute directly to one's well-being; hence, one has no direct, as opposed to contingent instrumental, reason to acquire and exercise them.[27] This being so, I do not think there is any cogent case to be made for Unrestricted-RAS. One has no noninstrumental PN-reason to acquire particular skills that one would not enjoy exercising, and this will be so for many means-end skills that are for one just tedious drudgery. Of course there will often be instrumental reasons for acquiring them, rather than relying on another person or device to exercise them one one's behalf; these have been noted, and put aside, not being our present topic. Moreover there is no reason to acquire and exercise them simply in order to avoid dependence on other people or the machines they have designed and manufactured. So far as I can see, there is nothing intrinsically bad about dependence as such; and as noted, relations with other individuals and groups that involve dependence are essential in giving rise to various distinctively human goods such as interpersonal trust, affection and friendship, features that contribute to human well-being.

It is important that the type of reason and associated value we are considering is PN-reason and value. If there is indeed such a thing as perfectionist value—the value an activity is said to have when exercising it is part of the excellence of the kind of thing in question, as determined by its active nature—then one might seek to mount an argument that any skill humans are capable of acquiring is part of their excellence. The most economical route to this, covering all humanly attainable skills, goes thus:

> The ability to seek and acquire knowledge is part of human excellence, and so any item of knowledge has some (perfectionist) value. For any skill, exercising it gives access to a certain kind of knowledge—what it is like to do so—that is not otherwise available; hence for every humanly attainable skill, one has some non-instrumental perfectionist reason to acquire and exercise it.

Perfectionist reason and value is not my topic, and I will not assess this argument further. Perfectionist value is not my concern because I am interested in reasons for acting that will motivate any rational human once they become aware of them. I do not see why the information that exercising a certain skill is part of excellence for humans should motivate one, unless one contingently has the desire to excel qua human in every possible respect; a desire which many of us lack.[28]

We may conclude that there is no noninstrumental PN-reason to do one's washing by hand, nor to acquire skills in clothes washing, when a washing machine is reliably available—assuming only, as is empirically plausible, that one would not enjoy the process of washing clothes by hand.[29] So there is nothing to regret about the invention of washing machines, no distinctive aspect of human well-being is threatened or curtailed by it; on the contrary, it frees up people, mainly women, from the drudgery of scrubbing, rinsing and mangling, to enable them to spend their precious time on other more rewarding and worthwhile activities. What goes for washing machines goes for many other labor-saving devices: they are an unalloyed good, and their invention and widespread availability constitute unambiguous human progress.

Just as there is nothing to regret about the invention and widespread diffusion of many labor-saving devices, there is nothing to regret about the extensive social division of skills of labor. Unless I would enjoy spending my Sundays tinkering around under the bonnet of my car, there is no noninstrumental reason for me to seek training as a mechanic so I can diagnose and fix the fault with my car myself. It is just fine, from my standpoint, for me to go on relying on the services of my mechanic, leaving me free to spend my weekends on things I enjoy doing. The division of labor and skills is a pervasive general good of civilization and economic advance—especially so if tastes are idiosyncratic, so some will gain satisfaction from exercising skills in activities that to others are just a boring chore.

From what I have said so far, the reader may have anticipated the case I will make for Certain-RAS. Each person has some PN-reason to acquire and exercise each in a certain set of skills, viz. each skill such that she would enjoy exercising it. What this set is varies from person to person—one person's enjoyable and exciting challenge is another's nightmare, for instance caving, mountaineering and skydiving. And one person's evening of intense, profoundly moving aesthetic appreciation is to another a complete bore—such as sitting through a performance of a lengthy Wagner opera.[30] So what one has PN-reason to do depends on one's tastes, what kind of thing one is disposed to enjoy.

The case that must be made for Certain-RAS, however, is not so quick. What contributes to well-being, on our uncontroversial view of some of its ingredients, is the enjoyment one gains from the skydiving or the opera. But is actually making the dive, or going to the opera, necessary to getting this? To get this result I need to invoke a specific conception of pleasure and enjoyment that I believe is correct but which is controversial. Here I can only make a quick sketch of an argument in its favor.

Pleasure and enjoyment are closely related, but are not identical. The same holds for pain and suffering.[31] Enjoying oneself is a global notion, in the sense that it entails that things are all-things-considered subjectively good for one during the period of one's enjoyment. In contrast, one may have a pleasant sensation while being uncomfortable or anxious or distracted and so not enjoy oneself overall. But if one gets pleasure from an activity, then one will enjoy it so long as there are not other aspects of one's current subjective state or background beliefs that interfere with this: pleasure suffices for enjoyment in the absence of interfering factors. Moreover, it is the pleasurableness of an activity that makes it enjoyable. Thus in what follows I discuss the nature of the pleasures of skilled activity and appreciation, which make for enjoyment of those activities and appreciations. If these distinctive pleasures of skilled activity can only be enjoyed by one who possesses the skill, then one cannot get the distinctive enjoyment of the activity without possessing the skill.

It may be that some pleasures are just sensations—of pleasant taste, for instance. These are phenomenal occurrences in consciousness lacking any representational content, caused by some activity (e.g., eating) but ontologically independent of this cause. If this is true of some pleasant sensations, then they could be had by someone hooked up to Nozick's notorious "experience machine," and the PN-reason to engage in any activity that causes them would be only instrumental.[32] I am skeptical that there are any such purely sensational pleasures—nice tastes would seem to be a prime candidate, but in fact experienced taste is highly dependent on cognitive setting—as you will know if you have ever sipped a glass of milk while expecting it to be water. This suggests, though it does not entail, that there is a representational element to the pleasant taste-experience itself.

Whatever is the correct account of pleasures of sensation, many pleasures are inherently representational and involve an intentional relation to their object—the appreciated object or the activity one is engaged in. This is true of all pleasures of skilled activity and of appreciation, such as the skills involved in skydiving and in listening appreciatively to Wagner. And these are the ones involved in the pleasantness of skilled activities. One's pleasure in listening to Wagner is an aspect of one's appreciation of his music, the pleasurable thrill of skydiving is the thrill of what one is now doing.

It may be objected here that although it is true that what is pleasant and enjoyable is one's appreciation of the music, the pleasantness itself is a distinct aspect of one's experience that is in principle separable. This might be argued for modally, by claiming that one could have an experience that is exactly similar in all representational content yet not pleasant. This line of argument is fallacious, and its conclusion is false. Just because one can conceive of a cat with a grin, and another cat that is exactly similar but not grinning, does not entail that the grin of the grinning cat is separable from the cat which grins.[33] So it is, I claim, with the pleasantness of experiences of skilled activity and skilled appreciation generally. Another line of argument stems from neurophysiology: that there is activity in a specific part of the brain associated with felt "positive affect." Again, I do not think this shows that the positive valence of the experience is separable from its other aspects; it is not an addition to them; rather, it suffuses them. (See discussion and references in Katz 2016.)

A Rylean account of the pleasantness of skilled activity and appreciation maintains that it is essentially relational: it is an aspect or manner of one's engagement in the activity, part of the way in which one is aware of what one is engaged in.[34] If this is so, there is no metaphysical possibility of getting the pleasure in question without engaging in the activity, since it is an aspect of one's manner of engagement in this. I am attracted by the Rylean view, but it is certainly controversial, and insofar as it has behaviorist overtones, unlikely to be accepted in our post-behaviorist philosophical environment.

Whether an activity is for one pleasant is undeniably a matter of how it is subjectively for one as one engages in it; it turns on the character of one's experience of the activity. This being so, to defend the Rylean view of pleasure as essentially relational in his strong sense—to enjoy an activity is to engage pleasurably in it, where "pleasurably" is a qualifier of one's engagement—requires insisting that one's pleasant experience of the activity is necessarily veridically perceptual—one cannot not have that precise kind of representationally rich pleasant experience, with its precise kind of representationally rich pleasantness, unless one is indeed doing what it subjectively seems to one that one is enjoyably doing and one's experience is a perception of this.

To hold this is to espouse a disjunctivist account of experience of the pleasantness of skilled activity and appreciation.[35] Although this view is attractive, it is certainly controversial. Rather than seeking to establish such disjunctivism, I will rest my case for Certain-RAS on a weaker externalist thesis about the representational content of experiences of skilled activity and appreciation.

With regard to the character of the experience of pleasant skilled activity and appreciation, I have suggested that these experiences have a rich representational content—of features of the appreciated object or of one's skilled activity, and that the pleasantness of the experience is an aspect of this: it is the manner in which those features are present in consciousness, not a separable further feature of one's total experience. This is why it is not metaphysically possible to obtain the pleasure of listening to Wagner except by either actually or seemingly listening to Wagner—that pleasure only comes as an aspect of an experience with that distinctive rich representational content. The same goes, mutatis mutandis, for pleasures of skillful activity. I do not here insist that it is impossible for it to seem to one just as if one is listening to Wagner or skydiving unless one is indeed doing so, but I do insist that one cannot have experiences with that rich representational content unless one has acquired the needed skills to appreciate Wagner or to effectively skydive; and that this is not possible except by actually learning to skydive, or actually listening to large chunks of Wagner and related music as part of an education in music in that classical tradition through which one comes to understand the musical language of his works.

If this is right, then two key points for my argument for Certain-RAS follow: first, that one can gain the distinctive pleasure of engaging in a particular enjoyable skilled activity only once one has acquired its skill; and to acquire its skill involves engaging in the activity, practicing it; second, that this pleasure is itself a distinctive good, the specific pleasure of skillfully skydiving or of listening appreciatively to Wagner—it is not just a case of pleasure, one kind of thing, contingently caused in this case by a particular worldly engagement.

If these two key points are correct, then Certain-RAS is established: each person has some PN-reason to acquire and exercise every skill such that she would enjoy exercising it; and this is direct, not merely instrumental reason, since it is not metaphysically possible to attain the distinctive enjoyments of the exercise of each skill, except by possessing that skill. (I have, however, left it as an open question whether it is metaphysically possible on some occasion to have the enjoyable experience as of exercising the skill when one is not in reality doing so, being instead the subject of some kind of illusion.)

So: one has some PN-reason, for every skill one is capable of acquiring and would enjoy exercising, to acquire and exercise precisely that skill, because each enjoyable activity generates its own sui generis kind of enjoyment, only attainable by engaging in that very activity. Thus, for instance, I have some reason to learn Russian in order to be able to exercise the skill of reading Russian poetry. This is so because I would enjoy doing so, and, since the enjoyment is an aspect of my appreciation of the literary qualities of the poetry, there is no other metaphysically possible way of achieving it.

8. A Well-Being–Based Case for Some-RAS and Core-RAS

I have made an enjoyment-based case for Certain-RAS and have claimed that no such case is forthcoming for Unrestricted-RAS. What of Some-RAS? It is plausible that, for humans with normal cognitive capacities, having some skills is necessary to leading a happy life, because this is required for self-respect, and self-respect is a general necessary condition for happiness for such individuals—lack of self-respect is a background interferer preventing one from being happy, and making it difficult to enjoy oneself. This counts as a noninstrumental reason for ensuring that one has some skills, on my definition.[36]

One may have some pleasant sensations while lacking any self-respect, but the more global property of leading a happy life requires that one have a reasonably positive self-image, and this requires that one knows oneself to have some skills. If one thinks of oneself as totally useless, lacking in any significant skills and achievements, then one lacks any self-respect. This entails being dissatisfied with oneself, which is inconsistent with being reasonably satisfied with one's life, one criterion of happiness, since being satisfied with one's life entails being satisfied with oneself.

That thinking of oneself as lacking in any skills means one lacks self-respect may be a contingent cultural feature, not a necessary aspect of human life in all possible circumstances, but it is a deeply entrenched one. If it is contingent, then the status of Some-RAS is as a nomological truth, not a metaphysically necessary one.

I now turn to Core-RAS, the principle of most interest to me. Core-RAS would be a contingent nomological truth if there were as a matter of nomological truth a certain set of skills—a core set—such that everyone enjoys their exercise. But I want to argue for a more tendentious proposition. Are there certain core skills whose possession is a precondition for human well-being? My thesis lying behind Core-RAS is that:

(CS) There exist certain core skills (broad skill-types) whose possession is a generally necessary facilitating condition for attaining and maintaining a happy human life.

The chief difficulty here is to find skills whose necessity for well-being is not a mere cultural contingency. Thus the argument for Core-RAS has a bit of a perfectionist flavor, appealing if not to human beings' essential nature, then at least to entrenched features of the human condition.

I propose (CS) not as a metaphysically necessary truth about all possible forms of existence of the human animal—it is very hard to afford a principle of any substance such status, since so much of what we are, and how we flourish, is due to our material, technological and social culture; and who can predict how much that may change over time? It is offered as a truth about what are core skills for the vast majority of us, leading the kinds of lives people now lead, but where this kind transcends a lot of contingent local cultural variation, fixing on relatively entrenched and stable features of the human condition. Even understood as relative to circumstances of a kind not radically unlike our current ones, it must be read as allowing exceptions. Someone paralyzed from the neck down after an accident may, despite this, lead what can be called a happy life if they successfully adapt to their new circumstances, adopting projects still open to them; however, on the account I offer next, there is at least one core skill that they can no longer exercise.

Core skills, if there are such, will be high-level abstracted skill-types, which receive more specific interpretations in particular cultural settings. To formulate a definitive list of core skills would be hubris that goes beyond my aspirations here. But here are some suggestions: language, interpersonal interpretative and communicative skills, theoretical and practical reasoning. And finally, to return to the autobiographical departure point of my enquiry: I suggest that basic spatial and navigational skills are core, because the capacity to understand where one is located in spacetime, and to navigate one's way around it, is a core skill. Not knowing where one is located in space makes for a sense of helplessness, of not being in control of one's life. In spy thrillers, a victim's being captured and blindfolded, and then taken to a place whose location within the objective spatial nexus she has no idea of, is both a fact of and a metaphor for helplessness. When one awakes from an operation, one's first questions are: "What time is it?" and "Where am I?"[37] Why is this so? Knowing one's location in one's spatial environment, of which one has a cognitive map locating features important to one, connects directly to being in control of one's life, because it affects directly and massively how one can proceed to fulfill one's projects and plans. If I am imprisoned, I cannot easily escape. But if I have a mental representation (or simply a map that I can interpret) of the layout of the prison, and more so if I also know where it is located in the broader environment with which I am familiar, I have much more chance of successful escape. Fulfilling one's basic needs (e.g. for food and sleep) typically turns on having a cognitive map of one's environment, and knowing what resources are available at what locations in it, and being able to navigate one's way to them. For this reason, the skill-based cognitive ability to maintain a mental map of one's environment, conjoined with the skill-based ability—on foot, in a motorized wheelchair or with the aid of other transport—to make one's way around in it is, I suggest, a background necessary condition for the ability to control the progress of one's own life, the fulfillment of one's projects.[38] So it is directly implicated in autonomy, being in control of one's life. On the plausible view that some degree of autonomy is a necessary condition for happiness for cognitively normal humans, this gives the result that the skill-based cognitive ability to maintain a mental map of one's environment, and hence to understand where one is and, when traveling, where one is proceeding to and from, is a general background condition necessary for and contributing to well-being for humans in cultural, material and social conditions broadly similar to our actual ones. Core-RAS is true because (CS) is true; and the skills involved in maintaining a mental map of one's environment, together with the skill to navigate one's way around in it, are among the core skills. In fact if (CS) is correct, then a stronger principle than Core-RAS is true: Core-RAS says only that there are core skills that each one of us has some reason to acquire; but if my argument is correct, the reason to acquire each core skill is a very strong one, overridden only in exceptional circumstances.

This of course does not mean that GPSs are a bad thing or that we should seek to avoid using them. It is just common sense to use a GPS in many circumstances, and many modern journeys would be impossibly difficult to achieve without resorting to them. But what it shows is that the spatial representational capacities and navigational skills that a GPS provides a surrogate for are something of core prudential value to humans, an extension of a core skill whose exercise is a needed facilitating condition of normal human well-being. We should not allow the availability of GPSs to erode our own navigational skills and ability to represent our spatial environment without limit; were we to do so, our control of our own lives would be eroded, and a core part of a paradigm happy human life, namely one that the agent herself exercises a large degree of control over the progress of, would be lost.

9. Conclusion

This chapter began by noting one's extensive epistemic dependence on others for much of what one knows. The inevitability of this dependence means that one must trust others, relying on them to exercise epistemic skills on one's behalf. The same goes for one's practical dependence on others, relying on them to exercise practical skills on one's behalf. However, over time, one makes choices about which of these skills to acquire oneself, and which to continue to rely on others for, to obtain the fruits of their exercise. This fact led me to consider what, if any, reason one has to seek to acquire and exercise skills oneself, rather than continuing to rely on others for their fruits.

I have made a case for five propositions. The first is that Unrestricted-RAS is false: there is no noninstrumental PN-reason for one to acquire and exercise noncore skills such that one would not enjoy exercising them. So the invention of labor-saving devices that eliminate the need for the exercise of such skills is an unqualified good.

The second is Certain-RAS: that one has some noninstrumental PN-reason to acquire and exercise any skill such that one would enjoying exercising it, since this is a distinctive pleasure attainable only through that exercise. My argument for this invokes no mere contingencies, and so if it is sound, this is a metaphysically necessary truth.

The third is Some-RAS: that one has some noninstrumental PN-reason to ensure that one is not skill-less, since this is nomologically necessary for self-respect, which is nomologically necessary for humans' well-being. If this argument is sound, then this second proposition is a nomological truth.

The fourth is Core-RAS: that there are certain core skills, highly abstract general ones, such that each one of us has strong PN-reason to acquire an instance of each of them; this is so because these core skills are generally necessary facilitating conditions for attaining a happy human life in any circumstances broadly similar to our own current cultural, material and technological conditions. This is also a nomological truth.

My fifth and final proposition, also a nomological truth, is that the skills involved in maintaining both a cognitive map of one's environment and one's ability to navigate one's way around it are among these core skills. They are so because of the intimate link between one's being able to find one's way about in one's environment and one's autonomy—the ability to be in control of one's life, to pursue one's plans and projects. This does not mean that satnavs (GPSs)—that is, reliance on them—are ipso facto bad; on the contrary, they are in many circumstances an indispensable aid to getting to one's destination. But it would be bad if their existence should lull one into completely abdicating from all pretensions to maintaining and sometimes exercising the spatial-navigational skills that they aptly provide a surrogate for in some circumstances. To do this would be to relinquish a key facilitating condition of one's control of the progress of one's own life, and this would detract from one's well-being as an intelligent human agent.

Notes

1. The ideas in this chapter have been a long time a-growing. My thanks for really useful discussion and ideas to audiences at conferences in December 2016 at the Ludwig Maximilian University in Munich and at the University of Innsbruck, in March 2017 at the Moral Sciences Club of Cambridge University, and in September 2017 at a graduate conference where I was keynote speaker at University College London. Thanks to my colleague Robert Audi for helpful comments on a draft. I am especially grateful to Roger Crisp for guidance and suggestions for reading on reasons and well-being. My ideas on skills and abilities benefited from discussions with Jennifer Hornsby and Julian Bacharach.
2. In (Fricker 2012) I argue that nonlinguistic communication of a message does not amount to testifying, since the utterer does not overtly take

responsibility for the truth of a communicated content. Groups can also testify, through the medium of a spokesperson.

3. (Fricker 2015) develops an account of how testimony works, which provides an account of which instances of testimony are apt to provide knowledge. I argue that the testifier must be expressing her knowledge. Although this view is common, it is contested by some, most notably in (Lackey 2008).

4. In contrast, there are other concepts for which accepting others' testimony is only a causally necessary condition for acquiring them, such as color concepts; once grasped, one's possession of them is free of epistemic dependence on others. Hence the fact that one learns one's first language through responding trustingly to others' utterances does not entail that absolutely all one's linguistically represented knowledge is epistemically dependent on testimony.

5. This is so, regardless of whether a reductionist or fundamentalist account of one's justification for accepting another's testimony is held. Even if one should have, and often does have, good noncircular grounds to trust another's testimony, one is still epistemically dependent on them for the knowledge they convey to one, in the sense explained later. See (Fricker 2017) for an explanation of reductionism and fundamentalism, and an argument for an inference-to-the-best-explanation local-reductionist account of justified testimonial belief.

6. The reader may here object that I beg a question, in assuming that any case to be made for the value of skill possession holds for both epistemic and practical skills. As is shown later, virtually all skills involve both practical and epistemic elements, so it would not work to make separate cases for the practical and the epistemic.

7. Why "canonical"? Because spreading knowledge through the recipient taking the speaker's word for what she asserts is what testimony is "for"—its function within a society. See (Fricker 2015, Graham 2010)

8. This felicitous phrase originates from (Graham 2015).

9. Why is this basis defeated, when all that is needed is that the testimony be true, not that it be known by the testifier? It is defeated, because the basis for the recipient's belief is that the speaker is expressing her knowledge, in conscientious conformity with the knowledge norm for assertion. If that supposition is defeated, she then has, absent other grounds, no reason to expect the testimony to be true. Compare: I take myself to be perceiving a dagger before me. Once I learn I am not perceiving, but hallucinating, though this is consistent with there being a dagger before me, I have absolutely no reason to think there is one. See (Fricker 2015).

10. I will not offer an explicit semantics for this notion. The idea of a type of event that would not easily occur, and conversely of one that might easily occur, is a folk notion we have a good grip on. As, for instance, when I say to my son as he arrives in the opera house just as the entrance doors are closing and the lights going down, "You should have set off earlier, you might easily have missed the whole first act." I, in contrast, departing from my home with hours in hand and arriving more than half an hour before the start, would not easily have arrived late. The same notion of what would not easily happen is used in Ernest Sosa's writings (Sosa 2011). Someone's having the property that not easily would she fail to φ on O, while it entails that it is very unlikely that she will fail to φ on O, does not entail that she will not fail to φ on O. A property that entailed this would not be knowable of someone in advance of O's occurrence.

11. Talk of "trust" is apt, because the recipient relies on the speaker to be expressing her knowledge due to her relevant epistemic and character virtues: she relies on the speaker both seeking conscientiously to conform to the

knowledge norm for tellings and being suitably competent in judging whether she has knowledge or not. See (Fricker 2016) for this account of trust.

12. More strictly, these conditions, and the account of testimony given earlier, hold only for what I call originating testimony—that is, when one learns from the testimony of a speaker who herself came to knowledge of her topic through her own epistemic resources, not by in turn trusting the testimony of yet another person. For what I call passing-on testimony, the crucial factor is that the testifier is passing on what is known, which may not be known by her. I neglect this complication in the present discussion, though it is important to take account of it in a full account of how testimony serves to spread knowledge iteratively through a society.

13. What one can understand of propositions of the domain in question puts limits on what one can know at second-hand. If I truly know nothing about how a car works, then I cannot really grasp what it means to say that the "big end" in the engine has gone. But one can certainly grasp the observational consequences of such theoretical facts, such as that a repair will involve ordering a part that may take three weeks to arrive and be very expensive.

14. This is not strictly true, since a layperson has various resources available to check the credentials of an expert, for instance getting a second opinion. What is strictly true is that if I know nothing of cars, I cannot evaluate the evidence and contest or corroborate her opinion myself.

15. Knowledge-getting skills do not exhaust epistemic skills since, for instance, in science the goal of enquiry may be a somewhat different one. In this chapter I am concerned with one's dependence on others for knowledge.

16. See (Scanlon 1998, Raz 1999, Crisp 2006, Parfit 2011).

17. See (Crisp 2006, Fletcher 2016).

18. See (Fletcher 2016) for an excellent critical introduction to different accounts of well-being and (Sumner 1996) for an interesting critique and theory.

19. This will be false just if the agent's getting what she wants will not in fact make her happier or otherwise contribute to her well-being.

20. We can say that the feature of an action that provides PN-reason to do it has PN-value.

21. Note that we are concerned with PN-value, not perfectionist value. This latter is that of a kind of thing achieving the excellence proper to its kind, as determined by its active nature. This idea originates with (Aristotle 2002). The account given later implies that I have some PN-reason to seek to improve my piano playing just if to do so would make me enjoy playing more, or allow me to get distinctive enjoyments from playing currently not available to me. Perfectionist value on the other hand is likely to say that, if I have some reason to acquire a skill at all, I always have some reason to seek to acquire it to the highest degree attainable by me.

22. This account of ability or competence (he treats these as equivalent terms) is offered in (Sosa 2015), where it plays a central role in his account of knowledge as the achievement of true belief whose truth is owed to competence. (If the earlier account of how skill and ability/competence relate, it is in fact the agent's skill rather than her competence that explains her success.)

23. For interesting discussion of the individuation of abilities, see (Small, forthcoming). Small observes that the ability exercised in an action is typically more general than the specific action-type intended by the agent on that occasion—for instance, when I bake a cake for Anna's birthday, the ability exercised is my general ability to bake cakes. The proprietary outcome of my cake-baking ability is nonetheless an intended outcome of my action.

24. Of course one may swim or whistle to serve some further purpose, but this further purpose is external to the identity of the skill of swimming or whistling.

25. Of course these skillful activities may be engaged in as a means to some further end, extrinsic to the skill itself, but they have no ontologically independent proprietary end result.
26. That is to say, obtaining the outcome will contribute to one's well-being.
27. This neglects the possibility that merely possessing them will enhance one's well-being in some manner. While I argue later that possessing some skills is a necessary condition for self-respect, which is a general necessary condition for an adequate level of happiness, this does not mandate possession of any particular skill.
28. The reader will see that I am unconvinced by attempts in the Aristotelian tradition to equate perfectionist value with well-being, or to argue that they are co-extensive. This is, however, a very important tradition that merits serious engagement, something I cannot do here. See (Aristotle 2002, Hurka 1993).
29. One would not enjoy it in the strong sense of looking forward to it, seeking to do it for its own sake. By not positively enjoying it in this way, one does not necessarily find it actively unpleasant; this will surely depend on circumstances—how much there is, how good the facilities are, and whether it is one's own or another's. One may get some satisfaction as one scrubs from knowing that one is getting competently through one's chores and keeping one's life under control. But this satisfaction arises from that broad fact—it is not the distinctive pleasure of clothes-washing specifically.
30. Enjoying classical music requires acquiring skills of aesthetic understanding and appreciation of the genre—a tradition of music is a distinctive language, no less than a spoken language.
31. For a perceptive discussion see (Sumner 1996).
32. See (Nozick 1981).
33. A logical category-incoherence beautifully exploited in Lewis Carroll's story (Carroll 2015/1865).
34. See (Ryle 2000/1949).
35. See (Soteriou 2016).
36. It may be objected that what is required for self-respect is that one believes oneself to have some skills, rather than actually having them. But belief that was not knowledge could not play the required role in one's psychology, because it would not connect with actual instances of exercise of the skills, which is part of what allows for self-respect.
37. At least this was my first question, when aged 29 I awoke from being operated on to have my appendix removed. Knowing where one is located in time and space is a first condition for feeling and being in control of one's situation.
38. This is why enabling mobility is a key issue for those with reduced physical ability.

References

Aristotle. 2002. *Nichomachean Ethics*. Oxford: Oxford University Press.

Carroll, Lewis. 2015/1865. *Alice's Adventures in Wonderland*. Vancouver, BC: Ostrich Books.

Crisp, Roger. 2006. *Reasons and the Good*. Oxford: Clarendon Press.

Fletcher, Guy. 2016. *The Philosophy of Wellbeing*. Oxfordshire: Routledge.

Fricker, Elizabeth. 2006a. "Second-Hand Knowledge." *Philosophy and Phenomenological Research* 73(3): 592–681.

———. 2006b. "Testimony and Epistemic Autonomy." In *The Epistemology of Testimony*, edited by Jennifer Lackey and Ernest Sosa, 225–50. Oxford: Oxford University Press.

———. 2012. "Stating and Insinuating." *Aristotelian Society Supplementary Volume* 86(1): 61–94.

———. 2015. "How to Make Invidious Distinctions Amongst Reliable Testifiers." *Episteme* 12: 173–202.

———. 2016. "Doing (Better) What Comes Naturally: Zagzebski on Rationality and Epistemic Self-Trust." *Episteme* 13(2): 151–66.

———. 2017. "Inference to the Best Explanation and the Receipt of Testimony: Testimonial Reductionism Vindicated." In *Best Explanations: New Essays on Inference to the Best Explanation*, edited by K. McCain and T. Poston, 262–94. Oxford: Oxford University Press.

Goldman, Alvin. 2001. "Experts: Which Ones Should You Trust?" *Philosophy and Phenomenological Research* 63(1): 65.

Graham, Peter. 2010. "Testimonial Entitlement and the Function of Comprehension." In *Social Epistemology*, edited by Alan Millar, Adrian Haddock, and Duncan Pritchard, 148–74. Oxford: Oxford University Press.

———. 2015. "Testimony as Speech Act, Testimony as Source." In *Moral and Intellectual Virtues in Western and Chinese Philosophy: The Turn toward Virtue*, edited by Chienkuo Mi, Michael Slote, and Ernest Sosa, 121–44. Abingdon, Oxfordshire: Routledge.

Hurka, Thomas. 1993. *Perfectionism*. Oxford: Oxford University Press.

Katz, Leonard D. 2016. "Pleasure." In *Stanford Encyclopaedia of Philosophy* (Winter 2016 Edition), edited by N. Zalta, *et al.*, Stanford, CA: Stanford University Press. https://plato.stanford.edu/archives/win2016/entries/pleasure. Accessed October 1, 2018.

Lackey, Jennifer. 2008. *Learning from Words: Testimony as a Source of Knowledge*. Oxford: Oxford University Press.

Nozick, Robert. 1981. *Philosophical Explanations*. Oxford: Clarendon Press.

Parfit, Derek. 2011. *On What Matters*. Oxford: Oxford University Press.

Raz, Joseph. 1999. *Engaging Reason*. Oxford: Oxford University Press.

Ryle, Gilbert. 2000/1949. *The Concept of Mind*. London: Penguin Books.

Scanlon, Thomas M. 1998. *What We Owe to Each Other*. Cambridge, MA: Harvard University Press.

Small, Will. Forthcoming. "Agency and Abilities." In *Philosophy of Action*, edited by Anthony O'Hear. Cambridge, UK: Cambridge University Press.

Sosa, Ernest. 2011. *Knowing Full Well*. Princeton, NJ: Princeton University Press.

———. 2015. *Judgment and Agency*. Oxford: Oxford University Press.

Soteriou, Matthew. 2016. *Disjunctivism*. Abingdon, Oxfordshire: Routledge.

Sumner, Leonard W. 1996. *Welfare, Happiness, and Ethics*. Oxford: Clarendon Press.

Section 2

Trust in Testimony

4 The Role of Trust in Testimonial Knowledge

John Greco

What is the role of trust, if any, in testimonial knowledge? More exactly: What is the *epistemic* role of trust in testimonial knowledge? The second formulation emphasizes that our question is epistemological. That is, we are asking whether trust plays some role or makes some contribution that is *epistemically* important or interesting. In this regard, some kinds of contribution would be clearly *un*interesting. For example, suppose it turns out that trust is necessary for human beings to achieve some minimal level of psychological development and that this minimal development is necessary for knowledge in general. Then it would turn out that trust is *psychologically necessary* for testimonial knowledge, but that would fall short of being epistemically interesting. Or suppose that some degree of trust is psychologically necessary for language acquisition. Then, again, trust would be psychologically necessary for testimonial knowledge as well, but in a way that is not interesting to epistemology per se.

Here is another way that trust might play a role in testimonial knowledge but in a way that might still fall short of being epistemically interesting. Suppose that knowledge in general requires some kind of reliable process and that a hearer's trusting the speaker contributes to the reliability of testimonial exchanges. For example, suppose that the hearer's trusting the speaker makes it more likely that the speaker will tell the truth.[1] In that case, trust would be "epistemically important" in a sense, but again not in a way that makes trust itself especially interesting. In effect, trusting the speaker would be just one way of fulfilling otherwise agreed-upon conditions for knowledge.[2]

This last point raises a question: What would it take for trust to be epistemically important or interesting? More specifically, what would it take for trust to make an epistemically interesting contribution to testimonial knowledge? So far, we have seen that it would take more than that trust is *psychologically necessary* for testimonial knowledge. Moreover, it would take more than that trust allows the knower to satisfy some otherwise agreed-upon condition for testimonial knowledge. In the latter case, trust would be contingently related to testimonial knowledge, so to speak, but would not be related to testimonial knowledge in any essential way. But suppose that the contribution to reliability, or to satisfying some other condition on testimonial knowledge, was not merely contingent. Suppose, for example, that it is a law of nature that trusting the speaker makes it more likely that the speaker will tell the truth, and suppose it were a law of nature that, absent such trust, nothing else would cause the speaker to reliably tell the truth. In that case, trust would be *nomologically necessary* for testimonial knowledge, but still in a way that would fail to be *epistemically* interesting in at least one important sense. Even in this scenario, we might say, trust would not be *essentially* related to testimonial knowledge, or to *what testimonial knowledge is*.

This suggests that "what it would take" for trust to be epistemically important, in the sense that we are requiring, is that trusting the speaker is somehow essentially related to the very nature of testimonial knowledge. And this, in fact, is what some trust theorists at least seem to be claiming. That is, they seem to be claiming that trust *itself* (rather than evidence or some other standard epistemic condition) is essential to the very nature of testimonial knowledge.[3] This interpretation is in line with Lackey's dilemma for the "interpersonal view of testimony (IVT)," including trust theories. Lacky writes,

> Thus, we have seen that there is a general dilemma confronting the proponent of the IVT: either the view of testimony in question is genuinely interpersonal but not epistemological, or it is genuinely epistemological but not interpersonal. In the former case, the IVT will be novel but useless for an epistemology of testimony; in the latter case, the IVT will be epistemologically useful, but not interestingly different from its so-called competitors. The bottom line is this: interpersonal features cannot create justification or warrant epistemologically ex nihilo and hence there is no room for a genuinely interpersonal view in the epistemology of testimony.
>
> (Lackey 2008, 239–240)

That is, there is no room for a view that makes interpersonal relations (such as trust) *themselves* essential to testimonial justification and knowledge, as opposed to underwriting some more properly epistemic condition, such as reliability, or sensitivity, or evidence, and so on.

Perhaps this way of framing our question sets the bar too high. Perhaps no one thinks, or no one should think, that trust is essentially related to the very nature of testimonial knowledge. Nevertheless, that is the thesis that I will defend in the remainder of the chapter.[4] In what follows I will explore two (related) lines of argument, each of which would establish that conclusion. Of necessity, the arguments will be programmatic. But each presents a promising line for understanding the essential role of trust in testimonial knowledge.

The first line of argument invokes the notion of knowledge transmission, claiming that knowledge transmission is an important epistemological phenomenon that is distinct from and irreducible to knowledge generation.[5] Knowledge transmission, it will be argued, essentially involves joint agency. More specifically, knowledge transmission essentially involves the kind of cooperation and coordination between speaker and hearer that is the hallmark of joint agency. Joint agency essentially involves trust, however, and therefore knowledge transmission essentially involves trust.

The second line of argument invokes a thesis that has been defended extensively in the recent literature—that knowledge in general is a kind of success from ability. Put better: knowledge is essentially a kind of success attributable to competent agency.[6] The next step in the argument makes a claim about transmitted knowledge. Whereas generated knowledge is true belief attributable to the competent agency of the knower, transmitted knowledge is true belief attributable to the competent joint agency of a speaker and hearer acting together. But because some knowledge is transmitted knowledge, it follows that some knowledge is true belief attributable to competent joint agency. That is, some knowledge is *essentially* true belief attributable to competent joint agency. And because joint agency essentially involves trust, it follows that some knowledge essentially involves trust.

Here are the two arguments in outline.

Main Argument A

1. Knowledge **transmission** is an important epistemological phenomenon and distinct from knowledge **generation**. In particular, knowledge transmission is not reducible to knowledge generation. (For example, it is not reducible to back-to-back cases of generation.)
2. Knowledge transmission (essentially) involves **joint agency**. Put differently: knowledge transmission essentially involves the kind of cooperation and coordination between speaker and hearer that is the hallmark of joint agency.
3. Joint agency (essentially) involves **trust** between the cooperating agents.

Therefore,

4. Knowledge transmission (essentially) involves trust. (2, 3)

Therefore,

5. An important and distinct epistemological phenomenon (essentially) involves trust. (1, 4)

Main Argument B

1. **Knowledge in general** is (essentially) a kind of success from ability—a kind of success attributable to competent agency. **Transmitted**

knowledge is (essentially) true belief attributable to the competent joint agency of a speaker and hearer acting together.
2. Some knowledge is transmitted knowledge.

Therefore,

3. Some knowledge is (essentially) true belief attributable to the competent **joint agency** (competent cooperation) of a speaker and hearer acting together. (1, 2)
4. Joint agency (essentially) involves **trust** between the cooperating agents.

Therefore,

5. Some knowledge (essentially) involves trust. (3, 4)

To make good on these two lines of argument, or at least to make them more promising, we will need to do several things. The first is to say more about the transmission/generation distinction and, in particular, more about the nature of knowledge transmission. The second is to say more about the nature of joint agency, and the third is to say more about the nature of trust. Finally, with regard to Argument B, it will be necessary to defend the general claim that knowledge is a kind of success attributable to competent agency and that transmitted knowledge in particular can be understood as success attributable to competent joint agency.

Here is the plan for proceeding. Sections 1 and 2 rethink some familiar categories in the epistemology of testimony. The purpose of this "rethinking" is to better understand, and better articulate, the central dispute between trust theorists in epistemology and their critics. With our revised categories in place, we can articulate the central claims of trust theorists as follows: knowledge transmission, as opposed to knowledge generation, is an important epistemological phenomenon that cannot be reduced to—cannot be understood in the same categories as—knowledge generation. In particular, knowledge transmission essentially involves the hearer trusting the speaker for what she is being told, where the trusting in question cannot be understood in terms of the usual categories of evidence, good reasons, and so on, at least not as these are traditionally understood. Trust theorists, then, are essentially making an anti-reductionist claim: that knowledge generation and knowledge transmission are irreducible phenomena. In their most radical form, trust theories go beyond this to claim that there can be no unified epistemology. That is, knowledge generation and knowledge transmission are not merely irreducible to each other—they cannot be given a theoretically unified account. For example, they are not irreducible species of a higher genus. Section 3 then makes the case that, properly understood, knowledge transmission essentially involves joint agency between hearer and speaker, and therefore trust between hearer and speaker. Section 4 reviews some arguments for the virtue-theoretic claim that knowledge is a kind of success attributable to competent agency and extends this approach to the claim that transmitted knowledge is a kind of success attributable to competent joint agency. Section 5 evaluates our two main arguments in light of Sections 1 to 4.

1. Some Categories for the Epistemology of Testimony

The issue that has perhaps most dominated the epistemology of testimony is the debate between so-called reductionists and anti-reductionists. Very roughly, reductionists think that testimonial knowledge can be subsumed under some other species of knowledge, for example, inductive knowledge. The idea here is that testimonial knowledge is just more inductive knowledge, distinguished only by the epistemically superficial fact that the induction concerns testimony and testifiers. The anti-reductionist idea is that testimonial knowledge cannot be understood as a species of some other kind of knowledge—that testimonial knowledge is its "own kind of thing" and cannot be reduced to something else.[7]

This kind of "source reductionism," then, is best understood as a claim about species of knowledge. Specifically, it claims that the genus *knowledge* has several species, such as *perceptual* knowledge, *inductive* knowledge, *introspective* knowledge, and so on, according to the different ways that knowledge can be generated. And it also claims that testimonial knowledge does *not* constitute a separate species alongside these others. Put differently, it claims that testimonial knowledge can be understood in terms of these other species of knowledge generation, perhaps as a subspecies of some one of the others, or perhaps as involving some combination of the others. Suppose we were to construct a diagram marking the various species of the genus *knowledge*. According to this kind of reductionism, you don't need a separate species for testimonial knowledge.

Source reductionism, then, divides the genus *knowledge* into species according to specific ways that knowledge can be generated and claims that testimonial knowledge can be understood entirely in terms of non-testimonial generative sources. "Source anti-reductionism" denies this by claiming that testimonial knowledge requires its own generative source. Put differently, it claims that testimonial knowledge cannot be understood entirely in terms of nontestimonial generative sources, and this is because testimony is its own kind of generative source. (See Figure 4.1.)

Source reductionism and source anti-reductionism will look somewhat different in different theories of knowledge, according to how they understand the various species in our diagram. For example, evidentialists will think that perceptual knowledge is grounded in perceptual evidence, inductive knowledge is grounded in inductive evidence, *a priori* knowledge is grounded in *a priori* evidence and so on. Process reliabilists, on the other hand, will think of our species as specifying different kinds of cognitive processes; perceptual knowledge is generated by reliable

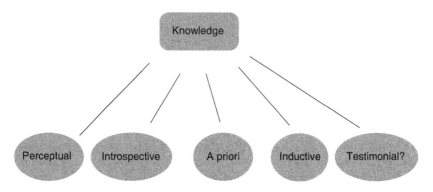

Figure 4.1 Species of Knowledge

perceptual process, inductive knowledge is generated by reliable inductive reasoning processes, and so on. But whatever their more substantive view about knowledge, source reductionists agree that testimony does not constitute an irreducible generative source of knowledge alongside other generative sources. Anti-reductionists agree that it does.

Another set of issues that has dominated the testimony literature regards the transmission of knowledge. As with the terminology of "reductionism" and "anti-reductionism," the term "transmission" is used in various ways in the literature. At times, it is used to mark an important and special function of testimony to transmit *as opposed to* generate knowledge in a community of knowers. On this use of the term, it is assumed that transmission is something epistemically distinctive and special.[8] At other times, however, the term is used to mark something that is not necessarily interesting at all—it refers simply to coming to know via testimony, without any connotation that this involves anything of special epistemic interest or importance.[9]

For purposes of clarity, let's begin with a neutral characterization of knowledge transmission. We can stipulate as follows, roughly following the literature:

> Knowledge that p is transmitted from a speaker S to a hearer H just in case (1) S knows that p, (2) S testifies to H that p, (3) H believes that p on the grounds of S's so testifying, and (4) as a result of conditions 1–3, H comes to know that p.

Our characterization is "neutral" in the sense that it leaves condition (4) entirely open; that is, it says nothing about *how* one comes to know as a result of conditions 1 to 3. For example, both source reductionists and source anti-reductionists can sign on to this general characterization, because it is entirely silent on whether testimonial knowledge is reducible to other generative species. Accordingly, the characterization is perfectly consistent with the position that testimonial knowledge is simply a species of inductive knowledge and that *the way* H comes to know in cases of transmission is via relevant inductive evidence about the speaker and the circumstances of testimony.

If we are working with this characterization of transmission, two questions naturally arise. First: *Is all testimonial knowledge transmitted knowledge?* For example, is it possible to get knowledge that p from testimony, even if the speaker does not know that p? If so, then not all testimonial knowledge will be transmitted knowledge. This is the question that has dominated recent discussions of transmission in the epistemology of testimony.[10]

But however this first question is answered, we may ask a second question that speaks more directly to present purposes: *How does transmission occur when it does occur?* That is, suppose that our neutral characterization correctly describes conditions for knowledge transmission, although it may not describe conditions for coming to know by testimony in general. If so, then it describes those conditions only in general and uninformative terms. And we can ask: *What, more specifically, is required for knowledge transmission to occur?*

On a conservative view, the transmission of knowledge simply reduces to two instances of generation. First, knowledge is somehow generated in the speaker. Then, on the basis of speaker testimony, knowledge is generated in the hearer. On this conservative view, nothing epistemically special is going on in transmission. On the contrary, the transmission of knowledge from speaker to hearer can be reduced to two instances of generation.

By denying this conservative view, we get a second kind of anti-reductionism, which we can label "transmission anti-reductionism." In this more radical view, knowledge transmission is not reducible to two instances of generation, but is rather a distinctive phenomenon. How radical does the more radical view have to be? Some philosophers, including some trust theorists, have argued that an adequate understanding of knowledge transmission requires a fundamental reorientation of epistemology. In this view, traditional epistemology lacks the theoretical resources for understanding the full range of epistemic phenomena, including testimonial knowledge and knowledge transmission.[11]

So far, we have distinguished two kinds of reductionism in the epistemology of testimony. Source reductionism is the claim that testimonial knowledge can be entirely understood in terms of familiar, nontestimonial generative species such as inductive knowledge, perceptual knowledge, introspective knowledge, and so on. Source anti-reductionism denies this, by claiming that testimony must be understood as a distinctive source of knowledge. Transmission reductionism claims that knowledge transmission is reducible to knowledge generation. In particular, knowledge transmission can be understood as back-to-back cases of knowledge generation: first knowledge is somehow generated in the speaker, then knowledge is generated in the hearer as a result of a testimonial exchange. Transmission anti-reductionism denies this, claiming that knowledge transmission is a distinctive phenomenon, irreducible to knowledge generation.

Using these categories, we may now see that there are two ways to be "an anti-reductionist about testimonial knowledge." (See Figure 4.2.) Let the most general anti-reductionist thesis be this: *testimonial knowledge cannot be understood as a species of some other kind of knowledge.* We may now see that there are two ways (actually three) to hold this thesis: one can endorse source anti-reductionism, one can endorse transmission anti-reductionism, or one can endorse both.

Here are some further observations. First, vis-à-vis traditional epistemology, the most conservative option is to be a reductionist on both counts. Second, it is clear that one can be a source anti-reductionist and a transmission reductionist. That is, one might consistently hold that testimony is an irreducible generative source of knowledge but still understand transmission in terms of back-to-back generation: first knowledge is somehow generated in the speaker, then knowledge is generated in the hearer via testimony, considered an irreducible source. Third, one can be a source reductionist and a transmission anti-reductionist. That

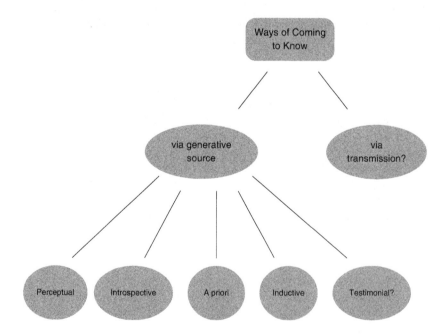

Figure 4.2 Ways of Coming to Know

is, one might endorse the claim that knowledge transmission is irreducible to knowledge generation but still be a reductionist on the level of generation.

And now we may ask, *Where do trust theories fit in?* That is, how should we best understand the claim that trust plays an epistemically interesting and important role in testimonial knowledge? One way to understand the claim is as a kind of *source anti-reductionism*—the idea would be that trust plays an essential role in the generation of testimonial knowledge, understood as an irreducible species of knowledge, alongside other species of generated knowledge, such as inductive knowledge and perceptual knowledge. Another way to understand the claim, however, is as a kind of *transmission anti-reductionism*. This, I believe, is the more interesting and fruitful way to understand trust theories. Their claim is that knowledge transmission is a distinctive and important epistemic phenomenon that is irreducible to knowledge generation and that essentially involves the hearer trusting the speaker regarding what she is being told.

Suppose that we embrace this kind of transmission anti-reductionism. Here now is a further question: Can knowledge transmission nevertheless be understood using traditional epistemological categories? That is, even if knowledge transmission is irreducible to knowledge generation, can we give a unified account of the two phenomena? This is not the same question as either of our reductionism questions. Our first question about reduction asked whether testimonial knowledge, considered as a generative source, can be reduced to some nontestimonial species of knowledge. Our second question asked whether knowledge transmission can be reduced to knowledge generation. Suppose we answer no to both of these questions. We may still ask whether a unified account of knowledge generation and knowledge transmission is possible. That is, we can ask whether both can be understood using the same theoretical resources, within a single theoretical framework.

A clear example of a unified account would be a reliabilist account. Thus, it is open to the reliabilist to distinguish transmission from generation but analyze both in terms of relevant reliable processes. The idea would be that the processes relevant to knowledge transmission are different from those relevant to knowledge generation and in such a way that neither can be understood in terms of the other. Nevertheless, what makes for both successful generation and successful transmission is to be cashed out in reliabilist terms.

At least some trust theories, I suggest, can be interpreted as proposing a nonunified account of knowledge generation and knowledge transmission.[12] Consider the structure of nonunified accounts. Like other forms of transmission anti-reductionism, such theories claim that there are two ways of coming to know—by generation and by transmission—and that neither is reducible to the other. But nonunified accounts make the further claim that there is no deeper theoretical unity between these two ways. For example, one might give an evidentialist account of knowledge generation in terms of true belief grounded in adequate evidence and then a trust account of knowledge transmission in terms of true belief grounded in morally proper trust of a speaker. On such a view, there would be two ways of "coming to know," but these would not be species of a theoretically interesting genus. Such a "no common genus" view is consistent with more superficial forms of unity. For example, one might define knowledge as "properly held true belief," but then go on to give nonunified accounts of "properly held" for generated knowledge and for transmitted knowledge. For example, one might define knowledge generation in terms of proper evidence and knowledge transmission in terms of morally proper trust. Such a view would be "unified," but only in a nominal sense.

But even if some trust theories can be fruitfully understood as offering a nonunified account, trust theories don't have to eschew theoretical unification. In Section 4, I defend a unified virtue-theoretic account of knowledge generation and knowledge transmission in terms of success attributable to competent agency. Before that, I present a general framework for understanding knowledge transmission (Section 2), and I argue that knowledge transmission should be understood as involving joint agency and therefore trust (Section 3).

2. A General Framework for Understanding the Generation–Transmission Distinction[13]

I suggest that we can understand the distinction between knowledge generation and knowledge transmission by invoking a technical notion of *epistemic community*, defined as a group of persons cooperating together with regard to some set of information-dependent tasks. For example, an epistemic community might be constituted by a medical research team, characterized by needs for information associated with its research agenda. Another example of an epistemic community is a business corporation, characterized by needs for information associated with conducting its business.

The first point to make is that such a community will be faced with two distinct tasks—that of *acquiring* relevant quality information and that of *distributing* that information to those who need it (Figures 4.3 and 4.4). For example, a business corporation will be tasked with acquiring quality information regarding product availability, supply chains, sales trends, competition, and so on and with distributing that information to the right people as needed.

The next point to make is that the norms and standards governing these two kinds of activity will be different, insofar as they answer to different purposes. Specifically, the norms and standards relevant to information acquisition answer primarily to concerns regarding quality

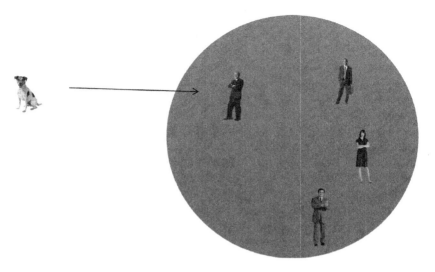

Figure 4.3 Information Acquisition

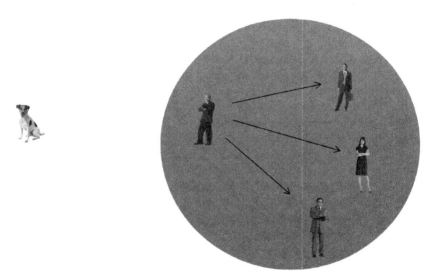

Figure 4.4 Information Distribution

control. That is, we want information in the system that is of adequate quality to be actionable, and the norms and standards of information acquisition answer to that concern. But once that actionable information is in the system, we want it to be available to those who need it. The norms and standards relevant to information distribution answer primarily to that concern.

Suppose that S and H are members of the same epistemic community and are therefore cooperating with respect to some set of relevant tasks. One way for them to cooperate will be in the distribution of relevant information. The idea is that testimonial exchanges between S and H will be cooperative exchanges in that sense and will be governed by norms and standards associated with that cooperative activity. The next point is that not all testimonial exchanges are like that. On the contrary, sometimes speaker and hearer do not share membership in some relevant epistemic community and are not cooperating so as to distribute information within such a community. For example, suppose that S is a job applicant and H is a personnel director charged with interviewing for the position. In that case, testimonial exchanges between S and H are at the service of information acquisition and should be governed by the norms and standards appropriate to that function. For example, if S tells H that he has ten years of experience as an engineer, H ought to evaluate this information accordingly. This is in contrast with a testimonial exchange in which H reports to his boss that S has ten years of experience as an engineer. That exchange ought to be governed by the norms appropriate to information distribution, which presume that H has done an adequate job at the acquisition stage. And in fact, all parties concerned will typically have a sense that these different norms and standards are in play. The job applicant, for example, will not take offense if the personnel director checks his references. But the personal director should take offense, or should be worried, if his boss checks his testimony in the same way.

Accordingly, some testimonial exchanges are in the service of information distribution, and this might be thought of as testimony's primary and characteristic function. But other testimonial exchanges are in the service of information acquisition, in which case they should be governed by the norms and standards associated with that function. (See Figure 4.5.)

The proposal is now this: we can understand the knowledge generation/knowledge transmission distinction in terms of the information acquisition/information distribution distinction. Specifically, knowledge generation is to be understood in terms of the norms and standards associated with the acquisition of information, whether for an individual or for an epistemic community. Knowledge transmission is to be understood in terms of the norms and standards associated with the distribution of information within an epistemic community.

This model is consistent with reductionism regarding testimony as a generative source. That is because the model proposes that, in contexts where a testimonial exchange is in the service of information acquisition, the hearer properly employs norms relevant for acquiring information. And these might very well be, for example, the norms of good inductive reasoning. However, the model *entails* anti-reductionism about transmission. That is because, as we have seen, the norms and standards governing information distribution are different from the norms and standards governing information acquisition, answering as they do to different purposes.

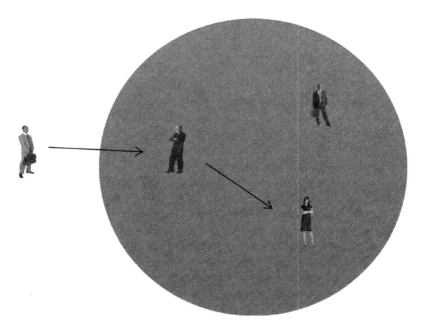

Figure 4.5 Testimony in the Acquisition and Distribution Functions

This general framework for understanding the knowledge generation/ knowledge transmission distinction is consistent with various normative epistemologies, including evidentialism, reliabilism, and virtue epistemology. On any of these views, we can make a distinction between activities relevant to information acquisition and activities relevant to information distribution, and we can endorse the idea that the two are governed by different norms or standards, answering to their respective purposes. And we can use those resources to understand the distinction between knowledge generation and knowledge transmission. Different normative epistemologies will fill in the details differently, but the general framework is neutral regarding these details.

In Section 3, I will argue that knowledge transmission, so understood, essentially involves a kind of joint agency between hearer and speaker, and therefore trust between hearer and speaker.

3. Knowledge Transmission as Involving Joint Agency and Trust

Suppose that two people are walking to the same restaurant at the same time, although neither is aware of what the other is doing.[14] This is compatible with the two persons walking side by side. Now imaging two people who are walking to the restaurant *together*. In this case, the two share an intention to walk to the restaurant together, and they share the knowledge that such an intention exists between them. This latter case is an example of *joint agency*.[15]

There are various accounts of joint agency in the literature, but there is broad agreement about its central features. First, and as already suggested, joint agency involves a "participatory intention" on the part of the joint actors—what John Searle calls a "we intention."[16] That is, the participants in joint agency intend their participation and understand their action as something that they are doing together. A second feature of joint agency is that it involves what Michael Bratman calls "sub-plans."[17] If we are to do something together, such as walk to the restaurant, we must have some plan for carrying that action out together. For example, we are not walking together if you decide to take one route to the restaurant and I decide to take another.

A third feature of joint agency is that it is *interactive*, in the sense that, if we are acting together, what I do depends on what you do, and what you do depends on what I do. For example, if we are walking together and one of us speeds up the pace, the other must speed up the pace as well. Likewise, it would be inappropriate for you to walk at a pace that I can't maintain.[18]

Finally, joint agency involves a kind of interdependence—if we are doing something together, then neither of us can do the very same thing alone, or at least not in just the same way. Put differently, in joint agency each of the joint actors is doing some of the work of the joint action, doing his or her part in it. Suppose we are painting a house together. We are not really doing that together if I am doing all the painting. The point is less obvious in the case of walking to the restaurant together, but it still holds. Thus, I can't walk *with* you unless you do your part in responding to my interactions, or at least staying within the parameters of pace and path that I can manage.[19]

This last characteristic of joint action involves a kind of *trust*, where that notion is understood in terms of both interpersonal dependence and expectation of success.[20] For example, in Jonathan Reibsamen's account, one person *depends* on another when the latter "bridges an ability gap" for the former.[21] Thus, S1 depends on another S2 to achieve some result A when S1 does not have the ability to achieve A himself, or at least not as easily or in just the same way. S1 *trusts* S2 to achieve A just in case S1 depends on S2 to achieve A and has some expectation that in so depending A will be successfully achieved. Clearly enough, joint agency involves trust in both directions. Thus, two people acting together involve a wedding of abilities to achieve a particular result in a particular way, with some expectation that so acting will be successful.

With these resources in place, we are now in a position to argue that knowledge transmission essentially involves a kind of joint agency between hearer and speaker, and therefore trust between hearer and speaker. First, the transmission of knowledge involves a communicative exchange, and it is commonplace that communication involves the kinds of shared intention, shared understanding, and cooperation between speaker and hearer that are characteristic of joint agency. Thus, in a communitive exchange, the speaker intends to be understood by the audience, and the audience understands that this is the speaker's intention. Moreover, speaker and hearer cooperate so as to achieve the intended result, each depending on the other to make appropriate contributions (communicative and interpretive) to the exchange.

In the case of knowledge transmission, however, joint agency goes beyond what is required for communication in general. Specifically, the transmission of knowledge involves the participatory intention to impart relevant information. S transmits knowledge that p to H, in the sense intended here, only if S intends to inform H that p and H understands and shares this intention. Thus, the transmission of knowledge is characterized by a particular kind of speech act, what we might variously characterize as "telling that p," "informing that p," "letting know that p," or "giving to know that p." The successful performance of that speech act requires that S and H each do their part in the exchange, with the result that H forms a true belief that p.

Accordingly, we may conclude that the transmission of knowledge essentially involves a kind of joint activity between speaker and hearer, one that is characterized by the shared intention that S informs H, or that S lets H know, or that S gives H to know. And because this kind of joint activity essentially involves the kind of interpersonal dependence and expectations constitutive of trust, we may conclude that knowledge transmission essentially involves trust between hearer and speaker.

4. Knowledge as Success From Ability

In Sections 1 through 3 we argued for a particular understanding of knowledge transmission and for the claim that knowledge transmission, so understood, essentially involves joint agency and therefore trust. In this section, we review some reasons for understanding knowledge as a kind of success from ability, and we consider some advantages of wedding this view to the account of knowledge transmission defended earlier. In particular, doing so allows us to answer a persistent objection to virtue epistemology—that the view is "overly individualistic" in the sense of not accommodating phenomena of social-epistemic dependence, as when hearers depend on speakers in testimonial knowledge. In the final section, we take the results of Sections 1 to 4 and apply them to our two main arguments regarding the role of trust in testimonial knowledge.

4.1. Some Theoretical Advantages of Virtue Epistemology

The idea that knowledge is a kind of success attributable to ability has considerable explanatory power regarding the nature and value of knowledge. Regarding the nature of knowledge, the account yields the following diagnosis of standard Gettier cases. In cases of knowledge, S's arriving at the truth is attributable to her own competent cognition. More exactly: S has a true belief, S's belief is formed by an exercise of cognitive ability, and S has a true belief *because* her belief is formed by an exercise of cognitive ability. In Gettier cases, S has a true belief, and S's belief is formed by an exercise of cognitive ability, but S does not have a true belief *because* her belief is formed by an exercise of cognitive ability. Rather, S's forming a true belief is merely lucky (Greco 2003, 2010). Consider the following two cases, which plausibly display this structure.

> **Perceptual Knowledge.** A man with excellent vision looks out over a field and sees what he takes to be a sheep. In fact, what he sees is indeed a sheep, he perceptually recognizes it as such, and forms a true belief to that effect.
> **Gettiered Perception.** A man with excellent vision looks out over a field and sees what he takes to be a sheep. Due to an unusual trick of light, however, what he takes to be a sheep is actually a dog. Nevertheless, unsuspected by the man, there is a sheep in another part of the field. (Adapted from Chisholm 1977, 105).

In **Perceptual Knowledge**, S's true perceptual belief is attributable to his excellent perception; that is, S has a true belief *because* S has exercised excellent perception. In **Gettiered Perception**, S exercises excellent perception and S ends up with a true belief, but S does not end up with a true belief because S has exercised excellent perception. On the contrary, it is just good luck that there is a sheep in another part of the field, unseen and unknown to S. Suppose we think of *achievements* as successes that are attributable to competent agency, as opposed to mere lucky successes that are not so attributable. Then **Perceptual Knowledge** describes a cognitive achievement, whereas **Gettiered Perception** describes a mere lucky success.

The idea that knowledge is a kind of success attributable to ability also yields an elegant explanation of the *value* of knowledge. That is because, in general, we think that achievements are both intrinsically and finally valuable. That is, we think that achievements are both valuable "in themselves" and "for their own sake." By understanding knowledge as a kind of achievement, we can explain the value of knowledge in terms of the value of achievements more generally. In the same way, the account elegantly explains the *superior* value of knowledge over mere true belief in terms of the superior value of achievements over mere lucky successes (Greco 2003, 2010, especially chapter 6).

Finally, the idea that knowledge is a kind of success attributable to ability yields insight into the nature of epistemic normativity and epistemic evaluation by understanding these within the context of a broader normative domain. That is, in any domain of human performance that allows for success and failure, we make a distinction between success due to competent agency and success that is merely lucky. The present account exploits this familiar distinction to understand epistemic normativity as simply a species of performance normativity more generally (Greco 2010, especially chapter 1; Sosa 2015). In fact, this final point is not unrelated to the considerations earlier regarding the value of knowledge, the superiority of knowledge over mere true belief, and the relationship between knowledge and luck. In all of these contexts, we get insight into the nature of epistemic normativity and epistemic evaluation by considering the contours of performance normativity more generally.

4.2. A Persistent Objection: Testimonial Knowledge and Anti-individualism

Our virtue-theoretic approach, then, has impressive explanatory power. That approach has been persistently criticized, however, as being unable to accommodate the social dimensions of knowledge, and especially testimonial knowledge.[22] Here is that objection in the voice of Jennifer Lackey, who considers the following example:

CHICAGO VISITOR: Having just arrived at the train station in Chicago, Morris wishes to obtain directions to the Sears Tower. He looks around, randomly approaches the first passerby that he sees, and asks how to get to his desired destination. The passerby, who happens to be a Chicago resident who knows the city extraordinarily well, provides Morris with impeccable directions to the Sears Tower.

Even if Morris is appropriately attentive to the speaker, and even if his reception of the speaker's testimony is appropriately discriminating, Lackey argues, it seems right to say that he forms a true belief *because of the speaker's testimony* rather than because of his own efforts. Alternatively, his true belief is attributable to the speaker's competent agency rather than his own.

But why not say that Morris gains a true belief *both* in virtue of his own efforts (his own exercise of relevant abilities) *and* in virtue of the speaker's efforts? Lackey argues that this would ruin the diagnosis of Gettier cases reviewed earlier. For in Gettier cases, too, S gains a true belief *partly* in virtue of her own efforts. Accordingly, Lackey's objection is best understood as a dilemma: either (a) we understand the attribution of success to S's own agency strongly, in which case we cannot account for standard cases of testimonial knowledge, or (b) we understand the attribution of success to S's own agency weakly, in which case we lose our diagnosis of Gettier cases.[23]

The inadequacy of the account in these respects is not obvious at first glance. After all, we can emphasize that many of our cognitive abilities are social cognitive abilities. Moreover, just as empirical knowledge requires a good fit between our perceptual faculties and our broader physical environment, we should expect that testimonial knowledge requires a good fit between our social cognitive abilities and our broader social environment. We rely on knowledgeable speakers, for example, but we also rely on the social norms and institutional structures that create knowledgeable speakers, make them available to us, and help us to monitor them for competence and sincerity. In all these regards, then, analogies to perceptual faculties and physical environments hold up well. Nevertheless, there is a sense in which our epistemic dependence on other persons is not adequately captured by what has been said so far. The point is nicely made in a remark by Sandy Goldberg, who notes that, when thinking about testimonial knowledge, we don't want to treat other people as "merely more furniture" in the environment.[24] Put differently, the present account does not yet accommodate the point that our epistemic dependence on others is a dependence on other *persons*—that it is an *interpersonal* dependence.

4.3. A New Proposal

Using the resources of Sections 1 to 3, however, we can now do better. The central claim of the new proposal is that, in cases of knowledge transmission, H's having a true belief that p is attributable to the competent joint agency constituted by S's telling H that p. Put differently, the joint agency in question *explains why* H has a true belief regarding p (rather than a false belief or no belief at all). Our new proposal involves a significant revision to the original achievement view of knowledge. For in the original view, the idea was that knowledge constitutes an *individual* achievement. That is, knowledge was understood as true belief attributable to the cognitive abilities of *the knower*. With the new proposal, there are in effect two ways of coming to know. First, one may come to know by means of one's individual competent agency. Second, one may come to know by means of one's competent participation in competent joint agency. In the second case, it is important to note one's having a true belief is attributable to the *competent joint agency*, as opposed to one's competent participation in that joint agency. Put differently, in the second case one's own competent agency does not adequately explain one's success. Rather, one's success is explained by *one's cooperation with others*, and is in this sense a joint achievement (an achievement attributable to joint agency) *rather than* an individual achievement (an achievement attributable to individual agency).

Finally, once these ideas are in place, it is easy to see that knowledge generation, as well as knowledge transmission, might sometimes be a joint achievement depending on joint agency. For it is easy to see that knowledge generation might sometimes involve the kind of intentional cooperation that characterizes joint activity. For example, we can conceive of a research team that cooperates in an investigation that is too complicated for any one person to undertake alone. If that cooperation is structured in the right way, and if the knowledge so produced is attributable to that cooperation, we will have a case in which knowledge generation is a joint achievement.

The proposed view is, of course, lacking in many details. For example, there is more to say about how we should characterize the details of joint agency in general, what constitutes *competent* joint agency as opposed to mere joint agency, and how we should understand the details of the kinds of joint activity that can result in knowledge transmission and knowledge generation. But the general idea is now in view.[25]

We next consider how the present proposal addresses concerns about social epistemic dependence and how it does so while preserving the theoretical advantages of the original achievement view.

4.4. Advantages of the Revised View

First, it should be straightforward that the revised view addresses concerns about epistemic individualism. For one, the view continues to invoke social cognitive abilities and social environments in its account of knowledge. But more importantly, in the revised view, knowledge is no longer understood solely terms of individual achievements, but in terms of joint achievement as well. Moreover, the revised view accommodates Goldberg's point that, in theorizing about social epistemic dependence, we should treat persons as persons, as opposed to merely more furniture in the environment. The present account does this by treating others on whom we depend as *agents*, and more specifically, as agents with whom we cooperate in joint activity.

Importantly, the revised achievement view also preserves the theoretical advantages that we noted for the original achievement view. For example, it preserves the original view's basic approach to the nature and value of knowledge. First, knowledge is still understood as a kind of success attributable to competent agency. We merely add that knowledge is sometimes a joint achievement, understood as success attributable to competent joint agency. This, in turn, preserves the achievement view's general approach to the value of knowledge: knowledge is intrinsically and finally valuable because achievements in general are intrinsically and finally valuable, and we value knowledge over mere true belief because in general we value achievements over mere lucky successes. We need only add that we value joint achievements in which we participate (we value such achievements in and for themselves) and that we value such achievements over mere lucky successes. In fact, the revised view potentially provides richer insights in these respects, insofar as the notions of joint agency and joint achievement afford more resources than do the notions of individual agency and individual achievement alone.

5. Back to the Main Arguments

We are now in a position to evaluate our two main arguments. Argument A begins with the premise that knowledge transmission is an important epistemological phenomenon, distinct from and irreducible to knowledge generation. This premise was clarified and supported by Sections 1 and 2. The argument continues with the claims that knowledge transmission essentially involves the kind of cooperation and coordination between speaker and hearer that is constitutive of joint agency and that joint agency essentially involves trust between the cooperating agents. These claims were supported by Section 3, which characterized transmission in terms of a special speech act of *telling* or *giving to know*, the execution of which, we argued, involves the kind of shared intention and requisite cooperation between speaker and hearer that is characteristic of joint agency. Because that intention and cooperation, in turn, require the kind of expectation and interpersonal dependence constitutive of trust, it follows that knowledge transmission essentially involves trust between speaker and hearer. Therefore, we may conclude, an epistemically important and distinctive phenomenon—knowledge transmission—essentially involves trust.

Argument B begins with a familiar theme from virtue epistemology—that knowledge is essentially a kind of success attributable to competent agency, as opposed to a mere lucky success, and is in that sense a kind of achievement. But Argument B extends this idea to the notion of knowledge transmission, claiming that transmitted knowledge is essentially true belief attributable to the competent *joint* agency of a speaker and hearer acting together (Section 4). We saw how this move preserves the theoretical power of the original virtue-theoretic claim that knowledge is a kind of achievement, while also addressing the persistent objection that virtue epistemology is overly individualistic. With that much in place, it then follows straightforwardly that transmitted knowledge essentially involves joint agency and trust, and that therefore some knowledge essentially involves trust. More exactly, some testimonial knowledge—that which comes about through knowledge transmission—essentially involves the hearer trusting the speaker, and that by its very nature.[26]

Notes

1. See Faulkner (2011) for an argument to this effect.
2. Here I have in mind Jennifer Lackey's objection to trust theories on which trust contributes to reliability and thereby explains justification. Lacky writes, "Thus, while the addition of [a reliability condition] places the Trust View on the epistemological map, trust itself turns out to be epistemically superfluous" (Lackey 2008, 238).
3. For some examples of trust theories, see (Welbourne 1986; Hardwig 1991; Hinchman 2005; Faulkner 2011).
4. That is not exactly right, because in fact I will be arguing that *some* testimonial knowledge essentially involves trust. More exactly, I will be arguing

that transmitted knowledge essentially involves trust, although not all testimonial knowledge is transmitted knowledge.

5. By "knowledge transmission," I mean specifically the kind of transmission that takes place between speaker and hearer in a successful testimonial exchange. Some authors have used the term "transmission" to talk about the transfer of justification from premises to conclusion in a competent inference (e.g., Wright 2015), and others have used the term in relation to the epistemology of memory (e.g., Burge 1997). My use of the term is here restricted to the epistemology of testimony, and I withhold any claims about there being an interesting common phenomenon that occurs across testimony, inference and/or memory.

6. This is the genus–species claim defended in (Greco 2010). See also (Greco 2003, 2012a; Sosa 2007, 2015)

7. In fact, there are many different "reductionism/anti-reductionism" debates in the testimony literature, as these terms have been defined in a myriad of ways. For discussion, see (Greco 2012b).

8. For example, see (Welbourne 1979).

9. For example, see (Graham 2000; Lackey 1999).

10. For example, see (Graham 2000) and (Lackey 1999, *op. cit.*).

11. For example, see (Hardwig 1985, 1991; Welbourne *op. cit.*).

12. Some assurance theories and speech act theories might also be interpreted this way. For example, see (Hinchman 2005).

13. The framework presented in this section is defended at length in (Greco 2015, forthcoming).

14. See (Gilbert 1990).

15. For a helpful overview, see (Roth 2011).

16. Searle (1990). As noted by Roth, *op. cit.*

17. Bratman (1992).

18. Gilbert, *op. cit.*

19. Gilbert, *op. cit.*

20. Here I intend a very general notion of trust. For example, the present notion is neutral between understanding trust as a cognitive, noncognitive, or hybrid phenomenon, depending on how one understands the central notions of dependence and expectation. This approach is, of course, consistent with the present purpose, which is to demonstrate that joint agency, however plausibly understood, essentially involves trust. For helpful overviews, see (McLeod 2015, and McMyler and Ogungbure 2018).

21. Reibsamen (2015).

22. See Lackey (2007, 2009).

23. Lackey (2009, 34) characterizes her objection this way.

24. In conversation.

25. The proposal put forward in this section is further defended in Greco (2019, forthcoming).

26. I am indebted to many people for comments and conversation, including Heather Battaly, Vincent Colapietro, Katherine Dormandy, Naomi Eilan, Lizzie Fricker, Sandy Goldberg, Georgi Gardiner, Peter Graham, David Henderson, Sahar Joakim, Jesper Kallestrup, Christopher Kelp, Jennifer Lackey, Duncan Pritchard, Jonathan Reibsamen, Joe Salerno, Ernest Sosa, Eleonore Stump, Deborah Tollefsen, John Turri, and my students in graduate seminars at Saint Louis University.

References

Bratman, Michael E. 1992. "Shared Cooperative Activity." *The Philosophical Review* 101: 327–41.

Burge, Tyler. 1997. "Interlocution, Perception, and Memory." *Philosophical Studies* 86: 21–47.

Chisholm, Roderick. 1977. *Theory of Knowledge*. 2nd ed. Englewood Cliffs, NJ: Prentice Hall.

Faulkner, Paul. 2011. *Knowledge on Trust*. Oxford: Oxford University Press.

Gilbert, Margaret. 1990. "Walking Together: A Paradigmatic Social Phenomenon." *Midwest Studies in Philosophy* 15: 1–14.

Graham, Peter. 2000. "Transferring Knowledge." *Nous* 34: 131–52.

Greco, John. 2003. "Knowledge as Credit for True Belief." In *Intellectual Virtue: Perspectives from Ethics and Epistemology*, edited by Michael DePaul and Linda Zagzebski, 111–34. Oxford: Oxford University Press.

———. 2010. *Achieving Knowledge: A Virtue-theoretic Account of Epistemic Normativity*. Cambridge: Cambridge University Press.

———. 2012a. "A (Different) Virtue Epistemology." *Philosophy and Phenomenological Research* 85(1): 1–26.

———. 2012b. "Recent Work on Testimonial Knowledge." *American Philosophical Quarterly* 49(1): 15–28.

———. 2015. "Testimonial Knowledge and the Flow of Information." In *Epistemic Evaluation*, edited by David Henderson and John Greco, 274–90. Oxford: Oxford University Press.

———. 2019. "Knowledge, Virtue and Achievement." In *The Routledge Handbook of Virtue Epistemology*, edited by Heather Battaly. New York: Routledge.

———. Forthcoming. *The Transmission of Knowledge*. Cambridge University Press.

Hardwig, John. 1985. "Epistemic Dependence." *Journal of Philosophy* 82: 335–49.

———. 1991. "The Role of Trust in Knowledge." *The Journal of Philosophy* 88: 693–708.

Hinchman, Edward. 2005. "Telling as Inviting to Trust." *Philosophy and Phenomenological Research* 70: 562–87.

Lackey, Jennifer. 1999. "Testimonial Knowledge and Transmission." *The Philosophical Quarterly* 49: 471–90.

———. 2007. "Why We Don't Deserve Credit for Everything We Know." *Synthese* 158: 345–61.

———. 2008. *Learning from Words: Testimony as a Source of Knowledge*. Oxford: Oxford University Press.

———. 2009. "Knowledge and Credit." *Philosophical Studies* 142: 27–42.

McLeod, Carolyn. 2015. "Trust." In *Stanford Encyclopedia of Philosophy* (Fall 2015 Edition), edited by Edward N. Zalta. https://plato.stanford.edu/archives/fall2015/entries/trust/. Accessed June 15, 2018.

McMyler, Benjamin, and Ogungbure, Adebayo. 2018. "Recent Work on Trust and Testimony." *American Philosophical Quarterly* 53 (3).

Reibsamen, Jonathan. 2015. "Social Epistemic Dependence: Trust, Testimony, and Social Intellectual Virtue." Dissertation, Saint Louis University.

Roth, Abraham Sesshu. 2011. "Shared Agency." In *Stanford Encyclopedia of Philosophy* (Spring 2011 Edition). http://plato.stanford.edu/archives/spr2011/entries/shared-agency/. Accessed June 15, 2018.

Searle, John. 1990. "Collective Intentions and Actions." In *Intentions in Communication*, edited by Philip R. Cohen, Jerry Morgan, and Martha E. Pollack, 401–15. Cambridge, MA: MIT Press.

Sosa, Ernest. 2007. *A Virtue Epistemology: Apt Belief and Reflective Knowledge*, vol. I. Oxford: Oxford University Press.

————. 2015. *Judgment and Agency*. Oxford: Oxford University Press.

Welbourne, Michael. 1979. "The Transmission of Knowledge." *The Philosophical Quarterly* 29: 1–9.

————. 1986. *The Community of Knowledge*. Aberdeen: Aberdeen University Press.

Wright, Stephen. 2015. "In Defence of Transmission." *Episteme* 12: 13–28.

5   Trust, Preemption, and Knowledge

Arnon Keren

1. Introduction

Trust, Annette Baier once noted, is like air: it is everywhere around us, necessary for our normal functioning, and yet we rarely notice it unless it becomes "scarce or polluted" (Baier 1986, 234). The comparison between trust and air seems particularly apt when thinking of the role of trust within our cognitive lives and of the epistemological treatment of trust. Hardwig's (1991) classic paper on the important, but neglected, epistemological role of trust thus aptly opens with a very similar comparison between trust and air (Hardwig 1991, 693).[1] Indeed, although we would know very little, if at all, if we had not trusted, and if people around us were not often trustworthy (Shapin 1994; Hardwig 1991), epistemologists have been much slower than their counterparts in other philosophical fields in their recognition of the importance of trust. Thus, although John Locke, already in the early 1660s, noted that "trust is the bond of society" (2002, 213), epistemologists only started acknowledging the importance of trust in the epistemic domain relatively recently. As late as 1991, Hardwig could present his claim that "a climate of trust . . . is required . . . to support much of our knowledge" as a novel claim, incompatible with the suppositions of most epistemologists, who view trust and knowledge as "antithetical" (Hardwig 1991, 693).

If Hardwig's claim was indeed novel and controversial in the early 1990s, it is no longer controversial today. Few contemporary epistemologists see trust and knowledge as antithetical, and there is widespread agreement among contemporary epistemologists that we would know much less than we actually do if we did not operate within a climate of trust. In recent decades, epistemologists have therefore exhibited a growing interest in the epistemological role of trust and in developing an epistemological account of trust-based knowledge and justified belief (Faulkner 2007, 2011; Hardwig 1991; Keren 2014; McMyler 2011; Moran 2005; Zagzebski 2012).

This chapter will try to do three main things: first, it will describe the central tasks of a nonrevisionist epistemological account of trust. Such an account, I will suggest, must answer two kinds of questions: the first concerns the nature of trust, and in particular, of trust when it functions as a source of knowledge and belief; the second concerns the epistemic significance of trust. I will then present the preemptionist account of trust (Keren 2007, 2014)[2] and explain why it is better fitted than alternatives to perform these tasks. I will end by considering a central challenge to this preemptionist account and to its claim to be able to explain the epistemological role of trust: the challenge to explain, within the preemptionist framework, not only why trusting makes us vulnerable to others in distinctive ways but also how trust could play a positive epistemic role.

2. Preliminaries

If we didn't trust, and if others hadn't often been trustworthy, we would know much less than we actually do know. On this, there is widespread agreement among contemporary epistemologists. Much of our knowledge thus depends upon trust.

However, that our knowledge depends upon trust might not mean that there is any need for an epistemological account of trust. For our knowledge might depend on trust in two distinct ways, and only one of them calls for an *epistemological* account. First, we might owe much of our knowledge to coordinated social action involving a complicated division of labor, which depends upon a climate of trust. Consider, for example, scientific research: scientists perform experiments in labs using expensive research materials, which are funded by universities, pharmaceutical companies and other funding agencies, who trust scientists to take proper care of equipment bought with the help of their funds; scientists, on their side, trust funding agencies to provide funds and salaries as promised. And this is, of course, only one node in an extensive chain of cooperation and trust: scientists hire research assistants, promising them payment, future employment, recommendation letters and so on. The latter trust the former to fulfill their promises; the former trust the latter to handle sensitive data and expensive material with care, to prepare experimental materials in accordance with preplanned protocols and so on. Thus, scientific research, like other forms of organized inquiry, and like other forms of coordinated social activity and division of labor, depends on trust (Baier 1986). Because much of our knowledge is owed to scientific inquiry and such inquiry requires trust, we would know much less than we actually do if this climate of trust did not exist.

However, as described here, trust's contribution to the acquisition of knowledge, although highly important, is, at most, indirect and does not call for an epistemological treatment: if, as a result of an experiment she has performed, scientist S comes to believe that scientific theory T is false, then the fact that trust was required to secure the funding used to purchase experimental equipment does not seem to matter for the epistemological evaluation of *S*'s belief. The epistemic status of her beliefs does not depend on the source of her funding, but rather on whether the results she obtained support the conclusion that *T* is false.

However, trust can also play a different and much more direct role in the formation of our beliefs and in the acquisition of knowledge. This is what happens when a speaker tells us that *p*, and we take her word for it; when we are told that *p* and we form the belief that *p* because we trust the speaker. Suppose that after reaching the conclusion that *T* is false, *S* tells her friend, *L*, that *T* is false, and suppose that *L* believes *S*. Believing S, that is, believing a person rather than merely believing a proposition, involves trusting the person for the truth of what she says (Anscombe 1979). In such a case it does seem that the fact that *L* arrived at his belief by trusting *S* may be highly relevant to the epistemological status of *L*'s belief. Call the kind of trust involved in a case where one person believes another, or trusts the other for the truth of what she says, "epistemic trust." Unlike the case of nonepistemic trust, the fact that a person's belief is formed through epistemic trust does seem, prima facie, to be relevant to its epistemological evaluation.

Although much of our knowledge depends on both epistemic and nonepistemic trust, it is epistemic trust which Hardwig seems to have in mind when he complains about the neglect of trust by epistemologists. For even if much of our knowledge depends on a climate of nonepistemic trust, there is no reason to think that this fact calls for an epistemological treatment or may require "basic changes in epistemology and the philosophy of science" (Hardwig 1991, 694). Moreover, it is far from clear why anyone might consider nonepistemic trust and knowledge "deeply antithetical" (693). We should therefore understand Hardwig as arguing for the claim that much of our knowledge is acquired through epistemic trust. It is this claim that is standardly accepted by epistemologists today and on which I shall focus here. Call this the *epistemic dependence* claim.

3. Revisionist and Nonrevisionist Accounts of Trust

Epistemological treatments of epistemic trust can be broadly divided into two main camps: revisionists and nonrevisionists.[3] Nonrevisionist epistemological treatments of epistemic trust accept, at least to a large extent, common intuitions about epistemic trust and its epistemological role[4] and common practices involving epistemic trust. While largely preserving these intuitions and practices, they attempt to account for them by trying to explain why these common intuitions are true, or almost true, and why these common practices are legitimate. Revisionist treatments, in contrast, reject central commonsense intuitions about epistemic trust and its epistemological role or imply that common practices should be significantly revised or eliminated. One of Hardwig's (1991) main points is that epistemological accounts that deny the epistemic dependence claim and maintain that knowledge and justified belief cannot be acquired through epistemic trust are highly revisionist because our common practices and common judgments often recognize beliefs formed on epistemic trust as constituting knowledge; moreover, he suggests that because they are revisionist in this way, such accounts must be rejected.

Contemporary epistemologists have largely agreed with Hardwig, both on the claim that an epistemological account that denies that knowledge is often obtained through epistemic trust would have highly revisionist skeptical implications and on the claim that any account with such revisionist implications should be rejected. Indeed, within the contemporary epistemology of testimony, it is often assumed that it is not merely a weighty consideration against an epistemological account that it entails a revisionist form of skepticism about testimonial knowledge; rather, it is a "constraint" on any satisfactory account that it not have such skeptical implications (Fricker 1994, 1995, 2016; Rowley 2012): any account that does not satisfy this constraint can be quickly dismissed (Anscombe 1979; Weiner 2003; Fricker 2002).

Although I reject the idea that revisionist and skeptical accounts of trust and testimony can be dismissed (Keren 2019b; see also Pritchard 2004), I agree that there are *methodological* reasons for focusing our efforts at this stage, when the epistemological study of epistemic trust is still in its infancy, on developing nonrevisionist accounts of epistemic trust. It is only on the basis of a richer understanding of our common intuitions and practices that we can properly evaluate skeptical arguments that call for their rejection. Accordingly, in what follows, I will try to describe some of the main tasks facing nonrevisionist accounts of trust and explain why one type of account, the preemptionist account, is better fitted than the alternatives to succeed in these tasks.

4. The Task

In general, the task facing nonrevisionist accounts of epistemic trust can be divided into a number of distinct, but related, subtasks: first, such accounts must provide answers to questions about the nature of trust and epistemic trust: What is epistemic trust? What kind of relation must hold between two persons, S and L, and a proposition, p, for it to be the case that L believes p because she trusts S? How does this relation differ from other ways in which L might rely on S when forming the belief that p? And what makes this relation a trusting relation?

Second, the account must answer questions about the epistemic significance of epistemic trust: Can it ever be epistemically rational for L to epistemically trust speaker S and to believe p because of this kind of trust? Are there situations in which it would be irrational not to trust? What is the relation between the supposed fact that L's belief that p constitutes knowledge and the fact that it was based on epistemic trust? And what kind of epistemic vulnerabilities are associated with epistemic trust?[5]

The challenge facing the nonrevisionist account of epistemic trust emerges from the fact that such an account must respect our common-sense intuitions with respect to both kinds of questions and that it is not clear how common judgments about the nature of trust in general, and epistemic trust in particular, can be accommodated with judgments about the epistemic significance of epistemic trust. On the one hand, there are reasons to think that trust, in general, and epistemic trust, in particular, involves holding a belief about the trusted person—either that she is trustworthy or that she will do what she is trusted to do (and in the case of epistemic trust: to tell the truth or to speak from knowledge); moreover, if epistemic trust is to play the kind of epistemic role often accorded to it, then the beliefs supposedly required for trust—call these "trusting beliefs"—must often be epistemically justified and thus sensitive to evidence. On the other hand, the relation between trust and evidence has certain features that might make it difficult to understand how, if indeed trust involves such trusting beliefs, these could be epistemically justified.

Accounts of the nature of trust can be broadly divided into two main camps, doxastic and nondoxastic, and their response to this challenge is what often underlies the division between them. On the one side are doxastic accounts of trust, which maintain that trusting a person to Φ involves holding a trusting belief about her (Adler 1994; Hardin 2002; Fricker 2006; Hieronymi 2008; McMyler 2011, 2018; Keren 2014, 2019c). Indeed, according to some doxastic accounts—pure doxastic accounts—to trust a person to Φ just is to hold a trusting belief about her (Hardin 2002; McMyler 2011). Nonpure doxastic accounts maintain that having such a belief is necessary, but not sufficient, for trust; such accounts might, for instance, maintain that trusting S to Φ requires, beyond having trusting beliefs about S, also relying on S in certain ways (Keren 2014). In contrast, nondoxastic accounts deny that trusting S to Φ requires having trusting beliefs about her. Although trust may often give rise to or be accompanied by trusting beliefs, trusting beliefs are not necessary for trust (Jones 1996; McLeod 2002; Holton 1994; Faulkner 2007; Kappel 2014; Simpson 2012). Such nondoxastic accounts either maintain that trust requires some mental state other than belief—for instance, an affective state or attitude (Jones 1996) or a moral attitude towards the trusted person (Holton 1994)—or they may deny that any kind of particular mental state is necessarily involved in trusting (Kappel 2014, Simpson 2012).

The claim that the relation between trust and evidence is very different from the relation between belief and evidence and that, moreover, the relation between *rational* trust and evidence is very different from the relation between *rational* belief and evidence, is one of the main reasons that has led many philosophers to endorse nondoxastic accounts of trust

(Holton 1994; Jones 1996; McLeod 2002; Faulkner 2007). A number of features are usually cited in this context: the first is what is known as trust's resistance to counter-evidence (Baker 1987; Jones 1996; Faulkner 2007). We tend to disbelieve accusations against those we trust and to interpret the behavior of those we trust favorably, disregarding evidence that could be taken as indications that they will not do what they are trusted to do; moreover, we tend not to arrive at such disbelief and such interpretations by weighing evidence for and against those accusations or for and against the claim that the trusted persons will fail to do what she is trusted to do. Indeed, seeking such evidence and weighing it seems to be incompatible with trust.

A second related feature of trust is the fact that trust is undermined by reflection on its basis: "[t]rust is a fragile plant, which may not endure inspection of its roots, even when they were, before the inspection, quite healthy" (Baier 1986, 260). Even when there is strong evidence supporting the trustworthiness of the person trusted, trust seems to be inconsistent with actively gathering this evidence.

Third, unlike belief, over which we arguably do not have direct voluntary control, it has been claimed that trust is subject to our voluntary control and that we can decide to trust for nonevidential reasons. Moreover, it has sometimes been claimed, such nonevidential reasons can make our trust rational. On the basis of these claims, several philosophers have argued for nondoxastic accounts of trust (Jones 1996; Holton 1994; Faulkner 2007; Simpson 2012).

However, there are also considerations supporting the claim that trust does require holding trusting beliefs about the trusted person (Keren 2014, 2019c; McMyler 2011, 2018; Hieronymi 2008). Indeed, denying this claim is particularly difficult when it comes to epistemic trust (Keren 2014, 2019c). For when we trust a speaker who tells us that *p*, we invariably form the belief that p. If trusting a speaker did not require believing that she will tell us the truth or that she is trustworthy, it would be unclear why this systematic relation between trusting the speaker and believing what she says holds; moreover, it would be difficult to see how beliefs obtained on the basis of such trust could be sustained while known by the thinker to be based on trust.[6]

Moreover, both the belief about the speaker involved in epistemic trust and the beliefs to which epistemic trust gives rise must be epistemically justified if epistemic trust is to play the positive epistemic role we often ascribe to it. Thus, it won't do to say that trust involves belief, but that because of its relations to evidence, trust systematically involves holding epistemically unjustified beliefs. For as noted earlier, any nonrevisionist account of trust must acknowledge that much of our knowledge is based on epistemic trust. If trust involved holding unjustified beliefs, then it would be difficult to see how beliefs based on trust could often constitute knowledge. Moreover, thinkers often explain how they know or why their beliefs are justified by noting that their belief is based on trust; again, it would be difficult to see how thinkers could present their reasons for belief in this way, unless the beliefs involved in trusting could be rational. Relatedly, our criticism of thinkers who refuse to trust certain experts, or their epistemic superiors, seems to involve the claim that such thinkers are not epistemically justified in their beliefs, or that their belief is not responsibly formed, because these thinkers do not trust their epistemic superiors. Prima facie, these thoughts seem to presuppose that if trust involves trusting beliefs, these beliefs can be justified.

This is the challenge that all nonrevisionist accounts of trust must face. In what follows, I will illustrate how one type of account—the preemptionist account of trust (Keren 2007, 2014)—addresses this challenge. As I will argue, the account suggests a more promising way of addressing this challenge than the alternatives. Moreover, I will argue that the account has the resources to meet the most serious challenge raised against it, namely, the claim that the account cannot explain the positive role played by epistemic trust.

5. Precaution and Preemption

The preemptionist addresses this challenge by presenting a general account of trust, which on the one hand, both neutralizes some central objections to doxastic accounts of trust and provides positive support to (nonpure) doxastic accounts. On the other hand, the account also explains why trust in general, and epistemic trust in particular, should involve beliefs that have seemed to be "blind" or resistant to evidence. In this account, trusting necessarily involves holding what we can call "trusting" beliefs about the trustworthiness of the trustee, and these can be supported by the evidence; however, in virtue of one's belief in the trustworthiness of the trusted person, trusting involves seeing yourself as having reasons for not taking precautions against the possibility that the trusted person will fail to do what she is trusted to do. This means that in trusting others, we see ourselves as having reasons for not being attuned to evidence for the proposition that the trusted person would fail to do what she is trusted to do, for not seeking such counter-evidence and for not deliberating on available evidence regarding the possibility that she will let us down. All these forms of insensitivity to evidence are a manifestation of a single feature of trust: namely, that trusting involves seeing yourself as having reasons for not taking precautions against the possibility of being let down by the trusted person.

The preemptionist account thus starts with the general question about the nature of trust. Both when we rely on a person to Φ and when we trust a person to Φ, we incur the risk that the person might fail to Φ. However, as is widely accepted, trust differs from other forms of reliance (Baier 1986; Jones 1996, Holton 1994; Hieronymi 2008). The preemptionist account of trust points at one important aspect of this difference: we can rely on a person to Φ while taking every precaution against the possibility that she will fail to Φ. Trust, in contrast, seems to be incompatible with taking such precautions. The preemptionist account takes this to be a constitutive feature of trust: trusting a person to Φ involves seeing oneself as having reason for not taking precautions against the possibility that she will fail to Φ.

As Elster writes (2015, 335), to trust someone is "to lower one's guard, to refrain from taking precautions against an interaction partner, even when the other, because of opportunism or incompetence, could act in a way that might seem to justify precautions". The preemptionist account of trust agrees with this observation, but notes that it is incomplete: in trusting, one does not merely lower one's guard; rather, one does so because one sees oneself as having reasons to do so. That is, in trusting, one does not merely lower one's guard as a result of, for example, being absent-minded, or of being tired: instead, one lowers one's guard because the trusted person's trustworthiness is *a reason for* lowering one's guard.

As an illustration, consider the following example. Suppose that John and Mary want to go out but have no arrangement for their kids. And suppose a friend, Tom, offers to come to their home to watch over the kids. "Trust me," he says, "I'll take good care of them and make sure they are in bed by nine." If John and Mary leave their kids with Tom but just before leaving, install CCTV cameras in their apartment so they can check that the kids are well taken care of, then they do not trust Tom to take good care of the kids. Surely if Tom were to discover that they have installed the CCTV cameras as a precaution, he would have the right to protest that they do not trust him.

The point is quite general. If you rely on a person to Φ but take every precaution against the possibility that she might not Φ—by seeking evidence that might indicate that she might fail to Φ and by acting in order to minimize the harm caused in case she fails to Φ—then you do not trust her to Φ. You might rely on her to Φ, but you do not trust her to do so.

Moreover, trust does not merely require not taking precautions against the possibility that the person would fail to do what she is trusted to do; trust requires seeing yourself as having reasons, because of the trusted person's trustworthiness, for not taking such precautions. If John and Mary both think that they should operate the CCTV cameras before Tom arrives but in their rush to get prepared, forget to do so, then they do not trust Tom, because they do not see themselves as having reasons for not taking this precaution. If we see ourselves as having every reason to take precautions but fail to take them nonetheless, then we do not trust. The preemptionist thus claims that not only is trust incompatible with taking every precaution against the possibility that the trusted person will fail to do what she is trusted to do but that, moreover, trust involves seeing oneself as having reasons against taking such precautions.

Furthermore, John and Mary do not seem to trust Tom to take good care of the kids if they both think that they should operate the CCTV cameras but fail to do so because each believes that the other has already done so. This is so, in spite of the fact that they do not take this precaution and, moreover, that they see themselves as having reason against taking this precaution. The preemptionist account explains why this is so by noting that their reason for not operating the CCTV camera—namely, that they think that someone else has already done so—has nothing to do with Tom's trustworthiness. Trusting a person to Φ necessarily involves seeing oneself as having reasons, *because of the person's trustworthiness*, for not taking precautions against the possibility that the trusted person would fail to Φ.

Because taking precautions is a matter of acting for certain reasons, according to the preemptionist account, trusting a person necessarily involves seeing oneself as having reasons against acting for certain kinds of reasons, namely, precautionary reasons. This means that trusting a person involves seeing oneself as having a preemptive reason. A preemptive reason for action (or belief) is a second-order reason against acting (or believing) on certain first-order reason (Raz 1986). A reason against taking precautions is a preemptive reason, because it is not merely a reason against acting in certain ways (e.g., against operating CCTV cameras) but rather, a reason against acting in certain ways for certain reasons, namely, for precautionary reasons.

On the basis of this general account of trust, the preemptionist account proceeds to explain features of trust to which supporters of nondoxastic accounts of trust have often pointed, such as trust's resistance to evidence, and the fact that trust is undermined by excessive reflection on the evidence supporting it. Both features of trust are a manifestation of a constitutive feature of trust, namely, that trust involves seeing oneself as having preemptive reasons for not taking precautions against the possibility of being let down. When we rely on others to act in certain ways, various precautions that we can take—such as operating CCTV cameras—serve as precautions precisely because they can provide us with evidence about the risk of being let down. Because trust involves seeing oneself as having preemptive reasons against taking such precautions, it involves seeing oneself as having reasons against being sensitive to evidence in this way. This is true of trust in general, but in particular of epistemic trust. For considering relevant evidence, seeking counter-evidence and being attuned to counter-evidence are the main forms of precaution that we can take in order to guard against the risk of being misled into forming a false belief when we rely on the testimony of a speaker. Therefore, if our reliance on speakers takes the form of epistemic trust, then we see ourselves as having reasons against taking such precautions. In the case of epistemic trust, preemptive reasons against taking precautions are therefore reasons for not basing our belief on consideration of available evidence, for not being attuned to evidence suggesting that the speaker is not speaking the truth and for not seeking and gathering further evidence relevant to the truth of the speaker's testimony. Let us use the umbrella term "evidential preemption" to refer to these different forms of cognitive behaviors which we see ourselves as having reasons not to engage in when we trust.

Thus, according to the preemptionist account of trust, trusting a speaker who tells us that p involves seeing her as trustworthy about p and seeing her testimony that p as good evidence for p;[7] moreover, it involves seeing her testimony as providing us with a second-order reason for evidential preemption: for not forming our opinion regarding p on the basis of our own weighing of certain other evidence that may be available to us and for not seeking further evidence, but rather, for forming our belief on the basis of the speaker's say-so. Correspondingly, a speaker who tells us that p thereby invites us to trust her about p, thus purporting to provide us with both evidence for p and a second-order preemptive reason for not forming our opinion regarding the matter on the basis of our own weighing of other evidence that may be available to us.

6. The Central Challenge to Preemption

What we have said so far about the preemptionist account of trust goes some way towards addressing the tasks facing nonrevisionist accounts of epistemic trust. First, it provides answers to questions about the nature of epistemic trust of the following sort: What is epistemic trust? How does this relation differ from other ways in which a person might rely on another when forming beliefs? And in virtue of what does this relation constitute a trusting relation? The account also goes *some* way towards answering *some* questions about the epistemic role of trust: in particular, it suggests an obvious answer to questions about the particular epistemic vulnerabilities associated with epistemic trust, given that in trusting we see ourselves as having reasons for not gathering evidence and not considering evidence available to us. The account can thus explain why trust is often described as "blind" (Hardwig 1991).

The preemptionist account can also explain in what way trust, and epistemic trust in particular, "is like air." Trust is like air not in the sense that we don't notice it until it becomes "scarce or polluted," as suggested by Baier (1986). After all, if John and Mary trust Tom and are asked by a friend whether they operated CCTV cameras before leaving the kids with Tom, they can answer that they did not do so because they trust him. Pace Baier, we can and often do notice our trusting relationships even when they are healthy and stable. What is right about the air analogy is that as long as we operate within healthy and stable trust relationships, we do not see the need to examine them and to gather evidence about the risk that trusted persons will fail us. Trust is what allows us to just take it for granted that other persons will do what they are trusted to do. In this sense, trust is like air: we normally see no need to consider whether there is breathable air surrounding us, but rather are naturally constituted so as to just take it for granted that there is.

However, as was noted from the start, accounting for the epistemic vulnerabilities associated with epistemic trust is only part of what a non-revisionist account of trust must do. Such an account must also explain how epistemic trust can have a positive epistemic role: how could it ever be epistemically rational for L to believe p because she trusts S? How can beliefs formed in this way constitute knowledge? And why might it sometimes be thought that thinkers *should* trust their epistemic superiors and that, epistemically speaking, their beliefs would not be responsibly formed unless they trusted the relevant speaker? How could all this be true if trust indeed involves evidential preemption, as suggested by the preemptionist account?

The central challenge facing the preemptionist approach comes from the idea that the epistemic status of beliefs is improved to the extent that they are well-based on more evidence, rather than on less. This idea is hard to deny. It finds its expression in a number of fundamental epistemological requirements. One is the evidentialist requirement of total evidence (TE): that one's beliefs should be responsive to all of one's evidence, rather than to only parts of one's evidence. Another is the very basic thought, which underlies evidence gathering and the rejection of the kind of dogmatism and closed-mindedness of those who refuse to consider further evidence: the idea that even if one's belief regarding p is justified by one's currently available evidence E, the epistemic status of one's belief regarding p would be improved if one obtained further evidence $E1$, such that one's belief would be well-based on the conjunction of E and $E1$. Call this the *more evidence is better* principle (MEB). The problem is that it may seem that the kind of evidential preemption involved in epistemic trust—the preemption of evidence gathering or of consideration of available evidence—necessarily involves either a violation of the TE requirement or the MEB principle, or of both. But if so, it would seem that if epistemic trust can play any significant epistemic role, it can only play a *negative* epistemic role. This indeed seems to be the most important objection to the preemptionist approach (see especially Jäger 2016; Dormandy 2018; Simpson 2017).[8] As Dormandy puts it: "[W]hen you have [evidence E] but preempt it, your basing behavior does not reflect the full force of your reasons and you forfeit doxastic justification" (2018, 778).[9] Call this "the forfeiture of justification" objection.

The first thing to note about the forfeiture of justification objection is that although it poses an important challenge to the preemptionist account, it is not only the preemptionist account that must face this challenge. Any nonrevisionist account of epistemic trust must acknowledge that trust involves a kind of "bracketing of evidence:" that trust is incompatible with gathering further evidence or with excessive deliberation on evidence available to one. Accordingly, any nonrevisionist account must explain how trust can have a positive epistemic role, given that trusting involves such a "bracketing" of evidence.

In fact, I argue, it is not only that the preemptionist account can meet this challenge; moreover, the account is in a better position to do so than other nonrevisionist accounts. For what sets the preemptionist account apart from other nonrevisionist accounts is that it does not maintain that trust involves some bare disposition or tendency to bracket evidence, but rather, that it involves seeing oneself as having *reason*, in virtue of the trusted person's trustworthiness, to bracket evidence or to not seek counter-evidence. According to other accounts, such as the affective attitude account of trust (Jones 1996) or the bracketing view of trust, according to which trust "is an attitude that constitutively involves bracketing certain evidential . . . considerations" (Kappel 2018), this "bracketing" is a matter of a bare disposition to fail to seek or bracket evidence. Indeed, the assumption that the kind of bracketing involved in trust cannot have a positive epistemic role is what often motivates such accounts (Kappel 2018, Jones 1996). But this leaves these "bare disposition" accounts ill-fit to explain normative evaluations of beliefs and actions that seem to presuppose the idea that trust does often have a positive epistemic role: evaluations that seem to presuppose not only that trust involves our being disposed to the bracketing of evidence, but, moreover, that because we trust, we have reason to bracket the evidence.

Consider, first, how we refer to trust in defending and criticizing action and belief. Suppose that you are flying to an unfamiliar country with a friend. To his question, "Aren't you packing umbrellas?" you might respond by saying, "Tina said that it never rains there in May, and I trust her." Here, you seem to try to explain the reasonableness of your not packing umbrellas by referring to your trust. Your response is not intended as a mere factual explanation of a fact about you, namely, that you did not pack umbrellas. Rather, we can respond by citing our trust—and this is the natural way of interpreting the kind of response described here—in a rationalizing explanation of your not packing umbrellas.

Moreover, the fact that Tina said that it wouldn't rain and that you trust her can serve not only as a rationalizing explanation of your decision not to take an umbrella; it can also serve as a defense of your decision not to gather further evidence. Thus, you can respond in the very same way even if your friend suggested that you gather more evidence about the weather at your destination. "Aren't you packing umbrellas? Don't you want to at least to call the hotel, to check about expected weather? It's a toll-free number, you know." Here, again, you might respond by saying that Tina told you that it never rains there in May and that you trust her. The preemptionist account can explain why this response seems to be at least an attempt to explain the reasonableness of not checking further about the weather: because you believe that Tina is trustworthy, you see yourself as having reasons against further checking. In contrast, accounts that deny that trusting involves seeing oneself as having reason for bracketing evidence do not seem to be in the position to explain this kind of response. On the one hand, accounts that deny that trust involves evidence bracketing cannot explain why your trusting Tina is at all relevant to your not calling the hotel in order to check; on the other hand, those that maintain that trust involves a bare disposition to bracket the evidence can explain why your response may explain what *caused* you not to check with the hotel, but they do not seem to explain why your response seems like an attempt to explain the *reasonableness* of your not checking.

Or consider criticisms of evidence gathering by reference to trust. Suppose that after you are told by Tina that there is absolutely no chance of rain in May, you nonetheless call the hotel to check whether it often rains there in May. Here your friend can criticize your inquiring with the hotel by saying, "But why did you call them? You know that we can trust Tina on such matters!" Again, this criticism can be explained by the preemptionist account, but it is difficult to see how it can be explained by nonpreemptionist accounts.

What is true of trust in general is also true in the case of epistemic trust. The way we refer to trust in defending and criticizing beliefs and forms of deliberation and evidence-gathering decisions that lead to them can be explained by the preemptionist account of trust, but would be difficult to explain on the basis of alternative accounts. We can try to explain the reasonableness of our not gathering further evidence by pointing to our trust both in cases where our interest is practical (e.g., where we must decide whether or not to take an umbrella) and in cases where we trust others for the truth of what they say and where our only interest in what is said emerges from our curiosity and desire to know. If Tina says that it never rains in a certain country in May and you have no plans of ever visiting that country but are only interested in inquiring about the local weather patterns out of curiosity, you can nonetheless explain why you don't make further inquiries by noting that Tina said so and you trust her.

Of course, that you trusted Tina does not mean that it was reasonable for you not to gather more evidence. Your friend can surely criticize you by noting that you shouldn't have trusted her. But it does not seem that your friend can both maintain that you should have trusted Tina for the truth of what she said and criticize you for not gathering further evidence before forming your belief.

Any nonrevisionist account of trust would have to explain why trust can figure in this way in explanations of the reasonability of not gathering evidence when relying on others for action and belief or why it can figure in criticism of evidence gathering. Because, in the preemptionist account, trust involves the avoidance of evidence gathering, along with other forms of evidential preemption, and involves seeing the trusted person's trustworthiness as providing a reason for not gathering evidence, the account is better suited for the task than its alternatives.

But even if the account can explain why trusting subjects see themselves as reasonable in avoiding further inquiry or in failing to deliberate on available evidence, it must still be asked whether evidential preemption can indeed be reasonable. In particular, can evidential preemption, and beliefs formed or sustained in this way, be epistemically justified? To the extent that evidential preemption is epistemically significant, can it involve anything other than forfeiture of doxastic justification? If not, how could trust have a positive epistemic role? That is the central challenge that the preemptionist account must face.

7. Forfeiting Doxastic Justification

To meet the central challenge to the preemptionist account, we must explain how evidential preemption can sometimes contribute to, rather than detract from, the epistemic standing of beliefs based upon trust. We must explain not only why trusting a speaker can be better, epistemically speaking, than disbelieving her; more than that, we must explain why trusting a speaker can be better than other forms of reliance on her that do not involve evidential preemption. And we must do so in a way that is consistent with a plausible interpretation of the TE requirement and of the MEB principle.

Now it might be suggested that sometimes trust might not involve the forfeiture of doxastic justification even if it involves a tendency to bracket the evidence, whether or not the bracketing involves seeing oneself as having reasons to bracket the evidence; for this bracketing, it might be suggested, may sometimes fail to have any epistemic significance. As Kappel (2019) suggests, a trusting thinker may enjoy environmental luck and may not encounter the kind of evidence that he is disposed to "irrationally disregard." In such a case, Kappel suggests, although he is disposed to irrationally disregard certain evidence, the epistemic irrationality involved in actually disregarding fails to materialize. Alternatively, it might be suggested that when part of the evidence available to a person makes no difference to the kind of doxastic state justified by the totality of her evidence, disregarding this part of one's evidence might not matter to the epistemic status of one's belief. That is, one's belief may be well-based even if one disregarded this part of one's evidence. For although a propositionally justified belief, it might be argued, must fit all available evidence, a belief need not be based on considerations of all the evidence to be well founded or doxastically justified.[10]

Although both these claims might be true, they fail as responses to the central challenge to the preemptionist account. For what we need to explain is how epistemic trust can sometimes have a *positive* epistemic role, whereas these responses can only explain how trust might sometimes fail to play a *negative* epistemic role. They do so by suggesting that even if trust generally plays a negative epistemic role, sometimes it can fail to play any significant epistemic role whatsoever. These responses therefore do not explain why it might seem natural to ask, when we encounter disagreement among experts, which experts we *should* trust:[11] Why assume that we *should* trust either of the experts, if trusting them would either forfeit epistemic justification or, in the best possible case, have no epistemic significance whatsoever? Similarly, these responses fail to explain how we are to make sense of the fact that thinkers sometimes refer to their trust in response to the question, "How do you know?" "She told me so, and I trust her" often seems to be a perfectly natural way of responding to this kind of challenge to a knowledge claim. However, if trust can either detract from the epistemic status of a belief or, in the best possible case, have no epistemic significance, then the fact that you arrived at a belief by trusting a speaker might seem, at best, irrelevant to your claim to know. Why cite this fact in support of your claim to know if the fact cannot contribute anything to the epistemic status of your belief?

So the preemptionist must provide a different kind of response to the forfeiture challenge if she is to explain the positive epistemic role of epistemic trust. She can do so, I suggest, by saying the following: beliefs based upon trust can sometimes have better epistemic status than beliefs formed by other forms of reliance, in virtue of the evidential preemption involved in trusting. This is so, because by believing as the trusted speaker does and not basing your belief on your own consideration of first-order evidence available to you, your opinion can become properly sensitive to *better* evidence than that which you yourself have: it can become appropriately sensitive to the better evidence available to the speaker.[12]

A proper response to the evidence is a matter of having doxastic attitudes that are well founded: that not only fit the evidence, but moreover, are ones whose fit with the evidence is not a matter of coincidence. When a speaker has better evidence than you have and when she properly responds to this evidence, then by preempting your own weighing of the first-order evidence available to you and believing as she does, you can form a belief that not only fits the better evidence available to her but, moreover, that is well founded on her evidence: a belief that achieves this fit with *her* evidence in a reliable, noncoincidental way.[13]

Trust and evidential preemption can have such a positive epistemic role because we don't generally have access to evidence that is available to others. In the context of the interaction with another thinker, when the other thinker's belief or testimony is supported by better evidence than that available to us, trust has a positive epistemic role, because weighing our own first-order evidence is just not a way that allows us to reliably form beliefs that fit the evidence that is available to the other thinker but that we do not possess. Thus, when you have better evidence than I do, trusting you for the truth of what you say allows me to properly respond to better evidence than that available to me, namely to that evidence which is available to you; and it allows me to form my belief in a way that most reliably fits this superior body of evidence.[14] Trusting you for the truth of what you say is what allows my belief to be well founded on your superior body of evidence.[15]

What are we to say then of the TE requirement and of the MEB principle? Our explanation of the positive epistemic role of epistemic trust is perfectly compatible with a plausible interpretation of what underlies both principles. Gathering new evidence and holding beliefs that are well founded on more evidence rather than less is a way of improving the epistemic status of our beliefs, because more evidence is better than less. For similar reasons, the totality of my evidence is the best body of evidence available to me and therefore is authoritative for me. What underlies both MEB and TE is the idea that more evidence is better than less and that we should be guided by the best body of available evidence. However, having better evidence is not always a matter of having more evidence. Sometimes others have evidence that is better than that available to me and hold beliefs that are well-formed on that evidence. Moreover, sometimes they are kind enough to share these beliefs with me. In such cases, trusting them, and the preemption of evidence weighing and gathering involved in trusting, is a way of basing my belief on a better body of evidence. In contrast, in such cases, forming my belief on my own weighing of the evidence available to me is not a way of forming beliefs on a better body of evidence. Thus, in such cases trust and preemption do not violate the TE and MEB principle, but rather contribute to the same kind of normative idea that underlines both: namely, that we should form our beliefs on the basis of the best available body of evidence. Thus, even on a plausible reading of the idea that underlies TE and MEB, the epistemic status of our belief can be improved, rather than forfeited, by preempting my own weighing of the evidence. Thus our response to the central challenge is perfectly consistent with a plausible understanding of what underlies both the TE and MEB: the idea that epistemically speaking, it is always better to hold beliefs that are well founded on a better body of evidence, rather than on an inferior body of evidence.

7. Conclusions

The preemptionist account can explain how epistemic trust can play a *positive* epistemic role. Moreover, it can explain the kind of positive epistemic role we tend to think it can have. As has been emphasized throughout this chapter, common intuitive judgments and common forms of speech seem to suggest that we think that much of our knowledge depends on epistemic trust. However, the common intuition is that our knowledge depends on trust in a very particular way: trust does not generate knowledge, but rather "transmits" knowledge from one person to another. "Because Tina told me that it never rains there in May, and I trust her" appears a natural answer to the question "How do you know that it wouldn't rain?", but only if you take it that Tina herself knows that it never rains there in May. The preemptionist account, and its explanation of the positive epistemic role of epistemic trust, can explain why we have this intuition (Keren 2007). If trust can have a positive epistemic role in virtue of the fact that it allows us to form beliefs that are supported by evidence available to the speaker, then our beliefs would be supported by knowledge-supporting evidence only if the speaker's own belief is supported by knowledge-supporting evidence. Hence, it would seem plausible to think that we can only claim to know through trust if the speaker knows that what she is saying is true.

Thus, the preemptionist account of trust seems able to meet all subtasks that a nonrevisionist account of trust must meet and seems better able to do so than alternative accounts. It provides an account of the nature of trust that can explain why trust may often be described as "blind" or compared with air, and it can explain, in particular, what sort of epistemic vulnerabilities are associated with epistemic trust. At the same time, it can explain why this "blindness" of trust, why the evidential preemption involved in trust, may play a positive epistemic role. Trust may involve this kind of blindness, but that it involves this blindness does not mean that the epistemic dependence claim is false. On the contrary. This preemptionist feature of trust helps explain why our knowledge depends on our trust as it does: why it is knowledge shared with us, or transmitted to us, rather than new knowledge generated by us, that depends on epistemic trust.[16]

Notes

1. It is unclear whether Hardwig takes the comparison between trust and air from Baier's classic paper. I have not found any explicit references to Baier in any of Hardwig's classic papers on trust; but the passage from Baier comparing trust and air has been quoted verbatim by more than 100 other papers and has probably been rephrased by many more, so Hardwig might have drawn the comparison indirectly from Baier.
2. See Siebert (2016) for a discussion of Aquinas's account of trust and testimony, which points at important similarities between Keren's (2014) preemptionist account of trust and Aquinas's account. On Siebert's interpretation, Aquinas's account might also count as a preemptionist account.
3. As I use the terms, a philosophical account is characterized as "revisionist" or as "nonrevisionist" depending on its treatment of our commonsense understanding of, and intuitions about, the relevant phenomena. Thus, a revisionist account of trust is one that rejects commonsense intuitions about trust and its epistemological role, whereas a nonrevisionist account largely preserves these intuitions. In this usage, philosophical tradition can be revisionist if it rejects our commonsense intuitions about relevant phenomena, as Hardwig claims was the case with mainstream epistemology in his time.

4. These include intuitions both about what trust is and its justification.
5. These are the primary tasks of a nonrevisionist account of epistemic trust, but they are not the only tasks. However, other tasks, such as that of responding to revisionist critics of our common conception of epistemic trust, depend on these two primary tasks, and hence might need to wait for some progress on these two primary tasks.
6. I am assuming here that epistemic trust is a species of trust. But it might be suggested that this assumption is mistaken, and that once we reject it, a simple solution to the challenge presented earlier suggests itself: epistemic trust and nonepistemic trust are not the same kinds of things. The suggestion then is that the considerations that seem to call for a nondoxastic account of trust apply to nonepistemic trust, which indeed admits of a nondoxastic account, whereas considerations that seem to pull in the doxastic direction apply to epistemic trust, which admits of a doxastic account.

   However, there are good reasons to accept the standard assumption that epistemic trust is indeed a species of trust. Our linguistic behavior, for one thing, indicates that we treat epistemic and nonepistemic trust as species of the same thing, namely, interpersonal trust. Thus, both forms of trust can be invited in the same way, by employing trust terminology: "trust me!" can both be used to invite someone to believe you as a speaker and to trust you to take good care of the kids. Similarly, the complaint, "But I thought that I could trust you!" is appropriate both when a trusted speaker speaks falsely and when a trusted babysitter fails to take good care of the kids.

   Moreover, there are reasons to doubt whether the alternative claim, that epistemic trust is not a species of trust, does offer a simple solution to the challenge described earlier. At least some of the central considerations that seem to pull us towards doxastic accounts of trust apply both to epistemic and to nonepistemic trust. Thus, beyond the systematic relation between trusting a speaker and believing what she says, there are other systematic relations between trusting a person to do Φ and holding certain beliefs about her, relations that are easily explained by doxastic accounts of trust, but which nondoxastic accounts of nonepistemic trust seem unable to explain (Keren, 2019c). Consider, for instance, the impossibility of trusting a person to Φ while holding the belief that the person will fail to Φ or that she is not trustworthy with respect to Φ-ing. Supporters of nondoxastic accounts typically agree that this is impossible (Holton 1994; Faulkner 2007; Frost-Arnold 2014), but nonetheless seem unable to explain this impossibility, which doxastic accounts can easily explain (Keren 2019c).

   Moreover, considerations that have attracted some philosophers towards accepting nondoxastic accounts of trust apply also to epistemic trust and so would not be accounted for by the supposedly simple suggestion. One such feature is trust's apparent resistance to the evidence, which seems to apply to epistemic trust no less than to nonepistemic trust. Trump supporters, for instance, are often criticized for trusting what he says, in spite of having strong evidence against what he says; but the claim made by supporters of nondoxastic accounts of trust is usually that this kind or resistance to counter-evidence is not something unique to supporters of any particular politician, but rather, that it is a general characteristic of trust that "beliefs formed on the basis of trust *are* abnormally resistant to evidence" (Jones 1996, 20; original emphasis).

   I conclude, therefore, that there are good reasons for taking epistemic trust to be a species of trust; moreover, rejecting this assumption would not offer a simple solution to the challenge presented earlier. I am grateful to Katherine Dormandy for pressing me on the issue.

7. In some views of trust, in particular, Richard Moran's (2005) assurance view, trusting or believing a speaker is inconsistent with treating her testimony that *p* is evidence for p. In contrast, the preemptionist claims that trusting a speaker is inconsistent with treating her testimony that *p merely* is evidence for *p*, but denies that it is inconsistent with treating it *also* as evidence for p. For in the preemptionist view a trusted speaker's testimony that *p* provides us *both* with evidence for *p and* with a preemptive reason for not basing our opinion regarding *p* on our own weighing of other first-order evidence available to us.

   Moran's assurance view has been extremely influential, and so many supporters of the view would likely reject my claim about what trusting a speaker consists of [However, not all interpersonalist accounts of testimony inspired by Moran insist on the claim that trusting a speaker is inconsistent with treating her testimony as evidence. See in particular McMyler (2011, 2019)]. Although I cannot pursue the matter here, I think there are good reasons to reject Moran's assurance view in favor of the preemptionist view. One reason for doing so is that Moran's assurance view is unable to explain the positive epistemological role of trust (on this see Keren (2019a), whereas, as I argue later, the preemptionist view is able to do so. Moreover, as I argue elsewhere (Keren 2012), Moran's argument against the evidentialist view of testimony is unsound.

8. See also Lackey (2018).

9. Or as Jäger puts it: "[W]ouldn't the agent be epistemically better off if he based his belief both on the fact that the authority shares his belief and on his own reasons (or set of reasons)? Basing a belief on two good reasons is better than basing it on one" (2016, 176).

10. See, e.g., Feldman and Conee (2004).

11. See, e.g., Goldman (2001)

12. I appeal here to the notion of better evidence but leave for elsewhere a detailed discussion of the notion. Ultimately, the account suggested here would need to appeal to a more detailed explication of the notion, which would allow us to specify when body of evidence *E1* counts as better than *E2*. But for the sake of the current discussion, such an account of "better evidence" is not required. It suffices that we accept that there are cases in which one person has a better body of evidence available to her than another, and moreover, that we are often in a position to recognize those who have better evidence than we do. The preemptionist account of trust can appeal to such cases to explain how it can sometimes be the case that our opinion would be supported by better evidence if we preempt basing our belief on our own consideration of the evidence.

13. I am suggesting that one person's belief can be supported by evidence available to another. This suggestion seems to radically depart from traditional evidentialist doctrine, which has been usually developed within an internalist framework and which has insisted that only evidence currently available to a thinker can support her current belief (Bonjour 2003). However, like many others, I believe that there are independent reasons for abandoning this internalist version of evidentialism. One reason for rejecting this version is that it cannot account for the justification of beliefs stored in memory, when the evidence for them is lost.

14. Note that if this defense of evidential preemption is successful, it not only establishes that trusting the speaker can be better, epistemically speaking, than disbelieving her; it also explains how trusting her can sometimes be better than other forms of reliance that do not involve evidential preemption. If you would mobilize your epistemic resources—considering the

speaker's testimony alongside all other evidence available to you—then your belief would not be supported by better evidence than if you trust the speaker, but rather, by weaker evidence: for if you trust her, then your belief would be supported by her evidence, which, we assume, is better than that available to you.

15. Of course, trust does not always play a positive epistemic role. It does not play a positive epistemic role when the speaker's testimony is not supported by evidence or when it is supported by evidence available to her but this evidence is not better than that available to the hearer.

16. This research was supported by the Israel Science Foundation (grant no. 650/18). I am grateful to Katherine Dormandy for helpful comments on previous drafts of this chapter.

References

Adler, Jonathan. E. 1994. "Testimony, Trust, Knowing." *The Journal of Philosophy* 91(5): 264–75.

Anscombe, Gertrude Elizabeth Margaret. 1979. "What Is It to Believe Someone?" In *Rationality and Religious Belief*, edited by Cornelius F. Delaney, 141–51. Notre Dame, IN: University of Notre Dame Press.

Baier, Annette. 1986. "Trust and Antitrust." *Ethics* 96(2): 231–60.

Baker, Judith. 1987. "Trust and Rationality." *Pacific Philosophical Quarterly* 68: 1–13.

BonJour, Lawrence. 2003. "A Version of Internalist Foundationalism." In *Epistemic Justification: Internalism vs. Externalism, Foundations vs. Virtues*, edited by Lawrence Bonjour and Ernest Sosa, 3–96. Malden, MA: Blackwell.

Dormandy, Katherine. 2018. "Epistemic Authority: Preemption or Proper Basing?" *Erkenntnis* 83(4): 773–91.

Elster, Jon. 2015. *Explaining Social Behavior: More Nuts and Bolts for the Social Sciences*. Cambridge: Cambridge University Press.

Faulkner, Paul. 2007. "On Telling and Trusting." *Mind* 116(464): 875–902.

———. 2011. *Knowledge on Trust*. Oxford: Oxford University Press.

Feldman, Richard, and Earl Conee. 2004. "Evidentialism." In *Evidentialism: Essays in Epistemology*, edited by Earl Conee and Richard Feldman, 83–100. New York: Oxford University Press.

Fricker, Elizabeth. 1994. "Against Gullibility." In *Knowing from Words*, edited by Bimal Krishna Matilal and Arindam Chakrabarti, 125–61. Dordrecht: Kluwer Academic.

———. 1995. "Telling and Trusting: Reductionism and Anti-Reductionism in the Epistemology of Testimony." *Mind* 104: 393–411.

———. 2002. "Trusting Others in the Sciences: A Priori or Empirical Warrant?" *Studies in History and Philosophy of Science Part A* 33(2): 373–83.

———. 2006. "Second-Hand Knowledge." *Philosophy and Phenomenological Research* 73(3): 592–618.

———. 2016. "Unreliable Testimony." In *Goldman and His Critics*, edited by Brian P. McLaughlin and Hillary Kornblith, 88–123. Oxford: Wiley Blackwell.

Frost-Arnold, Karen. 2014. "The Cognitive Attitude of Rational Trust." *Synthese* 191: 1957–74.

Goldman, Alvin I. 2001. "Experts: Which Ones Should You Trust?" *Philosophy and Phenomenological Research* 63(1): 85–110.

Hardin, Russell. 2002. *Trust and Trustworthiness*. New York: Russell Sage Foundation.

Hardwig, John. 1991. "The Role of Trust in Knowledge." *The Journal of Philosophy* 88: 693–708.

Hieronymi, Pamela. 2008. "The Reasons of Trust." *Australasian Journal of Philosophy* 86(2): 213–36.

Holton, Richard. 1994. "Deciding to Trust, Coming to Believe." *Australasian Journal of Philosophy* 72(1): 63–76.

Jäger, Christoph. 2016. "Epistemic Authority, Preemptive Reasons, and Understanding." *Episteme* 13(2): 167–85.

Jones, Karen.1996. "Trust as an Affective Attitude." *Ethics* 107(1): 4–25.

Kappel, Klemens. 2014. "Believing on Trust." *Synthese* 191(9): 2009–28.

———. 2019. "Trust and Disagreement." Forthcoming in *The Routledge Handbook of Trust and Philosophy*, edited by Judith Simon. London: Routledge.

Keren, Arnon. 2007. "Epistemic Authority, Testimony and the Transmission of Knowledge." *Episteme* 4: 368–81.

———. 2012. "On the Alleged Perversity of the Evidential View of Testimony." *Analysis* 72(4): 700–07.

———. 2014. "Trust and Belief: A Preemptive Reasons Account." *Synthese* 191: 2503–615.

———. 2019a. "Letting Hyde Loose: Testimony and the Second Person." Unpublished manuscript.

———. 2019b. "On Living the Testimonial-Skeptic's Life: Can Testimonial Skepticism Be Dismissed?" Unpublished manuscript.

———. 2019c. "Trust and Belief." Forthcoming in *The Routledge Handbook of Trust and Philosophy*, edited by Judith Simon. London: Routledge.

Lackey, Jennifer. 2018. "Experts and Disagreement." In *Knowledge, Belief, and God: New Insights in Religious Epistemology*, edited by Matthew A. Benton, John Hawthorne, and Dani Rabinowitz, 228–45. Oxford: Oxford University Press.

Locke, John. 2002. *Essays on the Law of Nature*, 3rd ed., edited and translated by Woflgang von Leyden. Oxford: Oxford University Press.

McLeod, Carolyn. 2002. *Self-Trust and Reproductive Autonomy*. Cambridge, MA: MIT Press.

McMyler, Benjamin. 2011. *Testimony, Trust, and Authority*. New York: Oxford University Press.

———. 2019. "Trust and Authority." Forthcoming in *The Routledge Handbook of Trust and Philosophy*, edited by Judith Simon. London: Routledge.

Moran, Richard. 2005. "Getting Told and Being Believed." *Philosophers' Imprint* 5: 1–29.

Pritchard, Duncan. 2004. "The Epistemology of Testimony." *Philosophical Issues* 14: 326–48.

Raz, Joseph. 1986. *The Morality of Freedom*. Oxford: Clarendon Press.

Rowley, William. D. 2012. "Evidence of Evidence and Testimonial Reductionism." *Episteme* 9(4): 377–91.

Shapin, Steven. 1994. *A Social History of Truth: Civility and Science in Seventeenth-Century England*. Chicago, IL: University of Chicago Press.

Siebert, Matthew Kent. 2016. "Aquinas on Testimonial Justification." *The Review of Metaphysics* 69(3): 555–82.

Simpson, Thomas. 2017. "Trust and Evidence." In *The Philosophy of Trust*, edited by Paul Faulkner and Thomas Simpson, 177–94. Oxford: Oxford University Press.

———. 2012. "What Is Trust?" *Pacific Philosophical Quarterly* 93(4): 550–69.

Weiner, Matthew. 2003. "Accepting Testimony." *The Philosophical Quarterly* 53(211): 256–64.

Zagzebski, Linda T. 2012. *Epistemic Authority: A Theory of Trust, Authority, and Autonomy in Belief*. Oxford: Oxford University Press.

6 Groups, Trust, and Testimony

Jesper Kallestrup

A prominent set of questions in social epistemology concerns the epistemic profile of groups: Are groups fit to constitute knowers and testifiers in much the same way as individuals? And if so, are such epistemic properties of groups, as so-called *divergence arguments* aim to show, *irreducible* to corresponding properties of their individual members? Another important set of questions in the epistemology of testimony concerns the role of *trust in testimony*: to what extent, if any, do individual testifiees acquire knowledge through trusting individual testifiers to speak the truth? And is such trust best understood, following the influential *assurance* view, in terms of the testifiers lending their assurance that their tellings are true? This chapter seeks to bring these hitherto distinct debates together. In the first section, we revisit the reasons that have been adduced in support of irreducible group knowledge and testimony. In the second section, a version of the Assurance view of trust is expounded with a view to testimonial knowledge. The aim is not to defend nonreduction about group knowledge and testimony, or indeed the Assurance view, against all extant objections in the literature. Rather, in the third section, an argument from cases is developed to the effect that groups can instantiate irreducible relations of testimonial trust, understood in accordance with the Assurance view, *provided* groups can serve as testifiers of knowledge over and above any knowledge testified by their members. Still, such a conditional claim is significant, because, on the face of it, such relations appear to obtain only between individuals, given that trust is a rational relation with normative and affective implications that would seem to pertain only to individuals. The contention is that, given our assumptions, this appearance is misleading: intergroup testimonial trust is a genuine phenomenon that deserves further exploration.

1. Group Knowledge and Group Testimony

A question of great import that theories of knowledge aim to answer is: What converts true (properly based and nondefeated) belief into knowledge? Prominent answers include being produced by a reliable cognitive process, being supported by mentalist evidence, and being true because of competence.[1] Despite favoring different epistemic properties as being responsible for the conversation, such competing theories could all accept that individuals (or persons) and groups alike are capable of being in states of belief and knowledge. Disagreement over what makes the difference between true belief and knowledge is compatible with shared *liberalism* about which entities can be in such states. Still, attributions in the literature of belief and knowledge to groups have historically been rare. That changed with the advent of social epistemology, which inter alia sought to explore the epistemic credentials of doxastic attitudes of groups.[2] Let's review some of the reasons why social epistemologists take groups to not only have knowledge that none of their members have but also to testify such knowledge.[3]

Our first question is: Why should we think groups can enjoy the epistemic status of knowledge at all? An important observation concerns *ordinary parlance*.[4] As any quick Google search will verify, we speak unproblematically about clubs, boards, firms, churches, governments, and so on as having knowledge.[5] The ubiquity and diversity of such talk present a genuine reason to take its content at face value. Were we invariably mistaken about groups having knowledge, a drastic revision of epistemic discourse would be called for. Of course, we also say "the flowers know when to blossom," or "my computer knows me better than my friends," but such talk is loose, as the *normative* aspect of the concept of knowledge is missing. Flowers and computers are neither epistemically responsible for what they do, nor do they deserve praise for getting things right. But might not some true attributions of knowledge lack a normative dimension, such as talk of knowledge had by sophisticated animals or young children? Both are arguably capable of forming true beliefs as a result of reliable cognitive processes, but such *low-grade* knowledge still involves some normative evaluation, as when one is rewarded for reliably produced cognitive success. Still, they are by any reckoning incapable of attaining an epistemic perspective on their first-order beliefs and so lack the kind of *high-grade* knowledge that implies a wider range of normative assessments. In contrast, we ordinarily speak as if groups are subject even to such reflective knowledge, say, in the way credit is assigned when groups are attributed knowledge on the basis of scrutinizing the credentials of their evidence. Although ordinary ascriptions of knowledge provide pro tanto reason to think groups can instantiate knowledge on a par with mature individuals, such reasons might be outweighed by other considerations. A proper vindication of group knowledge would require addressing the challenges raised within social epistemology by Wray (2001) and Meijers (2002) to do with the requirement of group belief for group knowledge, or by Lackey (2014) and Carter (2015) to do with epistemic defeat of group knowledge, as well as in the cognitive science literature by Rupert (2005; manuscript) to do with putative causal powers of group minds. Our discussion going forward is optimistically premised on the possibility of satisfactory answers. For example, Wray (2007) proposes that group knowledge merely requires justified true acceptances.

A second question is whether the knowledge that groups have may differ from the knowledge that some, or all, of their members have. The following view gives a negative answer:

(SUMMATIVISM$_{Know}$) Necessarily, a group g has knowledge K if and only if at least one individual i is both a member of g and has K ($Kg \leftrightarrow \exists i \ (i \in g \ \& \ Ki)$).[6]

However, so-called *divergence arguments* challenge (SUMMATIVISM$_{Know}$). One type of case concerns the possibility that *epistemic standards* apply to groups while failing to apply to their members.[7] Take criminal proceedings in a court of law for which the standards of evidence include that hearsay normally be excluded and that the standard of proof be beyond a reasonable doubt. These special standards govern how the criminal court must perform as devolved from the office of such courts. It can then happen that a jury finds the evidence, as adduced by the prosecution, not beyond a reasonable doubt, and hence insufficient to validate criminal conviction. Still, the jury members may have hearsay evidence from a reliable source, sufficient for knowledge, that the defendant is guilty, yet the judge instructs them to ignore such inadmissible evidence. Because evidence sufficient for knowledge is available to the jurors distributively but unavailable to them jointly, we have a counterexample to (SUMMATIVISM$_{Know}$) when read from right to left.

A different type of case exploits the common phenomenon of *distributed cognition*, involving a division of cognitive labor within a group such that the cognitive task of producing group knowledge is divided into subtasks, which are then assigned to individuals, or to subgroups in which individuals collaborate to pursue subgoals, depending on their respective areas of expertise. Bird (2014, 57; cf. 2010, 34–35) imagines Dr. X, a physicist, and Dr. Y, a mathematician, collaborating on a project to demonstrate the truth of the conjecture q. Dr. X shows p by conducting experiments and analyzing data, while Dr. Y solves the problem in pure mathematics of proving $p \rightarrow q$. The remaining part of the project is an application of modus ponens, for which Drs. X and Y provide a prewritten proof such that when their appointed assistant independently receives from Dr. X the demonstration that p and from Dr. Y the proof of $p \rightarrow q$, the assistant will upload and publish their joint paper.[8] The research team thus comes to know q, yet neither of its members, Dr. X or Dr. Y, knows q. Nor does the assistant, whom we assume lacks sufficient expertise to even grasp the demonstration that p and the proof of $p \rightarrow q$. So, we have a counterexample to (SUMMATIVISM$_{Know}$) when read from left to right.

Naturally, although the foregoing provides genuine reason to think (SUMMATIVISM$_{Know}$) is false in both directions, more needs to be said about our two cases for them to firmly establish epistemic divergences between groups and their individual members. We shall not here delve further into the details, but simply proceed on the plausible assumption that groups are able to possess knowledge that is *irreducible* to knowledge possessed by their members.

A third question is whether groups can function as testifiers, and if so, whether they can testify knowledge which their members lack. Because not all knowing agents need be able to testify, there is no swift inference from (irreducible) group knowledge to group testimony. Even granting that sophisticated animals and small children are subjects of knowledge, we would surely hesitate to regard them as testifiers, in part because they are unable to perform the required speech act of assertion. But ordinary epistemic discourse is replete with examples of groups being treated as testifying agents who can issue statements, draft reports, provide guidance, reply to queries and so on. Thus, the following seems eminently plausible:

(GROUP TESTIFIER) Groups can testify any proposition of which they have knowledge.[9]

One may attempt to explain away such indications of group testimony as mere metaphorical use of language.[10] The problem is that much of our knowledge stems from group testimony: our knowledge of tomorrow's weather is based on the Met Office's forecasts, and our knowledge of travel risks in the Middle East is based on advice by the Foreign Office. To insist that any appearance of group testimony is misleading would raise a question mark over large swathes of individual knowledge. An initially more promising proposal is that group testimony is nothing over and above the testimony of one or more group members. After all, just as with (SUMMATIVISM$_{Know}$), such purported reduction is *conservative* rather than *eliminative*. Thus, we can define a corresponding view about group testimony:

(SUMMATIVISM$_{Testifier}$) Necessarily, a group g testifies that p if and only if at least one individual i is both a member of g and testifies that p ($Tpg \leftrightarrow \exists i\, (i \in g \,\&\, Tpi)$).

For (SUMMATIVISM$_{Testifier}$) to be a serious contender, i's testimonies must be restricted to those (a) i is authorized by g to offer and (b) i actually offers qua member of g. Obviously, if i lacks a license to testify on behalf of g, i's testimony cannot constitute group g testimony, nor can it do so if i testifies qua private individual or qua member of distinct group g^*.[11]

Reflect that the falsity of (SUMMATIVISM$_{Know}$) does not entail the falsity of (SUMMATIVISM$_{Testifier}$) even on the assumption of (GROUP

TESTIFIER). It may be that for a group to testify propositions of which only it has knowledge is for at least one of its individual members to testify those propositions. After all, intuitions elicited by cases where an individual *i* testifies a proposition of which *i* lacks knowledge question the knowledge norm of assertion. Take Lackey's (2008, 110–13) religious science teacher whose acceptance of the Genesis creation myth rationally prevents her from knowing the theory of evolution, yet when in the classroom she reliably and conscientiously teaches her pupils about the origin of the species. In fact, the same can happen at the group level. Imagine that some members of the National Science Teachers Association (NSTA) form a subgroup for those with creationist leanings to discuss among themselves how best to reconcile their commitment to science education with their religious worldview. The subgroup may communicate new studies in evolutionary biology to keep their members abreast of recent developments, yet both the group and its members would be rationally prevented from knowing their contents.

Be that as it may. Our earlier counterexample to (SUMMATIVISM$_{Know}$) of a research group knowing q despite none of its members knowing q arguably also constitutes a counterexample to (SUMMATIVISM$_{Testifier}$). When the assistant publishes the paper containing the demonstration that q, he does so by merely following predrafted instructions. The testifier is the group itself. The point here is not so much that the assistant lacks knowledge of q, but that he even lacks the required expertise to grasp such a complex proposition. Because nobody can properly assert a proposition they do not understand, the assistant cannot be regarded as testifying that q. Nor can either of Drs. X and Y be said to testify q. Nothing about the way the case is described suggests their linguistic behavior amounts to an assertion that q. Dr. X asserts p but not $p \rightarrow q$, whereas Dr. Y asserts $p \rightarrow q$ but not p, and so neither asserts q on the basis of modus ponens. The upshot is therefore that (SUMMATIVISM$_{Testifier}$) is false when read from left to right, in that our research team testifies a proposition that none of its members testify.[12]

2. The Role of Trust in Testimony

Section 1 argued that group knowing and testifying are irreducible. That nonsummativism is false of such epistemic properties is a familiar claim. What remains largely unexplored in the literature is whether groups can also serve as *testifiees of knowledge* and, if so, whether nonsummativism about such property is plausible.[13] Section 3 provides affirmative answers to both questions, but first we must explore the critical role of trust in testimony. One may suspect that any agent who is capable of testifying is also *eo ipso* capable of being testified to, but these roles are markedly different. In particular, testimonial exchanges typically involve the testifiee *trusting* the testifier, where such trust is a *rational* relation with normative and affective implications. A pressing worry is then that relations of trust seem essentially *interpersonal*, in that they appear to obtain only between individuals qua sources of rationality and emotion.[14] Because groups are not individuals, groups would seem incapable of entering into the receiving end of testimonial relations unless summativism about group trust is true. Section 2 outlines an *Assurance view* of the epistemology of testimonial trust. Although the argument of Section 3 does not hang on any particular view about trust, Assurance serves to illustrate the aforesaid worry, while also allowing for the possibility of irreducible group trust, or so we shall argue.

Let's develop the trust relation, that is, the tertiary relation between a truster, a trustee and some action φ, in more detail.[15] First off, trust involves the truster *relying* on the trustee to φ so as to enable the truster to pursue some goal, in the sense that the trustee φ-ing is *necessary* for the truster to achieve that goal. In particular, testimonial trust involves the testifiee relying on the testifier to speak truly in order to facilitate the testifiee pursuing some epistemic good. Such epistemic reliance is typically manifested by the testifiee basing beliefs on a testifier's say-so. So, trust is about the act of relying on someone (or something) to act, but trust also involves the attitude of *expectation* towards this reliance, that is, trust implies the expectation that the trustee will (try to) do what the truster is relying on the trustee to do. In the case of testimony, the testifiee expects the testifier to (attempt to) speak the truth.[16] Two different sets of reasons for the expectation mark two distinct types of trust.[17]

When a truster *predictively trusts* a trustee, the truster not only relies on the trustee to φ (call that "other-reliance"), the truster is also confident that the trustee is likely to φ. If one is compelled to rely on someone φ-ing but regards φ-ing as an improbable occurrence, one does not predictively trust that person. Predictive trust is more demanding than mere reliance. The justification for the truster to adopt such an attitude of expectation comprises *trust-independent evidential reasons*, which are inferred from background empirical knowledge about the trustee. Such reasons, if undefeated, rationalize the truster's expectation and make its content more likely to be true. One can expect the alarm clock to ring at 6:00 a.m. because one knows it has done so reliably in the past, or one can expect Sophie to help organize the Christmas fair because one knows how much she enjoys the festive season and how eager she always is to be involved. Possessing such knowledge renders one's expectation reasonable and makes its content more probable. Predictive trust thus involves relying on a trustee, which may or may not be a person, but lacks a distinctive *normative* dimension, in that certain reactive attitudes are misplaced. One may rightly be *annoyed* that the alarm clock did not go off, or *disappointed* that Sophie did not offer her assistance, but one should not feel *betrayed* by either failure.[18] Because no normative expectations are required, predictive trust is not essentially an interpersonal relation: a person may predictively trust a nonperson. Moreover, to be *predictively trustworthy* with respect to φ is for the trustee to reliably φ, where the *motivating reason* for (or cause of) φ-ing has nothing to do with other-reliance. Neither the alarm clock nor Sophie does what one expects them to do because of one's reliance on them.

Consider *predictive testimonial trust* as a special instance. Suppose one walks to the office without an umbrella on the basis of earlier *overhearing* a conversation in which a friend, who is known to be reliable, claimed that the weather would be fine. One could, on the basis of the friend's word, come to learn about the weather even though one was not being testified to. If instead one's friend ought to have known it was going to rain heavily, one is entitled to feel frustrated, but not let down, because one's expectation is merely inferred from, as it happens, misleading eavesdropping evidence. The motivating reason for the friend's assertion has nothing to do with one's reliance on this piece of say-so.

When a truster *affectively trusts* a trustee to φ, the truster also relies on the trustee to φ. Where affective trust differs from predictive trust is that the former requires not only that the truster expects that (a) the trustee recognizes that the truster relies on the trustee to φ but also that (b) the reason for which the trustee φ-s (or at least attempts to φ) is such other-reliance. Put differently, affective trust involves an expectation that the trustee is favorably moved by recognizing that the truster is counting on the trustee to φ.[19] Crucially, the justification for these expectations pertains to the relation of trust itself. More precisely, this justification consists in *trust-dependent nonevidential reasons*, which the truster acquires when the trustee φ-s in response to the truster's implicit need or explicit request for the trustee to φ. The trustee φ-ing is not a piece of evidence, but rather *assurance* that acting on φ is a safe policy. In that sense, trusting and promising are analogous. But for the trustee to φ is also to *affirm* the earlier contents (a) and (b) of the truster's expectations. To be *affectively trustworthy*, the trustee must reliably φ, but only for the *motivating reason* of other-reliance. A trustee who φ-s for some other reason, for example, out of self-interest, conformity to social norms or fear of repercussions, may be relied upon, perhaps reliably so, but is undeserving of affective trust.[20] Unless the truster suspects the trustee is insincere or incompetent, seeing that the trustee φ-s thus implies having reason that the trustee recognizes the dependency in (a) and that (b) the trustee φ-s for the reason of other-reliance. Such reasons rationalize the truster's expectations, as well as indicate the truth of their contents. If, despite such reasons, the truster fails to φ while having both the ability and opportunity to φ, or φ-s for reasons other than other-dependency, then the truster is entitled to feel *betrayed* by the trustee, who in turn is subject to blame. Such a reactive feeling of *resentment* is appropriate, as the trustee lent their assurance that φ-ing was motivated out of concern for the truster's reliance, such that following through on φ would not lead the truster astray. Affective trust involves the truster holding the trustee *responsible* for acting for the right reason, and so comes with an opportunity for the trustee to harm, and hence with a risk for the truster of betrayal.[21] Thus understood, affective trust seems to be essentially *interpersonal*. A person cannot affectively trust a nonperson (e.g. a technological device) because a nonperson cannot act for reasons of other-dependency, nor a fortiori does a nonperson deserve blame for failing to fulfill its obligations vis-à-vis the trustee. Likewise, a nonperson cannot affectively trust a person, because a nonperson cannot normatively expect a person to act for reasons of other-dependency, nor a fortiori can a nonperson feel betrayed by a person failing to do what is expected of them. In short, the trust relation demands that any relata be governed by epistemic norms, which require being a source of rationality and emotion as characteristic of persons.

Consider *affective testimonial trust* as a special case, where the testifiee relies on the testifier to speak truly, but also expects that (a) the testifier recognizes that the testifiee so relies and (b) the testifier speaks truly (or at least attempts to speak truly) for the reason of such other-reliance. The testifier is in turn to be regarded as worthy of affective trust just in case the testifier reliably speaks truly for the *motivating reason* of other-reliance. The justification for the testifiee's expectations originates in the testimonial relation itself, in that offering testimony is to *assure* the testifiee of its truth and to affirm that the reason for which the testifier speaks truly is other-reliance. To testify is to perform the illocutionary speech act of *telling*, to *give* someone one's word that they can *take* one's word for it out of consideration for their epistemic need for the truth. In the normal run of things, telling provides the testifiee with reason for the expectations in (a) and (b), making their acceptance reasonable and indicative of truth. Paradigmatically, the testifiee will have such reason if, upon asking a question, the testifier provides a sincere and competent answer. A lost tourist asking a local resident for directions is a case in point. Because telling is the offer of a guarantee of truth, telling involves acceptance of the *responsibility* to honor the trust invested in the testifier such that if the testifier speaks falsely through epistemic fault on their part, blame is in order for having betrayed the testifiee's trust.[22] Affective testimonial trust involves holding the testifier to expectations and implies vulnerability to betrayal and associated feelings of resentment when these are unfulfilled.[23] Importantly, such trust seems to be essentially a relation only between people, in that no nonperson can tell for reasons of other-dependence, nor can any nonperson form normative expectations about someone's telling, or indeed display reactive attitudes upon being let down by a testifier.

Both predictive and affective trust are also *voluntary* in a way mere reliance need not be. If one is literally forced or compelled by circumstance to depend on someone else, one is not in a relationship of trust, even if one is confident that the person will φ because of one's counting on them to φ. Trust involves two separate acts of volition to do with whom or what to trust and whether or how to act on the truster φ-ing.[24] The first decision is typically constrained by knowledge of the person's trustworthiness. An employee might choose to trust a colleague at work for career advice, as that person is known to be knowledgeable about such matters.[25] But lack of antecedent knowledge of untrustworthiness may suffice for (affective) trust at will, as when a traveler asks a stranger in the airport to look after their luggage while going to the toilet; indeed, prior knowledge of (fairly limited) untrustworthiness need not prevent one from placing (affective) trust in them, as in the case of a reformer who employs someone recently discharged from prison for petty theft.[26] After all, the stranger does not appear utterly untrustworthy to the traveler, and the reformer may hold the standing belief that everyone deserves a second chance. The second decision is based on the trustee φ-ing together with what else is known about the subject matter in question. Obviously, assuming doxastic involuntarism of some stripe, which beliefs the truster forms on the basis of the trustee's φ-ing, is much less up to the truster than what further action to take in response thereto.

Our last question concerns the epistemology of trust. Restricting attention to testimonial trust, the question is what justifies a *belief* when formed on the basis of a trustee's testimony. The answer is straightforward in the case of predictive trust. Suppose again one overhears a conversation in which someone known to be reliable asserts the content p. Assuming one has no independent evidence indicating its falsity, such testimony amounts to nondefeated evidence of truth. Consequently, a belief in *p* formed on that basis is *epistemically justified*, as it is likely to be true. The answer is less obvious in the case of affective trust. In the absence of independent evidence to question an assurance of *p*'s truth, the truster has a nondefeated reason to believe *p*, and so a belief formed on that basis is *rational*. For it is rational to believe content offered by someone whom one affectively trusts to tell the truth when one has no countervailing evidence. To wit, assurance provides one with reasonable belief, that is, belief for which one can offer reasons to do with someone speaking truly because of their recognition that one depends on them to do that. In short, assurance provides the trustee with *epistemic rationality*. But affective trust cannot bootstrap *justification* for belief. From the fact that a person, whom one affectively trusts, offers testimony that *p*, nothing follows about whether belief in *p* is likely to be true. To see that reasons furnished by assurance need not be conducive to truth, suppose that unbeknownst to a testifier, an assertion that *p* by that testifier is produced by an unreliable cognitive process. A belief formed by the testifiee on the basis of the testifier's say-so is thus unjustified. However, the testifiee may still affectively trust such an unreliable testifier: she may rely on the testifier to speak truly, and she may reasonably expect not only that the testifier recognizes that she so relies but also that the testifier speaks truly for that reason. After all, such a testifier may take herself to be speaking out of trust. For example, our petty thief may appear to be motivated to speak truly out of regard for the reformer's epistemic needs, who, remember, went out on a limb to trust the thief. But suppose the thief incorrectly takes himself to be reliable when, in fact, his sincere and competent assertions are unwittingly a result of doubtful processes from his criminal past. In that case, our reformer's testimonial beliefs will unjustified, due to the poor credentials of the etiology of these assertions. Still, such beliefs would be rational (and not gullible), as they arise out of affective trust.[27]

Let's summarize the foregoing. We argued that trust plays an indispensable role in testimony. Predictive testimonial trust involves independent evidence of trustworthiness, which constitutes both rational and probabilistic reason for belief, whereas affective testimonial trust has it that telling is an assurance which provides nonevidential, rational reasons for belief. Each type of trust is characterized by distinct expectations about motivating reasons, as well as associated reactive attitudes, should those expectations be frustrated. Crucially, one might suspect that whereas a person can predictively trust a nonperson, only people can affectively trust each other. After first detailing two necessary conditions on group agency, the next section argues that groups are capable of entering into irreducible relations of such trust.

3. Trusting Groups

Not any old collection of individuals forms a proper group, even if they share certain unifying features. When knowledge is attributed to, say, the British electorate, we ascribe *aggregate, mutual* or perhaps even *common* knowledge to all or most entries on the UK electoral registers. The falsity of (SUMMATIVISM$_{Know}$) is compatible with the existence of such knowledge: the fact that group knowledge neither entails nor is entailed by knowledge had by at least one individual member is consistent with collections of individuals being such that most or all of their members share knowledge, or indeed such that each member knows that all the other members share some knowledge. Because a collection of individuals who merely have certain features in common constitutes no group, there is no question of attributing group knowledge. Exactly what converts such a collection into a group is a vexed question. We shall restrict attention to two sets of constraints to do with *organizational structure* and *joint intentions*. Bearing in mind the different ways groups operate, the details are bound to vary from group to group, but some general characteristics are worth highlighting.

Consider first what Schmitt (1994, 273) calls a "chartered group." When a group has a *charter*, as constituted by the intentions of its founding members, its actions aim to fulfill its *office* as specified by that charter. The office of a group can roughly be understood as its task, goal or purpose, as determined by its charter (i.e. the rules, norms or standards by which the group is governed) such that a chartered group would not exist without its office. Particular chartered groups are characterized in terms of the specific intentions that are common to their members, as well as the actions that aim to fulfill their office as fixed by their charter. A group's charter is sometimes formally enshrined in a system of laws, other times evidenced by the practice of the group and its members. Either way, a collection of individuals is a group agent only if its (founding) members jointly set up common goals and agree on how to proceed in order to meet them. An adequate organizational structure within the group is thus needed to facilitate the means that are carried out for the purpose of achieving its end.

Second, certain joint intentions (or we-intentions) are called for, which are best understood as individual intentions joined together when shared by members of the collective.[28] A collection of individuals is a group agent only if (a) these individuals intend that the collection acts and forms attitudes together, that is, each of these individuals must intend that they together enact the joint performance and come to a group attitude.[29] Moreover, (b) each must intend to do their part and (c) intend to do so because of their belief that others intend to do their bit. Importantly, these joint intentions need not involve individual intentions to form *particular* output attitudes of the group. That is to say, although each individual member must intend that the group form attitudes as a result of joint action, no single member need intend to form, let alone accept, any specific attitudes that the group forms.[30]

Let's assume that these two sets of constraints are individually necessary and jointly sufficient for a collection of individuals to unite in forming a rational agent in its own right. They are the glue that joins individuals together as an agent with a cohesive mind of its own. The British electorate meets none of them, but our examples from Section 1 of a scientific research group and a jury in a criminal court meet both. When transposed into an epistemic setting, we can say that a collection of individuals constitutes a sui generis epistemic agent just in case (a) its actions aim to fulfill its epistemic office as specified by its epistemic charter and (b) its individual members form the required joint intentions in so far as they bear epistemically on the group.

Equipped with this rudimentary conception of group agency, let's revisit the question of whether groups can enter into relations of testimonial trust. The first observation to make is that, just as in the case of group knowledge and group testimony, we speak uncontroversially as if groups can serve as both affective trustees and trusters in the context of testimony and beyond. First, individuals trust groups (e.g. students trust their universities) and so experience *institutional betrayal* when the university management fails to prevent sexual assault on campuses.[31] Second, groups trust individuals (e.g. banks trust their employees) and so experience *individual betrayal* when a rogue trader abuses that trust for personal gain. Third, groups trust other groups (e.g. health services trust public service broadcasters to report impartially) and so experience *group betrayal* when they parrot government spin as uncontested fact. Obviously, while such parlance counts in favor of taking its content literally, at least when widespread and systematic, an explanation is needed of how groups can satisfy the specific conditions on testimonial trust that were outlined in Section 2. We deal with predictive and affective trust in turn and focus on establishing the strongest claim that relations of trust can obtain between groups and not merely between individuals and groups.

For a group g to predictively trust another group g^* in the context of testimony is (a) for g to rely on g^* speaking the truth, and (b) for g to expect g^* to reliably speak truly for reasons that have nothing to do with other-reliance. That groups can satisfy (a) and (b) should be fairly straightforward. Universities rely on the Office for National Statistics (ONS) to deliver accurate economic data that enable strategic planning of student intake, future hires, and so on. Investment firms rely on the Dow to correctly report the state of the markets, without which they would not know when to sell or buy stocks. The Royal Navy relies on the Met office to provide up-to-date shipping forecasts when deciding how to deploy its fleet. Having accurate data, correct reports and updated forecasts is necessary for these groups to fulfill their respective offices as specified by their charters. Moreover, groups are also able to have reasonable and justified expectations about their reliance on other groups. Universities are optimistic that the ONS report accurate figures, because they are the largest independent producer of official statistics with a strong track record; investment firms are confident that these stock market indices are reliable, as they are widely known to be of good repute; and the Royal Navy is pretty certain that the Met office continually updates its forecasts, as it has done so in the past. Provided none of this supporting evidence is defeated, these testifying groups should be regarded as worthy of predictive trust—indeed, the contents of their testimonies are likely to be true, given such evidence. If, nevertheless, the testified groups are misinformed through inadvertence, neglect or deceit, they are entitled to express disappointment. But there is no betrayal of trust, as the testified groups do not expect the testifying groups to act out of concern for their *particular* epistemic needs. And rightly so: as ONS, Met or Dow provide generic information on a massive scale, which is utilized by a huge number of diverse groups worldwide, they typically do not recognize any *specific* other-reliance, and even if they did, such reliance would rarely be a motivating reason. So, these three cases illustrate predictive, but not affective, group testimonial trust.

The next question is whether group predictive trust is reducible to individual predictive trust, that is, whether summativism about group predictive trust holds. Consider:

(SUMMATIVISM$_{\text{P-Trust}}$) Necessarily, group g predictively trusts group g^* to φ (tell the truth) if and only if there are individuals i and i^* such that i is a member of g and i^* is a member of g^* and i predictively trusts i^* to φ (tell the truth) $(T_p gg^* \leftrightarrow \exists i \exists i^* (i \in g \ \& \ i^* \in g^* \ \& \ T_p ii^*).$

Reflection on our three cases shows that they constitute counterexamples to (SUMMATIVISM$_{\text{P-Trust}}$) when read from left to right. Although they illustrate the possibility of g and g^* instantiating the relation of predictive trust with respect to testimony, there is no guarantee that this relation is also instantiated by two individual members of g and g^*. Take the first example of a university relying on the ONS to make available accurate economic data. There is no single university employee who is relying on a single ONS statistician in this regard. The admissions office is relying on student loans data, the human resources (HR) department is relying on employability data, the estates are relying on interest rates and inflation data and so on. Not only do different staff work in those three parts of the university, making all those data available is a collaborative exercise involving multiple staff at the ONS collecting, analyzing and disseminating statistics.[32] The same is true *mutatis mutandis* of the other two cases involving group predictive trust.

Let's turn to group affective trust, which on the face of it is more problematic, in that such trust, unlike the predictive variant, seems to be essentially an interpersonal affair. For a group g to affectively trust group g^* in the context of testimony is (a) for g to rely on g^* to speak the truth and (b) for g to expect g^* to recognize the reliance in (a) and to be motivated to speak truly for reasons of such other-reliance. For g^* to be affectively trustworthy is in turn to speak truly and to do so reliably only for such a reason. The justification for g's expectations vis-à-vis g^* stems from the assurance of truth and affirmation of the motivating reason which g^*'s telling offers.[33]

Our argument for (irreducible) group affective trust also proceeds from cases. Let's tweak our examples from Section 1. Suppose the aim of research team g comprising Drs. X and Y is to establish a famous conjecture c. The physicist Dr. X shows that a, and the mathematician Dr. Y demonstrates the proof $(a \ \& \ b) \rightarrow c$. Because neither Dr. X nor Dr. Y has sufficient expertise in the area of b-type propositions, g approaches research team g^* comprising Drs. Z and W to ask whether they are able to show the lemma b. As g^* knows that confirming b is necessary for g to fulfill its office as specified by its charter, g^* agrees to assist their long-term collaborators in this matter. When physicist Dr. Z eventually shows d and the mathematician Dr. W demonstrates the proof $d \rightarrow b$, g^*'s assistant passes on to g's assistant the information that b holds, after which the latter publishes the proof of c in a paper that acknowledges the contribution of g^*. The two assistants are not sufficiently competent to be able to testify b and c, nor is there any robust sense in which they can serve as spokespersons. Instead, g^* is to count as testifier of b (and g as testifier of c). Moreover, Drs. Z and W intend to testify b *if* this lemma turns out true and to do so out of consideration for the reliance of g on g^* to show b. That means g^*'s testifying constitutes lending assurance of b's truth and affirmation that g^* acted for reasons of other-reliance. Not only are the expectations g forms as to g^*'s testimony and motivating reasons thus reasonable, g^* is also worthy of g's trust, provided those expectations are correct and that g^* correctly established b as a result of relevant reliable processes. What is more, the belief g forms on the basis of g^*'s testimony is reasonable and justified, given that g possesses no countervailing evidence and that those processes are reliable. Our example of the two research teams thus demonstrates that groups can instantiate the relation of testimonial affective trust.[34] Before we revisit our second example from Section 1, let's ponder the question of whether group affective trust is reducible to individual effective trust. Consider:

(SUMMATIVISM$_{\text{A-Trust}}$) Necessarily, group g affectively trusts group g^* to φ (tell the truth) if and only if there are individuals i and i^* such that i is a member of g and i^* is a member of g^* and i affectively trusts i^* to φ (tell the truth) $(T_A gg^* \leftrightarrow \exists i \exists i^* \ (i \in g \ \& \ i^* \in g^* \ \& \ T_A ii^*))$.

Our amended example of trust between scientific groups shows that (SUMMATIVISM$_{\text{A-Trust}}$) is false when read from left to right. Group g affectively trusts group g^*, but no affective trust with respect to b is obtained between individual members of these respective groups. The reason is that no single member of g relies on a single member of g^* to tell the truth about b. First, b is a lemma, which neither Dr. Z nor Dr. W can establish on their own; indeed, b is not even a statement to which they (or their assistant) are individually positioned to testify, because neither is aware that their group g^* has shown b. So, no individual member of g^* can replace g^* as an affective trustee. Second, neither Dr. X nor Dr. Y relies on b for their subtasks of showing a and $(a \ \& \ b) \rightarrow c$, respectively, and their assistant lacks scientific knowledge to even count as a testifiee of b. So, no individual member of g can replace g as an affective truster.

A consequence of the falsity of (SUMMATIVISM$_{\text{A-Trust}}$) is that group g^* can betray group g's trust without any individual member of g^* betraying the trust of any individual member of g. However, there is nothing mysterious about irreducible group betrayal. Suppose in our example that due to the careless organization of g^* Dr. Z is tasked with proving $d \rightarrow$

b while Dr. W is assigned the task of showing *d*. As Drs. Z and W lack sufficient acumen in mathematics and physics, respectively, both fail, and so *g** reports to *g* that *b* cannot be shown. Consequently, *g* is unable to establish the conjecture *c*. When *g**'s error is discovered, *g* is entitled to feel betrayed, and not merely disappointed, by *g**'s conduct, because *g** assured *g* to judge correctly on *b*. As *g** is accountable to *g* for speaking truly, *g** is worthy of blame for being epistemically irresponsible in leading *g* astray. But because Drs. Z and W are not to be held individually responsible for the wrongly assigned subtasks, neither should be considered as individually betraying a trust. Moreover, because Drs. X and Y's assigned su-tasks are not affected by *g**'s error, neither should be regarded as undergoing an individual betrayal of trust. Only *g*'s goal of establishing *c* is thwarted.

Consider now an amended version of our other example from Section 1. Take a jury in a criminal court of law that convicts a defendant chiefly on the basis of a police report, including forensic evidence, an interrogation transcript and a description of the crime scene. Different units within the local police force are responsible for these distinct parts of the report. The jury is thus relying on the local police drafting a comprehensive and correct report, but the jury can also reasonably expect that the reason for which this report was shown to the court is that the police recognizes that the jury depends on its availability as evidence for conviction. What motivates the police is precisely the dependency of the jury on the police: for in the absence of the police's findings, the jury could not satisfactorily fulfill its office as specified by its charter. Upon presenting the report to the court, the police assure the jury in writing of its veracity and completeness, which suffices for the jury's expectation that the police be motivated by such other-reliance to be rationally and probabilistically justified; indeed, provided the expectation is correct, the police are also thereby worthy of the jury's trust. Moreover, the beliefs the jury forms on the basis of the report are reasonable and justified on the assumptions that the jury has no evidence to the contrary and that the DNA analyses, fingerprinting technique, and so on are reliable. In sum, the jury and the police are two groups instantiating the relation of testimonial affective trust.

Reflect again how such group trust is irreducible to individual affective trust, in that there need not be any corresponding trust between a particular juror and a particular police officer. First, given that the report is a complex document drawing on multiple units within a police force, there is no single individual whom the jury trusts for the report in its entirety. Nor does the jury trust multiple individuals for different parts of the report, as the jury may lack knowledge of which police officers are responsible for which parts. Moreover, given that the court is simply presented with the document itself, there is no identifiable spokesperson to whom the jury could direct their trust. Second, no individual juror need trust the police to provide a credible report. Suppose instead the jurors individually have hearsay evidence from a known reliable source that much of the information in the report is fabricated, so as to frame the defendant for a crime someone else committed. Even so, because such evidence is deemed inadmissible in a criminal court, the jury (as a group) may still trust the police with respect to the report. Our refined example of the jury thus illustrates once again that (SUMMATIVISM$_{A\text{-Trust}}$) is false. It follows that the jury may undergo a betrayal of trust by the police without any particular jurors sharing such an affective attitude, but that should by now come as no surprise. Suppose further that the reason the police produced their report is that they were secretly paid a large sum of money to frame an innocent person. In that case, the jury (as a group) will rightly feel betrayed by police assurance to the contrary. Individual jurors may, of course, feel the same way, but the jury's affective attitude is not conditional on any member sharing that attitude. Certainly, if no individual juror trusted the police in the first place, any such individual attitude would be misplaced. The jury case, as well as the science case, thus shows that irreducible group betrayal is a possibility nonsummativists about affective trust can safely embrace.

4. Concluding (Metaphysical) Remarks

The upshot of Section 3 is that neither predictive nor affective trust is essentially an interpersonal relation. Groups are not persons, yet groups can instantiate relations of predictive and affective trust. Still, there are important differences in the nature of the *relata* of these two trust relations. Not with respect to which entities count as trusters: only individuals and groups can, predictively or affectively, trust, in that only individuals and groups have expectations about the reasons for which others act. But although technological devices (or indeed natural objects) can serve as predictive trustees, only individuals and groups can serve as affective trustees. It makes no sense for an alarm clock to recognize that others are relying on it to ring at a certain time, let alone for the reason for its ringing to be that they so rely. Human artifacts do not act for reasons of trust, but groups do so irreducibly. What makes groups different from artifacts is that groups are ultimately composed of individuals, and although affective trust between groups is irreducible to relations of trust between their respective members, such *intergroup* trust plausibly *supervenes* on joint actions and the joint intentions of their members. Here is a first stab at a supervenience claim:

> (SUPERVENIENCE$_{A\text{-Trust}}$) Necessarily, if group g affectively trusts group g^* to φ, then there are members of g who (a) jointly rely on g^* to have members whose cognitive abilities in suitable circumstances are jointly sufficient for g^* to φ and (b) jointly expect g^* to

have members who jointly intend to φ for the reason of the reliance in (a), such that any other g' whose members (b) jointly rely on g^* to have members whose cognitive abilities in suitable circumstances are jointly sufficient for g^* to φ and (c) jointly expect g^* to have members who jointly intend to φ for the reason of the reliance in (a) is a group that affectively trusts g^*.

Note that this is a *weak* supervenience claim: there is no possible world within which individuals are indiscernible with respect to their joint actions and joint intentions, but rather where the groups these individuals compose are discernible with respect to relations of affective trust. The reason is that any particular relation of intergroup affective trust is only obtained against a broader background of *extragroup* relations of such trust. As Baier (1986, 258) argued, any two-party trust relationship presupposes a "network" or "climate" of trust as a society-wide phenomenon, such that a social environment permeated by mistrust undermines any such relationship.

What is more, because group members are individuals, (SUPERVENIENCE$_{A\text{-}Trust}$) has it that relations of affective trust are obtained between groups only if *individual* members have properties of joint intentional states and joint action. As mentioned, nothing that is not an individual or a group of individuals can have expectations about the reasons for which others intend to act, or indeed (intend to) act for reasons of other-dependence. For instance, we have no room for the thought that a technological device should be able to do either. But that is unproblematic in the case of individuals, and also in the case of groups provided that (SUPERVENIENCE$_{A\text{-}Trust}$) holds. Obviously, because this principle only pertains to the covariance (within possible worlds) of relations of affective trust with properties of joint intentions and joint action, more would need to be said about how such trust can be obtained between groups by way of being *grounded* in such properties of their individual members. Such an account is for another occasion.

Reflect finally that (SUPERVENIENCE$_{A\text{-}Trust}$) holds in our examples of group affective trust involving a scientific team and a jury, even though, as argued in Section 3, (SUMMATIVISM$_{A\text{-}Trust}$) fails in those two cases.[35] Consider again the former example of team g affectively trusting team g^* to tell whether b holds. Such trust is obtained in virtue of the joint reliance and joint expectations of individual group members: the members of g (a) together rely on g^* having members who, in appropriate conditions, will determine the truth-value of b, and (b) together expect the members of g^* to do so out of regard for the other-reliance in (a). But just as the affective trust between g and g^* is irreducible to relations of affective trust between individual members of these respective groups, such intergroup trust is irreducible to particular joint expectations and joint reliance of these members. After all, group g could have been constituted (at least partially) by individuals other than its actual members, in which case those other individuals would have jointly relied on g^* and would have had joint expectations vis-à-vis g^*, so as for g to affectively trust g^*.[36] There is thus no question of reducing the affective trust between g and g^* to any *actual* joint reliance and joint expectations. Moreover, if we suppose that Drs. Z and W were equally competent in both physics and mathematics, there would be more than one way in which those members of g^* could arrange the cognitive labor so as to establish b, and any one of these ways would suffice as far as g is concerned; indeed, different possible members of g^* could well establish b as long as they would make the right contribution towards that goal, given the assignment of labor within g^*. That means there is no prospect of reducing the way g relies on g^* to any particular joint reliance among their respective members.[37]

Notes

1. See Goldman (1986), Feldman and Conee (2004), and Sosa (2007, 2009), respectively.
2. Early highlights include Tollefsen (2002), Gilbert (2004), and Goldman (2004).
3. Gilbert (2013), Knorr Cetina (2009), Tollefsen (2006), Tuomela (1995) Wray (2007) and the author (forthcoming) all argue that group knowledge is irreducible to individual knowledge. Tollefsen (2007, 2009), Lackey (2014, 2018) and Fricker (2012) all argue that group testimony (or group assertion) is irreducible to individual testimony (or individual assertion).
4. See for example Goldman (2004, 12), Schmitt (1994, 257–58) and Lackey (2012, 245).
5. We shall use "group" as a catch-all label for all such collectives.
6. Quinton (1975: 17) required that a group has some propositional attitude only if "all or most" of its members have that attitude. In his view, ascriptions of attitudes to a group are an indirect way of ascribing them to its members. Note that his more demanding formulation avoids the problem that a group is ascribed inconsistent attitudes if (i) two (or more) of its members hold inconsistent attitudes and (ii) the group holds an attitude if at least one of its members does. Our discussion has no bearing on this qualification.
7. See also Schmitt (1994, 274), and Lackey (2014, 66–70) for a survey of cases.
8. This example helps fix ideas, but in reality, research groups typically involve distributed cognition on a huge scale. The detectors at the Large Hadron Collider at CERN have a sprawling collaboration involving physicists, engineers and other researchers from dozens of institutions and countries. Research based on these particle accelerators recently resulted in the publication of a joint article in *Physical Review Letters* with a record 5,154 authors.
9. There are at least three accounts of group testimony (or assertion) in the literature: Tollefsen's (2009) assurance account, Fricker's (2012) joint commitment to trustworthiness account and Lackey's (2018) spokesperson account. We shall not here adjudicate between these accounts, except to note that either of the first two will serve our purposes.
10. See for example Quinton (1975, 17).
11. (SUMMATIVISMTestifier) is not the only reductive model on the table. For example, Lackey (2014, 2018) suggests that group testimony (or assertion)

is nonsummatively reducible to the testimony (or assertion) of the group's spokesperson, who need not be a group member. It follows that any epistemic credentials of group testimony are reducible to epistemic credentials of the spokesperson's testimony. But Lackey also holds the view that group knowledge requires member knowledge, and so because a group may testify a proposition of which none of its members are even aware, a group can testify a proposition of which it lacks knowledge.

12. See also Tollefsen (2007) for a real-life example of distributed cognition.
13. Fricker's (2012) is an exception, in which she applies Craig's (1990, 36) distinction between a source of information and a good informant at the collective level, but Lackey (2012, 2018) argues that the purpose of group knowledge attributions is not to identify or flag reliable informants. Our argument going forward makes no reference to Craig's work.
14. See, for example, Hawley (forthcoming), who claims that "every proper attitude of trust or distrust is directed interpersonally. Or so it seems."
15. The following owes much to the Assurance views of Faulkner (2007, 2014) and Moran (2005a, 2005b), who in turn build on Jones (1996), Baier (1986), Holton (1994), Coady (1992) and Ross (1986). Other recent defenses of this view include Fricker (2012) and Hinchman (2005). Hawley (2014) objects to some of these views, in that they fail to account for the distinction between distrust and mere nonreliance. A thorough reply to Hawley would take us too far afield. Our goal is to show that an influential account of trust, such as Assurance, applies to groups, and to that end the distinction between (affective) trust and mere reliance (or predictive trust) suffices.
16. Or speak knowledgeably if knowledge is the norm of assertion. As noted earlier, such a norm would rule out the possibility of testimony serving as a knowledge-generating source and not merely as a knowledge-transmitting source.
17. We borrow Faulkner's (*op. cit.*) terminology of predictive and affective trust, but see also Hollis (1998, 10). The following is not exhaustive of all types of trust. For instance, we shall not discuss the trust one can place in someone to do something for someone else for reasons that concern them rather than oneself. See Fricker (2012, 257) and Hawley (2014, 11) for examples.
18. I owe the distinction between disappointment and betrayal to Baier (1986, 235), but see also Holton (1994).
19. See also Jones (1996) and Walker (2006).
20. Pace Hardin (2002, 53) and Pettit (1995), who defend what Jones (1999, 68) dubbed "self-assessment views." Our claim is that the sole motive for which affectively trustworthy people act is regard for the truster's reliance on them. No additional care or goodwill on the part of the trustee is needed, nor need the truster be optimistic that such sentiments are in play. After all, affective trust can be obtained between people who otherwise display no friendly feelings or personal liking for each other. Holton (1994, 2) offers several examples.
21. As Hinchman (2005, 565, 568) and Fricker (2007, 5) have noted, (affective) trust also comes with an opportunity for the truster to "slight," "wrong" or "abuse" the trustee when the former fails to react appropriately to the latter's φ-ing. To simplify things, we shall not further dwell on the harm or injustice done to the trustee when not treated properly by the truster. For extensive discussion see Goldberg (manuscript).
22. Less ambitiously, assertions are widely regarded as conferring responsibility on the assertor for the truth of their contents; see for example Williamson (2000, 268–69).
23. One could safeguard against the testifier failing one by trying to independently ensure that the testifier speaks truly and acts for reasons of

other-dependency, but the more evidence one was able to amass to that effect, the less one would affectively trust the testifier. At some point the relationship would transform into one of predictive trust.

24. According to Hawley's commitment account (2014), to trust someone to do something is to believe that she has a commitment to doing it and to rely upon her to meet that commitment. Because belief typically involves no such act of volition, her account offers no straightforward explanation of the way in which trust is voluntary.

25. Hardin (2002, 112) seems to assume that trust is rational only if the trustor has estimated the likelihood on the basis of prior evidence that the trustee will be trustworthy in the relevant circumstances and then updates the estimate as new evidence emerges.

26. The last example is from Holton (1994, 63).

27. Lackey (2008, 222) and Schmitt (2010, 227) criticize Assurance views for failing to explain how an invitation to trust can produce (or bootstrap) an epistemic reason for belief.

28. The following owes much to Pettit and Schweikard (2006), following Bratman (1999), Gilbert (2001, 2013) and Tuomela (1995, 2005).

29. We only consider noncoerced and nondeceived groups. Everything is above board.

30. The joint intentions that we require for group agency differ from Gilbert's (1989, 306) so-called *joint acceptance account*, according to which a group believes p just in case its members jointly accept p.

31. Baier (2013, 175–76) is explicit that her account of interpersonal trust, in terms of vulnerability, competence and goodwill, cannot easily encompass trust in organizations.

32. One may think that shifting the scope of the second quantifier in (SUMMATIVISM$_{\text{P-Trust}}$) makes for a more plausible summativist account of group predictive trust: necessarily, group g predictively trusts group g^* to φ just in case there is an i such that i is a member of g and i predictively trusts that there is an i^* such that i^* is a member of g^* and i^* φ-s. Although this formulation accommodates cases where g predictively trusts g^* even though no individual member of g knows which particular member of g^* is responsible for φ-ing, it does not help with our three cases. For example, because the provision by the ONS of relevant economic data necessitates the pooling of staff resources, and because different university staff are relying on different sets of data, there is no *single* university employee who predictively trusts that there is a statistician at ONS who is singlehandedly responsible for *all* those data.

33. Hawley (forthcoming) argues that we can vindicate our epistemic practices vis-à-vis groups without resorting to a distinction between trust and mere reliance, although she admits her conclusion is tentative. Hawley restricts attention to group reliability and group trustworthiness, without considering the possibility of intergroup trust in cases of nonsummativist group knowledge. Her point is that although we do in fact direct trust-related reactive attitudes towards groups, we could more appropriately direct these towards their individual members.

34. One might insist that the example rather illustrates the possibility of testimonial predictive trust. After all, if the two research teams are indeed long-term collaborators, the reasons for which g expects g^* to pronounce on b may instead concern g^*'s well-known expertise, track record, etc. However, g^* still recognizes that g relies on g^* in respect of b, and such reliance is exactly the reason for which g^* seeks to show b. Remember that affective trust is characterized in terms of other-reliance as a motivating reason for action.

Having said that, nothing in principle prevents one group from expecting that another group speaks truly for a mix of reasons, including other-reliance, and in that sense predictive and affective trust would be compatible.

35. See also Tuomela (2004) and List (2014), who subscribe to the supervenience of group judgment or agency on the contributions of individual members without embracing a corresponding reductive claim. ·

36. We assume not only that groups exist, and hence that nihilism about mereological composition is false, but also that groups can survive gradual change to their memberships (across times and worlds), and hence that mereological essentialism is false.

37. I'm very grateful to Sandy Goldberg, Lizzie Fricker, John Greco and Christoph Jäger for helpful discussion, and especially Katherine Dormandy and an anonymous reviewer for Routledge, for detailed comments on an earlier draft.

References

Baier, Annette C. 1986. "Trust and Antitrust." *Ethics* 96: 231–60.

———. 2013. "What Is Trust?" In *Reading Onora O'Neill*, edited by David Archard, Monique Deveaux, Neil Manson, and Daniel Weinstock, 175–85. London: Routledge.

Bird, Alexander. 2010. "Social Knowing: The Social Sense of 'Scientific Knowledge.'" *Philosophical Perspectives* 24: 23–56.

———. 2014. "When Is There a Group that Knows? Scientific Knowledge as Social Knowledge." In *Essays in Collective Epistemology*, edited by Jennifer Lackey, 42–63. Oxford: Oxford University Press.

Bratman, Michael E. 1999. *Faces of Intention: Selected Essays on Intention and Agency*. Cambridge: Cambridge University Press.

Carter, J. Adam. 2015. "Group Knowledge and Epistemic Defeat." *Ergo* 2: 711–35.

Coady, Cecil Anthony John. 1992. *Testimony: A Philosophical Study*. Oxford: Clarendon Press.

Conee, Earl, and Feldman, Richard. 2004. *Evidentialism: Essays in Epistemology*. Oxford: Oxford University Press.

Craig, Edward. 1990. *Knowledge and the State of Nature: An Essay in Conceptual Synthesis*. Oxford: Oxford University Press.

Faulkner, Paul. 2007. "On Telling and Trusting." *Mind* 116: 875–902.

———. 2014. "The Practical Rationality of Trust." *Synthese* 191: 1975–89.

Fricker, Miranda. 2007. *Epistemic Injustice: Power and the Ethics of Knowing*. Oxford: Oxford University Press.

———. 2012. "Group Testimony? The Making of a Collective Good Informant." *Philosophy and Phenomenological Research* 84: 249–76.

Gilbert, Margaret. 1989. *On Social Facts*. London: Routledge.

———. 2001. "Collective Preferences, Obligations, and Rational Choice." *Economics and Philosophy* 17: 109–19.

———. 2004. "Collective Epistemology." *Episteme* 1: 95–107.

———. 2013. *Joint Commitment: How We Make the Social World*. Oxford: Oxford University Press.

Goldberg, Sanford. Manuscript. "Understanding the Expectation of Trust."

Goldman, Alvin I. 1986. *Epistemology and Cognition*. Cambridge, MA: Harvard University Press.

———. 2004. "Group Knowledge Versus Group Rationality: Two Approaches to Social Epistemology." *Episteme* 1: 11–22.

Hardin, Russell. 2002. *Trust and Trustworthiness*. New York: Russell Sage Foundation.

Hawley, Katherine. 2014. "Trust, Distrust and Commitment." *Noûs* 48: 1–20.

———. Forthcoming. "Trustworthy Groups and Organisations."

Hinchman, Edward. 2005. "Telling as Inviting to Trust." *Philosophy and Phenomenological Research* 70: 562–87.

Hollis, Martin. 1998. *Trust within Reason*, Cambridge: Cambridge University Press.

Holton, Richard. 1994. "Deciding to Trust, Coming to Believe." *Australasian Journal of Philosophy* 72: 63–76.

Jones, Karen. 1996. "Trust as an Affective Attitude." *Ethics* 107: 4–25.

———. 1999. "Second-Hand Moral Knowledge." *Journal of Philosophy* 96: 55–78.

Knorr Cetina, Karin. 2009. *Epistemic Cultures: How the Sciences Make Knowledge*. Cambridge, MA: Harvard University Press.

Lackey, Jennifer. 2008. *Learning From Words: Testimony as a Source of Knowledge*. Oxford: Oxford University Press.

———. 2012. "Group Knowledge Attributions." In *New Essays on Knowledge Ascriptions*, edited by Jessica Brown and Mikkel Gerken, 243–69. Oxford: Oxford University Press.

———. 2014. "Socially Extended Knowledge." *Philosophical Issues* 24: 282–98.

———. 2018. "Group Assertion." *Erkenntnis* 83(1): 21–42.

List, Christian. 2014. "Three Kinds of Collective Attitudes." *Erkenntnis* 79: 1601–22.

Meijers, Anthonie. 2002. "Collective Agents and Cognitive Attitudes." *ProtoSociology* 16: 70–85.

Moran, Richard. 2005a. "Getting Told and Being Believed." *Philosophers' Imprint* 5: 1–29.

———. 2005b. "Problems of Sincerity." *Proceedings of the Aristotelian Society* 105: 341–61.

Pettit, Philip. 1995. "The Cunning of Trust." *Philosophy and Public Affairs* 24: 202–25.

Pettit, Philip, and David Schweikard. 2006. "Joint Actions and Group Agents." *Philosophy of the Social Sciences* 36: 18–39.

Quinton, Anthony. 1975. "Social Objects." *Proceedings of the Aristotelian Society* 76: 1–27.

Ross, Angus. 1986. "Why Do We Believe What We Are Told?" *Ratio* 1: 69–88.

Rupert, Robert D. 2005. "Minding One's Cognitive Systems: When Does a Group of Minds Constitute a Single Cognitive Unit?" *Episteme* 1: 177–88.

———. Manuscript. "Individual Minds as Groups, Group Minds as Individuals."

Schmitt, Frederick. 1994. "The Justification of Group Beliefs." In *Socializing Epistemology: The Social Dimensions of Knowledge*, edited by Frederick Schmitt, 257–87. Rowman and Littlefield.

———. 2010. "The Assurance View of Testimony." In *Social Epistemology*, edited by Adrian Haddock, Alan Millar, and Duncan Pritchard, 216–42. Oxford: Oxford University Press.

Sosa, Ernest. 2007. *A Virtue Epistemology*. Oxford: Oxford University Press.

———. 2009. *Reflective Knowledge*. Oxford: Oxford University Press.

Tollefsen, Deborah. 2002. "Challenging Epistemic Individualism." *Protosociology* 16: 86–117.

———. 2006. "From Extended Mind to Collective Mind." *Cognitive Systems Research* 7: 140–50.

———. 2007. "Group Testimony." *Social Epistemology* 21: 299–311.

———. 2009. "Wikipedia and the Epistemology of Testimony." *Episteme* 6: 8–22, special issue edited by Don Fallis and Larry Sanger.

Tuomela, Raimo. 1995. *The Importance of Us: A Philosophical Study of Basic Social Notions*. Redwood City, CA: Stanford University Press.

———. 2004. "Group Knowledge Analyzed." *Episteme* 1: 109–27.

———. 2005. "We-Intentions Revisited." *Philosophical Studies* 125: 327–69.

Walker, Margaret Urban. 2006. *Moral Repair: Reconstructing Moral Relations after Wrongdoing*. Cambridge: Cambridge University Press.

Williamson, Timothy. 2000. *Knowledge and Its Limits*. Oxford: Oxford University Press.

Wray, K. Brad. 2001. "Collective Belief and Acceptance." *Synthese* 129: 319–33.

———. 2007. "Who Has Scientific Knowledge?" *Social Epistemology* 21: 337–47.

Section 3

Trust and Epistemic Responsibility

7 Reconciling Epistemic Trust and Responsibility

Heidi Grasswick

Few would question the position that human beings form a large portion of their beliefs through trusting others. The human condition is one of deep epistemic dependence. Increasingly, numerous epistemologists interested in testimony have framed their discussions explicitly in terms of the role of trust (Faulkner 2011; Jones 2002; McMyler 2011). To acquire either well-grounded belief or knowledge on the basis of someone's testimony is to trust another in the formation of one's beliefs in the matter at hand. At first glance, an acknowledgement of the important role for trust in our epistemic lives might appear to create tensions with understandings of what it means to be an epistemically responsible inquirer. Trusting others is not always a good epistemic strategy; it makes us vulnerable in ways that have the potential to harm us epistemically, especially if one's social environment is hostile to one's well-being, such as can be experienced by those who are marginalized in society. Furthermore, in some interpretations, epistemically trusting another may appear to abdicate our epistemic responsibilities by turning them over to others.

In this chapter I examine the relationship between forms of epistemic trust and a broad construction of epistemic responsibility that refers to how we conduct ourselves as inquirers who seek to satisfy our epistemic goals in a thoroughly social world. I first offer a general account of epistemic trust as a normative and affective trust and consider two forms of it—trust in testimony and trust in inquiry—noting that they are conceptually independent though also deeply intertwined with each other in our trust relationships. I then set out two interpretations of epistemic responsibility: a narrow interpretation that focuses on one's accountability to the available evidence at the moment of belief formation and a more common, broader interpretation that refers to one's epistemic conduct over time and includes considerations of how our activities of inquiry help *position* us to access those epistemic goods that are significant for us from a practical point of view. I explain various ways in which our epistemic responsibility can be exercised, first in the formation of, but more importantly from within, ongoing relationships of epistemic trust. Finally, I discuss three layers of epistemic responsibility that pertain to our relations of epistemic trust within a social world of knowing.

Although much of what I argue supports the need for an analysis of communal epistemic responsibility, for the purposes of this chapter, I focus on the implications of the important role of epistemic trust in our practices of inquiry for understanding what it is to be an epistemically responsible (individual) inquirer within a social world of knowing.

1

1.1. Epistemic Trust: General Accounts of Trust

In developing their understanding of the role of trust in the case of testimony, epistemologists have drawn from analyses of the general concept of trust (many having originated in ethics and social political philosophy), attempting to clarify trust's particular meaning and function with respect to testimony specifically, and our epistemic lives more generally. These general analyses of trust tend to recognize that although the term "trust" is sometimes used as a synonym for simple reliance on another, in what could be considered a "predictive" sense of trust (Faulkner 2011), there is a richer concept of trust that involves more than mere reliance. This richer concept is said to be normative, in that it involves placing normative expectations on the trustee (Faulkner 2011). One of the key features of trust in this richer, normative sense is the possibility of betrayal that accompanies trust (Baier 1986; Jones 1996). For example, if I simply rely on someone or something, I can be disappointed but not betrayed. If I rely on my car's gas tank gauge to indicate the amount of gas I have, I may be disappointed and frustrated with my situation when the gauge fails to operate properly, causing me to run out of gas unexpectedly. But I do not experience such reactive attitudes as resentment and a sense of betrayal such as I might if, after finding myself stranded without gas, I text my friend who responds that she will come right away to rescue me but then never shows up. My friend has let me down, and in the absence of her providing some convincing explanation for why she could not follow through, I would rightfully feel resentment towards her and a sense of betrayal.

In an attempt to explain the difference between mere reliance and this richer sense of trust, many have argued that trust itself involves a particular affective attitude (Jones 1996; Faulkner 2011). Karen Jones characterizes this attitude as having two components. First, one has an attitude of optimism in the goodwill and competence of the trusted (Jones 1996).[1] But additionally, in trusting another, one expects that the trusted one "will be directly and favorably moved by the thought that we are counting on her" (Jones 1996, 4). It is this richer sense of trust as involving an affective attitude through which we place certain expectations on each other that I investigate with respect to our epistemic pursuits and our epistemic responsibilities. Though frequently we trust only in the thin predictive sense of relying on another for epistemic goods, normative and affective trust has an important role to play in maintaining long-standing trust relations within epistemic practices. Epistemic relationships and systems involving affective and normative expectations of each other are part of what keeps our epistemic practices "on the rails" over time, functioning productively for us and supporting our epistemic goals of knowing well in the world through each other's efforts. Because of this important role of epistemic trust relationships, we need to assess how they can be reconciled with the demands that come with being epistemically responsible as in individual agent.

Trust theorists recognize that drilling down to a core conception of trust is difficult, given the wide variety of types of things that we entrust to others and the vastly different contexts within which we trust. We trust teachers, sitters, relatives, and neighbors with the care and safety of our children; we trust bank tellers with our money; we trust strangers to respect our personal space as we walk down the street; we trust our friends to treat us well and not undermine our pursuits by backstabbing us in the company of others; and we trust many different kinds of people, positioned in many different kinds of relationships with us, for their testimony of many different types of claims. To simply say that I trust someone does not yet specify the scope of that trust or what kinds of things I'm entrusting them with. Trust theorists have typically articulated the relationship of trust in terms of a three-place structure: A trusts B for C, where C is some good that A cares about (Baier 1986).[2] Correspondingly, trust can take different forms, depending in part on the nature of the good entrusted. And though I do not discuss the point in detail, a crucial feature of trust that underlies my analysis is that trust is rarely absolute, but rather comes in degrees, being easier or harder to break depending on the context and nature of our interactions and our epistemic needs.

1.2. Epistemic Trust: Two Forms

Among the different kinds of trust, naturally it is epistemic trust that epistemologists are particularly interested in. Epistemic trust needs to be identified and distinguished from other types of trust because we need to understand cases where I might epistemically trust someone without trusting them for other types of goods and vice versa. For example, I may consider an acquaintance of mine who is an expert on fly fishing and loves to share her knowledge of it to be a very trustworthy testifier on the topic of fly fishing, even though I do not find her trustworthy as a friend, given that throughout my social interactions I have found her character to be quite self-serving and manipulative. But I am perfectly comfortable trusting her with respect to her testimony on the topic of fly fishing, and I believe she has goodwill toward me when interacting with me on this topic and is responsive to my dependence on her for learning about fly fishing; her love of the sport overrides any self-serving tendencies she has that may make me more wary and less confident in her goodwill towards me in other aspects of our interactions. On the other hand, I may trust my cousin (whom I know well) to take excellent care of my children and treat them with kindness and respect, without trusting him for certain epistemic matters. I know that he is not a detail-oriented person, not just in terms of his capacities but also in that he is impatient with in-depth explanations and has little interest in pursuing forms of understanding that require grappling with complex details. These latter traits create good reasons for my hesitation in trusting his reporting on complex issues. Distinguishing epistemic trust from other forms of trust helps clarify the features of situations and inquirers that appropriately ground our epistemic trust, while ruling out those features that might be relevant to grounding other forms of trust, but not epistemic trust. Epistemologists have long been interested in identifying the types of reasons, judgments, and interactions that are relevant to serving our epistemic goals and distinguishing them from those that serve us poorly in our epistemic pursuits. For example, we generally think that I should not believe a person on a matter of grave importance simply because I think they are a nice person.

All this may seem rather obvious. Yet as I argue throughout this chapter, because trust relations are inherently social and involve expectations of goodwill and responsiveness to others, features that are typically considered more moral rather than epistemic, and because we need trust to access epistemic goods in order to solve practical problems, the reasons we have available to support or withhold epistemic trust are in fact broader than those typically conceptualized as purely epistemic.

I define *epistemic trust* as:

> those forms of normative or affective trust that are involved in the care of and achievement of a variety of epistemic goods, such as knowledge, understanding, true beliefs, justified or well-grounded beliefs, and reliable practices of inquiry.[3]

Trust in someone's testimony is the most obvious form of epistemic trust, and is considered by many to be the classic form of epistemic trust. In trusting another for their testimony, I am relying on them to provide me with at least a well-grounded belief (perhaps even knowledge itself), making me vulnerable to them for that epistemic good. If they let me down, they can harm me epistemically. Additionally, when I trust epistemically in another for their testimony, I do so with an attitude of optimism that they will fulfill the expectations I have for them in providing me with, or caring for, the epistemic good in question and a sense that they bear me goodwill, or at least not ill will, within the scope of these expectations. Again, there will, of course, be times when we merely rely on others epistemically, but throughout this chapter I reserve the term "epistemic trust" for cases of the richer sense of normative or affective trust applied to epistemic goods, involving more than just reliance.

In spite of the dominance of discussions of trust in testimony in the literature, cases of testimony do not comprise the only form of epistemic trust. Another very important form of epistemic trust concerns trusting another to *do the knowing* for me. I might think it is very important for society in general, as well as important for myself, that *someone* be investigating some field of knowledge or understanding, though not necessarily myself, and I will often trust another to undertake the activities and practices of inquiry for a particular area. We can call this form of epistemic trust *in inquiry*. Perhaps I think it is important that there are people studying quantum mechanics and developing a robust understanding of that field, yet I do not consider it important that *I* understand quantum mechanics. I epistemically trust quantum physicists to be investigating this field of knowledge that I think is important, and I trust that they understand how quantum mechanics plays out in the world on the basis of their inquiry. But I can trust them with this epistemic good without ever expecting them to provide me with testimony of their findings. It is plausible that I will never find myself in a situation where I need their testimony on quantum mechanics or be particularly interested in it. Yet if I were to find out that they were doing a poor job in their inquiry—perhaps I was to learn about a scandal concerning widespread fabrication of data among the researchers—I could easily feel a certain level of resentment, in that I trusted them to be doing such epistemic work in a conscientious and responsible manner. They have violated the trust I placed in them to care for an epistemic good that I valued.[4]

There are also cases where I trust someone else to do the knowing for me, but rather than simply not expecting that they will share that knowledge with me, I actually expect them *not* to share the results of their inquiry, given that there are good reasons not to. For example, intelligence agencies are trusted to do the work of obtaining information that concerns national security, but precisely because the goal of national security depends on the information not circulating widely, we expect the results of their inquiries to be withheld from the public.[5] There are many different types of inquiry we trust others to undertake that are coupled with the expectation that some form of confidentiality or secrecy will be maintained, from anonymous academic journal review practices to medical research on patients where confidential records are in play and practices of double-blind studies are valued.

Furthermore, the epistemic goods others generate in their inquiries are often valued by us because they are crucial in allowing these inquirers to put that knowledge to work through particular actions in the world that we value, not necessarily because we care that the results of inquiry are widely shared. Almost all undertakings in the world have epistemic dimensions to them. When we trust others in practical affairs, this includes trust in their abilities to generate the necessary epistemic goods relevant to those undertakings through inquiry. Many of those epistemic goods will be trivial on their own, their relevance possibly fleeting, and never in need of sharing with others. For example, imagine all the bits of information required for a chef to make us a delicious meal—everything from knowing which ingredients on the counter are the freshest and ought to be selected, to tell-tale signs of when the particular dish they are preparing is cooked just right. Trust in inquiry abounds throughout our dependencies on the practical activities of others.

When I offer trust in inquiry in isolation from trust in testimony, I am adopting an attitude something like "this inquiry is important, and I expect with optimism that the people I am trusting will undertake the inquiry well, but as long as they come to know or understand the results, I (and possibly others) don't need to." Such a situation makes it clear that trust in inquiry is a different form of trust than trust in testimony. Yet it is still an *epistemic* trust insofar as there are epistemic goods I am entrusting to another. Trust in inquiry forms an important part of our networks of relations of epistemic trust and our systems that employ a cognitive division of labor, placing epistemic demands on others that affect how we understand our own epistemic responsibilities, and at times lightening our load when we are able to trust others to undertake inquiries that are crucial to our human flourishing.

It is worth noting that although the paradigm cases of trust in inquiry will involve either specialized inquiries, or at least cases where I recognize that the person I trust is more competent for the inquiry at hand than I am, trust in inquiry can also be placed in those whom I consider to have weaker relevant epistemic skills than myself. For example, as a manager of a construction company with a full slate of work, I might delegate the job of calculating a rough estimate of a project to one of my employees, knowing full well that I am more experienced with construction planning and sharper with numbers than they are. Yet I delegate this inquiry to them because I trust them to be able to do the job adequately, within the range of quality that is required to generate a "good-enough" estimate at this stage of the project. If, as manager of the project, I do not need to see this estimate (imagine it is simply a rough estimate presented to the client by members of my team and by the time I expect to be involved again at the fine-tuned budgeting stage, we will have moved on past this initial estimate), then it is only trust in inquiry that has been employed, not trust in testimony.

This latter example makes clear that the degree to which we are willing to trust others for inquiry depends on many pragmatic and contextual details, including how high the stakes are in achieving a certain level of accuracy or understanding. The placement of my trust in another for an inquiry will depend on my belief in their ability to pursue the inquiry *well enough*, given what I take to be at stake, and such distinctions in what counts as well enough appropriately depend on the context of the inquiry. Furthermore, my willingness to trust another for a particular inquiry (and its appropriateness) will depend on whether I find there to be some additional value in my performing the inquiry for myself instead of trusting another for it. For example, we might think that there is important value in each of us performing some degree of research or inquiry as to various electoral candidates' positions on issues prior to casting a vote. Even though we could place our trust in another friend or family member who is more interested in politics than we are to do such research, and then, following their inquiry, be willing to trust their testimony simply by asking them "whom should I vote for?", many would argue that such trust in their inquiry (and resultant testimony) would be inappropriate, given our civic duties.[6]

1.3. Inquiry and Testimony: Intersections of the Epistemic Trust Forms

Though I have stressed that trust in inquiry can stand on its own, separate from trust in testimony, most often the two intersect, as in the voting advice example given earlier. To begin with, trust in testimony almost always involves a component of trust in inquiry. If I trust your testimony, it is in part because I trust that you have the relevant competence in inquiry that would result in you having achieved an epistemic good (such as knowledge or understanding) to offer me. I say that trust in testimony "almost" always involves trust in inquiry in order to allow for cases where there isn't much inquiry involved or much complexity to the inquiry. What I have in mind are very simple cases such as reporting to another a direct perception that one has. There is certainly a perceptual competence involved in such a case, but this can only be interpreted as inquiry in an extremely minimal sense, if at all. The idea of inquiry that I have set out in my articulation of trust in inquiry involves activities and practices undertaken to access epistemic goods, and sometimes our trust in the testimony of certain types of knowledge claims would push the limits of this understanding of inquiry as something required. Such cases show that occasionally we may trust testimony without having expectations of much (active) inquiry having taken place. Nevertheless, most cases of trust in testimony necessitate trust in inquiry, insofar as trust in testimony includes trust in another's competence in undertaking the inquiry that is necessary to be able to provide reliable claims. If someone is untrustworthy in inquiry due to their incompetence, they will also be untrustworthy in their testimony on such matters.

Additionally, trust in inquiry hooks onto trust in testimony in the other direction, with trust in inquiry implying a kind of trust in testimony. To clarify this point, we must distinguish trust in testimony in a weak sense from a strong sense. A weak sense of trust in testimony simply involves trust in the testimonial reports that someone *does* offer me; when they tell me something in a particular area, I trust them. More importantly though, trust in testimony can also be understood in a strong sense that involves trusting that the person *will* report to me those things (within a particular scope) that will be relevant to me when they have access to them. When I trust someone in this strong sense of trust in testimony, then when my interlocutor is silent, I trust that their silence indicates that they have nothing relevant to report to me. This stronger sense of trust in testimony is deeply connected to why we trust in inquiry, and it is the sense of testimony that we most often use when we are discussing *relationships* of testimonial interaction that are maintained over time rather than a single encounter of testimony with a stranger. In cases of trust in inquiry where I am trusting another to do the knowing for me for a particular range of topics, circumstances may arise, perhaps even unexpectedly, in which the results of their specialized inquiry will become relevant to me and thus of interest to me. Such potential interest may lead me to either hope or expect (depending on the circumstances) that the results of a specialized inquiry will be shared with me in some form of testimony when appropriate. For example, if I trust health scientists to undertake inquiries that progress our understanding of our nutritional needs, and they discover results that run counter to the current government recommendations and public understanding of a nutritionally balanced diet, I would expect that they would make that knowledge publicly available in recognition of and in response to the public's (and my) interest in coming to know this. The trust in inquiry I have placed in them brings with it the expectation that should they make such discoveries that are significant for me, they will be responsive to my epistemic interest in that knowledge.[7] This is part of having entrusted them with epistemic goods that I care about. If I learn that they have not made efforts to provide such knowledge (or worse, tried to hide the knowledge), I may well feel a sense of betrayal that will in turn lessen the trust in inquiry I am prepared to offer them in the future.

Finally, in cases where I never have a personal interest in receiving the testimony of the results of another's inquiry (and never expect to), trust in inquiry involves the strong sense of testimonial trust I mentioned earlier in an additional way that does not involve the truster directly. In cases where I do not expect to ever need to know the results of the inquiry, my trust in inquiry is still grounded in the (strong testimony) expectation that the inquirer will share their knowledge with the relevant people when those people need it. Such people include collaborators in the inquiry itself, as well as the relevant parties in society for whom the knowledge generated could be significant. This could include policymakers or specific populations within society, for example. In short, I entrust epistemic goods in other inquirers in part because I expect that these goods will be able to make their way to those who need access to them, even when those who need or want access do not include me. I care about those epistemic goods that I do not want or need myself because these epistemic goods can, when they reach the appropriate persons, have impacts on actions and practices that connect us to the way the world is and help us solve practical problems. If it becomes apparent that an inquirer (or community of inquirers) has withheld from the relevant parties epistemic goods that they have developed, a sense of betrayal and a lessening of my trust in their inquiry may reasonably ensue.

In practice, there will be many circumstances in which I trust in inquiry without expecting that I will ever need or want to be testified to on the relevant matters. This fact alone makes it worthy of recognition as a different form of trust from trust in testimony. Nevertheless, it is deeply connected to the strong interpretation of testimony, in that placing such epistemic goods in the care of another brings with it an expectation that should a situation arise where it is appropriate to share those epistemic goods that have become relevant to others, they will be shared through testimony with those others.

Epistemic trust in having others undertake particular epistemic work through specific inquiries crucially underwrites our knowledge practices that involve large systems of cognitive divisions of labor. Its connections with our expectations concerning potential moments of relevant testimony explain why it is important to entrust epistemic goods to others through their inquiry and protects against a problematic interpretation through which trust in inquiry might be understood as fostering epistemic silos.

2

2.1. Epistemic Responsibility: Responsibility for Beliefs

In her 1987 book *Epistemic Responsibility*, Lorraine Code acknowledges that there are different ways in which humans can make sense of the world, and from this fact she reasons that accounts of knowledge must "recognize a need for cognitive imperatives to limit what kinds of sense can *responsibly be made of the world*" (Code 1987, 9). The point of epistemic responsibility is "to ensure that knowledge claims are well-grounded in the world, that they respect the constraints the world imposes upon those who would know it" (Code 1987, 6). At its most basic core, the concept of epistemic responsibility amounts to being guided by a respect for evidence in virtue of evidence's crucial role in ascertaining what is true of the world. Being epistemically responsible involves being motivated by such a respect for evidence and desire for the truth, rather than allowing other motivations to influence belief formation. Perhaps the clearest violation of epistemic responsibility is wishful thinking, whereby I form a belief because I want the world to be as my belief would claim. Even if we reject the doctrine of doxastic voluntarism and its claim that humans are capable of believing at will, the concern about wishful thinking and related psychological tendencies such as motivated reasoning remains. Wishful thinking inclines us to ignore or turn our attention away from evidence that might be available. It can also interfere in the epistemic process by having an untoward influence on how quickly or slowly I commit to a particular belief when there is available evidence supporting it. Similarly, when there is mixed evidence present (both in favor of and against a claim), wishful thinking and related forms of motivated reasoning can influence how one weights such varying evidence, pushing one's beliefs in one direction or another. Confirmation bias, whereby we tend to favor the evidence that supports the hypothesis or claim that we already hold, is one example of this. For many epistemologists, such influences constitute an epistemic impropriety by the agent failing to be fully accountable to evidence.

For epistemologists who focus on questions concerning the epistemic status of our particular beliefs (asking such questions as "is this belief justified?" and "does it constitute an instance of knowledge?"), epistemic responsibility has sometimes been interpreted in a particularly narrow sense of one being accountable solely to the evidence one has available at the time of forming a particular belief. For example, many of those who work with a deontological theory of justification directly connect the idea of a justified belief with having satisfied one's epistemic responsibilities or duties.[8] When epistemic responsibility is understood in this narrow sense concerning the relationship between the evidence at hand and the formation of belief, and furthermore is coupled with a traditionally individualistic and internalist orientation to epistemology that understands reasoning and evidence to be things that must be directly available to the individual epistemic agent, trusting another's testimony seems to present a tension. As John Hardwig has noted, for those wedded to a traditional individualist model of knowing, some of the epistemological resistance to allowing a role for trust in testimony has had its source in the fact that trust has long been conceptualized as antithetical to knowledge because it is "partially blind" (Hardwig 1991). To trust another is to lack the direct evidence for the claim oneself. If trust is considered antithetical to having the direct evidence, and that evidence is what is needed in order to responsibly form the belief that p, then trust cannot be responsibly employed in building the epistemological case for p.

Not surprisingly, an important focus for many testimony theorists then has been to demonstrate how we can understand another's testimony as offering a kind of evidence, or else a different kind of reason, but still a legitimately epistemic reason for holding p. As Frederick F. Schmitt points out, "It is uncontroversial that testimony that p can give the hearer of the testimony an epistemic reason to believe p, and indeed make the hearer epistemically justified in believing *p*" (Schmitt 2010, 216). If trust in testimony can justify one believing *p*, then surely it is possible to be epistemically responsible in believing on the basis of another's testimony. The task then becomes to develop an analysis of testimony that explains how and when one can be epistemically responsible in adopting a particular belief in testimony. Testimony theorists have employed different strategies in this regard, from reductive accounts, to entitlement and assurance theories, to second-person knowledge accounts. Much of this work conceptualizes trust in the predictive sense of (mere) reliance on another's testimony, and some of it employs the normative and affective sense of trust that I employ. Excellent work has been done here, with promising results that themselves go some distance to explaining how cases of testimony can be supported by types of reasons and evidence that can make it compatible with epistemic responsibility in the moment of belief formation. But I do not discuss this literature here, because my focus in this chapter takes up a different epistemological orientation, as I explain later. Although the task of reconciling trust at the moment of belief formation with the demands of the narrow interpretation of epistemic responsibility remains an important part of the overall project of coming to terms with epistemic trust and responsibility, I turn instead to a different dimension of trust that warrants attention: examining the epistemic role of trust relationships that last over time and reconciling this role with the broader contours of epistemic responsibility.

2.2. Epistemic Responsibility: Responsibility in Epistemic Conduct

The narrow interpretation of epistemic responsibility described earlier concerning the relationship between evidence at hand and the formation of belief at a particular time has been useful for those epistemologists who focus on questions concerning the epistemic status of particular beliefs and the requirements of good reasoning. However, it is more common to interpret epistemic responsibility in a much broader sense that goes beyond synchronic belief formation. Epistemic responsibility is commonly applied not just to the moment of forming a particular belief, but rather is taken to describe how we ought to conduct ourselves more generally as inquirers who seek epistemic goods such as knowledge and understanding about the world. In this broad sense, the demands of epistemic responsibility that speak to how we reason with respect to the evidence in front of us, in a particular moment and with respect to a particular belief, are only a small part of leading an epistemically responsible life; the demands of epistemic responsibility importantly involve how conscientious we are in *pursuit* of would-be relevant evidence from which to form our beliefs. Being epistemically responsible requires that we undertake particular actions and investigations over time, being conscientious and exercising care in coming to know the world by seeking out evidence that can then support those claims we are prepared to make about the world. It involves how best to *position ourselves* to be capable of knowing well in the world, and such positioning takes work. The general gloss of epistemic responsibility that I began with—understanding it as a general respect for evidence and its role in grounding our beliefs in the world as we seek truth—in large part involves working to ensure that one is positioned well to be able to support those beliefs about the world that are important for us through evidence and reasons. Ongoing relationships of epistemic trust with worthy partners play an important role in that positioning, in many cases allowing us to access epistemic goods that we could not obtain except through trust.

This attention to our activities of inquiry that results from this broader concept of epistemic responsibility is invoked extensively among virtue epistemologists, especially those identified as responsibilists who are interested in the character traits of knowers (such as consciousness, open-mindedness, and carefulness) that allow us to know and understand our world well. Code, one of the early developers of responsibilism, argues that we need a sense of epistemic responsibility because "ensuring the accountability of knowledge claimants requires imperatives of responsibility to regulate epistemic carelessness, dogmatism, and *akrasia*" (Code 1991, 72). For responsibilist virtue epistemologists, epistemic responsibility involves one's conduct over time and one's engagement in the activities of inquiry through which we pursue knowledge and understanding of the world. For those responsibilists who also take seriously the extent to which our epistemic lives are deeply social, our epistemic responsibilities will include developing habits and practices of social interaction that support our epistemic goals by positioning ourselves to know well through each other. The virtues that support epistemic responsibility include certain "other-regarding" virtues, such as honesty and integrity, traits that help support healthy epistemic relations between community members (Kawall 2002). But additionally, the structures of our epistemic trust relations need to be examined, given their crucial role in our social activities of inquiry.

The difference between the narrow interpretation of epistemic responsibility, as answerability to evidence at the time of belief formation, and the broader sense that captures a larger picture of our overall conduct and, in turn, generates analyses of how practices and activities of inquiry themselves can embody a respect for evidence and its connection to the world reflects a larger difference in epistemological orientation. Though concern with how we handle the evidence available at the time of belief formation remains an important component of this broader sense of epistemic responsibility (after all, it would be odd for someone concerned with an epistemically responsible life of inquiry to leave out issues of one's ability to reason through the implications of the evidence available at the time of belief formation!), the questions asked by those who adopt the broader version of epistemic responsibility tend to have a different focus.

Christopher Hookway articulates this difference in the contrast he draws between what he calls the doxastic paradigm of epistemic evaluation with an alternative understanding of epistemology as "theory of inquiry." While the doxastic paradigm focuses on the evaluation of beliefs, Hookway's alternative framing of epistemology as a theory of inquiry offers a broader reading of the evaluative work of epistemology. Within this broader framework, Hookway claims that "the target for epistemic evaluations lies in our ability to carry out inquiries, to reason effectively and solve problems, rather than in how far our beliefs are justified, or whether we possess knowledge" (Hookway 2006, 98). Because such reasoning is a goal-directed activity, "the norms that govern reasoning and inquiry will include norms of *practical* reason" (Hookway 2006, 100). Under this framing of the work of epistemic evaluation, concern with how we respond to the evidence at hand in our formation of beliefs will, of course, continue to be a relevant dimension of our exercise of epistemic responsibility. But a larger focus of analysis will form around the kind of practices we participate in and the habits we develop, assessing the degree to which they help us position ourselves well in order to obtain, over the long run, the kinds of epistemic goods that will help us lead a flourishing life.

Hookway's framework has implications for our understanding of the relationship between epistemic trust and epistemic responsibility. In my earlier discussion of epistemic trust, I argued that we needed to distinguish forms of epistemic trust from other forms of trust, in part to be able to distinguish those features of situations that would appropriately support the placement of epistemic trust from features that, though they may be relevant to placing other kinds of trust in another, should not be taken to be relevant to placements of epistemic trust. Hookway's point that norms of practical reason are involved in epistemic evaluations concerning our inquiries opens the possibility that some factors that might have classically been considered nonepistemic will need to play a role in (at least some of) our epistemic evaluations. For example, the epistemic standards we employ in our evaluations within a particular inquiry, including our standards of evidence and evidence gathering, might be in part dependent on the relative seriousness of the practical consequences of "getting things wrong" versus the need to deliver some level of knowledge or understanding to solve a practical goal.[9] Practical reason concerns our decisions to act in certain ways, and inquiry itself involves action. Hence, if we are interested in how we can be epistemically responsible in our inquiries, practical reason will play a role alongside theoretical reason. The inclusion of practical reason opens up the scope of what features of a situation will be relevant to include when analyzing appropriate or responsible placements of epistemic trust. For example, my earlier discussion of the relationship between trust in inquiry and trust in testimony suggested that the practical ramifications of inquirers sharing their epistemic goods with the appropriate people generates a standard I can properly appeal to when assessing the trust in inquiry I have granted; I can responsibly withdraw my trust in inquiry if the inquirer fails to share the epistemic goods they have generated with those well placed to use the epistemic goods in the service of practical goals which are also relevant to me.

2.3. *The Implications of Epistemic Responsibility in Inquiry: A Matter of Knowing and Living Well*

Hookway's point that inquiry itself is about our abilities to generate epistemic goods that can help us solve practical problems also points to the fact that epistemic responsibility is not about maximizing epistemic goods, but rather requires prioritizing the attainment of those areas of knowledge and understanding that are important for a good life. Our epistemic responsibilities have never been conceptualized by epistemologists as involving the need to know everything or pursue inquiry on a particular matter endlessly. That would be impossible, even for a group of people who distribute their cognitive labor among themselves. But it would not only be impossible, it would be unwise. We need to be able to direct our epistemic attentions and develop understandings of those features of the world that are important for us to survive and flourish. Hence, many epistemologists have pointed out that the goals of our epistemic life revolve around the generation of *significant* truths, not just any random or trivial collection of truths (Anderson 1995; Kitcher 2001).

The broad sense of epistemic responsibility with its analyses of our activities of inquiry targets our epistemic decisions, habits, and practices in relation to our epistemic goals, and in practice the achievement of some of those goals requires prioritizing some epistemic goods over others. A responsible inquirer is one who, among other things, can do a good job prioritizing her epistemic work in order to attain the understandings that are important and relevant to her and her epistemic communities. Epistemic responsibilities concern how to *know well* in the world, with knowing well being "a matter both of moral-political and epistemic concern" (Code 1991, 72). Epistemic responsibilities involve directing our energies towards knowledge that matters, that can help solve our problems, and that can lead to human flourishing.

For that to happen, an epistemically responsible life will involve accepting many states of ignorance, including those that result from ending an inquiry or redirecting efforts to other inquiries. Of course, this is not to say that all states of ignorance are compatible with having fulfilled one's epistemic responsibilities. Clearly, many forms of ignorance will be epistemically vicious and culpable—cases where I should have known or I should have been more scrupulous in my inquiry. But epistemic responsibility and its appropriate limits, given the overall epistemic goals that it serves, will involve the acceptance of certain states of ignorance, including ignorance of some forms of evidence or counter-evidence that might have been unturned if one's inquiry had been continued.

This feature of epistemic responsibility has important ramifications for those who worry that the attitudes that permeate trust relations are inherently incompatible with the demands of inquiry and the seeking of evidence that come with epistemic responsibility. As prominent trust theorists have noted, a core feature of engaging in a trusting relationship is that in having adopted an attitude of trust towards another, one commits to not checking up on them (Townley 2011; Hawley 2014). For example, if I trust my significant other when they tell me they did not visit their ex when they were out of town, and we both understood me as trusting in this regard, they would rightfully be upset with me if they were to discover that I later made some investigations into their visit and checked their phone to ensure that no contact was made. Such check-ups would suggest I had not actually trusted them in their testimony.[10] To trust another epistemically involves being *willing* to stay in a state of ignorance about certain forms of evidence that I have not yet acquired; in trusting, I commit to refraining from working to seek further evidence regarding either the claim itself or the trustworthiness of the one I trust.[11]

Yet this discussion of epistemic responsibility and its demands that we prioritize epistemic goods appropriately makes clear that epistemic responsibility does allow for the maintenance of certain states of ignorance when they are consistent with our larger epistemic goals. In this regard, if the trust relation is well placed and capable of serving our larger epistemic goals, then its inherent "restraint" feature that brings with it sustained ignorance of evidence that I could have obtained through checking up on my trustee can be understood as compatible with one's epistemic responsibilities.[12]

3

3.1. *Epistemic Responsibility in a Social World of Trust Relations*

Having discussed two main forms of epistemic trust and explained how a broad conception of epistemic responsibility results in the need to develop analyses of our activities of inquiry, taking into account our practical needs for specific kinds of epistemic goods, I am now poised to articulate more clearly how epistemic responsibility plays a role in our trust relations. Traditionally, modern Western epistemology has been highly individualistic, reserving states of the individual, as opposed to states of others, as relevant to epistemic evaluations. Accordingly, the concept of epistemic responsibility has been commonly interpreted as involving only the individual and their epistemic conduct as they encounter the world. But for those who recognize the wide extent of the social dimensions of our epistemic pursuits, including the important role of placing epistemic trust in others, the concept of epistemic responsibility needs some adjusting to accommodate the role of others in our knowledge-seeking endeavors and our epistemic vulnerabilities as individual epistemic agents. As Catherine Elgin puts the point, "epistemic success requires that agents be properly attuned not just to the objects of knowledge but also to one another" (Elgin 2014, 245).

With respect to trust relations, our epistemic success clearly depends on the trustworthiness of those in whom we place our epistemic trust and how well matched the extent of the trustworthiness is with the degree of trust we place in them. Healthy epistemic trust relations involve just such a balance. Unhealthy trust relations result when there is a mismatch—when the truster exhibits an attitude that is either too skeptical of the trustee or too gullible relative to the trustee's epistemic trustworthiness.[13] In Elgin's terms, trusters must be "properly attuned" to the trustees.

To have a relationship of epistemic trust with another is to have developed certain *habits and practices of engagement* with them. To recap, for affective and normative trust in the epistemic case, these habits and practices will involve making myself vulnerable to the trustee by optimistically depending on them for certain epistemic goods, and doing so by placing a normative expectation on them that they will be responsive to my epistemic needs. Given that healthy trust relations offer powerful ways of succeeding epistemically, our epistemic responsibilities will involve the development and maintenance of such trust relations as part of *positioning ourselves well* for accessing epistemic goods through our relations with others. When I am able to participate in a healthy trust relationship, the trustee will be responsive to my epistemic needs, making it possible for me to access such epistemic goods that in most cases would otherwise be out of reach.

One obvious way my epistemic responsibility can be exercised is during the process of *forming* trust relations. It is clear that we often can and do reason about the trustworthiness of others with respect to epistemic goods, and at times we decide on the basis of such reasoning whether or not to place our trust in others—trust which could then be long-lasting (McMyler 2017).[14] As we *form* a specific relationship of epistemic trust with another and seek to do so responsibly, we often will be looking for indicators of our potential trustee's trustworthiness and the scope of that trustworthiness.[15] These indicators involve not just evidence concerning the trustee's likely reliability on the relevant matters but also indicators that they likely care about and will be responsive to our epistemic needs, making evidence of their moral character relevant to our assessment of their trustworthiness as a partner in epistemic pursuits. Also important will be indicators of whether or not they are likely to grasp what my epistemic needs are that I am hoping they will become responsive to. If, for example, I consider myself to be in a very different social position from a potential trustee, one that brings with it a particular set of epistemic needs, indications that they are unaware of or do not understand my needs (because of their different social position from me) will be important to consider in judging the likelihood of their epistemic trustworthiness. Without a grasp of my epistemic needs, a potential truster will be unable to respond to them. Furthermore, it is worth noting that a potential trustee's activities of inquiry for a given domain also will involve interactions with others through their own networks of trusting relationships, and their success in turn will depend on their ability to judge the trustworthiness of others in whom they may place epistemic trust (Daukas 2006). This means that to the extent that I have any indicators regarding my potential trustee's ability to judge the trustworthiness of others with whom they are interacting and depending upon epistemically, these, too, will be relevant to my assessment of their epistemic trustworthiness as I begin to form a trust relationship with them.

In most cases of the formation of trust relations, the trust is built over time. Trust, by its nature, always exceeds the evidence available to me. Yet in building a relationship of trust, one may extend to a potential trustee a limited degree and scope of affective trust, or may begin by simply relying on the person (in the predictive sense of trust). When results from such strategies are positive and the trustee begins to earn one's trust, the trust relationship may deepen, expand, and grow into a deeper affective trust. At the same time, as a trust relation is built, its parameters become clearer; the truster develops a good sense of what they are willing to trust the trustee with and what not, and habits of trust within those parameters take shape. Trust deepens when one comes to have confidence in one's understanding of its appropriate boundaries.

By seeking a range of indicators relevant to another's epistemic trustworthiness and being responsive to such (indirect) evidence, we can (and often do) exercise epistemic responsibility when developing trust relationships. However, to focus on the seeking of evidence of trustworthiness that will then serve as baseline support for the responsible formation of (and then continuation of) trust relations would be to obscure the fact that in reality, each of us inherits a place within a vast array of already functioning social practices that embody networks of epistemic trust in inquiry and testimony, with social norms and expectations of the various parties already in play. In this more common case, we begin exercising our epistemic responsibilities *from within* these practices, already working as a participant within various relationships of trust that may be more or less healthy. We find ourselves already socially expected to trust particular others, and we understand others as being held to normative expectations of trustworthiness by many of those around us, not just ourselves.

In the following sections, I articulate three different layers of epistemic responsibility that are implicated in trust relations that we are already in. The first briefly returns to my early consideration of the component of epistemic responsibility that zeroes in on accountability to the evidence available in the moment of belief formation—the component that I originally identified as a very narrow interpretation of epistemic responsibility when taken on its own. The second and third focus more specifically on how to understand our epistemic responsibilities within our ongoing relationships of trust with others and the limitations of the social practices of trust that we inherit.

3.2. Implications of Trust: Belief Formation and the Distribution of Epistemic Responsibilities

In keeping with my focus on the role of long-standing trust relations and their implications for that portion of epistemic responsibility that concerns our activities of inquiry, I have been clear that I will not say much about the workings of epistemic responsibility at the level of individual belief formation. But I do want to note one major repercussion of what I have said thus far for understanding epistemic responsibility at the level of belief formation.

The extensive role of trust in both inquiry and testimony makes it obvious that epistemic responsibility is rarely simply the affair of an isolated individual, and this has implications even at the level of epistemically responsible belief formation at a specific moment. This is where many epistemologists have understood an individual's capacities of reasoning through the available evidence to be paramount to epistemic responsibility. Yet several testimony theorists have made the point that when I adopt a particular belief (at a particular time) on the basis of trust in another's testimony, the speaker whom I am trusting bears some epistemic responsibility for my belief. As Linda Zagzebski describes it,

> [T]he teller asks for trust and counts on the recipient to trust her. In return, she assumes the responsibility that goes with that trust, taking upon herself the epistemic burden of believing in a conscientious fashion, and doing so not only for herself, but for the recipient.
>
> (Zagzebski 2012, 124)

Similarly, Benjamin McMyler argues that when one adopts a belief on the basis of trust in testimony, the truster bears responsibility for deciding to trust the speaker and form the belief, but if they are met with a challenge to the claim and its warrant, they can rightly defer to the responsibility of the speaker in their having made the claim (McMyler 2011). Here we see a distribution of different responsibilities at work through testimonial belief formation. Our relationships of trust mean that speakers and hearers ultimately share epistemic responsibility for the quality of the particular beliefs that are adopted through trust, with each playing their part.

The distribution of epistemic responsibilities that Zagzebski and McMyler articulate effectively lightens the load of the epistemic responsibilities to be fulfilled by the truster compared with individualistic epistemic analyses of belief formation. The truster's role in the interaction doesn't do all the epistemic work (and isn't expected to), and this is an important feature of this first layer of epistemic responsibility at the level of belief formation to note.

3.3. Implications of Trust: The Presumption of Trustworthiness Within Epistemic Practices

A second layer of epistemic responsibility involves how we engage with others in extended relationships of normative and affective epistemic trust that last over time, range over whole areas of potential beliefs, and become the backdrop for many of our activities of inquiry. As I noted earlier, we inherit positions as participants within many social epistemic practices that involve relationships of trust, complete with the normative expectations that are central to affective forms of trust and that help sustain these relationships.

Within relationships of trust that are already formed or inherited, the need for positive evidence of the trustworthiness of the trustee begins to fade into the background. One simply engages in the habits and practices of these trust relations, optimistically expecting trustees to come through. Epistemic responsibility within these relationships manifests itself instead through other forms of discernment, such as noting when counter-evidence to another's trustworthiness appears through our history of interactions.

That counter-evidence to my trustee's trustworthiness can emerge within relationships of trust, and that trusters can respond to such counter-evidence reminds us that though trust is—as Hardwig puts it— "partially blind," it is not completely blind; we often can and do exercise discernment as we maintain trusting relations with other inquirers. Such discernment demonstrates that we continue to engage our epistemic responsibilities within relationships of trust. Importantly, however, the ways in which we exercise such discernment is often a matter of established social epistemic practices and our positions within them that we inherit. We go about our epistemic business constantly immersed in social exchanges where actors comply with the social norms that serve to establish our epistemic expectations of each other, and in so doing, define our accountability to each other. These are the expectations of affective trust that will result in resentment and betrayal if we are severely let down.

Paul Faulkner argues that in conversation, we operate according to the twin norms of trustworthiness (in the form of truth telling) and trust (in the form of credulity) (Faulkner 2011). They are the core social norms that allow for our cooperation in the exchange of information.

But these core social norms are supplemented by more nuanced norms specific to particular epistemic practices. For example, we have high expectations for the truthfulness of professors when they are asked about their area of expertise. We expect them not only to be honest and not mislead us but also that they be careful in their explanations to ensure accuracy. We tend to expect less truthfulness and care from politicians, knowing that although we can certainly successfully ascertain some information from them, they are likely to spin the facts in their political favor, and we often take this into account as we interpret their communications. We apply different epistemic expectations to others in virtue of the specific social and epistemic roles we understand them to be performing. These expectations help guide us not only in determining the degree of trust we ought to offer them but also in defining the relevant scope of the epistemic goods that we entrust them with and interpreting their specific communications, considering, for example, the degree of accuracy or comprehensiveness we can reasonably expect them to be able to deliver and then determining if those satisfy our particular epistemic needs within a given context. The expectations of each other that are embedded in our social epistemic practices also give us reference points from which we can sometimes discern if a particular player is violating the specific conditions of trustworthiness that underwrite the trust we have placed in them. For example, cases of scientific misconduct offer instances where a researcher has violated the terms of the trust they have been offered by many members of society. Such a researcher has failed to live up to identifiable social expectations in the form of a set of professional standards of epistemic conduct related to their research (such as maintaining high standards for the quality of the data used). When such a failure becomes known, a restriction of our trust is warranted. The failure provides counter-evidence to the trustee's trustworthiness that needs to be considered. Within our epistemic practices, the circulation of those social norms that capture the expectations that are considered *appropriate* to demand of our trustees also makes it reasonable to assume that those in trustee positions are at least to some degree aware of these expectations that they are being asked to be accountable to (something that is necessary if they are to be responsive to my expectations).

My argument, then, is that many of the epistemic trust relationships that we inherit and simply find ourselves in are supported by those social norms in circulation that capture the expectations that are understood to be appropriately placed on trustees. They are specific to particular epistemic practices. When I say these trust relationships are "supported," I mean that the presence of these social norms provides some reason for trusters to operate with an initial presumption that their trustees are trustworthy players within the parameters of the epistemic practice in question. Their presumption of the trustworthiness of the players is an epistemically responsible starting point from their inherited place within a social epistemic practice that has been historically (relatively) successful.

The backdrop of the historical epistemic success of particular epistemic practices, along with their social norms that set out our expectations of each other that help keep the practice on the rails, make it epistemically acceptable (and responsible) to presume the trustworthiness of the participants within the context of those practices. I can responsibly join in these epistemic trust relationships without having to first establish positive reasons for trusting individual trustees who are functioning in specific roles within the practice.

Of course, any particular player may not in fact be trustworthy, and the presumption of their trustworthiness is only an epistemically responsible starting point. Epistemic responsibility will demand that any episodes or cues that raise suspicions about the trustworthiness of one of my trustees be either adequately addressed or incorporated into a reassessment of their trustworthiness and the degree of trust I am willing to offer. Here again, once we are *within* trusting relations, it is a responsiveness to counter-evidence of another's trustworthiness that plays the main role in our exercise of epistemic responsibility, not the search for positive reasons for trusting in the first place.

Elsewhere, I have discussed "responsibly placed epistemic trust" in terms of a preponderance-of-evidence standard for assessing a trustee's trustworthiness for the relevant range of epistemic goods (Grasswick 2014, 2017, 2018). Importantly, given that often there is not a lot of evidence available in trust relationships, this standard of support for trustworthiness can actually be quite a low standard. My argument earlier concerning the presumption of trustworthiness is meant to suggest that for those trust relations that form a part of larger social epistemic practices, the presumption of trustworthiness, supported as it is by the presence of social norms and the historical successes of the practice, offers a preponderance of evidence in favor of the trustworthiness of trustees, at least at first.

Part of the epistemic power of affective relationships of trust is that they can withstand small failings or indiscretions. For example, if I am in a fairly robust relationship of trust and it becomes apparent to me that an occasion has arisen in which my trustee has made an epistemically relevant misstep, this will likely not destroy my relationship of trust. Such mistakes, or even oversights that demonstrate a lack of care for my epistemic needs, are survivable for the trust relationship if they only occur occasionally. This is a good thing for me epistemically in the long run. From the truster's point of view, continuing such a relationship of trust with occasional errors being generated can still be easily understood as within the bounds of epistemic responsibility when epistemic responsibility is understood in the broad sense of being in the service of one's long-term epistemic goals.

However, if the missteps are more serious and common and the truster becomes aware of this pattern, the demands of epistemic responsibility to position oneself well epistemically and be responsive to evidence begins to put pressure on the relationship. Counter-evidence to the trustworthiness of my trustee may begin to build, suggesting that I have not placed myself well within this particular relationship of trust. At this point, one epistemically responsible option will be that I adjust my expectations of the trustee. Perhaps I have been expecting too much of them—more than they are properly positioned to deliver. Or perhaps the pattern of errors suggests a weakness in my trustee's commitment to being responsive to a certain subset of my needs and I need to adjust my expectations accordingly. Such adjustments to the trust relationship are consistent with the exercise of the truster's epistemic responsibility within a range of degrees of seriousness of the patterns of failings, and they are compatible with the maintenance of the trust relationship itself, even as it is adjusted in scope and degree.

Finally, there are also cases where the counter-evidence to my trustee's trustworthiness as an epistemic partner is so strong and persistent that the epistemically responsible course of action would be to withdraw from the trust relationship altogether. These are the same cases where strong senses of betrayal are likely reactions on the part of the truster, which in turn will make it very difficult to rebuild a relationship of trust. Betrayals of trust can be very costly to the social epistemic economy.

3.4. Implications of Trust: Responsibility as Critical Reflection on Our Practices

The two layers of epistemic responsibility that I have described thus far explain ways in which we exercise epistemic responsibility *within* social epistemic practices involving epistemic trust. But we must also recall that the broad sense of epistemic responsibility concerns our overall conduct as inquirers and how well that conduct serves our epistemic goals of providing us with appropriately prioritized epistemic goods such as forms of knowledge and understanding that help us survive and flourish. Should we discover that some of our epistemic practices are regularly failing to serve our epistemic goals well, conducting oneself in an epistemically responsible manner may require resisting current epistemic practices and the trust relations embedded in them.

Because of this, I suggest that a full account of epistemic responsibility needs to include a layer of critical reflection with respect to the relative strengths and weaknesses of our epistemic practices themselves, occasionally stepping back and assessing whose epistemic goals are being met and how well. Such critical reflection is too onerous to be expected to be engaged often. But nevertheless, critical reflection on our socially embedded epistemic practices has an appropriate place in a full account of epistemic responsibility, given that our epistemic practices are only as good as they manage to serve our epistemic goals. As Lorraine Code writes, "[t]hinking individuals have a responsibility to monitor and watch over shifts in, changes in, and efforts to preserve good intellectual practice" (Code 1987, 245). Our commitments to the norms of our epistemic practices, including those that affect our trust relations, only reach as far as we are confident that they are helping us in pursuit of our epistemic goals, and full epistemic responsibility demands occasional consideration as to whether our epistemic practices are satisfactory. Accordingly, when we see epistemic practices involving trust failing in such ways, a commitment to epistemic responsibility and our epistemic goals must push us in the direction of challenging these practices and finding ways to make them more reliable and more responsive to our needs, in part by building healthier and more robust relations of epistemic trust.

The problem, of course, is that unless our epistemic practices are failing tremendously, their failures will not be all that easy to discover. They will more likely involve pockets of failure, and such pockets are likely to affect some knowers more than others and be more likely to be noticed by those who are affected. This means that one's epistemic responsibility to occasionally reflect on the strengths and weaknesses of our epistemic practices will, in practice, include paying attention to the complaints of others who might be more directly affected by these failures.

An example of a problematic feature of an epistemic practice directly involving the structure of trust relations is that of testimonial injustice. Testimonial injustices refer to cases in which members of nondominant groups suffer deflated credibility assignments due to identity prejudices—such as racial and gender biases—that are widely internalized in society. These are cases where members of these nondominant groups who should be viewed as trustworthy knowers are inappropriately (and often systemically) denied their due credibility, resulting in a mismatch between the degree of trust assigned and actual trustworthiness, signally unhealthy trust relations that are epistemically problematic. While unhealthy trust relations epistemically harm all involved (in that epistemic goods cannot be successfully shared), those who are denied proper credibility suffer an additional harm, in that without this credibility, it is difficult for them to get epistemic uptake on those issues that have particular epistemic significance for them and that they are trying (through their testimony) to bring to the table. Testimonial injustices both affect the capacity of members of marginalized groups to be full participants in society's epistemic pursuits and have their epistemic needs addressed and also make our epistemic practices less reliable and, hence, less trustworthy for everyone involved.[16] Because of the direct effect on those who suffer the testimonial injustice, however, it is at least more likely (though not guaranteed) that the injustice will be noticed by those who are subjected to this form of injustice rather than others.

4. Conclusion

We know most of what we do about the world and ourselves because of the epistemic contributions of others and the social organization of our communities of inquiry. Given this reality, it is clear that no individual is fully responsible for their epistemic successes, even though they participate in those successes in many ways. My discussion of epistemic trust in relation to epistemic responsibility has sought to bring some clarity to the different ways in which we employ epistemic trust and the tools we have available as epistemically responsible agents when we engage in social practices involving trust. A key feature of my analysis has been its attempt to set the questions of our epistemic responsibilities and epistemic trust relationships within an epistemic framework that understands our epistemic choices and evaluations as made within the contexts of our practical needs, prioritizing some epistemic goods over others on the basis of how we can know and live well.

I began this chapter by setting out a normative and affective conception of epistemic trust, arguing that this is a much-needed tool in coming to understand both the value and functioning of ongoing relationships of epistemic trust. Throughout the chapter I continually referred back to this conception and how its affective and normative dimensions play out in epistemic trust relations, including the fact that the relevant expectations placed on trustees in epistemic trust often extend beyond what might be considered the purely epistemic. My discussion of trust in testimony and trust in inquiry demonstrated both important distinctions and connections between them and revealed that there are, in fact, many manifestations of these forms of epistemic trust that need to be understood. In the case of epistemic responsibility, I opted to work with the broad conception that considers our overall conduct of inquiry and understands part of this work of inquiry as *positioning ourselves well* to be able to access epistemic goods, something that can be done through healthy trust relationships. I was then able to distinguish how epistemic responsibility is employed during the formation of a trust relationship as one looks for indicators of trustworthiness, from how it plays a different role—now responding to counter-evidence—once we are already in relationships of trust and have already taken up an attitude of trust. Finally, I considered three layers of epistemic responsibility—at the level of belief formation, at the level of determining trust in another within a social practice involving trust relations, and at the level of critiquing the adequacy of the norms and social practices of epistemic trust that we have available. This three-tiered account is able to reconcile the idea of individual epistemic responsibility with the significant and widespread role epistemic trust relations play in our deeply social epistemic lives.

Notes

1. This first component builds on Annette Baier's claims that in trusting another, one expects the trustee's goodwill, or at least their lack of ill will (Baier 1986, 235). Jones characterizes this more clearly as an attitude of optimism towards their goodwill.
2. One exception to this is Faulkner's conceptualization of trust relations as fundamentally two-person relations between person A and person B, without the good C being specified. He adopts this position in his attempt to solve the "problem of trust" by finding intrinsic rather than merely instrumental value in trust and trustworthiness. He argues that a three-place structure formulates the trust relation as merely having instrumental value in order to obtain the good that is entrusted (Faulkner 2017). Even if one accepts his arguments from the point of view of grounding trust relations, it is still important to recognize that when we identify existing trust relations in practice, they are bound in scope, depending on the goods entrusted.
3. One can accept that there is a variety of epistemic goods without necessarily accepting all that I have mentioned here. For this chapter, I set aside debates about how best to conceive of epistemic goals (such as the discussions and debates concerning understanding versus knowledge).
4. Some trust theorists would take issue with this example because it introduces questions of whether the dominant model of interpersonal trust on which the theory of affective trust is based can be extended to groups and communities and to those with whom I do not have a personal relationship. For now I shall just state that I think that the affective theory of epistemic trust can be extended to communities and organized groups, though I do not have the space to take up these issues here. For an example of an attempt to avoid some of the problems of extending this sense of trust to groups by stressing how much mileage one can get out of reliance on groups, see (Hawley 2017).
5. Some might view this as a controversial example, since there are certainly some segments of the public who do not trust government intelligence agencies with this line of inquiry or the act of maintaining the classified status of what they find. There are many reasons people might distrust government authorities producing knowledge that is kept secret, including histories of the abuse of such powers. But regardless, this case serves as a clear example of the kind of situation where there is, at least in practice, a separation of trust in inquiry and trust in the transference of the inquiry's results (though I complicate this relationship in the next section).
6. Civic duties are moral and political responsibilities, not epistemic responsibilities per se, though they may well have epistemic dimensions. One might hold the position that as a citizen I have a moral responsibility to engage in some level of investigation into the positions of electoral candidates; but if part of that moral responsibility involves undertaking inquiry myself, then I have an epistemic responsibility that is derived from this moral responsibility.
7. See (Grasswick 2010, 2011) for a discussion of knowledge-sharing norms as part of epistemic practices.
8. For an example of one who explicitly links justification with epistemic responsibility see (Bonjour 1978).
9. The literature on inductive risk is pertinent here. See for example (H. Douglas 2000; H. E. Douglas 2009; Elliott and Richards 2017).

10. I have implied nothing in this example regarding whether or not there are other targets of my distrust here (for example, whether or not I trust my partner to maintain an appropriate emotional distance from their ex). Other forms of distrust may or may not be involved, but my actions of checking up on their movements and communications and considering the consistency of their testimony with what I find out is all that I'm interested in with this example.

11. Recognizing degrees of trust will, of course, mean that there will be degrees of this commitment to refrain from further evidence gathering.

12. On the other hand, the situation is quite different if I accidentally fall upon some evidence that my significant other had in fact visited their ex. In this case, I would not have violated the expectations of the trust relationship, though this newfound evidence should not be ignored, but instead should contribute to my reassessment of the trustworthiness of my significant other.

13. I exclude from the idea of "healthy trust relations" extreme circumstances of social practices that consist of people offering no trust or distrust, coupled with poor trustworthiness of potential trustees. Though the trusters' lack of trust may be in balance with the trustees' lack of trustworthiness, it would be a mistake to consider these relationships of trust at all. Both trust and trustworthiness are absent. In a social world where both lack of trust and lack of trustworthiness are common, our epistemic lives would be extremely impoverished.

14. McMyler argues that the fact that we can decide to trust on the basis of reasons for another's trustworthiness does not amount to a voluntarism about trust. Trust is akin to belief in that although we cannot trust (or believe) purely through will, we can and do decide to trust (or believe) on the basis of available reasons.

15. Cases of "hopeful trust" and "therapeutic trust" will also sometimes play a role in the formation of trust relations without depending on finding evidence of trustworthiness. Hopeful or therapeutic trust can be placed as a way of fostering a healthy trust relationship by creating an environment of trust that the trustee may respond to positively by becoming trustworthy, or more trustworthy than they have been (Frost-Arnold 2014; McLeod 2015).

16. For a sampling of the extensive literature on epistemic injustice see (Fricker 2007; Pohlhaus 2014, 2012; Medina 2013; Kidd, Medina, and Pohlhaus 2017; Dotson 2012, 2014; Origgi 2012).

References

Anderson, Elizabeth. 1995. "Knowledge, Human Interests, and Objectivity in Feminist Epistemology." *Philosophical Topics* 23(2): 27–58.

Baier, Annette. 1986. "Trust and Antitrust." *Ethics* 96(2): 231–60.

Bonjour, Lawrence. 1978. "Can Empirical Knowledge Have a Foundation?" *American Philosophical Quarterly* 15(1): 1–13.

Code, Lorraine. 1987. *Epistemic Responsibility*. Hanover, NH: Published for Brown University Press by University Press of New England.

———. 1991. *What Can She Know?: Feminist Theory and the Construction of Knowledge*. Ithaca, NY: Cornell University Press.

Daukas, Nancy. 2006. "Epistemic Trust and Social Location." *Episteme* 3(1–2): 109–24.

Dotson, Kristie. 2012. "A Cautionary Tale: On Limiting Epistemic Oppression." *Frontiers: A Journal of Women Studies* 33(1): 24–47.

———. 2014. "Conceptualizing Epistemic Oppression." *Social Epistemology* 28(2): 115–38.

Douglas, Heather E. 2000. "Inductive Risk and Values in Science." *Philosophy of Science* 67(4): 559–79.

———. 2009. *Science, Policy, and the Value-Free Ideal*. Pittsburgh, PA: University of Pittsburgh Press.

Elgin, Catherine Z. 2014. "The Commonwealth of Epistemic Ends." In *The Ethics of Belief: Individual and Social*, edited by Jonathan Matheson and Rico Vitz, 1st ed., 244–60. New York: Oxford University Press.

Elliott, Kevin Christopher, and Ted Richards, eds. 2017. *Exploring Inductive Risk: Case Studies of Values in Science*. New York: Oxford University Press.

Faulkner, Paul. 2011. *Knowledge on Trust*. Oxford and New York: Oxford University Press.

———. 2017. "The Problem of Trust." In *The Philosophy of Trust*, edited by Paul Faulkner and Thomas Simpson, 109–28. New York: Oxford University Press.

Fricker, Miranda. 2007. *Epistemic Injustice: Power and the Ethics of Knowing*. Oxford and New York: Oxford University Press.

Frost-Arnold, Karen. 2014. "The Cognitive Attitude of Rational Trust." *Synthese* 191(9): 1957–74.

Grasswick, Heidi. 2010. "Scientific and Lay Communities: Earning Epistemic Trust through Knowledge Sharing." *Synthese* Online First, September 9.

———. 2011. "Liberatory Epistemology and the Sharing of Knowledge: Querying the Norms." In *Feminist Epistemology and Philosophy of Science*, edited by Heidi Grasswick, 241–62. Springer Netherlands.

———. 2014. "Climate Change Science and Responsible Trust: A Situated Approach." *Hypatia* 29(3): 541–57.

———. 2017. "Epistemic Injustice in Science." In *The Routledge Handbook of Epistemic Injustice*, edited by Ian James Kidd, José Medina, and Gaile Pohlhaus, 313–23. London and New York: Routledge.

———. 2018. "Understanding Epistemic Trust Injustices and Their Harms." *Royal Institute of Philosophy Supplements* 84.

Hardwig, John. 1991. "The Role of Trust in Knowledge." *The Journal of Philosophy* 88(12): 693–708.

Hawley, Katherine. 2014. "Partiality and Prejudice in Trusting." *Synthese* 191(9): 2029–47.

———. 2017. "Trustworthy Groups and Organizations." In *The Philosophy of Trust*, edited by Paul Faulkner and Thomas Simpson, 230–50. New York: Oxford University Press.

Hookway, Christopher. 2006. "Epistemology and Inquiry: The Primacy of Practice." In *Epistemology Futures*, edited by Stephen Hetherington, 95–110. Oxford: Oxford University Press.

Jones, Karen. 1996. "Trust as an Affective Attitude." *Ethics* 107(1): 4–25.

———. 2002. "The Politics of Credibility." In *A Mind of One's Own: Feminist Essays on Reason and Objectivity*, edited by Louise Antony and Charlotte Witt, 154–76. Boulder, CO: Westview Press.

Kawall, Jason. 2002. "Other—Regarding Epistemic Virtues." *Ratio* 15(3): 257–75.

Kidd, Ian James, José Medina, and Gaile Pohlhaus, eds. 2017. *The Routledge Handbook of Epistemic Injustice*. Routledge Handbooks in Philosophy. London and New York: Routledge, Taylor & Francis Group.

Kitcher, Philip. 2001. *Science, Truth, and Democracy*. Oxford Studies in Philosophy of Science. New York: Oxford University Press.

McLeod, Carolyn. 2015. "Trust." In *The Stanford Encyclopedia of Philosophy*, edited by Edward N. Zalta, Fall 2015. http://plato.stanford.edu/archives/fall2015/entriesrust/.

McMyler, Benjamin. 2011. *Testimony, Trust, and Authority*. Oxford and New York: Oxford University Press.

———. 2017. "Deciding to Trust." In *The Philosophy of Trust*, edited by Paul Faulkner and Thomas Simpson, 161–76. New York: Oxford University Press.

Medina, José. 2013. *The Epistemology of Resistance: Gender and Racial Oppression, Epistemic Injustice, and Resistant Imaginations*. Studies in Feminist Philosophy. Oxford and New York: Oxford University Press.

Origgi, Gloria. 2012. "Epistemic Injustice and Epistemic Trust." *Social Epistemology* 26(2): 221–35.

Pohlhaus, Gaile. 2012. "Relational Knowing and Epistemic Injustice: Toward a Theory of *Willful Hermeneutical Ignorance*." *Hypatia* 27(4): 715–35.

———. 2014. "Discerning the Primary Epistemic Harm in Cases of Testimonial Injustice." *Social Epistemology* 28(2): 99–114.

Schmitt, Frederick F. 2010. "The Assurance View of Testimony." In *Social Epistemology*, edited by Adrian Haddock, Alan Millar, and Duncan Pritchard, 216–42. Oxford and New York: Oxford University Press.

Townley, Cynthia. 2011. *A Defense of Ignorance: Its Value for Knowers and Roles in Feminist and Social Epistemologies*. Lanham, MD: Lexington Books.

Zagzebski, Linda Trinkaus. 2012. *Epistemic Authority: A Theory of Trust, Authority, and Autonomy in Belief*. New York: Oxford University Press.

8 Proper Epistemic Trust as a Responsibilist Virtue

Benjamin McCraw

This chapter defends an account of epistemically proper trust modeled along virtue-theoretic lines. Specifically, I shall argue that epistemic trust (ET), when well placed, is an epistemic virtue. Much work has been done on the nature of intellectual trust and, given its role in testimony, its epistemic status. Yet virtue epistemologists haven't given a systematic, distinctively virtue-theoretic treatment of ET.[1] Doing so will form a robust intersection between virtue epistemology and social epistemology. This chapter, then, joins these two fields—a benefit given the rise of interest in both social and virtue-theoretic approaches to epistemology. A trust-based social, virtue epistemology illuminates both approaches by showing how they can interconnect and provides some tools to address issues arising within both fields. My position on proper ET thus allows one to socialize virtue epistemology by offering a robust virtue-theoretic maneuver within social epistemology.

Let me make an important proviso at the outset. I assume here and throughout this chapter a responsibilist version of epistemic virtue. Virtue responsibilism construes virtues as traits of character, whereas virtue reliabilism—the main counterpoint in virtue epistemology—takes a virtue to be any general (truth-conducive) epistemic disposition, ability, or competence.[2] By assuming virtue responsibilism (rather than reliabilism), I'm taking for granted that virtues have a psychologically robust structure, as we'll see in Section 2. I don't intend this proviso as grounds to favor responsibilism over reliabilism, and no claim in what follows will offer such grounds. However, I endorse responsibilism overall and for independent reasons,[3] and I assume it here primarily to make the following discussion of a manageable length and specificity.[4]

Section 1 lays out the general analysis of ET upon which I model the arguments in subsequent sections. One pair of arguments for proper ET as a virtue occurs in Section 2. They are based on the structure of responsibilist virtue(s). In Section 3, I give another pair of arguments showing that proper ET promotes the epistemic good life and that it forms part of the motivational structure of the paradigmatic person of virtue. In Section 4, I suggest some implications of my claim that PET is a virtue. I end by addressing peer disagreement, testimony, and low-grade knowledge, showing how the virtue of (proper) ET provides attractive and philosophically fruitful positions regarding these topics.

1. Epistemic Trust in General

My discussion of ET in this section will be brief, because I offer a full defense of the following account in my (2015). It's crucial to the discussion at this stage to note that I'm offering an analysis of a truster's placing ET *in* some trustee (emphasis on the "in"). My account does not attempt to explicate something we might instead call ET *that p*. Taking seriously the trust-in *analysandum*, we need something that is not (exhaustively) equivalent to a belief about the trustee. I'm happy to admit that (epistemic) trust-*that p* is some kind of belief that some trustee is reliable (vis-à-vis *p*), but that attitude is not the target of the model I defend here. If we take the trust-in/-that distinction seriously, we have good reason to accept the only partially doxastic view of epistemic trust that I will defend later. Moving from this quick proviso, I offer only a quick sketch of ET on which I build a case in the remainder for well-placed ET as an epistemic virtue. My last comment is crucial: nowhere do I defend ET *simpliciter* as a virtue (indeed, I do not think it is one). Instead, I argue that *proper* ET (PET) is an epistemic virtue. Unlike many traditional virtues (like courage), we have no distinct term or name for properly placed ET,[5] but *that* is the target of my arguments.[6] This section, however, concerns only what it means to place ET in someone—not what it means to do so *well*. That further discussion will occupy the remaining sections.

Any account of PET must begin with some notion of ET in general. Let's begin with the sketch and develop it in what follows. In my view, hearer *H* places ET in speaker *S* that p[7] iff:

(1) *H* takes *S* to communicate that p;
(2) *H* believes that p;[8]
(3) *H* depends upon *S*'s (perceived) communication for *H*'s belief that p; and
(4) *H* sees S as epistemically authoritative with respect to p.[9]

(1) and (2) express the *epistemic* elements of ET, and (3) and (4) pick out the *trust-based* aspects. Because trust typically doesn't obtain *ex nihilo* and always involves some trust*ee* (even in cases of self-trust), we must include some ground on which trust is extended or given: I can't trust you for some belief if I don't take you to communicate its content (to me). This point motivates (1): by trusting in some *S* for one's belief that p, *H* takes *S* to communicate (the content of) p.[10] I include (2) to ensure that ET is *epistemic*—that is, that we can use it to explain directly the formation, maintenance, revision, etc., of beliefs. For the *trust*-based element

of ET captured in (3) and (4), I extend Annette Baier's (1995) influential model of *moral* trust. For her, trusting S requires that one rely/depend on S's goodwill—mere reliance is insufficient for genuine trust. (3) and (4) work to explicate a Baier-ian analysis of *epistemic* trust. Epistemologically speaking, part of what H does by relying on S (for H's belief that p) is that H takes herself to be in a worse epistemic position with respect to p than S, so that it's S's (perceived) communication that explains why H believes that p. Hence, we get (3).

Yet how does Baier's account of trust as relying on another's goodwill yield (4)? Assuming that only agents can have goodwill and that *epistemic* trust need not require an assessment of the *moral* character of the trustee, we shouldn't take ET to involve ascribing goodwill to the trustee. Rather, if ET parallels something like moral trust but is not identical to it,[11] as I suggest here, we need something like a functional parallel or analogy to Baierian goodwill ascriptions. To see how this parallel can work, let's see why Baier requires such ascriptions in the first place.

She makes ascribing goodwill necessary for trust so as to distinguish it from mere reliance or dependence. Relying on S is consistent with actively *dis*believing that S will come through for the truster.[12] For Baier, trust requires some kind of positive assessment of the trustee (more than mere reliance on her), and what's more, given that Baier construes trust as a moral relation, this assessment must attach to the trustee *qua* person or agent. What does this positive assessment involve for Baier? As she describes it, when one "depends on another's good will" (i.e., trusts), then one "leaves others an opportunity to harm one when one trusts, and also shows one's *confidence* that they will not take it" (1995, 99; emphasis mine). Reading the "leaves others an opportunity to harm" as the "relying" element of trust, discussed in (3), I suggest her "confidence" is the key to the positive assessment of the trustee included in trust. For her purposes in clarifying the *moral* notion of trust, reading 'confidence' as something like ascribing goodwill makes sense. Yet we are interested in the *epistemic* dimensions of trust and giving it an *epistemic* model.

Recognizing Baier's confidence as central to trust enables us to give a functional parallel in epistemology—one that doesn't require goodwill ascriptions or assessing the moral character of the trustee. Part of the role of confidence in Baier's analysis of (moral) trust, and what I attempt to capture in ET via epistemic confidence, is seeing the object of one's confidence under a positive aspect. Because I take moral confidence and epistemic confidence to be distinct, the nature of that aspect will differ; but some kind of positive aspect will be central to both accounts. What does it mean to be epistemically confident in S *qua* epistemic agent? Here's my suggestion: epistemic confidence in a person is seeing her as an epistemic authority. In being (epistemically) confident *in* S, one sees S, and thus her pronouncements, under the positive aspect of being authoritative. Accordingly, we can motivate (4) in the account earlier.

Some brief remarks on confidence and 'seeing as authoritative' are needed. Crucially, I don't parse confidence as equivalent to a propositional attitude (i.e. as equivalent to belief that S is competent, trustworthy, authoritative, or what have you). This is because, as mentioned earlier, ET *in* S has S as the direct object of ET (rather than *propositions* about S). Keeping this point in mind explains how we can read confidence without reducing it to a belief about the trustee. Taking epistemic confidence in S as "seeing S as authoritative/well-placed" as partially constituted by a nonpropositional attitude distinguishes between having ET *in* S and having ET *that what S says is true*. Rejecting the idea that epistemic confidence is just a propositional attitude (the belief that S is reliable) will also make it possible to include an affective (noncognitive) component in ET *via* confidence (e.g. loyalty, commitment, optimism, etc.). Unlike my (2015), this chapter doesn't analyze epistemic confidence as necessarily having an affective element, but I simply want to note that the present account of confidence is compatible with an affective aspect.[13]

We may contrast my account with what Paul Faulkner (2007) calls "predictive trust:" a model on which trust is reliance plus a predictive expectation that the trustee will deliver. Because predictive trust is cashed out as the *belief that* the trustee will act in certain ways, this account offers an analysis of what I call trust-*that p*. My model of ET and such predictive trust thus are distinct and dissimilar, and this is due to the fact that these models work to explicate different kinds of concepts or attitudes. My view of ET (in S) is simply out to perform a different task than predictive trust (that what S says is true). As I try to keep in mind, I aim to analyze ET in some S, whereas wholly propositional (doxastic) predictive trust has a natural extension in ET *that* some p. These different attitudes, I have suggested, call for different analyses. And the task here is to analyze the former rather than the latter. ET in S is thus more psychologically robust in the sense of involving more or other types of attitudes, than ET that p. If the *analysandum* is of the form H has ET in S, then there must be some constitutive element of ET-in that differs from any purely propositional attitude directed only towards some p. In my view, confidence will make this attitude (of ET *in* S) possible.

Let me highlight one important structural point about the analysis of ET I sketch earlier before moving on to arguments for PET as a virtue. Nothing in the account I provide entails that H or S must be distinct individuals. That is, my proposed model of ET is neutral with respect to self- or other-ET. It's possible for one to display all of the conditions for ET I detail—belief, (perceived) communication, dependence, and confidence—to oneself (just as one could to others).[14] Hence, ET can be utilized to define both other- and self-ET.

At this point, I need to say more about the *object* of self-ET. Should we take it to be oneself (*qua* agent) or one's faculties (in general)?[15] We may leave this question open. Many (e.g. Holton 1994) conceptualize trust as an essentially interpersonal relation, saving something like mere reliance for nonpersonal objects. Suppose, though, that one takes the sort of approach in epistemology. If epistemic trust were understood this way, then such a move would rule out self-trust in one's *faculties*. Similarly, it would be false—in such a view—to say that I can place ET in, say, my GPS to get me to some unfamiliar location. I don't follow these strict lines: obviously ET can hold between persons, but it can be extended to nonpersons as well. Suppose I need directions. I can place ET in another person to form beliefs as to the correct route. But what of my GPS? A view that insists that trust can only be extended to persons cannot construe my cognitive relation to my GPS as (epistemic) *trust*. However, it seems tremendously counterintuitive to reject that one can epistemically trust one's GPS. It seems clear, to me anyway, that if one believes that X is the best route to Y on the basis of one's GPS, this is a plausible expression of one's ET in the GPS. My view can easily accommodate this (to my lights, commonsensical) usage.[16] My conditions (1)–(3) are easy enough to apply here. As for (4), I can certainly see my GPS as "epistemically well-placed" or "authoritative," and this is all that we need.[17]

One final matter must be clarified: What *is* the relation between epistemic confidence in S and one's beliefs about S? Such confidence often or typically issues in beliefs, I take it, about the object seen as authoritative or statements we take that object to communicate (to us). Yet I'm arguing that (A) confidence or seeing-as-authoritative is not equivalent to belief that the source is reliable and (B) confidence doesn't *entail* such belief. I've laid out my reasons for (A) earlier at length, but (B) needs some work. One quick reason to see why confidence doesn't entail belief is the possibility of defeaters. H may see S as authoritative, but H may also have some good, albeit rare and unexpected, reason to think that S is wrong in some particular instance. What seems reasonable in light of this possibility is to make a weaker claim: epistemic confidence need not entail belief, but being confident in S typically or paradigmatically involves a disposition to believe various propositions (about S or S's pronouncements).[18] I recognize that epistemic confidence is crucial for guiding our beliefs, but, as I suggest, we shouldn't go so far as to say that such confidence *is* a belief or *entails* beliefs. Using a disposition to believe strikes exactly the right kind of balance needed.

A similar story to the one earlier regarding ET in my GPS holds for ET in one's faculties. I may lack (extant) propositional belief that my faculties are reliable, yet (insofar as I use them, fully integrating them into my life) I see them as epistemically worthy. This attitude is distinct from the belief <my senses are reliable>, grounding legitimate *trust in* my cognitive faculties.[19] So, even if self-ET does target one's faculties, my account still classifies such trust in the same way as interpersonal other-ET. Because I aim to defend PET as a virtue, it should be able to tell us when ET is displayed well to both others and ourselves, that is, as an account of proper other- *and* self-trust. Now I can turn to arguments for that claim in the next sections.

2. Proper Epistemic Trust and the Structure of Responsibilist Virtues

In this section, I focus on how virtue responsibilism analyzes the nature or structure of virtue, showing that PET satisfies the theoretical conditions necessary and sufficient for epistemic virtue. Take Linda Zagzebski's (1996) influential responsibilism. Given that Zagzebski's account makes rigorous conceptual demands for any putative trait to be a virtue (as we shall soon see), if PET satisfies it, it would very likely satisfy laxer or less restrictive versions of character virtues. Hence, if PET is a Zagzebskian (responsibilist) virtue, it very likely will be a responsibilist virtue *simpliciter*. In her definition, a virtue is identical to the following: a

(a)   "deep and
(b)   enduring
(c)   acquired excellence of a person,
(d)   involving a characteristic motivation
(e)   to produce a certain desired end and
(f)   reliable success in bring about that end." (137)[20]

Taking each condition (a)–(f), we shall see that PET satisfies them all. First, let us address (a).

I follow Zagzebski in taking "deep" to mean that if a trait is a virtue, it must be characteristic of that agent or, alternatively, part of that agent's identity *qua* that particular person (1996, 136). That is, one's courage makes one a distinctive sort of agent (namely, *courageous*). Now, in this conception of what it means for a trait to be 'deep,' can PET satisfy this criterion? It seems to me that the answer is an obvious 'yes.' We may all display *some* level of ET *some* of the time, but there are people whose trust is part of what makes them the (intellectual) agent they are; moreover, some are characteristically disposed to extend ET *well*. For instance, one may display appropriate, dispositional ET in climate scientists for beliefs in climate change or medical researchers for the safe efficacy of vaccines even when one couldn't possibly possess (much less understand) the evidence backing up these views. These agents, given certain contexts, are (characteristically) trusting. This parallels the virtue of courage: in certain contexts, the agent with the virtue is (characteristically) courageous. This seems good reason to consider well-placed trust—including the *epistemic* variant thereof—as a characteristic trait of certain persons (in certain situations). PET thus has no problem with (a). And if we are willing to accept that PET can be 'deep,' then we should accept that it can be enduring as well. If PET is part of Jones's character, then if Jones endures *qua* Jones, Jones's PET may (will?) endure as well. Put differently: virtues are elements of character distinctive of the sort of agent one is. So, if PET is (or can be) characteristic of Jones (insofar as Jones is the sort of agent she is), then Jones's PET will endure as long as Jones is *Jones*. So, insofar as PET satisfies (a), it satisfies (b) as well.

PET must also be an "acquired excellence of a person" if it is to satisfy (c). How should we understand the acquisition element of (c)? A few comments should help. First, recall that *proper* ET rather than ET *simpliciter* is the target. Perhaps ET (in general) is a kind of unacquired Reidean default trusting disposition, but PET would be the perfection of that disposition. So, I suspect that anyone thinking of trust as a congenital, natural faculty or disposition will likely be thinking of ET rather than PET. And because I'm arguing that PET—not ET in general—satisfies (c), my view is not threatened if ET is faculty-like.

Second, we have good reason to think (c) is true of PET: empirical studies suggest that PET is learned, acquired, and developed. There is evidence that we track the reliability of others as children and shape our epistemic responses accordingly, with the effect that we filter out for more reliable speakers in whom we place ET. Melissa Koenig and others with her have conducted experiments with infants concerning how they deal with reliable and unreliable sources.[21] They determine that children do not have a default "trust mode" out of which they operate indiscriminately, showing that even small children display what Koenig and Harris (2007) call "selective trust" in others that focuses upon the reliability or trustworthiness of a speaker via his or her utterances. They claim that "developmental evidence demonstrates that a generalized credulity is not true of young children, even infants" (2007, 265). Selective trust, to use Koenig's term, shows that PET is not a faculty that we either possess or lack or something in which we engage or do not engage. Instead, we perfect and develop PET over time—meaning that PET is not like an inborn, congenital faculty even for infants. Rather, *if* we are to associate it with talk of faculties, the only way (given Koenig's research) would be to see it as the *perfection* or *development* of a certain faculty or disposition as opposed to a faculty itself. That is, even if ET is faculty-like, PET is not; keeping them distinct is crucial to my claim that only the latter counts as a virtue. Thus, PET would not be a natural disposition or faculty—it is, at most, the acquired excellence of that disposition, making PET seem much closer to something like a virtue *qua* acquired excellence than a faculty. Yet even if we have reason to think that PET is not faculty-like, we need more to show that it is acquired or perfected.

Koenig also finds evidence that children are "capable of evaluating both positive reasons for accepting as well as negative reasons for rejecting a particular speaker's claim" (2010, 254). These results suggest that young children are fairly sophisticated with respect to PET, but their sophistication has limits. To see this, we find Koenig and Harris claiming that "very young children, even toddlers, are capable of selective trust *but may not be as competent or efficient as older children*" (2007, 273; emphasis added). This means that children can (and frequently do) progress and perfect PET over time, suggesting that it is a trait capable of acquired development. Koenig's (et al.) experiments give us the evidence to make two important claims here: (A) PET is not an inborn faculty we have as part of our natural endowment from birth and (B) ET requires development over time to function properly as PET. (A) and (B) imply that PET satisfies (c). PET may *appear* to be something that we are just born using, but rather, PET is a habituated trait that we must perfect over time and experience to use properly. Granted, this time and experience occur so early in our cognitive life that we do not give it much reflection, but I suspect this is due to the importance of PET in cognition more widely.

Other sorts of studies give us similar grounds to accept the 'acquisition and development' thesis central to (c) outside of studies on small children. Susann Wagenknecht (2016) reports a series of surveys for scientific researchers regarding their ET in colleagues. One important result is that one's ET in collaborators "is over time, specific, and adapted to the experiences of collaboration" (136). Her work on ET in scientific practice supports my contention that PET is developed even in adults.

Let us move on to (d)—how can we construe the characteristic motivation of PET? Zagzebski defines a 'motive' as "an emotion or feeling that initiates and directs action towards an end" and understands a 'motivation' as "a persistent tendency to be moved by a motive of a certain kind" (1996, 131–32).[22] The definitions of 'motive' and 'motivation,' then, require an account of emotion. For Zagzebski, an emotion has both an affective (i.e., feeling-based) aspect and a cognitive aspect. The affective side of emotions seems obvious: emotions are states with distinctive *feelings* like anger, joy, or disgust. But an emotion "is distinguished from moods or sensations in that it has an intentional object. That is, an emotion is a state of feeling a certain away *about* something or *at* something or *toward* something" (2004, 60). Emotions are like perceptions insofar as they are ways of 'seeing' something as having a particular quality, and they are like feelings insofar as the quality that we 'see' is affective. In short, an "[e]motion is a type of value perception that feels a characteristic way" (2004, 69). Thus, we need to ask: Does PET have this sort of emotional basis? Our definition of ET from Section 1 points the route to a positive answer.

ET requires that the trust*er* see the trust*ee* as epistemically well placed (authoritative)—this is how I cash out the epistemological import of confidence. By glossing confidence as a way of *seeing* someone as (epistemically) authoritative, ET fits neatly into the Zagzebskian model of a motivation. As we saw earlier, for Zagzebski, an emotion is a way of affectively 'seeing' the world. ET, accordingly, is a way that we 'see' others and ourselves as worthy of our confidence—forming the characteristic motivation for PET. That is, we are motivated to depend upon others and ourselves for our beliefs, and when we extend ET to them, we *see* them as (epistemically) authoritative. To do so *well* gives PET a characteristic motivation and, accordingly, it satisfies (d).

And, next, we have (e): a virtue must work towards some desired end. We can consider two different kinds of ends here. Consider a moral virtue as an analogy: benevolence has a twofold end structure. Following classical virtue ethics, we might think of benevolence as contributing to or partially constitutive of that agent's *eudaimonia*. But we can also construe benevolence more specifically: where the agent has the particular end of promoting the welfare of the *specific* target of one's benevolence. What we see, for any virtue, is a dual-end structure—there's an overall end (e.g. *eudaimonia*, or the good life) that is identical for every virtue of the same type, but there's also a specific aim or target (e.g. benevolence aims at helping some specific person in a particular way), which will differ for each distinct virtue.[23]

PET has the same twofold structure of ends. First, we can think of the *general* end of PET as some putative epistemic good, like true belief, knowledge, wisdom, understanding, rational belief, and so on. As we saw earlier, our ET is an extension of our confident reliance on the trustee for something we lack. If I trust in you to tell me the correct time, I see you as worthy of my confidence and dependence for a truth I lack—namely the time. My relying confidence is a way of coming to know something when I cannot directly obtain knowledge of it myself. Thus, we can see that PET has the same (general) end of *any* epistemic virtue. Depending on your epistemic value system, this end could be truth, knowledge, "cognitive contact with reality" (Zagzebski 1996), understanding, or whatever your preferred theory takes to be the fundamental epistemic good. But ET has a (distinctive) aim that is specific to it as well. When I trust you for the time, I am not merely aiming at knowledge in general, but, insofar as I am trusting, part of my aim is to place the proper kind or amount of reliance on someone trustworthy and display a level of confidence appropriate to the situation in which I find myself.[24] How I rely and how much confidence I have will vary according to what is appropriate for the circumstance. Asking a stranger for the time in a (literally) 'life or death' context would alter the epistemic standard(s) I should satisfy to display PET in the stranger (i.e. I should be in a better epistemic position to assess her and her words than otherwise). The way, the amount or kind of confidence I display must be sensitive to a range of crucial contextual features. To trust *well* means that I don't just aim at knowing something but also that my aim is to display the *right* amount/kind of dependence with the *appropriate* attitude of confidence,[25] marking out the end specific to PET. Accordingly, PET satisfies condition (e).

Finally, is PET reliable? Of course, PET isn't reliable without riders about its circumstances. But I seriously doubt *any* belief forming practice would be reliable without similar provisos. When we think about the reliability of sense perception or inductive reasoning, our best bet is to reflect on our own perceptual or induction-based beliefs and consider their record.[26] Generally, we think they are reliable because otherwise we would have to face a deep skepticism about the external world. I suggest the same procedure and result here. If we think about our reliance on and ET in others, do we think that trust generally leads us to the truth? I think the answer (keeping in mind the "generally") must be "yes" for the same anti-skeptical reasons as for sense perception, induction, and the like. We know much of what we think we know via testimony or the words of others. Similarly, I must place ET in myself for memory-based beliefs (for example). If we don't properly trust ourselves to remember, it's hard to see how we can preserve our memorial knowledge. If PET is (were) generally un- or nonreliable, we (would) lose massive stores of knowledge, resulting in a skepticism that undermines a large number of beliefs overall and certainly a large number of beliefs we take to be significant. So, as with perceptual (et al.) beliefs, we have good reasons to take PET to satisfy (f) on pain of skepticism. We have thus seen that PET satisfies (a)–(f). Thus, PET counts as a responsibilist virtue in Zagzebski's account (or any less specific trait-based responsibilism).

Given a general responsibilist virtue epistemology and Zagzebski's specifically neo-Aristotelian theory in particular, virtues will have two corresponding vices—one excessive and one deficient with respect to the virtue's characteristic motivation. For instance, the moral virtue of courage requires proper fear in the courageous agent. One (characteristically) disposed to feel too much fear is cowardly, and the agent (characteristically) disposed to feel too little fear is rash—each vice is defined by its inappropriate state with respect to the characteristic motive of the virtue. If PET lacks such vices, then this would count against classing it as a responsibilist virtue. On the other hand, if we can find intellectual traits (states or dispositions) that have (intuitively) vicious excessive and deficient ET, then this provides us with a strong reason to think PET itself is a virtue. The characteristic motivation of confidence or seeing someone as authoritative at work in (e) provides us with the tools to see how PET has characteristic vices, just as any other virtue.

If PET is characterized by seeing the trustee as epistemically authoritative, then deficient ET would amount to seeing too few people as authoritative or granting them too little authority. Accordingly, deficient ET has an affinity for Miranda Fricker's (2007) notion of a credibility deficit. My view counts deficient ET as vicious even if not motivated by the sociopolitical prejudices that drive Fricker's analysis, though I certainly agree with including those as plausible sources of viciously deficient ET. When framed that way, we have a plausible description of epistemic suspiciousness or Frickerian injustice: the trait of a person who's characteristically overly doubtful (of others or oneself, even).

Similarly, excessive ET involves seeing too many people as authoritative or granting them too much authority when they do not deserve such status. Again, we have a plausible commonsense term for this defect: gullibility. In my view, it's not about whether you trust too many or few *simpliciter* but whether you trust too many/few *who merit your trust*. And given that suspiciousness and gullibility seem like textbook examples of epistemic vices, they provide us with good reason to think that the appropriate mean between them (i.e. PET) counts as a virtue. Hence, we have another line of reasoning built on the structure of epistemic virtue to class PET among them. We can move on to my next argument based on the meta-epistemology of virtues.

3. Proper Epistemic Trust and the Meta-Epistemology of Virtues

I shall argue in this section that meta-epistemological considerations regarding how epistemic virtues function give reason to count PET among them. Zagzebski, following Michael Slote, distinguishes two different types of virtue theories: good based and agent based (1996, 80). A theory is good based if the notion of some good life or nonpersonal end serves as the fundamental value in the theory. Aristotle's use of *eudaimonia* to define and ground his concept of virtue provides a good example of this kind of virtue theory. On the other hand, a theory is agent based if it takes some essentially personal property as the bedrock value.[27] Zagzebski's own (2004) view takes the motives of a perfect moral agent (in her case, God) as the basic ground of moral value. The difference between these theory types is not whether virtues promote the good life or whether motivations have value, but rather which sort of value is more fundamental than the other. I think either view is plausible, so I shall remain on the fence regarding which is preferable. My neutrality here, though, means that I have two arguments to make: one fitting PET into a good-based account of virtue and one fitting it into an agent-based view. Let us first turn to the former.

Does PET promote epistemic *eudaimonia*?[28] Naturally enough, we can't answer that question without some notion of the good life in question and the epistemic values associated with any such life. Of the various plausible candidates of epistemic values (e.g. truth, knowledge, justification, understanding, wisdom, et al.), it seems clear that PET is necessary for a robust store of them. Without proper *other*-ET, it's hard to see how we can have testimonial beliefs with positive epistemic status. And if we lack appropriate confidence in ourselves, and thus proper *self*-ET, then beliefs based on our own cognitive functioning, like memory and sense perception, will lack positive epistemic status, too. Now, can we construe the epistemic *eudaimonia* without including at least some justified, warranted, true, etc., testimonial, memorial, and perceptual beliefs?

The answer is 'clearly not.' Hence, no matter which end(s) we pick for the epistemic good life and no matter how many are basic or fundamental, it will turn out that PET promotes them and therefore the epistemic *eudaimonia*.[29]

Let me dismiss a potential objection straightaway: PET cannot be necessary for a good bit of knowledge because, *qua* responsibilist virtue, it requires time to acquire and develop. Children and the generally vicious can have epistemically justified beliefs about testimony or sense perception without possessing any such virtue. To resolve this, we need to add some precision. For Aristotle, an action of some virtue *V* is virtuous just in case that *action* is what the agent with *V would* do in that context, but the *V-ous person* must actually *possess V* (*Nicomachean Ethics* II:4, 1105b5). Thus defined, a virtuous action doesn't require actually *being* virtuous: only that the earlier subjunctive is true—*S* acts as would the *V*-ous agent in *S*'s situation. I suggest a parallel setup for virtue epistemology: a virtuous belief doesn't entail that the agent in question *actually be* virtuous. She need only believe as the virtuous agent *would* in her circumstances. Hence, an agent need not *have* PET to have a PET belief; she need only *express* PET as the virtuous agent would.[30] Children, a generally vicious agent (but believing/acting) out of character, and people still in the acquisition or development stage have no problem expressing PET even if they don't have it (yet, at least). Hence, PET can be definitive of beliefs with positive epistemic status, but we need not be committed to overpredicating virtue for too many agents who obviously do not or cannot possess it. Hence, we need to be more careful than we have been earlier: *possession* of PET isn't necessary for a robust store of beliefs with positive epistemic status, but *expression* of PET is. Hence, there's still a crucial way that PET is required for the epistemic good life.

An agent-based approach takes some feature(s) of the ideal agent or exemplar as the fundamental concept used to ground one's virtue theory. Consider what sort of traits the paradigmatic person of epistemic virtue would possess, if actual. I suggest that we frame this issue by asking what sorts of motives such persons would possess.[31] For any paradigmatically virtuous agent, I take it that her guiding motive is to think well and to obtain a robust (but not necessarily exhaustive) store of whatever epistemic goods there might be—like the putative examples listed earlier. So, if we investigate the characteristic motives of the epistemically ideal agent, will she display and possess PET? I think so. If she is motivated to obtain either true or justified beliefs, then she must be motivated to use her belief-forming/maintaining practices, procedures, faculties, skills, etc., well. And if we recall the importance of testimony, we should expect our epistemic exemplar to place PET in others. When we consider some cognitive or intellectual exemplar, I take it that such a person displays ET in several contexts: she will listen to experts in fields about which she claims no expertise, she trusts others for a range of beliefs, and so forth.

And, again, proper *self*-ET follows an exactly similar line of argument: we ubiquitously and continually trust our own perceptions, memory, etc. It seems clear that the paradigmatically virtuous person trusts herself in those circumstances at least some time and probably quite often.[32] That is, displaying appropriate (relying) confidence (i.e. ET) in a variety of contexts is just what the person of virtue does, and so PET works in that person's cognition and intellectual functioning just as any other epistemic virtue. Hence, the essential features of PET work into the motivational structure of the paradigmatic person of virtue, and so we must conclude that the virtuous epistemic agent will display PET. In either account of virtue, whether it be good or agent based, we find that PET works in precisely the ways that *any* epistemic virtue does. PET turns out as a virtue by considering both the structure of virtue and the meta-epistemological roles virtues play in our cognition.

4. Implications

If PET is a responsibilist virtue, then some important implications follow. First, as mentioned at the end of Section 2, PET has two correlated vices: deficient ET (suspiciousness) and excessive ET (gullibility).[33] The former gives us an account of overly rigid dogmatism and the latter of epistemically improper *blind* trust. We shall fall victim to all sorts of intellectual ills if we trust everyone with everything they say but cannot obtain various epistemic *goods* or think well if we do not trust some people (and ourselves) some time. Thus, the virtue of PET explains why gullibility and dogmatism are epistemically faulty, strengthening my virtue-theoretic model of PET.

Related to this consequence, classical (especially neo-Aristotelian) approaches to virtue involve a sensitivity to contexts. Virtues are a mean between excess and deficiency, but what constitutes an appropriate mean is, in part, a function of the context in which the agent finds herself. For instance, Aristotle notes that what counts as an appropriate mean between too much and too little food is different for a weightlifter than for a person on a different diet and exercise regimen.[34] Similarly, what counts as appropriate (read: virtuous) ET is sensitive to contexts. The level of trust I have in my spouse is appropriately higher than the trust I might place in a complete stranger. There is a mean in both cases, but such a mean differs because the context in which that mean occurs differs as well. Thus, what counts as PET, as opposed to suspiciousness or gullibility, must have this same context sensitivity as well. I find this implication extremely instructive, for it allows a nuanced approach to how we trust others that does not come down along hard-and-fast rules. We have the kind of context-sensitive 'wiggle room' to deal with hard cases of trust. We shall see later on in Section 5 just what results this implication has for selected epistemological debates.

Another implication concerns PET's relation to evidence. Evidentialists with respect to ET hold that one's PET for some belief is epistemically good (warranted, justified, etc.) just in case (and *because*, presumably) one has good evidence for that belief regarding the epistemological status of the one in whom you trust (or the belief for which you trust). Nonevidentialists (with respect to ET) can adopt a range of other ways to explain when ET is (epistemically) well placed. Reliabilists will think of PET as a truth-conducive cognitive disposition, process, or faculty, and universalists claim that one's PET is in epistemic good standing if (and only if) one lacks defeaters for the belief or testifier in question.[35] A virtue-theoretic approach provides another model of PET but without reducing its epistemic status to evidence, truth conduciveness, or default universal ET. Instead, it is PET's nature *qua* virtue and its function as part of a virtuous character or cognition that explains the epistemic status of PET-based beliefs. Yet a virtue approach can still appeal to some motives driving each competing model.

For virtue-theoretic PET, *H*'s ET in *S* has positive epistemic status when and only when (and *because*) *H*'s trusting (in *S*) expresses virtue.[36] So, virtuous PET isn't identical or reducible to any of the views noted earlier.[37] However, each theory does find some of its motivation reflected in a virtue epistemology of PET. Many epistemic virtues are necessarily or essentially bound up with the obtaining, weighing, using, and maintaining of evidence and must be operating (at least in one's cognitive background). Thus, *at a minimum*, PET cannot conflict with these virtues: one's PET must fit with the evidence one has and/or should have.[38] As such, my account of PET, which is not evidentialist, nevertheless recognizes a crucial role evidence plays in PET(-based belief). Also, PET is more than a merely reliable cognitive disposition (as we see in Section 2), but it is *at least* that. And, finally, regarding universalism: PET doesn't entail that one's ET-based-belief must have evidence supporting it, so we find an important connection there, too.

What seems most intriguing in this discussion is how a virtue-theoretic PET accepts elements and motives from *all* of these other accounts. If virtue-theoretic PET doesn't imply that evidence is both necessary and sufficient for PET, then it can capture a core universalist motive. But if there *is* some positive, central role that evidence plays, then virtue-theoretic PET can utilize an important evidentialist insight. However, a virtue account of PET remains both separate and distinct from each theory. Often, PET will mix these accounts: some of the warrant, justification, etc., for one's ET will be from *both* the evidence one has (should have) *and* from the defeasible (universalist) presumption of trust—the two buttressing each other.[39] That is, one's PET itself will contribute to the positive epistemic status for a belief, but there will be some contribution to that status from one's evidential state (produced by one's wider virtuous functioning). What determines the appropriate mix? Naturally, the context sensitivity of virtue-theoretic PET has a role: differences in contexts call for different intellectual responses to them. Depending upon the particularities of the situation, our evidence, and our own cognitive sophistication, the other virtues in operation will determine what positive evidence and negative evidence (defeaters) I have for my ET in that particular case and what evidence I *should* have in those particular circumstances. Even in cases where my PET may be default, as universalism suggests, evidential concerns play *some* role as a limiting condition regarding what evidence I ought to possess, given the circumstances. But, *pace* evidentialism with respect to ET, evidence is not the *only* or *fundamental* good-making epistemic criterion here, though it is important (and often necessary). More exactly, it's one's epistemically virtuous functioning—including (expressions of) PET—that confers positive epistemic status even if adequate evidence is a necessary part of that story. Thus, we have a nonevidentialist, nonuniversalist (but also non–process-reliabilist) model of PET that can capture central motives from virtue theory's counterparts, while doing so consistently and in a theoretically principled way. These implications follow conceptually from taking virtue theory's insistence on the context sensitivity of virtues and their expressions seriously. Particular details of one's epistemic context suggest a nuanced approach like the one PET provides and entails.

Most of these implications are straightforward and follow directly on my account of PET. Thus, it benefits our understanding and the depth of the position to discuss them, and they provide some indirect reasons for my view. In the next section, I extend PET to several heated disputes for epistemology, finding interesting and fruitful consequences.

5. Proper Epistemic Trust and Epistemological Issues

In this section, I look at some issues in contemporary epistemology and argue that PET provides some philosophically beneficial responses. My purpose here is twofold: first, I want to show how my account has application to certain theoretical issues in the field and, second, if the view can informatively address some thorny philosophical disputes, this only adds to its force. In what follows, I shall indicate some of the inroads that PET can provide to the problem of low-grade knowledge, epistemology of testimony, and peer disagreement. I do not intend an exhaustive analysis of any of these theories, so my concern will be to give the general philosophical landscape of the issue and briefly extend PET to it.

5.1. Epistemic Trust and the Problem of Low-Grade Knowledge

Many critics object to responsibilism by appealing to the ease with which we typically obtain perceptual knowledge.[40] Simple perceptual beliefs do not seem to require (cognitively robust) *responsibilist* virtues. When I look out of my window and see a tree, it's unclear that any virtue is necessary to form that belief. Instead, it seems more plausible to think that my *faculty* of perception produces the belief without any need for responsibilist virtues. But if there is no need for virtue(s) in this case and if this perceptual belief is justified, warranted, grounded, etc., then responsibilism will have trouble accounting for perceptual (or any 'low-grade') knowledge. So, how can virtue responsibilism plausibly account for 'easy' instances of low-grade knowledge?

Zagzebski (1996, 281) tries to solve this worry by discussing the person of intellectual virtue. If we 'see' as this exemplar does, then we are virtuous. The problem is that Zagzebski's account of virtuous 'seeing' is really an account of nonvicious 'seeing.' She claims that what counts is that we do not exemplify certain *vices*, like *not* being prejudiced and *not* being in the grips of wishful thinking. The worry is that Zagzebski gives us a case of virtuous φ-ing without giving a single virtue that has φ-ing as an end. PET, though, gives us the means to rebut this argument from low-grade knowledge with a simpler, more principled response.

If we suppose that PET extends to trust in our own faculties, then there is a major virtue operating for perceptual knowledge—PET itself. Such trust in one's cognitive functioning must operate, even if it is only implicit.[41] I see a tree outside and I trust my eyes, thereby forming the belief that there is a tree. Because there are virtues operating here rather than mere lack of vices, it is certainly a good candidate for knowledge on virtue responsibilism. And, what's more, if knowledge requires credit, then we have a virtue operating for both testimonial and perceptual beliefs.[42] We can preserve attributions of credit that merely *appear* too easy—answering another criticism of virtue theory. So, on the virtue-theoretic account of PET I offer, we can answer the problem of low-grade knowledge—strengthening both virtue responsibilism on the whole and my own virtue-theoretic account of PET in particular.[43]

One might worry that my account of virtuous PET is still too thick or cognitively robust to explain low-grade knowledge. And I think that the *possession* of PET (*qua* virtue) is not necessary for justified (warranted, etc.) perceptual beliefs. However, as I argue in Section 3, it's not the possession of a virtue that's required for virtuous belief (or action), but merely that one believe (or act) as one possessing the full virtue *would* in one's circumstances. We may utilize the same point here to help neutralize the objection at hand: though fully possessed PET seems too robust for 'easy' perceptual knowledge, one's believing in what one's eyes present to one (for instance) certainly *is* what the person with fully developed, reflective possession and use of PET *would* believe. Hence, use of a fully robust character trait (i.e. PET) has no difficulty in explaining low-grade knowledge, which is precisely all the (responsibilist) virtue epistemologist needs to resolve the current worry.[44]

5.2. Epistemic Trust and Testimony

Virtue-theoretic PET also provides a ready-made way to reframe the reductionism vs. nonreductionism debate regarding testimony. Reductionists claim that the good epistemic standing of a testimonial belief reduces to or supervenes upon nontestimonial grounds—usually some standard source of epistemic justification like sense perception, memory, inductive inference, and others.[45] The evidence from these nontestimonial sources of justification may be inductive or *a priori*.[46] Accordingly, this reduction thesis implies that a testimony-based belief must have positive, nontestimonial justification.[47] Nonreductionists argue for the negation of this—namely, that testimonial beliefs (can) have good epistemic standing without any positive, testimonial-independent grounds, usually attaching a 'no defeater(s)' rider. I shall not catalog the worries with each position, but it should suffice to note there is no shortage of well-argued disagreement.[48] Instead, I shall mention what I consider a main driving motivation for each account and how the account of PET I defend here can shed light on the theoretical impasse.

To deal with reductionism first, my account of PET allows us to talk about well-formed (here, virtuous) belief without *reducing* this epistemic standing to the evidence for that belief. Epistemic virtues confer positive epistemic status—not *evidence itself*. (Though, as I describe in Section 4, evidence can play a key or even necessary role in at least some instances where such status obtains.) If one's ET is in epistemic good standing (= one displays PET), then (*qua* virtue) beliefs it causes are *prima facie* good (justified, warranted, etc.), too. Hence, we can capture a core intuition from the nonreductionist camp. However, we must not forget that other non-PET virtues, some dealing with evidence, must be in operation—at least as a limiting condition. Displaying PET entails seeing the testifier a certain way—namely, as authoritative—but this seeing cannot (in principle) conflict with one's evidence, because PET *qua* virtue cannot conflict with any other virtues (including whatever evidence they yield). And if the virtues are unified by something stronger than mere consistency, as is natural for anyone inspired by classical virtue theories, then PET would have to cohere with whatever evidential state one is in via other virtues.[49] Hence, we must be concerned with evidence *in some respect* with regard to testimony, thus preserving some of the motive behind reductionism (even if *pace* evidentialism, evidence itself doesn't confer positive epistemic status). If I place my ET in someone when I could or should have good defeating evidence by using other virtues, then my ET will not be good (i.e. express genuine PET) in this case. By requiring reduction for a testimonial positive epistemic status, reductionists explicitly aim to avoid *gullibly* accepting false, misleading, or unfounded communication(s). PET easily undercuts this worry—one cannot be gullible in extending the epistemic *virtue* of *proper* ET. And nonreductionists are concerned that reductionistic constraints undermine knowledge and lead to testimonial skepticism. Context-sensitive PET, denying strict reductionism, implies that skepticism-based worries about strict reductionism are unfounded. Hence, the context-sensitive and excess/mean/deficiency structure of PET can accommodate motivations for *both* reductionism and nonreductionism coherently, while giving a nuanced account that fits a virtue-theoretic approach.

When we are young and haven't developed virtues that govern how we process evidence, PET will function with a broader reign.[50] In contexts like this, the nonreductionist view seems right to posit default yet defeasible PET. Later, we can develop more sensitive 'eyes' to the testifier, as well as the epistemically pertinent features that surround the testimony, in addition to a large catalog of inductive evidence that can fit or clash with our PET. In these different contexts, quasi-default PET without requiring positive evidence is no longer all that compelling. So, while PET affirms part of reductionism and nonreductionism, it also rejects key elements of each; namely, their universal scope. PET implies neither universal default ET (*pace* nonreductionism) nor universal reduction of ET to other epistemic features of one's cognition (*pace* reductionism). Again, the proper epistemic status of ET is highly context sensitive to the evidence we (should) have and virtues we use in those circumstances, which we should expect on some accounts of testimony.[51] Because both reductionism and nonreductionism disregard such sensitivity in favor of necessary and sufficient conditions for *all* cases of trusting in testimony *simpliciter*, they cannot allow for this kind of approach.

The moral we should learn from the reductionism vs. nonreductionism debate, I suggest, is that neither side provides the right answer for *every* case of testimonial justification. There are some situations where reductionism gives the right answer (i.e. the agent should have positive evidence for his or her belief), and we see this in cases where the trusting agent appears gullible. PET can handle cases like this because gullibility is an expression of excessive—and hence vicious—trust. Nonreductionism seems to provide the proper account for other situations, though. Obvious candidates are certain historical beliefs and my knowledge that 'cat' refers to certain types of furry, four-legged mammals. Requiring positive (especially nontestimonial or non–trust-based) evidence in cases like these undercuts knowledge that we intuitively want to maintain. Again, PET can handle these cases because, *qua* epistemic virtue, PET can confer some kind of epistemic value on beliefs of this kind.

5.3. Epistemic Trust and Peer Disagreement

I shall examine the epistemology of peer disagreement in the same manner that I discussed the epistemology of testimony earlier. An epistemic or cognitive 'peer' is defined with respect to both a subject of disagreement (or difference in belief) and the general epistemic circumstances surrounding one and one's peer in this disagreement. So, consider some belief you may have about some proposition p. Your epistemic peer would be some person, S, such that S believes not-p or q—where q entails not-p—and S is in the same epistemic circumstances in which you find yourself. That is, you and S have the same evidence, cognitive function, epistemic abilities, and whatever else one wishes to specify that determine a belief's epistemic status. Given that there are genuine deep disagreements, epistemologists work to explain various aspects of them. One key question: Can a (deep) disagreement be *rational* (for both parties)?

There are (at least) two main types of theories addressing this question. I follow Jennifer Lackey's (2008, 2010) labels for these two theory types (for ease of expression). Let us call a theory 'nonconformist' if it allows two (disagreeing) epistemic peers to hold their respective, inconsistent beliefs *rationally*.[52] That is, for some two peers, A and B, A can rationally believe that p where B can rationally believe that not-p in nonconformism. In nonconformism, rationality does not necessarily force two peers to revise either the beliefs each has or the strength with which they believe them. Conformism, on the other hand, denies this core thesis behind nonconformism.[53] A and B must engage in some kind of belief revision in order to preserve their respective rationality.[54] Conformism implies, in motto form, that there is no rational disagreement between epistemic peers.

This debate becomes seemingly intractable because both conformism and nonconformism each have a very unattractive consequence. Consider the idealized situation sketched earlier. Given nonconformism, A and B are perfectly rational or within their epistemic rights in continuing to believe p and not-p, respectively. Neither must revise either the beliefs they hold or the degree to which they hold them. We have what Catherine Elgin calls a "symmetrical" situation regarding peers' beliefs (2010, 55). It seems rather more like a kind of epistemic 'stand-off' than symmetry. Both A and B can draw their doxastic lines in the sand. Generalizing here, we end with a situation of doxastically and intellectually isolated individuals. I take this sort of situation to be quite unappealing, for it, too, easily licenses a potentially vicious dogmatism in each.

But conformism fares no better. It yields a dilemma. In this view, A and B must either suspend belief or revise their relative strength(s) of belief. The first horn of the dilemma implies skepticism for any case of peer disagreement because both sides must relinquish their beliefs.[55] The second horn implies a state of continual doxastic self-monitoring.[56] Because peer disagreement could potentially occur for *any* belief, this implication means that there is no belief of which we can be *really* confident—even those beliefs that are deeply characteristic of oneself, one's view of the world, and how one places oneself in the world.[57] We end up being possible 'doxastic nomads' because we are never really 'at home,' cognitively speaking, when faced with the possibility of deep change in our doxastic commitments. As should be clear from my criticism of nonconformism, I'm not endorsing dogmatism or a dogmatic approach to one's beliefs. Rather, I worry that conformism takes calls to belief revision too lightly. For instance, consider moral beliefs. These are typically deeply held and can usually be quite divisive. With conformism, I can never commit fully to any moral judgment, practice, etc., because I can always come across an epistemic peer who disagrees. Because I take it that both horns of this dilemma imply unattractive results, we can conclude that both conformism and nonconformism are saddled with fairly nasty worries.

Now that we have examined the epistemological landscape of peer disagreement as well as the quagmires that such a landscape contains, let us examine how PET fits in this map. The first thing to notice is that my view is inconsistent with conformism. Virtue-theoretic PET implies that there is no "one-size-fits-all" modeling how PET confers positive epistemic status in a belief. Rather, particular elements of one's context are necessary to how one displays PET in that context. Thus, such a position cannot endorse a view that makes *every* case of disagreement fall under the same specific standards, as does conformism. But PET cannot be nonconformist either, for exactly the same reason. Both views entail unilateral epistemic principles in rational belief that cut across all cases of disagreement, ones that cannot properly handle specific and epistemically vital differences in particular cases of disagreement. Call the conformist's and nonconformist's endorsement of such unilateral epistemic principles "Uniformity."[58] Precisely by rejecting Uniformity, virtue-theoretic, *context-sensitive* PET is incompatible with both approaches to peer disagreement.

So, how does PET help with the epistemology of disagreement in a way that simply rejecting Uniformity does not? First, PET gives us an extra reason to deny Uniformity. Lackey's (2008) argument against Uniformity relies on various thought experiments to show that conformism works in some but nonconformism in others. Although I find (many of) her cases convincing, PET can further our theoretical reasons for giving up Uniformity. The context sensitivity of PET serves as a good general explanation for why we have varying cases of peer disagreement eliciting different intuitions. Second, PET can explain why cases like the ones she develops work. Differences in context mean differences in the *proper* extension or expression of ET, so we should expect different instances of disagreement to pull in different directions. Moreover, we can explain why the conformism vs. nonconformism debate seems impossible to settle. The debate seems intractable because, so long as each view 'seesaws' regarding the same response to different cases, the debate *really is* intractable. We find an exactly similar situation to the epistemology of disagreement as we do to the epistemology of testimony: the major sides of the debate get some cases correct, but neither gets all correct. Thus, each view has some significant degree of plausibility, but neither is plausible in its totality.[59]

Also, PET shifts the terms and landscape of the disagreement debate. Instead of battling principles with cases, we must adopt an agent-centric focus. The crucial issue about disagreement here is when (if ever) one ought to keep to one's beliefs or change them in recognition of the epistemic authority of another. In short, how does one strike the proper balance between self-ET and other-ET in cases of conflict? Instead, we focus on the agent, her ET, and her (more) particular context. Recall that nonconformism's unattractive implication is a situation of epistemic 'standoff' wherein both sides to the disagreement dig in their doxastic heels and take no heed of the other side's claim. This results in a doxastic isolationism or, worse, dogmatism. I assume that, because such isolation impedes proper cognitive functioning, it will not contribute to or constitute (even in part) either the epistemic good life or motivational structure of the person of epistemic virtue. Indeed, I suspect it would be part of the epistemic 'bad life' and something that the person of virtue would avoid. It would be conceptually impossible in this case to display *proper* self- or other-ET. At least one person (or both) then fails to display PET—the proper diagnosis of which side and what way, of course, depending upon the context in which those peers find themselves. Similar considerations tell against conformism: it will imply *either* skepticism in cases of disagreement *or* a kind of doxastic homelessness. As with the isolationism implied by nonconformism, I take both results to contribute to the epistemic 'bad life' and run contrary to the motives of the person of virtue. As such, they cannot, *in principle*, be the result of PET even if we cannot describe *how* this works without the specifics of the situation.

One important issue arises at this point: the setup for any putatively *problematic* instance of peer disagreement requires some aspects of two agents' contexts to be the same. If *A* possess sufficient evidence for *p* and *B* does not, we likely won't feel the intuitive pull to call this a *rational* disagreement. Thus, in any standard setup, *some* elements of the contexts must be held constant. Can this setup (with such constants) allow for some contextual variation to which PET (*qua* virtue) can be attuned? What I suggest is that the question yields a dilemma. If the setup holds most of one's circumstances constant, there won't be (m)any differences to which PET is sensitive. So, it can't explain the rationality of the disagreement. But if the constants are *so* nearly identical, then it's *far* less obvious that the disagreement *is* rational (and thus needs to be explained) in the first place. If we can find no epistemically relevant differences, we have, in effect, the same (or a functionally equivalent) agent holding inconsistent doxastic attitudes. To make it more plausibly rational (and, thus, in need of explanation), the contexts cannot be so nearly identical, and there we have some 'wiggle room' to find a possible context variation of which one's PET can note. So, if the disagreement is plausibly rational,

PET can get some traction. But the contrapositive holds as well—if PET gets no traction—then it's less plausible to think of the disagreement as rational. In either case, the issue poses no problem for the model of PET I propose.

In short, there is much work to do regarding PET as a solution to the problem of peer disagreement—my analysis is just a sketch that outlines what a view would look like in full. But I think it is informative enough to make its consequences attractive and thus worth more sustained development. Again, my analysis here mirrors that regarding testimony. I aim not to solve these debates, but rather only to give a plausible and potentially fruitful general approach to the disputes we've discussed. Perhaps, I hope, with more work, analysis, and argument, these consequences can help positively redress the worries catalogued in this section.

6. Conclusion

In this chapter, I've argued for the plausibility of PET along virtue responsibilist lines. With a model of ET in hand, we can see how properly placed or extended ET fits with the overall structure of epistemic virtue and that PET satisfies core meta-epistemological functions of such virtues. These points, I suggest, count as direct arguments for virtue-theoretic PET. Additionally, we've seen that virtuous PET both has plausible implications and opens up fruitful and interesting lines of response to certain significant epistemological points of debate. Such considerations, too, count in favor of my theory, even if indirectly. Thus, we have what I hope to be an attractive cumulative case for PET counted as a responsibilist epistemic virtue.[60]

Notes

1. One noteworthy exception is Laura Frances Callahan and Timothy O'Connor (2014): they defend "well-tuned" trust as an epistemic virtue. My view in what follows differs from their account in at least two key ways. First, they defend the virtue of trust *simpliciter*—not just *epistemic* trust. In this chapter, I have nothing to say about nonepistemic forms of trust. (Though I suspect similar considerations from moral theory can be made to count *moral* trust as a virtue, too. However, nothing here hangs on any of that.) Second, and more importantly I think, they work with a very general notion of an epistemic virtue as an "excellence" in "*practices of belief formation and revision over time*" (246). I agree that virtues are such excellences, but my view goes much further in the specifics of what exactly makes a property such an excellence in Section 2. Hence, the view defended in this chapter is more *systematic* with respect to the *responsibilist* virtue of *epistemic* trust.
2. Classical statements of virtue reliabilism are John Greco's (2010) and Ernest Sosa's (2007, 2010, 2015) lengthy treatments. Also of note are Sosa's (1980, 1991) earlier shorter works. For virtue responsibilism, Lorraine Code (1984) originates the term, and she expands her theory in (1987). James Montmarquet (1993) and Linda Zagzebski (1996) also provide important book-length

analyses and defenses of epistemic virtue along responsibilist lines. Other views (e.g. Baehr 2011 and Battaly 2008, 2015) take both responsibilist and reliabilist virtues as equally legitimate subsets of the whole of virtue epistemology.

3. For some of these independent reasons, see McCraw (2018).

4. As I mention in note 2, some accept both responsibilist and reliabilist virtues, so the dilemma here needn't be exclusive.

5. However, even Aristotle (in the *Nicomachean Ethics* II:7), the (grand)father of virtue responsibilism, affirms that there are "nameless" virtues without specific terms: so, the lack of a name for a trait doesn't count against it being a legitimate virtue.

6. In exactly the same way that no one would argue that fearing (*simpliciter*) is virtuous (rather, only appropriate fear—courage), I focus on appropriate ET rather than ET (*simpliciter*).

7. I am open to the possibility that there could be ET that does not involve believing a proposition. So, my view provides a model for one kind of ET, noting that there may be others.

8. There's some reason to think that a weaker propositional attitude than belief can work here—something along the lines of acceptance (which I take to be a propositional attitude towards *p* weaker than belief that *p*). This doesn't change the substance of the account.

9. So construed, this model defines an occurrent *instance* of ET. By making (1)–(4) *dispositional* properties (i.e. dispositions to believe, rely, etc.) and letting *p* denote a field (of study), area, or domain, one gets a dispositional model of ET—one suited to be the basis of a responsibilist virtue.

10. Note, however, that I require only that the truster *take* the trustee to communicate. The trustee need not actually assert p. We have good reason to think we can have ET-based beliefs for content never actually asserted or transmitted. I'm thinking of Jennifer Lackey's (2006) case of someone reading another's private journal. You can trust the words of someone's journal, thereby coming to ET-based beliefs, even though the journal is *private* and thus never intended by its author to communicate anything. Further, we can communicate without assertion: conversational implicature, well-placed pauses or silence, gestures, and so forth can all communicate content to a hearer without uttering any statements.

11. Because this account models ET *in S*, something other than belief that S is reliable is needed. But given that the trust at issue is *epistemic*, the model need (and should) not adopt purely moral concepts, attitudes, etc. I'll do more later in this section to show how ET in S goes beyond the belief that S is reliable.

12. Baier's (1995, 98) example is a local shopkeeper. If she or he runs the only show around, then one has no choice but to rely on him or her for the necessities of life. However, this relying doesn't mean we *trust* the shopkeeper. Past experience with poisoned goods, in her example, prevents legitimate trust but not reliance. I defend a similar line of thought in McCraw (2015, 420), where relying on S alone is insufficient for having ET in S.

13. However, it's important that epistemic confidence at least allows for the possibility of an affective component. The reason is that, as I show in the next section, my account of ET is compatible with Linda Zagzebski's (1996) virtue epistemology, and she defines epistemic virtues, in part, by their characteristic motivational or emotional components. Additionally, many philosophers see ET as having an affective component (e.g. Jones 1996 and Faulkner 2007) and a cognitive element (e.g. Frost-Arnold 2014, Hieronymi 2008, Kappel 2014, McMyler 2011). There's also precedent for construing ET as a way of seeing or interpreting someone (e.g. Govier 1992, 1993).

Yet others analyze ET as having both affective and cognitive components (e.g. Zagzebski 2011). My account of ET, via confidence, can explain why these models of ET are so construed.

14. Objection: How can I depend on myself for something that *I* lack? And how can I view myself as more authoritative than *myself*? My answer: a straightforward way to see how self-dependence/-confidence is possible appeals to self-trust over time. I can have ET in my past self for something I remember but (now) cannot recall the reason. Accordingly, I depend on my past self, and I also take me-in-the-past to be better epistemically placed towards belief in question than my present self (who is no longer in possession of the same evidence). For more see my (2015, 425–426). Another way to see how one may lack both self-dependence and self-confidence would be with instances of gaslighting.

15. We could also say that one directs ET to one's faculties and, *via them*, to oneself.

16. I take this result to be a significant advantage to my model over a 'mere reliance' account. Assuming that it's *very* plausible to think of my relation to the GPS as trust, it's a theoretical benefit for a theory that can accommodate and explain this usage over another theory that cannot do so. I don't 'merely rely' on my GPS, I have (and act on) a *positive* attitude towards it being a *good* source of information.

17. This story may not track with some or all people's experiences with a GPS, but it's certainly *mine* and, I suspect, indicative of enough of others' to make it worth serious philosophical examination.

18. I defend the same position on confidence as a disposition to believe in my (2015, 424).

19. Hence, we can see where my view on ET (in) differs from both predictive trust and 'mere reliance' accounts.

20. For ease of reference throughout this section, I've added my own lettering to Zagzebski's definition.

21. See Clément, Koenig, and Harris (2004), Koenig and Harris (2005, 2007), Koenig (2010), Cole, Harris, and Koenig (2012), and Stephens and Koenig (2015).

22. I assume that the characteristic motivation for an *epistemic* virtue initiates and directs a *belief* to its end (whatever that end may be: truth, understanding, wisdom, etc.).

23. For more on how the general end vs. specific aim/target distinction works out for epistemic virtues, see Sarah Wright (2009, 2013, 2014).

24. Like other specific targets, I take (P)ET's aim to direct one's proper (relying) confidence and also, *qua* means, towards the overall goal of cognition (truth, knowledge, understanding, etc.). Courage, too, has the same structure: the courageous aims at both proper fear and (as a result) to live well more generally.

25. That is, my aim is to have my dependence on S fit my overall context and for my 'seeing-S-as-authoritative' (= confidence) to track S's actual status.

26. Use of similar analogical or parity arguments connecting testimony with memory and/or sense perception has a well-documented track record in Western analytic epistemology (e.g. Reid, Alston, Coady, and others), but the same sorts of maneuvers have a much longer history in Indian philosophical reflections on testimony. See Chakrabarti (1992), Phillips (2012, ch. 6), and Ganeri (2006, chs. 4 and 5).

27. What I call an essentially personal property refers to properties only possessed by an *agent*: motives are a clear, commonsense example of one.

28. Given the rigorous debate in epistemology on the nature, number, and structure of epistemic values, aims, or goods, I don't want my words or argument to assume any *specific* notion of the epistemic good life. Let's say that the epistemic *eudaimonia* or good life is the life actualizing epistemic values—whatever and however many they may be.

29. See Laura Frances Callahan and Timothy O'Connor (2014, 257–262) for a similar line of reasoning focusing on how trust makes possible the attainment of goods directly rather than my focus on the epistemic *eudaimonia* more generally.

30. In making this point, I disagree with any virtue epistemology *requiring* that the positive epistemic status for a belief stem from the virtue(s) the agent must have. For instance, Ernest Sosa (2015, 26–32; 2018, 132–33) argues that apt (= epistemically well formed) beliefs must "manifest" competence (= virtue), such that manifesting a competence entails possessing it. My use of "expressing" virtue doesn't imply possession of a virtue as does Sosa's use of "manifestation."

31. This procedure falls in line with Zagzebski's motivation-based approach.

32. However, the person of virtue needn't trust herself at all times in the same way. She will defer to others or suspect her confidence in her own senses, memory, etc., as features of her context warrant: she may note that another is more authoritative than she or she may notice that her memory for certain details may be unreliable. Yet, *generally speaking*, she will trust her own cognitive functioning.

33. Perhaps excessive ET in oneself is more like intellectual arrogance than gullibility. However, deficient ET seems to yield the same flaw—one can be overly *self*-suspicious. See Govier's (1993) insightful discussion on the epistemic harms of lacking (appropriate) self-trust.

34. *Nichomachean Ethics* II.6, 1006b.

35. For reliabilist models of PET see Kappel (2014) and Goldberg (2013). See Foley (2001) for the universalist camp.

36. We can easily alter the details to fit belief: *H*'s belief that *p*, via *H*'s ET in *S*, has positive epistemic status just in case *H*'s belief expresses PET in *S*.

37. Assuming, of course, epistemic virtues don't reduce to evidence, truth conduciveness, and so on.

38. And given that I accept *some* version of the reciprocity of the virtues, I think *coherence* with other virtues beyond mere consistency strengthens the point that PET *qua* virtue and one's evidential state will (necessarily) dovetail.

39. I suspect this mixed option is more frequently the appropriate mean of ET, but the evidentialist and universalist options are probably plausible expressions of ET in some context or other.

40. See, for instance, William Alston (2000, 187).

41. As I argue in Section 1, my model of ET can apply to self-trust no matter whether one sees one's *faculties* or one's *self* as the direct object of ET. Accordingly, I read "one's cognitive functioning" earlier very broadly and as noncommittal on this issue.

42. For more on how my account of PET can address testimony and credit-based objections to virtue epistemology, see McCraw (2014).

43. Other nonresponsibilist virtue epistemologies could construe PET as a skill, ability, competence, disposition, or what have you and resolve the problem at hand, too. But such a result doesn't cause problems for my view: all I need is some responsibilist virtue that can account for low-grade knowledge (even if reliabilist virtues can as well). And I've argued that PET and, more exactly, its *expression* can account for such knowledge.

44. I also suspect that the same subjunctive maneuver I use to disarm the problem of low-grade knowledge can come to the aid of responsibilists dealing with the situationist objection in epistemology. According to the epistemic situationist, psychological experiments show that it's one's *situation rather than one's character traits* that explain one's beliefs, thus casting doubt on any empirical claims of virtue epistemologists to explain positive epistemic status in terms of the character traits of agents. If we don't have these sorts of traits, or if it's the situation rather than them that explains the belief, the situationist objects, then virtue epistemology cannot work. However, by making the *expression* of character traits necessary (rather than the traits themselves), such traits can define positive epistemic status even if the empirical psychological claims to which situationists appeal are true. But this a discussion for another place. (For more on the situationist challenge to virtue epistemology, see Alfano 2012 and Alfano and Fairweather 2017).

45. In describing these sources as 'nontestimonial,' I do not mean to exclude Elizabeth Fricker's local reductionism. Here, testimony can provide evidence for *other* testimony, making this evidence independent of the *specific* testimony in question. See her (1987, 1994, 1995).

46. See, e.g., Coady (1992).

47. In this respect, reductionism regarding testimony makes similar claims as evidentialism regarding PET.

48. See Duncan Pritchard's (2004) for a good overview of the worries facing each view.

49. I've suggested in the previous section that one's evidential state may (or may not) include a great deal of evidence due to the context sensitivity of virtues (or virtuous cognitive functioning).

50. See Section 3 for more on how PET can account for children's trust-based beliefs even if they haven't (yet) developed any virtues themselves.

51. See, for instance, Catherine Elgin's (2002) Gricean account of testimony.

52. Examples of nonconformist theories can be found in van Inwagen (2010), Thomas Kelly (2006), and Richard Foley (2001, ch. 4).

53. Instances of conformism are David Christiansen (2007), Adam Elga (2007), Richard Feldman (2006), and Hilary Kornblith (2010).

54. Some conformists, like Feldman, argue that the revision in question must be suspension of both peers' beliefs, whereas other conformists, like Christensen, require only a revision in the strength with which each peer holds his or her belief.

55. And given the extent of possible disagreement, the skepticism threatened is significant and worrisome.

56. Callahan and O'Connor call this sort of result epistemologically "crippling" (2014, 250). I find their assessment right on the mark and a result that an adequate theory of disagreement ought to guard against.

57. What follows, I suggest, is an epistemological parallel to Bernard Williams and Smart's (1973) worry about the loss of one's moral integrity in utilitarianism. Assuming that intellectual integrity is an epistemic value or even a virtue, we have an analogous objection in conformism.

58. Here, I follow Jennifer Lackey's (2008) language. Like my theory, hers objects to both theories insofar as they accept Uniformity.

59. Perhaps the way to frame my proposal is that we need a both/and to transcend the either/or that conformism and nonconformism implies.

60. I would like to thank Jennifer Baker, Richard Combes, Kevin DeLapp, Jeremy Henkel, David Holliday, Casey Woodling, the audience at the 2013 Southeastern Epistemology Conference, and the editor of this volume for comments on earlier drafts of this chapter.

References

Alfano, Mark. 2012. "Expanding the Situationist Challenge to Responsibilist Virtue Epistemology." *Philosophical Quarterly* 62(247): 223–49.

Alfano, Mark, and Abrol Fairweather, eds. 2017. *Epistemic Situationism.* Oxford: Oxford University Press.

Alston, William P. 2000. "Virtue and Knowledge." *Philosophy and Phenomenological Research* 60(1): 185–89.

Baehr, Jason. 2011. *The Inquiring Mind: On Intellectual Virtues and Virtue Epistemology.* Oxford: Oxford University Press.

Baier, Annette C. 1995. "Trust and Antitrust." In *Moral Prejudices: Essays on Ethics,* edited by Annette Baier, 95–129. Cambridge, MA: Harvard University Press.

Battaly, Heather. 2008. "Virtue Epistemology." *Philosophy Compass* 3(4): 639–63.

———. 2015. *Virtue.* Malden, MA: Polity Press.

Callahan, Laura Frances, and Timothy O'Connor. 2014. "Well-Tuned Trust as an Intellectual Virtue." In *Religious Faith and Intellectual Virtue,* edited by Laura Frances Callahan and Timothy O'Connor, 246–76. Oxford: Oxford University Press.

Chakrabarti, Arindam. 1992. "On Knowing by Being Told." *Philosophy East and West* 42(3): 421–39.

Christiansen, David. 2007. "Epistemology of Disagreement: The Good News." *Philosophical Review* 116(2): 187–217.

Clément, Fabrice, Melissa Koenig, and Paul Harris. 2004. "The Ontogenesis of Trust." *Mind & Language* 19(4): 360–79.

Coady, Cecil Anthony John. 1992. *Testimony: A Philosophical Study.* Oxford: Clarendon Press.

Code, Lorraine. 1984. "Toward a 'Responsibilist' Epistemology." *Philosophy and Phenomenological Research* 45(1): 29–50.

———. 1987. *Epistemic Responsibility.* Hanover, NH: University Press of New England.

Cole, Caitlin A., Paul L. Harris, and Melissa A. Koenig. 2012. "Entitled to Trust? Philosophical Frameworks and Evidence from Children." *Analyse & Kritik* 34(2): 195–216.

Elga, Adam. 2007. "Reflection and Disagreement." *Nous* 41(3): 478–502.

Elgin, Catherine. 2002. "Take It from Me: The Epistemological Status of Testimony." *Philosophy and Phenomenological Research* 65(2): 291–308.

———. 2010. "Persistent Disagreement." In *Disagreement,* edited by Richard Feldman and Ted A. Warfield, 53–68. Oxford: Oxford University Press.

Faulkner, Paul. 2007. "On Telling and Trusting." *Mind* 116(464): 875–902.

Feldman, Richard. 2006. "Epistemological Puzzles about Disagreement." In *Epistemology Futures,* edited by Stephen Hetherington, 216–236. Oxford: Oxford University Press.

Foley, Richard. 2001. *Intellectual Trust in Oneself and Others.* Cambridge: Cambridge University Press.

Fricker, Elizabeth. 1987. "The Epistemology of Testimony." *Proceedings of the Aristotelian Society, Supplementary Volumes* 61: 57–83.

———. 1994. "Against Gullibility." In *Knowing from Words: Western and Indian Philosophical Analysis of Understanding and Testimony,* edited by Bimal K. Matilal and Arindam Chakrabarti, 125–61. Dordrecht: Kluwer.

———. 1995. "Telling and Trusting: Reductionism and Anti-Reductionism in the Epistemology of Testimony." *Mind* 104(414): 393–411.

Fricker, Miranda. 2007. *Epistemic Injustice: Power and the Ethics of Knowing.* Oxford: Oxford University Press.

Frost-Arnold, Karen. 2014. "The Cognitive Attitude of Rational Trust." *Synthese* 191: 1957–74.

Ganeri, Jonardon. 2006. *Artha: Meaning.* Oxford: Oxford University Press.

Goldberg, Sandford. 2013. "Self-Trust or Extended Trust: A Reliabilist Account." *Res Philosophica* 90(2): 277–92.

Govier, Trudy. 1992. "Trust, Distrust, and Feminist Theory." *Hypatia* 7(1): 16–33.

———. 1993. "Self-Trust, Autonomy, and Self-Esteem." *Hypatia* 8(1): 99–120.

Greco, John. 2010. *Achieving Knowledge: A Virtue-Theoretic Account of Epistemic Normativity.* Cambridge: Cambridge University Press.

Hieronymi, Pamela. 2008. "The Reasons of Trust." *Australasian Journal of Philosophy* 86(2): 213–36.

Holton, Richard. 1994. "Deciding to Trust, Coming to Believe." *Australasian Journal of Philosophy* 72(1): 63–76.

Jones, Karen. 1996. "Trust as an Affective Attitude." *Ethics* 107: 4–25.

Kappel, Klemens. 2014. "Believing on Trust." *Synthese* 191: 2009–28.

Kelly, Thomas. 2006. "The Epistemic Significance of Disagreement." In *Oxford Studies in Epistemology*, vol. I, edited by Tamar Szabó Gendler and John Hawthorne, 167–96. Oxford: Oxford University Press.

Koenig, Melissa A. 2010. "Selective Trust in Testimony: Children's Evaluation of the Message, the Speaker, and the Speech Act." In *Oxford Studies in Epistemology*, vol. III, edited by Tamar Szabó Gendler and John Hawthorne, 253–73. Oxford: Oxford University Press.

Koenig, Melissa A., and Paul L. Harris. 2005. "The Role of Social Cognition in Early Trust." *Trends in Cognitive Sciences* 9(10): 457–59.

———. 2007. "The Basis of Epistemic Trust: Reliable Testimony or Reliable Sources?" *Episteme* 4: 264–84.

Kornblith, Hilary. 2010. "Belief in the Face of Controversy." In *Disagreement*, edited by Richard Feldman and Ted A. Warfield, 29–52. Oxford: Oxford University Press.

Lackey, Jennifer. 2006. "The Nature of Testimony." *Pacific Philosophical Quarterly* 87: 177–97.

———. 2008. "A Justificationist View of Disagreement's Epistemic Significance. In *Social Epistemology*, edited by Adrian Haddock, Alan Millar, and Duncan Pritchard, 298–325. Oxford: Oxford University Press.

———. 2010. "What Should We Do When We Disagree?" In *Oxford Studies in Epistemology*, vol. III, edited by Tamar Szabó Gendler and John Hawthorne, 274–93. Oxford: Oxford University Press.

McCraw, Benjamin W. 2014. "Virtue Epistemology, Testimony, and Trust." *Logos & Episteme* 5(1): 95–102.

———. 2015. "The Nature of Epistemic Trust." *Social Epistemology* 29(4): 413–30.

———. 2018. "A (Different) Virtue Responsibilism: Epistemic Virtues without Motivations." *Acta Analytica* 33(3): 311–29.

McMyler, Benjamin. 2011. *Testimony, Trust, and Authority.* Oxford: Oxford University Press.

Montmarquet, James. 1993. *Epistemic Virtue and Doxastic Responsibility*. Lanham, MD: Rowman & Littlefield.

Phillips, Stephen H. 2012. *Epistemology in Classical India*. New York: Routledge.

Pritchard, Duncan. 2004. "The Epistemology of Testimony." *Philosophical Issues* 14: 326–48.

Sosa, Ernest. 1980. "The Raft and the Pyramid: Coherence Versus Foundations in the Theory of Knowledge." *Midwest Studies in Philosophy* 5(1): 3–26.

———. 1991. *Knowledge in Perspective*. New York: Cambridge University Press.

———. 2007. *A Virtue Epistemology: Apt Belief and Reflective Knowledge, Volume I*. Oxford: Oxford University Press.

———. 2010. *Knowing Full Well*. Princeton, NJ: Princeton University Press.

———. 2015. *Judgment and Agency*. Oxford: Oxford University Press.

———. 2018. *Epistemology*. Princeton, NJ: Princeton University Press.

Stephens, Elizabeth C., and Melissa A. Koenig. 2015. "Varieties of Testimony: Children's Selective Learning in Semantic Versus Episodic Domains." *Cognition* 137: 182–88.

van Inwagen, Peter. 2010. "We're Right. They're Wrong." In *Disagreement*, edited by Richard Feldman and Ted A. Warfield, 10–28. Oxford: Oxford University Press.

Wagenknecht, Susan. 2016. *A Social Epistemology of Research Groups*. Basingstoke: Palgrave Macmillan.

Williams, Bernard, and John Jamieson Carswell Smart. 1973. *Utilitarianism: For and Against*. Cambridge: Cambridge University Press.

Wright. Sarah. 2009. "The Proper Structure of the Intellectual Virtues." *The Southern Journal of Philosophy* 47(1): 91–112.

———. 2013. "A Neo-Stoic Approach to Epistemic Agency." *Philosophical Issues* 23: 262–75.

———. 2014. "The Stoic Epistemic Virtues of Groups." In *Essays in Collective Epistemology*, edited by Jennifer Lackey, 122–41. Oxford: Oxford University Press.

Zagzebski, Linda. 1996. *Virtues of the Mind: An Inquiry into the Nature of Virtue and the Ethical Foundations of Knowledge*. Cambridge: Cambridge University Press.

———. 2004. *Divine Motivation Theory*. Cambridge: Cambridge University Press.

———. 2011. "Epistemic Self-Trust and the *Consensus Gentium* Argument." In *Evidence and Religious Belief*, edited by Kelly James Clark and Raymond J. Van Arragon, 22–36. Oxford: Oxford University Press.

9   Virtuous and Vicious Intellectual Self-Trust

Alessandra Tanesini

Some people have the measure of themselves. They come across as confident without being cocky. They are self-assured but not self-satisfied. They are steadfast in their convictions without being dogmatic or closed-minded about novel information that potentially undermines their views. They are proud of their achievements, but humble enough to accept or own their limitations. These individuals are rare. Three other kinds of people are more common.[1] The first two include those who lack in self-confidence and whom I describe as intellectually obsequious, and also others who are best characterized as intellectually timid. Individuals belonging to either of these two types are very often unsure of their views. They do not know what they think about important issues. Even when an opinion can be extracted from them, they are not prepared to defend it. Instead, they easily change their minds and, at least in the case of servility, uncritically defer to the views espoused by other people.

The third kind concerns those who are full of themselves and who are best thought of as intellectually arrogant. They are opinionated and pay little attention to criticisms or views opposed to their own. We can think of these three categories of people as exhibiting behaviors characteristic of different kinds of intellectual self-trust. Individuals who are confident, but not arrogant, trust their intellectual abilities. Further, this trust is often apt. Those who lack in self-confidence mistrust their capacities, but this diffidence is often unjustified. Finally, individuals whose self-confidence is self-satisfied put a lot of trust in themselves, but their trust is often unwarranted.[2]

These considerations suggest that some intellectual vices are closely connected to deficiencies in intellectual self-trust.[3] To my knowledge, this is a phenomenon that has been largely ignored in the philosophical literature to date. The main aim of this chapter is to fill this gap by throwing light on the pathologies of self-trust caused by intellectual arrogance, obsequiousness, and timidity. The chapter also defends two further theses which are subservient to its primary goal. First, it supplies an account of intellectual self-trust as composed of dispositions to rely on the deliverances of one's epistemic faculties and abilities, together with confidence

in one's willpower and a propensity to experience positive epistemic feelings of certainty and truth.[4] Second, it argues that appropriate self-trust
depends on attitudes to the self which are not defensive.

The chapter consists of five sections. The first offers an analysis of
intellectual self-trust. The second describes the sort of ill-placed self-
confidence characteristic of those who are intellectually arrogant. It con-
trasts this with the lack of confidence typical of those who are obsequious
or intellectually timid, and also with the well-placed confidence of those
who are humbly proud of their abilities. The third section introduces the
social psychological notion of an attitude and identifies three forms of
self-esteem: defensive, damaged, and secure. Section 4 argues that self-
trust is sensitive to agents' appraisals of their vulnerability to threats.
These evaluations are among the constituents of subjects' self-esteem (i.e.
their attitudes to the self). Finally, Section 5 details why the self-trust
resulting from secure self-esteem is well-placed, whereas the self-trust
characteristic of arrogance and the mistrust typical of servility and timidity are ill-placed.

1. Intellectual Self-Trust

In this section I argue that intellectual self-trust conceived as a three-
place relation between agents, their faculties, and a domain or context
is composed of at least three elements. These are, first, a propensity to
rely on one's epistemic faculties and abilities (which are implicitly taken
as reliable); second, a tendency to be confident in one's willpower; and
third, a disposition to experience positive epistemic feelings.[5] I show that
each of these three elements of self-trust plays a distinctive role in intellectual inquiry. Reliance on one's epistemic faculties is necessary to carry
out any investigation; confidence in the strength of one's will is required
to persevere in one's endeavors; finally, epistemic feelings of certainty
and doubt provide essential guidance when deciding whether to continue
or terminate one's examination of the issues. In this section I make no
distinction between intellectual self-trust that is well-placed or misplaced;
I return to the issue in the final section of the chapter, where I explain
why the self-trust of those who are humbly self-confident is warranted
but the self-satisfied trust that the arrogant places in himself is not.

First and foremost, intellectual self-trust is a form of reliance on one's
epistemic faculties such as memory or perception, one's intellectual abilities such as mathematical or writing skills, and on the accuracy of one's
belief system. The person who trusts herself intellectually relies on these
features not to let her down. She implicitly takes them to be reliable and
to be suited to the intellectual challenges that she must face. If confronted
with an easy task, such as the addition of small numbers, she deploys
her mental arithmetical skills without feeling the need to verify the result
by using a calculator. When faced with harder problems, she chooses

strategies for solving them that she thinks are suitable. These may include consulting an expert or engaging in extensive investigation of the relevant issues. In sum, her behavior manifests a reliance on her faculties, skills, and relevant beliefs that consists in taking these as suitable means to find truthful answers to the intellectual questions which interest her. This person may also be aware of vulnerabilities. She does not think that her reasoning skills or her memory are perfect, but she fully expects that they reliably deliver accurate outcomes. Hence, the self-trusting individual does not fret or endlessly double-check her judgment.

Second, the person who trusts herself in matters of the intellect is also confident in her willpower. She trusts herself to last the course. She relies on her capacity to stick to the intellectual endeavors upon which she embarks. Intellectual inquiry often requires that one focus on a single task and avoid distractions; it is frequently painstaking and time consuming. Thus, concentration and perseverance are crucial to success in intellectual activities. The person who trusts herself, therefore, in addition to treating her epistemic faculties as being up to the task of acquiring knowledge, takes herself to be able to control her mental activities in order to carry out her plans and projects to their conclusion.

Thus, self-trust is a cluster of behavioral dispositions that exhibit an implicit reliance on one's faculties and skills to deliver true outcomes and that manifest confidence in one's will to exercise the kind of control required to execute one's problem-solving strategies. Success in one's inquiries requires strength of commitment to one's plans, realistic goal setting, and suitable and reliable epistemic faculties and abilities.[6] The person who is intellectually talented because her faculties are reliable may achieve very little if she sets goals for which her talents are not suited. For instance, a gifted mathematician may not succeed in her inquiry because she stubbornly refuses computer assistance in her attempts to prove a complex conjecture. She may also fail despite choosing good problem-solving strategies and possessing reliable epistemic faculties if she is often distracted and gives up too soon. However, the individual who, through sheer strength of will, perseveres in her inquiries may also get nowhere if her faculties are not very reliable or she has set unrealistic goals.

These two facets of self-trust, therefore, may come apart. Some may trust their intellectual competence but mistrust their willpower. Hence, for example, the Italian poet Giacomo Leopardi as a young child was said to have asked his tutors to tie him to his chair because he did not trust himself not to want to wander off. At the same time he had no doubt that his intellectual abilities were up to the task. Conversely, one may trust one's ability to persevere but have reservations about one's intellectual prowess.[7]

These distinct elements of intellectual self-trust may also exhibit different relations of dependence. The person who trusts herself relies on her faculties and abilities in the same manner in which she relies on telescopes or microscopes. She takes these to be suitable to the task and treats them as reliable. She adopts an optimistic stance toward them by having predictive expectations that they will deliver. In short, our trust in our faculties is trust as mere reliance.[8] This is why, although our trust in them may be disappointed, it cannot be betrayed. If a person trusts her memory and it turns out to be unreliable, it would seem apt for her to regret the trust she put in her cognitive faculties, but resentment would be inappropriate.[9]

The relation of dependence that the self-trusting individual has to her will is not that of mere reliance. Rather, it exhibits the features of trust as confidence. The person who trusts her will but is let down feels disappointed in herself. However, she may also plausibly feel betrayed by herself because she has failed to live up to her commitments. Such a person does not merely expect, in the sense of predict, that she possesses enough self-discipline to persevere in her endeavors. She also expects, in the sense of commitment, to follow and execute the plans that she has set for herself. Hence, intellectual self-trust includes confidence in one's willpower, understood to include reliance on one's ability to commit and to fulfill one's commitments.[10] In what follows I largely ignore the distinction between these two kinds of reliance because my focus in this chapter lies primarily with the third component of intellectual self-trust, which is a disposition to experience positive epistemic feelings.

There is more to self-trust than reliance on one's faculties and abilities and confidence in the strength of one's will. A person may possess these dispositions and yet fail to trust herself. For instance, imagine a person who, on her way to the airport, keeps checking that her passport is in her bag.[11] She knows it is there because she distinctly remembers seeing it. This person does not genuinely believe that her memory is not reliable; nevertheless, she cannot help feeling anxious over the whereabouts of her documents.[12] This individual may be confident in the strength of her will and rely on her faculties, which she fully believes to be reliable. Nevertheless, she cannot shake this anxious doubt. In these circumstances, this person may steel herself—give herself a talking to—and resolve to stop checking. If her trust in her will is well placed, she may succeed in regulating her behavior. We may now imagine that a person who often finds herself in this kind of predicament can successfully resolve never to give in to her anxious feelings. She thus develops new habits despite, at least for a while, continuing to experience epistemic anxiety. This person has dispositions to rely on her faculties and the confidence to trust her willpower, but she has not fully shaken her self-mistrust.

I do not know whether those who suffer from compulsions of this sort can, in reality, adopt the resolute stance of ignoring their feelings, relying on their faculties and being confident in their willpower. The mere conceptual possibility of the resolute, but mistrusting, individual is sufficient to show that intellectual self-trust requires more than reliance on one's abilities and faculties and confidence in the strength of one's will. It also includes an affective dimension. In order to trust oneself, one must also often experience epistemic feelings of certainty and truth regarding the deliverances of one's epistemic faculties.[13]

I have claimed earlier that intellectual self-trust consists of at least three elements: a tendency to rely on one's intellectual faculties and abilities, a disposition to count on one's strength of will, and a propensity to experience positive epistemic feelings about some of one's beliefs. These three elements of self-trust are supplemented in reflective, mature human beings by beliefs about the level of one's intellectual competence and about one's capacity for self-discipline. Intuitively, however, these beliefs about one's own cognitions do not seem to be an essential component of self-trust because young children and other creatures that lack the cognitive tools for reflective self-knowledge nevertheless are capable of some form of self-trust.

It may be objected that examples concerning individuals suffering from epistemic anxiety do not support the conclusion that positive affect is an essential element of self-trust. One may argue that we can explain these cases by attributing inconsistent beliefs to the anxious. The person who continually verifies whether her passport is in her bag believes, based on her memory, that it is there. However, one may interpret her as also believing that the passport may not be in her bag. Her feeling of uncertainty would be a manifestation of this contradiction in her belief system. If this is right, intellectual self-trust would not require the presence of feelings of confidence, certainty, or correctness. Instead, the absence of feelings of doubt, anxiety, or uncertainty indicating an underlying inconsistency in one's belief system would be sufficient.

This objection misrepresents the dynamic of the family of examples under consideration. Those who are in the thrall of epistemic anxiety do not persist in checking whether the deliverance of their memory is accurate because they also believe that it is unreliable. Rather, these are cases where individuals find it difficult to terminate their inquiries and to take the question they are trying to address as settled.[14] The reason why they cannot stop is that they implicitly set the standards of evidence required to reach a conclusion unreasonably high. Epistemically anxious individuals take the deliverances of memory to be reasonably reliable. Nevertheless, they feel that memory must be supplemented with the additional evidence provided by perception. They proceed in this manner within contexts in which memory alone would satisfy other agents. Their anxious behavior is not based on inconsistent beliefs about the required standards of evidence. Rather, they would endorse the claim that the testimony of memory is sufficient for confident belief in this instance. Nonetheless, they experience a feeling of unrest, which prompts them to carry out additional checks.

One may also object that, although something must motivate agents to initiate and terminate their inquiries, this function may be fulfilled by mental states other than feelings. In response, I wish to show that this role cannot be played in every instance by rational deliberation. We cannot always deliberate about when to stop deliberating because such a process would give rise to an unstoppable regress.[15] Suppose I am trying to ascertain whether p, and I have evidence in support of p. If the evidence is sufficient, my investigation could stop and I could take myself to know that p. But in order to halt the deliberating process, I need to consider whether the evidence for p is sufficient to bring the process to an end. Suppose now that I deliberate about this question. I have some evidence that my evidence about p is quite strong, but is that evidence about the strength of my evidence itself sufficient to stop my deliberation about whether to stop deliberating whether p? Well, I could deliberate about that also. As it should be clear, given that this deliberative process cannot be halted by deliberation alone, each deliberative step generates another step dedicated to its evaluation.

Presumably, decisions to terminate inquiries and take their deliverances to settle the issue are not arbitrary. So they are not mere decisions. They must be grounded in appraisals or evaluations of whether the evidence in one's possession is sufficient. These evaluations, as I have argued, cannot themselves be based exclusively on deliberations. They must therefore be also grounded in something else. Sometimes investigations are largely carried out without much conscious reflection about one's problem-solving strategy. In these cases, the halting mechanisms that terminate inquiries may well be automatic and not conscious. But in other instances we need to make conscious choices about whether to stop an investigation. Because the decision is hopefully not wholly arbitrary and cannot be exclusively based on deliberation, it must be guided by intuitions or gut feelings. These are often experienced as epistemic feelings of ease, competence, certainty, or confidence.

These feelings are sensitive to heuristic cues which are indicative of the accuracy, truth, validity, or reliability of doxastic states and cognitive processes. In this manner, feelings are sources of information about the epistemic properties of mental states and processes, although their contents are not represented by the feelings. For example, feelings of ease or fluency in processing usually generate an impression of truth or validity (Alter and Oppenheimer 2009). The rationale for this heuristic is that fluency indicates familiarity or frequency, which, in turn, is some evidence of truth. The idea is that if a claim is frequently encountered, it must be widely held in society. Further, widespread consensus is at least *prima facie* evidence of truth. For this reason, claims whose processing feels easy and sound familiar also feel truer than claims that are harder to process. Sadly, this heuristic is easily manipulated by engendering fluency by means of spurious variables, such as font size or background color. Nonetheless, it can be epistemically valuable in a vast range of circumstances.

The conclusion that self-trust should include at least these three components (as well as an additional doxastic element in self-reflective, mature human beings) is supported by the foundational role played by self-trust in all intellectual pursuits. Some kind of pre-reflective self-trust must already be in place if we are to carry out any inquiry. Without it, we would be paralyzed. But any intellectual investigation presupposes three distinct capacities: the ability to form beliefs by means of reason, perception, memory, or any combination of our faculties; the ability to persist until one has reached a conclusion; and the ability to recognize whether one's answer is adequate to settle the issue.

Intellectual self-trust therefore consists of our propensities to rely on those aspects of our cognitive lives (cognitive capacities, will, and affect) that make our epistemic inquiries possible. Our reliance on, and confidence in, these aspects of the self is pre-reflective. We trust that they are up to the task of giving us truthful answers and accurate solutions to intellectual puzzles even though we do not possess independent evidence of their reliability, effectiveness, or accuracy. No independent evidence is available because we need to trust our capacities to discover whether those same capacities are trustworthy (Cf., Zagzebski 2012, p. 49). In short, as Alston (2005) argued, any attempt to justify our beliefs in the reliability of our belief-forming faculties ultimately suffers from epistemic circularity.[16] I address the question whether pre-reflective self-trust can be warranted in the final section of this chapter. For now, suffice it to say that self-trust is inevitable if we are to engage in any kind of investigation.

2. Virtuous and Vicious Types of Intellectual Self-Confidence

In this section I turn to a description of three different stances or attitudes that an individual may take toward her own ability to engage successfully in epistemic activities. These are the optimistic confidence exhibited by those who are humbly proud of their achievements, the self-satisfied and smug confidence of those who are arrogant, and the pessimistic outlook characteristic of individuals who are intellectually obsequious or timid. In the final section of this chapter, I explain why arrogant self-trust and obsequious mistrust are epistemically vicious, whereas optimistic self-trust is virtuous.

Intellectual arrogance is generally associated with overbearing or self-satisfied confidence. Here I wish to highlight five behaviors typical of those who possess this character trait: extreme self-confidence, feelings of invulnerability, superior attitudes, self-satisfaction or smugness, and a propensity to anger.[17]

First, individuals who are arrogant are often full of themselves. They appear supremely confident and come across as cocky. They give the impression of believing that they know it all and that they are right on every issue. They appear certain of their views and seem to overestimate the degree to which others agree with them.[18]

Second, some arrogant individuals behave as if they were invulnerable to threats. They may in a detached manner calculate risks accurately but fail to feel their salience to their own case. They are aware of the possibility of failure and disappointment, but they experience it as a mere possibility that does not need to be factored in their decisions. Hence, despite knowing about possible pitfalls, they are prepared to take enormous risks.

Third, arrogant people usually feel superior to others and act accordingly. They tend to behave as if no one could possibly teach them anything. They largely ignore the views of other people, and they dismiss any criticism raised against them. Although arrogant individuals feel superior to other people, this feeling need not be accompanied by a belief in one's superiority. A person may be able to judge that he is not actually cleverer than everybody else; nevertheless, he might in the heat of discussion always end up believing that his arguments are better, his position more interesting, than anything put forward by others. Conversely, a person may believe, rightly or wrongly, that he is intellectually superior to other members of his epistemic community without necessarily being arrogant.[19] For instance, he may be accurate in his judgment or he may have made an honest mistake.

Fourth, arrogant people usually appear to be very pleased with themselves. They seem to gain more pleasure from having the last word than from discovering the truth. They always give the impression that they care more about the feelings of self-satisfaction they gain from any success than about the objective worth of their achievements.

Fifth, arrogant individuals are prone to anger. They take criticisms very badly, as if they were personal affronts. They seem to arrogate for themselves the right not to be challenged, and thus consider disagreements as failures to acknowledge their privileges.[20]

These five manifestations of arrogance offer evidence in support of the view that arrogance is associated with a special kind of supreme self-confidence, which can be described as self-satisfied self-trust.

It is instructive to contrast arrogant self-trust with the optimistic stance adopted by those who are proud of their abilities but acknowledge their limitations.[21] The optimist exhibits self-trust because she relies on her faculties and is confident in her willpower. However, unlike the arrogant person, she is not a cocky know-it-all. Instead, there are occasions when she experiences feelings of doubt and uncertainty. She does not attempt to deny their existence, but rather treats them as a motive to seek to improve. Further, the optimist is not crippled by anxiety or fear that she may not be up to the task.

In addition, the person who is intellectually self-confident without being arrogant is not likely to experience feelings of superiority. She is proud of her achievements without exhibiting the smugness that is typical of the arrogant. In ordinary circumstances, she is open-minded in her response to criticisms, while remaining steadfast in her views when she feels certain about them.

Whereas intellectual arrogance is associated with a kind of self-confidence that is overbearing in its smugness, those vices—such as intellectual timidity and obsequiousness—that are in some sense opposed to arrogance are characterized by the lack of confidence typical of self-mistrust.

Individuals who are intellectually servile or who are timid lack self-confidence. They have a negative stance toward their intellectual abilities, which they expect, in the sense of prediction, not to be up to the challenges of intellectual inquiry. This inability to trust their faculties is likely to be associated with frequent experiences of epistemic feelings of doubt or uncertainty. In the more severe cases, this lack of confidence can take the form of crippling epistemic anxiety that makes one feel that one has never accumulated sufficient evidence to make up one's mind. In addition, these feelings of uncertainty often are taken not as an incentive to improve, but as evidence that one is stupid and unable to do better. Thus, at least in those who are intellectually timid, lack of self-confidence manifests itself not merely in an expectation of failure but also as resignation to it as inevitable and unchangeable.

People who suffer from servility or timidity have heightened awareness of their vulnerabilities.[22] They do not expect, in the sense of prediction, their abilities and faculties to serve them well consistently and on matters of importance. Those who are timid primarily respond to this awareness with fear of the harms that may accrue to them as a result. Intellectually servile individuals react to these perceived shortcomings by developing an increased sense of dependency on others to supply the answers to any questions that they may have.[23]

If arrogant people feel superior, those who are obsequious suffer from feelings of inferiority. They tend to capitulate in the face of criticism because they feel that others must be right, because they are better than them. Thus, intellectually servile individuals tend to defer too uncritically to the views put forward by other people. On their own, they are very unsure of their views, and because of their persistent feelings of uncertainty, may become prone to endless rumination about what to believe or do.

In addition, those who are obsequious seem to derive any sense of self-confidence that they may have from others' judgments of their abilities. Thus, they turn themselves into "yes-men" who always agree with those whom they are very keen to please and ingratiate themselves to.

Finally, if arrogant individuals are prone to anger, those who are timid are dominated by fear. They have negative expectations of their abilities and are afraid that their weaknesses (as they perceive them) may be apparent to others, who may exploit these in order to harm them.

Although more could be said about each of these types of intellectual self-confidence and lack of it, these brief characterizations are hopefully sufficient to home in on different kinds of personality, each of which exhibits a different sort of self-trust or mistrust.

3. Secure, Defensive, and Damaged Self-Esteem

The three forms of self-trust discussed in the previous section are underpinned by three kinds of self-esteem, which I will outline in this section. Social psychologists label them as secure, defensive, and damaged. I will argue that these kinds of self-esteem, respectively, underpin optimistic self-trust, intellectual arrogance, and intellectual servility and timidity.

Self-esteem can be thought of either as a transient state of momentary self-confidence or as a trait reflective of a stable self-evaluation. It can be global when it concerns the self as a whole or domain specific when it assesses the self, for example, for its competence or for its likeability. Social psychologists often think of self-esteem as an attitude directed toward the self (Zeigler-Hill 2013).

Attitudes are defined by psychologists as associations of valences (positive or negative) with representations of attitude objects. Attitudes are summary evaluations that are based on information supplied by one's evaluative beliefs about an object, one's emotional and affective responses to it, and one's behavioral dispositions with regard to that object based on past experiences. Attitudes thus function as cognitive shortcuts; they help subjects call to mind how they feel about or evaluate something— including oneself—without having to reconsider each time afresh all the relevant evidence (Maio and Haddock 2015).

Attitudes can be measured explicitly or implicitly (Maio and Haddock 2015). Explicit measures of attitudes are direct and include self-reports and answers to questionnaires using Likert scales. Self-esteem measures may include asking subjects whether they agree with statements about their likeability or their competence. They are intended to measure subjects' positive or negative conscious self-evaluations. By contrast, implicit measures of attitudes are indirect; they measure attitudes by measuring factors associated with them. These measures include evaluative priming and implicit association tests (IATs). With regard to self-esteem, psychologists often rely on the name-letter test (NLT) (when participants are asked how much they like the first letter of their first name) and the name-liking effect (when subjects are asked how much they like their name) to measure self-esteem (Zeigler-Hill and Jordan 2010). Individuals who like their name or its first letter are said to have high self-esteem as implicitly measured. Implicit measures of self-esteem are poorly correlated, raising concerns about the validity of the construct (Bosson, Swann, and Pennebaker 2000).[24] Nevertheless, each of these measures has predictive value, and thus cautious reliance on them is generally thought to be appropriate.

My focus in this chapter is on one kind of congruent self-esteem—namely secure high self-esteem—and two kinds of discrepant self-esteem: defensive high and damaged. Secure self-esteem is the kind of trait self-esteem typical of those who are positive about the competence and/or likeability of the self when their attitudes are measured explicitly and implicitly (Jordan et al. 2003).[25] Defensive or fragile high self-esteem is characteristic of individuals whose self-esteem is positive when measured explicitly but is negative when measured indirectly (Haddock and Gebauer 2011, Jordan et al. 2003, Zeigler-Hill 2006). Damaged self-esteem pertains to individuals whose self-esteem is negative when measured explicitly but positive when measured implicitly (Schröder-Abé, Rudolph, and Schütz 2007a).[26]

Secure self-esteem has been associated with a number of positive outcomes, including psychological health, life satisfaction, and persistence at difficult tasks (Jordan et al. 2003). This kind of self-esteem is said to be secure because it is not a mask or a defense hiding underlying insecurities. Those whose high self-esteem is secure are also less subject to fluctuations over time about their levels of self-esteem (Zeigler-Hill 2006). They are less prone to endlessly and inconclusively mulling things over (Phillips and Hine 2016) and are more disposed to trust their intuitions (Jordan, Whitfield, and Zeigler-Hill 2007).

Defensive or fragile self-esteem is generally thought to be predictive of behaviors that are intuitively associated with arrogance. These include a predisposition to anger (Schröder-Abé, Rudolph, and Schütz 2007a) and aggression (McGregor et al. 2005), a tendency to boast (Olson, Fazio, and Hermann 2007) and to self-enhance (Bosson et al. 2003), and higher levels of social prejudice (Jordan, Spencer, and Zanna 2005). Defensiveness and heightened vigilance to real or imagined threats are the most distinctive characteristics of this kind of self-esteem (Haddock and Gebauer 2011). Individuals whose high self-esteem is defensive experience their own sense of self-worth and competence as being under threat; they respond to this perceived potential harm in an aggressive manner. In short, their high self-esteem is a defense mechanism that hides underlying insecurities about the self.

Damaged self-esteem has received less attention in the psychological literature than either secure or defensive self-esteem. Nevertheless, there is evidence that individuals whose self-esteem is damaged exhibit some of the behaviors that are characteristic either of servility or of timidity. For example, they attribute any success that they may have either to good luck or to the limited difficulty of the task, but see any failures as a consequence of their lack of ability (Schröder-Abé, Rudolph, and Schütz 2007a).[27] They are also more nervous and have worse physical health (as measured by the number of sick days) than other people (Schröder-Abé, Rudolph, and Schütz 2007a). They are very sensitive to social rejection and live with persistent feelings of personal inadequacy (Schröder-Abé,

Rudolph, and Schütz 2007b). Researchers have concluded that individuals whose self-esteem is damaged feel constantly under threat and are rather defensive as a result. Their anger, however, tends to be suppressed rather than expressed (Schröder-Abé, Rudolph, and Schütz 2007a). In addition, there is evidence of a correlation between low self-esteem and behavior that seeks to ingratiate oneself to powerful others (Wu, Li, and Johnson 2011).[28]

In sum, there is empirical evidence linking secure high self-esteem to some manifestations of optimistic self-trust, intellectually arrogant behaviors to defensive high self-esteem, and conduct that exhibits intellectual servility and timidity to damaged self-esteem.

4. Self-Esteem as Underpinning Self-Confidence

The framework of attitude psychology can help to explain the three kinds of self-trust which I have described as optimistic, self-satisfied, and pessimistic. It can also reveal the basic psychological mechanisms that underpin intellectual self-trust. Although self-trust itself is a complex hybrid cluster of three-place relations of dependence between an agent, some aspects of her psychology, and some domains or contexts of inquiry, it is causally dependent on a more basic evaluative appraisal of the self (i.e., self-esteem), which moderates subjects' reliance on their faculties, confidence in their will, and dispositions to experience epistemic feelings of certainty or of doubt.[29] My aim in this section is to argue that optimistic, self-satisfied, and pessimistic intellectual forms of self-trust are, respectively, expressions of secure, defensive, and damaged self-esteem. Because both defensive and damaged self-esteem are associated with heightened alertness to threats, it is hardly surprising that intense awareness of one's vulnerability has profound effects on individuals' ability to trust their own intellectual abilities.[30]

I mentioned earlier that both defensive and damaged self-esteem are associated with increased vigilance to threats and a tendency to perceive situations as threatening. Individuals with discrepant forms of self-esteem are extremely good at detecting threats to the self, but are also prone to interpreting situations as threatening when they are not (Haddock and Gebauer 2011). It is extremely plausible therefore that these individuals are especially alert to any possible vulnerability they may have.

Those whose self-esteem is defensive have high self-esteem as explicitly measured. It is likely that implicit measures that show their self-esteem to be low reveal their insecurities. These individuals would respond to this feeling of vulnerability by "bigging themselves up." Explicit measures of self-esteem would thus tap into the protective conception of the self that these individuals have built up as a defensive response to their underlying insecurity. Those whose self-esteem is damaged, in contrast, show their vulnerability overtly and report feeling nervous and stressed

(Schröder-Abé, Rudolph, and Schütz 2007a). In both cases the evidence suggests that discrepant self-esteem is closely related to conscious or non-conscious heightened sensitivity to the vulnerability of one's sense of self-worth and self-confidence.

Trait self-esteem is a stable cluster of attitudes toward the self and aspects of it that are central to one's self-understanding. These attitudes are not identical to the dispositions constitutive of self-trust or mistrust. Rather, they underpin them, because the attitudes are causally responsible, together with situational and other factors, for the manifestations of self-trusting or mistrusting dispositions. That is, attitudes are the psychological properties that explain why people have dispositions to behave and feel in ways that are characteristic of self-trust or mistrust. In short, if self-trust is a complex disposition, self-esteem is among its causal bases.

Optimistic self-trust presupposes that one does not experience one's sense of self-worth as being under threat. It is only if one appraises oneself as being competent without feeling that this competence is at risk, that one can stably rely on one's faculties, feelings, and the strength of one's self-discipline. We can think of well-placed or secure self-trust as something that one can possibly develop only if one generally feels that what matters to one is not constantly in danger.

However, when individuals have defensive attitudes toward the self, they are disposed to perceive many aspects of their surroundings as potentially threatening. Hence, they consciously or nonconsciously feel that their identity is continually under threat. These individuals cannot adopt an optimistic stance about their abilities, because they have a heightened sensitivity to the vulnerability of their self-esteem. The absence of a secure sense of self-worth should be expected to impede the formation of those dispositions, commitments, and feelings that are constitutive of self-trust.[31]

Defensive and damaged self-esteem are two possible responses to this basic sense of insecurity. Defensive self-esteem is tantamount to the pursuit of a strategy of denial.[32] Those whose self-esteem is defensive cover up their vulnerabilities by developing an inflated—albeit unstable—sense of self-worth as a defensive shield. This interpretation of defensive self-esteem as a defensive mechanism to boost one's own sense of self-worth in order to banish feelings of insecurity helps explain why self-satisfied self-trust is a distinctive manifestation of intellectual arrogance. Those who are arrogant attempt to compensate for an overactive feeling of vulnerability by developing a high opinion of themselves. They thus appear exceedingly self-confident. However, these feelings of superiority and invulnerability serve the function of enhancing a sense of self that is always at risk of being overwhelmed by insecurities. The defensive or self-enhancing function of arrogant self-confidence explains why it comes across as self-satisfying. Its sole purpose is to make the arrogant individual feel good about himself.

Individuals whose self-esteem is damaged, in contrast, are aware of their vulnerabilities; this awareness is reflected in their conscious low opinions of their own global worth and competence. This heightened sense of vulnerability makes it hard for these individuals to develop an appropriate form of self-trust. This mistrust of one's own abilities, in my opinion, may take two distinct forms, although many individuals may exemplify both at the same time. The first is intellectual timidity, which consists of a resigned acceptance of one's own alleged shortcomings. Those who are timid adopt the depressive attributional style of interpreting failures as a consequence of their own lack of ability and interpreting successes as due to good fortune or to other properties of the situation external to the self. The second is intellectual servility, which consists of a response to vulnerability by seeking to ingratiate oneself to more powerful others so as to be accepted in their social group and perhaps bask in their glory.

The relation between attitudes to the self and the constituents of self-trust is not unidirectional. The dispositions to rely (or not) on one's epistemic faculties, to be confident or unconfident in one's will, and to have positive or negative epistemic feelings feed into the process of revising attitudes. For example, a person who often experiences feelings of doubt about her beliefs may take these feelings as evidence of the unreliability of her reasoning. She may as a result revise down her estimate of the trustworthiness of some of her epistemic faculties. This appraisal in turn may lead her to revise in a negative direction her attitudes toward herself.

What we have here is a kind of epistemic circularity in appraisal that mirrors the deliberative epistemic circularity highlighted by Alston (2005). We base our pre-reflective self-appraisals of the trustworthiness of our faculties and will on pre-existing evaluations of the self's vulnerability to threats. However, self-esteem is, in turn, responsive to dispositions to trust our faculties and will. In the next section, I highlight how this mutual dependency can lead to secure self-trust, which is calibrated to the trustworthiness of those aspects of the self that one trusts. Alternatively, with regard to self-satisfied trust and mistrust, this interdependence can lead to increasing decalibration.

5. Well-Placed and Ill-Founded Self-Trust

So far I have argued that optimistic self-trust flows from, and sustains, secure self-esteem. I have shown that it differs both from self-satisfied self-trust, which is associated with defensive self-esteem, and from pessimistic self-mistrust, which is closely related to damaged self-esteem. In this section, I argue that the first kind of trust is apt, or calibrated, and that the remaining two are unwarranted, or decalibrated.

There is substantial evidence that individuals whose attitudes (including those directed at the self) serve defensive purposes have a propensity to engage in cognition that is biased by a motive of self-defense. Individuals whose self-esteem is defensive tend to discount evidence contrary to their inflated self-conception and seek evidence in support of their high self-esteem. I have already noted that these individuals have the highest rate of self-delusion (Jordan et al. 2003). Two styles of thinking characteristic of defensive high self-esteem are especially illuminating in this context. First, individuals with this form of self-esteem gauge their level of ability by comparing themselves to others (Mussweiler and Rüter 2003).[33] However, when offered the opportunity these individuals prefer to compare themselves to people whose level of attainment is low so that they can seem accomplished in comparison (Vohs and Heatherton 2004). If forced to compare themselves to high achievers, defensive high-self-esteem individuals will do so by seeking evidence that they are similar to these exemplars. Because of a shared human tendency to confirmation bias, these comparisons result in unrealistically positive self-evaluations (Corcoran, Crusius, and Mussweiler 2011).

Second, when faced with a difficult task that may force them to form a realistic view of their competence, these individuals often opt for self-sabotage. Instead of applying themselves to a challenge by practicing and putting forth some effort, these people often prefer not to prepare. In this way they are able to attribute failure to lack of application and any unlikely success to their innate talents (Lupien, Seery, and Almonte 2010). What these results strongly suggest is that people whose high self-esteem is defensive are likely to form attitudes about their abilities that are out of step with reality. These delusive attitudes inform their behavior, their confidence in their strength of will, and their epistemic feelings of certainty. As a result their self-trust is not calibrated to the trustworthiness of their faculties and abilities. Further, because the dispositions that constitute self-trust in turn contribute to the information agents use to update their attitudes, these inputs are likely to set in motion a process of decalibration that causes subjects' self-appraisal to become increasingly inaccurate.

Individuals whose self-esteem is damaged are also prone to processes that decalibrate their self-assessments of their own intellectual skills and abilities. They prefer to compare themselves to people whom they think are better than they are, thus confirming their low opinion of themselves. Further, if forced to compare themselves to individuals of limited abilities, they do so by seeking evidence that they are similar to them (Vohs and Heatherton 2004). These comparisons are likely to produce inaccurate results and lead these individuals to evaluate themselves as being less intellectually able than they are. These assessments are then likely to contribute to the development of mistrustful dispositions and epistemic feelings of uncertainty and self-doubt. Further, these dispositions and feelings in turn feed into novel assessments of the self, giving rise to a downward spiral of ever lower self-esteem as explicitly measured. That said, individuals whose implicit self-esteem is high and who suffer from low explicitly measured self-esteem are responsive to positive feedback and thus able to reverse this downward trend (Jordan et al. 2013).[34]

These considerations show why self-satisfied trust and pessimistic mistrust are unwarranted. They are integral parts of appraisals that serve motives of defensiveness rather than accuracy and which lead those who engage in them to develop dispositions to rely (or not) on their faculties and abilities. These dispositions do not reflect the reliability of these psychological components of the self and do not serve those who have them, because they obstruct their ability to engage in inquiries that effectively lead to knowledge. For example, such people may experience feelings of certainty and of doubt which are not sensitive to the epistemic status of the beliefs and problem-solving strategies that they assess (Clarkson et al. 2009; Schröder-Abé, Rudolph, and Schütz 2007a); they may also exhibit a tendency to be uncertain of their intuitions (Jordan, Whitfield, and Zeigler-Hill 2007). Given their role in obstructing knowledge-conducive and responsible inquiry, these forms of self-trust are aptly characterized as vicious.[35]

Whereas high or low self-esteem that is motivated by defensive mechanisms has disabling effects on intellectual self-trust, high self-esteem which is secure serves as a prerequisite for trusting attitudes that are broadly accurate or well-placed. There is evidence that individuals whose high self-esteem is secure respond to negative feedback about their performance with added motivation to do well (Lambird and Mann 2006). These same individuals show more persistence when faced with a difficult task and are able to exercise better self-control than less secure individuals (Vohs, Baumeister, and Ciarocco 2005). These considerations suggest that individuals whose self-esteem is secure are able to regulate their mental activities and to form reasonably accurate evaluations of their abilities. In addition, they possess both the motivations to improve and to persevere that are essential elements of becoming deserving of one's own self-trust. Because secure self-trust plays such an essential role in enabling inquiry that is knowledge conducive, this kind of self-trust is aptly characterized as virtuous.[36]

In conclusion, in this chapter I offered an account of three forms intellectual self-trust and mistrust and traced their sources to three varieties of self-esteem. I have argued that secure high self-esteem grounds self-trusting dispositions that promote knowledge-conducive and responsible inquiry. I have also explained that defensive and damaged self-esteem facilitate the formation of dispositions to rely on one's epistemic faculties, to be confident in one's will, and to experience epistemic feelings, which inhibit successful epistemic activities. In this manner I have shown how some pathologies of self-trust can be explained as one manifestation of more encompassing intellectual character vices.[37]

Notes

1. I do not intend these claims about frequency to have any firm empirical footing. They are anecdotal.
2. I do not describe arrogant individuals as overconfident, because a person could be smugly confident while being, because of sheer luck, epistemically justified in his self-confidence.
3. The influence is reciprocal. Vices negatively affect self-trust, and decalibrations of self-trust facilitate the formation of intellectual vices.
4. I do not intend to suggest that these elements alone are sufficient. Instead, I defend the view that each of them is necessary.
5. In what follows, my talk of self-trust in one's abilities or in the strength of one's will should be read as a shorthand for trust in one's own abilities in most contexts and domains.
6. I do not assume that self-trust per se is a virtue. Instead, I presume that it consists of a cluster of dispositions which are minimally required to carry out any inquiry.
7. I include confidence in the strength of one's will as part of intellectual self-trust because I take it to be the kind of trust required to carry out with some degree of success one's intellectual activities.
8. Much more would need to be said to substantiate this point. My discussion later of the role of epistemic feelings indirectly speaks to this issue but does not fully address it. Be that as it may, it is generally agreed that intellectual self-trust at least involves reliance on one's epistemic faculties.
9. The distinction between disappointed and betrayed trust was first developed by Baier (1994). I owe to Jones (2004) the idea that trust as mere reliance requires only predictive expectations that what one trusts will deliver.
10. See Hinchman (2017) for an exploration of some of these themes.
11. I owe the example to Jones (2012).
12. De Sousa (2008, pp. 197–98) suggests that in these cases one remembers having done what one is anxious about, for instance, putting the passport in the bag. One may even be sure that one's memory is correct and yet be unable to shake a feeling of uncertainty.
13. There is a small literature on epistemic or noetic feelings. In addition to De Sousa (2008) prominent discussions include Proust (2013), Dokic (2012), Arango-Muñoz and Michaelian (2014), and Carruthers (2017). My discussion later makes it clear why these are not best thought of as intellectual seemings.
14. I owe to Jennifer Nagel (2010) this notion of epistemic anxiety as the feeling that current available evidence is insufficient to warrant full belief so that further investigation is necessary. In this chapter I reserve the label "epistemic anxiety" for cases where this feeling persists even though one possesses enough evidence to stop worrying. Kurth (2018), instead, uses "practical anxiety" to refer to feelings of uncertainty prompting reflection, which may often be warranted.
15. What I have in mind is not a regress of justification, but a regress in the process of ascertaining whether one is justified.
16. These considerations are undoubtedly too quick because one may be able to rely on one epistemic faculty to assess the reliability of another. Although I have doubts about the viability of this strategy, addressing this issue is beyond the scope of this chapter.
17. These behaviors are manifestations of arrogance but do not define it. Someone may on occasion exhibit them, and thus behave arrogantly, without being arrogant. This conduct might be, for example, an attempt to deal with a hostile environment.

18. There are circumstances in which arrogant individuals may mask these tendencies to avoid social sanctions. That said, arrogance often manifests itself in a belief that common norms, including those of politeness, do not apply to oneself.
19. I have argued for this point in my Tanesini (2016b).
20. I have discussed the privileges that arrogant individuals arrogate for themselves in my (2016a).
21. See my (2018) for the view that intellectual humility requires pride in one's abilities, as well as acceptance of one's limitations.
22. These two vices are different in several respects. Here I focus on similarities before highlighting some differences later.
23. It should not be presumed that they are confident in their ability to detect trustworthy sources. Rather, they accept the views of the majority or those of people the majority holds in high esteem.
24. This fact alone should not be taken as sufficient evidence that the two kinds of measures tap into distinct constructs (Cf., Buhrmester, Blanton, and Swann 2011, Olson, Fazio, and Hermann 2007).
25. Thus, these two measures are congruent.
26. In these cases there are discrepancies in the measures of self-esteem.
27. These tendencies are usually labeled as depressive attributional style.
28. There is some evidence in the empirical literature to suggest that individuals whose self-esteem is damaged are responsive to positive encouragement (Jordan et al. 2013; Spencer et al. 2005). If this is right, this kind of self-esteem does not conform to the resigned outlook I have attributed to intellectually timid individuals. It may be more in keeping with the stance adopted by those who are intellectually servile and responsive to the positive feedback of those whom they try to ingratiate.
29. Kidd's (2016) view that intellectual humility is, broadly speaking, a virtue calibrating confidence in one's intellectual capacities, those of one's peers, and in the fruitfulness of one's tradition bears some deep connections to the position that I present here.
30. The view that self-trust presupposes basic self-esteem is also defended by Govier in her (1993).
31. I owe the idea that trust depends on a more basic sense of safety to Jones (2004). In that paper, however, Jones does not consider the possibility that some forms of self-satisfied self-trust may also emerge as a response to a heightened feeling of vulnerability.
32. These individuals have the highest rate of self-deception (Jordan et al. 2003, 975–6).
33. This strategy is not exclusive to this category of individuals, but is widely adopted.
34. Attempts to reduce the cognitive dissonance created by discrepant self-esteem may also contribute to these processes. It is beyond the scope of this chapter to discuss the role of cognitive dissonance and harmony for well-placed and ill-founded intellectual self-trust. See Zagzebski (2012) for a discussion of rationality as dissonance reduction. For objections to Zagzebski, see Fricker (2016). As should be clear from the earlier text, in my opinion, dissonance reduction could drive decalibrating processes that take one further and further away from accurate self-assessments.
35. The view that vices are obstacles to knowledge-productive and responsible investigation has been defended by Cassam (2016).
36. See Battaly (2016) for some characterization of virtues as traits that reliably produce good effects.
37. I would like to thank Katherine Dormandy and two anonymous referees for some helpful comments on an earlier version of this chapter.

References

Alston, William P. 2005. *Beyond "Justification": Dimensions of Epistemic Evaluation*. Ithaca, NY: Cornell University Press.

Alter, Adam L., and Daniel M. Oppenheimer. 2009. Uniting the Tribes of Fluency to Form a Metacognitive Nation. *Personality and Social Psychology Review* 13(3): 219–35.

Arango-Muñoz, Santiago, and Kourken Michaelian. 2014. "Epistemic Feelings, Epistemic Emotions: Review and Introduction to the Focus Section." *Philosophical Inquiries* 2(1): 97–122.

Baier, Annette. 1994. *Moral Prejudices: Essays on Ethics*. Cambridge, MA and London: Harvard University Press.

Battaly, Heather. 2016. Epistemic Virtue and Vice: Reliabilism, Responsibilism, and Personalism. In *Moral and Intellectual Virtues in Western and Chinese Philosophy*, edited by Chienkuo Mi, Michael Slote, and Erneset Sosa, 99–120. New York and London: Routledge.

Bosson, Jennifer K., Ryan P. Brown, Virgil Zeigler-Hill, and William B. Swann. 2003. "Self-Enhancement Tendencies among People with High Explicit Self-Esteem: The Moderating Role of Implicit Self-Esteem." *Self and Identity* 2(3): 169–87.

Bosson, Jennifer K., William B. Swann, and James W. Pennebaker. 2000. "Stalking the Perfect Measure of Implicit Self-Esteem: The Blind Men and the Elephant Revisited?" *Journal of Personality and Social Psychology* 79: 631–43.

Buhrmester, Michael D., Hart Blanton, and William B. Swann Jr. 2011. "Implicit Self-Esteem: Nature, Measurement, and a New Way Forward." *Journal of Personality and Social Psychology* 100(2): 365–85.

Carruthers, Peter. 2017. "Are Epistemic Emotions Metacognitive?" *Philosophical Psychology* 30(1–2): 58–78.

Cassam, Quassim. 2016. "Vice Epistemology." *The Monist* 99(2): 159–80.

Clarkson, Joshua J., Zakary L. Tormala, Victoria L. DeSensi, and S. Christian Wheeler. 2009. "Does Attitude Certainty Beget Self-Certainty? *Journal of Experimental Social Psychology* 45(2): 436–39.

Corcoran, Katja, Jan Crusius, and Thomas Mussweiler. 2011. Social Comparison: Motives, Standards, and Mechanisms. In *Theories in Social Psychology*, edited by D. Chadee, 119–39. Oxford: Wiley Blackwell.

De Sousa, Ronald. 2008. Epistemic Feelings. In *Epistemology and Emotions*, edited by Georg Brun, Ulvi Doguoglu, and Dominique Kuenzle, 185–204. Aldershot: Ashgate.

Dokic, Jérôme. 2012. "Seeds of Self-Knowledge: Noetic Feelings and Metacognition." In *Foundations of Metacognition*, edited by Michael J. Beran, Johannes L. Brandl, Josef Perner, and Joëlle Proust, 716–61. Oxford: Oxford University Press.

Fricker, Elizabeth. 2016. "Doing (Better) What Comes Naturally: Zagzebski on Rationality and Epistemic Self-Trust." *Episteme* 13(2): 151–66.

Govier, Trudy. 1993. "Self-Trust, Autonomy, and Self-Esteem." *Hypatia* 8(1): 99–120.

Haddock, Geoffrey, and Jochen E. Gebauer. 2011. Defensive Self-Esteem Impacts Attention, Attitude Strength, and Self-Affirmation Processes. *Journal of Experimental Social Psychology* 47(6): 1276–84.

Hinchman, Edward S. (2017). "On the Risks of Resting Assured: An Assurance Theory of Trust." In *The Philosophy of Trust*, edited by Paul Faulkner and Thomas Simpson, 51–69. Oxford: Oxford University Press.

Jones, Karen. 2004. "Trust and Terror." In *Moral Psychology: Feminist Ethics and Social Theory*, edited by Peggy DesAutels and Margaret Urban Walker, 3–18. Lanham, MD: Rowman and Littlefield Publishers.

———. 2012. "The Politics of Intellectual Self-Trust." *Social Epistemology* 26(2): 237–52.

Jordan, Christian H., Christine Logel, Steven J. Spencer, Mark P. Zanna, Joanne V. Wood, and John G. Holmes. 2013. "Responsive Low Self-Esteem: Low Explicit Self-Esteem, Implicit Self-Esteem, and Reactions to Performance Outcomes." *Journal of Social and Clinical Psychology* 32(7): 703–32.

Jordan, Christian H., Steven J. Spencer, and Mark P. Zanna. 2005. "Types of High Self-Esteem and Prejudice: How Implicit Self-Esteem Relates to Ethnic Discrimination among High Explicit Self-Esteem Individuals. *Personality and Social Psychology Bulletin* 31: 693–702.

Jordan, Christian H., Steven J. Spencer, Mark P. Zanna, Etsuko Hoshino-Browne, and Joshua Correll. 2003. "Secure and Defensive High Self-Esteem." *Journal of Personality and Social Psychology* 85(5): 969–78.

Jordan, Christian H., Mervyn Whitfield, and Virgil Zeigler-Hill. 2007. "Intuition and the Correspondence between Implicit and Explicit Self-Esteem." *Journal of Personality and Social Psychology* 93(6): 1067–79.

Kidd, Ian James. 2016. "Intellectual Humility, Confidence, and Argumentation." *Topoi* 35(2 (Special issue on Virtue and Argumentation)): 395–402.

Kurth, Charlie. 2018. "Emotion, Deliberation, and the Skill Model of Virtuous Agency." *Mind and Language*. doi:10.1111/mila.12186.

Lambird, Kathleen Hoffman, and Traci Mann. 2006. "When Do Ego Threats Lead to Self-Regulation Failure? Negative Consequences of Defensive High Self-Esteem." *Personality and Social Psychology Bulletin* 32(9): 1177–87.

Lupien, Shannon P., Mark D. Seery, and Jessica L. Almonte. 2010. "Discrepant and Congruent High Self-esteem: Behavioral Self-Handicapping as a Preemptive Defensive Strategy." *Journal of Experimental Social Psychology* 46: 1105–08.

Maio, Gregory R., and Geoffrey Haddock, G. 2015. *The Psychology of Attitudes and Attitude Change*, 2nd ed. London: SAGE.

McGregor, Ian, Paul R. Nail, Denise C. Marigold, and So-Jin Kang. 2005. "Defensive Pride and Consensus: Strength in imaginary Numbers." *Journal of Personality and Social Psychology* 89(6): 978–96.

Mussweiler, Thomas, and Katja Rüter. 2003. "What Friends Are For! The Use of Routine Standards in Social Comparison." *Journal of Personality and Social Psychology* 85: 467–81.

Nagel, Jennifer. 2010. "Epistemic Anxiety and Adaptive Invariantisms. *Philosophical Perspectives (Epistemology)* 24: 407–35.

Olson, Michael A., Russell H. Fazio, and Anthony D. Hermann. 2007. "Reporting Tendencies Underlie Discrepancies between Implicit and Explicit Measures of Self-Esteem." *Psychological Science* 18(4): 287–91.

Phillips, Wendy J., and Donald W. Hine. 2016. "En Route to Depression: Self-Esteem Discrepancies and Habitual Rumination." *Journal of Personality* 84(1): 79–90.

Proust, Joëlle. 2013. *The Philosophy of Metacognition: Mental Agency and Self-Awareness*. Oxford: Oxford University Press.

Schröder-Abé, Michela, Almut Rudolph, and Astrid Schütz. 2007a. "High Implicit Self-Esteem Is Not Necessarily Advantageous: Discrepancies between Explicit and Implicit Self-Esteem and Their Relationship with Anger Expression and Psychological Health. *European Journal of Personality* 21(3): 319–39.

Schröder-Abé, Michela, Almut Rudolph, Anja Wiesner, and Astrid Schütz. 2007b. "Self-Esteem Discrepancies and Defensive Reactions to Social Feedback." *International Journal of Psychology* 42(3): 174–83.

Spencer, Steven J., Christian H. Jordan, Christine Er Logel, and Mark P. Zanna. 2005. "Nagging Doubts and a Glimmer of Hope: The Role of Implicit Self-Esteem in Self-Image Maintenance." In *On Building, Defending, and Regulating the Self: A Psychological Perspective*, edited by Abraham Tesser, Joanne V. Wood, and Diederik E. Stapel, 153–70. New York and Hove: Psychology Press.

Tanesini, A. (2016a). I – 'Calm Down, Dear': Intellectual Arrogance, Silencing and Ignorance. *Aristotelian Society Supplementary Volume, 90*(1), 71–92.

———. 2016b. "Teaching Virtue: Changing Attitudes." *Logos and Episteme* 7(4): 503–27.

Tanesini, A. (2018). Intellectual Humility as Attitude. *Philosophy and Phenomenological Research, 96*(2), 399–420.

Vohs, Kathleen D., Roy F. Baumeister, and Natalie J. Ciarocco. 2005. "Self-Regulation and Self-Presentation: Regulatory Resource Depletion Impairs Impression Management and Effortful Self-Presentation Depletes Regulatory Resources. *Journal of Personality and Social Psychology* 88(4): 632–57.

Vohs, Kathleen D., and Todd F. Heatherton. 2004. "Ego Threat Elicits Different Social Comparison Processes among High and Low Self-Esteem People: Implications for Interpersonal Perceptions." *Social Cognition* 22(1): 168–91.

Wu, Keke, Chenwei Li, and Diane E. Johnson. 2011. "Role of Self-Esteem in the Relationship between Stress and Ingratiation." *Psychological Reports* 108(1): 239–51.

Zagzebski, Linda T. 2012. *Epistemic Authority: A Theory of Trust, Authority, and Autonomy in Belief*. Oxford and New York: Oxford University Press.

Zeigler-Hill, Virgil. 2006. "Discrepancies between Implicit and Explicit Self-Esteem: Implications for Narcissism and Self-Esteem Instability. *Journal of Personality* 74(1): 119–44.

———. 2013. "The Importance of Self-Esteem." In *Self-Esteem*, edited by V. Zeigler-Hill, 1–20. Hove: Psychology Press.

Zeigler-Hill, Virgil, and Christian H. Jordan. 2010. "Two Faces of Self-Esteem: Implicit and Explicit Forms of Self-Esteem." In *Handbook of Implicit Social Cognition*, edited by Bertram Gawronski and B. Keith Payne, 392–407. New York and London: Guilford.

Section 4

The Vulnerabilities of Trust

10 Exploitative Epistemic Trust

Katherine Dormandy

1. Introduction

Relationships of trust incur vulnerability, and vulnerability can be exploited. Epistemic trust is no exception. This chapter maps out four forms of exploitation in epistemic-trust relationships involving testimony. Several theses of relevance to social epistemology emerge.

One important form of trust in testimony consists in a hearer trusting a speaker for knowledge: he believes what she says on the basis of the fact that she says it, making himself vulnerable to insincerity or error on her part. Less discussed but equally important is that speakers standardly trust hearers too: testifying makes a speaker vulnerable in various ways, for example to not being taken seriously (Hinchman 2005; Dotson 2011; M. Fricker 2007; Frost-Arnold 2016; Medina 2013), so a speaker standardly trusts her hearer for epistemic recognition. Because both hearers and speakers are vulnerable in their capacity as trusters, each can have their trust exploited by the other.

But it is not just a trustee who can exploit a truster—a truster can also exploit someone whom he trusts. After all, accepting trust is burdensome: it incurs an obligation and so makes a trustee vulnerable to difficulties that may arise in discharging it. This holds for both parties to a testimonial relationship: a hearer, in his capacity as a truster, can exploit a speaker by imposing his trust for knowledge on her, and a speaker, in her capacity as a truster, can exploit a hearer by imposing on him her trust for epistemic recognition. Because both speakers and hearers are vulnerable in their capacity as trustees, each can be exploited in their acceptance of the other's trust.

Four possibilities for epistemic exploitation in relationships of testimony have emerged: (a) a speaker can exploit a hearer by accepting his trust for knowledge or (b) by imposing on him her trust for epistemic recognition, and (c) a hearer can exploit a speaker by accepting her trust for recognition or (d) by imposing his trust for knowledge on her.

One might think that exploiting a truster—forms (a) and (c)—involves *betraying* him (or at least letting him down). One might also think that exploiting a trustee—forms (b) and (d)—involves imposing your trust under false pretenses (for example, pretending to trust when you are really out to manipulate). These two suggestions are right insofar as betrayal and deceit are much-loved tools of exploitation. But as we will see, they are not necessary: a trustee can exploit a truster by fulfilling his trust, and a truster can exploit a trustee by trusting her in good faith.

This chapter forges links between discussions about trust in general (Baier 1986, 1991; Jones 2004; Hinchman 2017; Hawley 2014), about testimony (E. Fricker 2006; M. Fricker 2007; Goldberg, unpublished manuscript; Hinchman 2005), and about the epistemic effects of power dynamics in social contexts (M. Fricker 2007; Mills 2007; Spelman 2007; Dotson 2011, 2012, 2014; Medina 2013; Berenstain 2016; Frost-Arnold 2014). Section 2 discusses trust and exploitation in nonepistemic settings. Section 3 introduces exploitative trust in testimony. Section 4 discusses how a speaker can epistemically exploit a hearer, and Section 5 how a hearer can return the favor. Section 6 concludes.

2. Exploitative Trust

2.1. Trust

The form of trust at issue is interpersonal: one person trusts another person. It is also a three-place relation: one person trusts another for some end. Trust involves *relying* on the trustee for the end in question; but trust is more than reliance, for you can rely on a person without trusting him. You can rely on me not to steal your cake on the grounds that I wouldn't touch lemon drizzle anyway. But if your cake is amaretto, which you know is my favorite, then you cannot merely rely on me—you had better trust me. The difference? Mere reliance is a matter of planning on someone's predictable behavior, whereas trust involves a cooperative relationship, in which she accepts your trust.

One characteristic feature of this relationship is that it is governed by special norms above and beyond the norms governing mere reliance (Baier 1986, 1991; Holton 1994; Becker 1996; Jones 2004; Hinchman 2005; Faulkner 2007; Nickel 2007; Darwall 2017). We can see this by imagining that I do steal your cake. If you were merely relying on me not to (as in the lemon-drizzle case), I violate the moral prohibition on steal-ing, but nothing more—I might not even know the cake is yours. When you trust me (as in the amaretto case), I violate this prohibition, but I also violate a second norm: I betray your trust.

Trust relationships come with their own package of norms. One man-dates that the trustee do whatever she can, within reason, to come through for the truster (Hinchman 2017); I'll refer to this as the *trying-your-best-within-reason* norm. Another, which I'll call the *authenticity norm*, for-bids either party from deceiving the other (Frost-Arnold 2014, 791).

Additional norms permit (or perhaps mandate) reactive attitudes, such as feelings of betrayal or gratitude (Baier 1986; Ruokonen 2013; Holton 1994).

What sort of norms are the norms of trust? I suggest (and others agree[1]) that they are for the most part a special kind of moral norm, making the betrayal or letting down of trust a special kind of moral violation. This might sound strange—for surely it can be *good* to betray trust and *bad* to fulfill it, for example when it sustains a mafia or other immoral enterprise (Baier 1986; Frost-Arnold 2014; Jones 2017). But this observation does not show that the norms of trust are not moral; it shows only that they are *pro tanto*: they can be outweighed by stronger moral norms.

A second distinguishing feature of trust, beyond having special norms, is that it is characterized by a certain psychological profile. The truster for his part premises his reliance on the trustee on the assumption that she will be responsive to some aspect of their trust relationship. This might be himself personally (Baier 1986; Darwall 2017), the fact that he is depending on her (Jones 1996; Faulkner 2011), a shared project (Baier *ibid.*), or simply the obligation or commitment that she has incurred by accepting his trust (Nickel 2007; Hawley 2014). A trustee who accepts the trust, for her part, characteristically is responsive in these ways.

Although thinner construals of trust relationships are possible (see the Introduction), I will characterize them in terms of the previously mentioned norms and psychological profile. For my aim is to show that relationships of trust are compatible with exploitation; if I can show this for a strong notion of trust, it will automatically hold for weaker ones.

In preparation for the following, we must clarify how a trust relationship might succeed or fail. In the paradigm case of a trust relationship gone right, one party trusts another in good faith, and the latter, doing her best within reason, delivers the end that she is being trusted for. For example, I fulfill your trust to pick you up at the airport by double-checking your arrival time, leaving in time to beat the traffic, and waiting at our arranged spot. In such cases we may say that the trustee has *fulfilled* the trust.

We may contrast this with two ways in which the trustee may fail to fulfill the trust: by *disappointing* it or by *betraying* it.[2] One disappoints trust by failing to deliver the end in question. One betrays it by not trying one's best, within reason, to come through (thus violating the trying-your-best-within-reason norm). Disappointment and betrayal often overlap, but neither entails the other. In our airport case, I would disappoint your trust by failing to turn up. If I do this because I failed to try my best (say, I lost track of time because I was engrossed in a novel), then it is also a betrayal. But some disappointments of trust are not betrayals (Hinchman 2017): I might fail to make it to the airport because I had a flat tire or had to witness to a car accident. Similarly, one can—at least arguably—betray trust without disappointing it (Hinchman *ibid.*). For example, I could pick you up at the airport after all, but accidentally: having forgotten our arrangement, I went there seeking my lost briefcase and happened to see you waiting. Although I delivered the end that you were trusting me for, I did it despite my carelessness and so arguably wound up betraying you (even if you never find out).

To simplify matters, in the cases discussed below, all betrayals of trust will also be disappointments: the trustee's culpable behavior will result in her failing to deliver the end that she is being trusted for, and all cases in which the trustee delivers the end in question will be a case of trust fulfillment: he will have delivered it by trying his best within reason.

An important issue in the following concerns what distinguishes a relationship as one of trust. This matters because I want to show that bona fide trust relationships can be exploitative—and I want to do so without needing to appeal to borderline cases. I have already said that trust is governed by special norms and is characterized by a cooperative, other-directed psychology. Yet sometimes a case might diverge from the ideal without thereby ceasing to count as a relationship of trust. For example, the truster might violate the "no-nagging" norm too much, or the trustee may flag in his sense of obligation or enthusiasm for the common project. Yet I will suppose that a necessary condition for a relationship to count as one of trust is that *both parties obey the authenticity norm*: both agree, and intend, to abide by the norms of trust. This criterion for bona fide trust includes any relationship in which the trust is fulfilled, but it also includes some cases in which it is betrayed: namely, those in which the betrayal is unintentional. Cases of intentional betrayal, by contrast, do not count as trust relationships—for the trustee cannot truly be said to *accept* the other's trust. That bona fide trust relationships admit exploitation should not come as a surprise. For interpersonal relationships, including trust relationships, encompass many dimensions of power and vulnerability (Baier 1986, 1991), which are already two of exploitation's main ingredients.

I will discuss how relationships of trust in general can be exploitative and will then move on to epistemic trust in particular.

2.2. Exploitation and Trust

The account of exploitation best suited to understanding this phenomenon in trust relationships is Wood's (1995, 2014, chapter 12).[3] One person exploits another when he takes advantage of her vulnerability, typically by exercising power over her, in order to achieve some gain. The exploited person typically gains too, though at a gouging price. For example, a water seller encounters a hiker lost in the desert and exploits her by selling her a bottle of water for €1,000.[4] I'll use *exploiting a person* and *exploiting his vulnerability* interchangeably.[5]

There are many forms of power and vulnerability that can feature in exploitation. One example is social; think of supervisors and students, members of majority or minority ethnicities, and so forth. Another is legal; think of someone's legal claim being upheld and enforced against another. Another form of power and vulnerability is emotional: one person might be manipulative, whereas another is emotionally needy and so vulnerable to manipulation. Exploitation can occur along these dimensions of power and vulnerability, as well as others.

Vulnerability might come about as a result of coercion or manipulation. Coercion forces a person's will by narrowing his acceptable alternatives, and manipulation covertly influences the deliberations that shape his will (Wood 2014, chapter 12). The water seller might have the hiker brought to the desert at gunpoint or slyly convince her that the trail is lined with potable streams. But vulnerability can arise independently of coercion or manipulation: one party may simply enjoy a powerful bargaining advantage. The seller, for instance, might set up shop and wait for desperate hikers.

Exploitation is sometimes used as a moral concept, implying the badness of the situation that it applies to (e.g. Wertheimer 1996; Sample 2003). But it can also be used neutrally: a debater exploits the weaknesses in her opponent's argument; a rescuer exploits a kidnapper's vanity. This neutral sense is what I am interested in here. What typically distinguishes bad from neutral or good exploitation is that, in the former, the exploiter disrespects or degrades the exploitee (Wood 1995). Though most of my examples are of bad exploitation, I'll discuss one virtuous case.

Relationships of trust necessarily incur vulnerability. They do so for the truster, because by definition he puts himself in the hands of the trustee—and she might fail to come through with the trusted-for end, or hurt him emotionally by not doing her best for him. On top of these vulnerabilities incurred by trust, the truster might have vulnerabilities that pre-exist it; they might even have made trust the best course of action to begin with (Baier 1986). The truster may, for instance, badly need the thing for which he trusts and be unable to obtain it alone.

Yet trustees are vulnerable too (Baier 1986, 1991). Accepting trust incurs obligation, which is a mental and emotional burden and perhaps, should things not go to plan, an inconvenience.[6] In addition to vulnerabilities incurred by trust, a trustee may have vulnerabilities apart from it, perhaps even accepting trust on account of them; she might, for instance, be lonely and welcome the emotional connection of being trusted or might need the truster's financial support.

Because both truster and trustee are vulnerable to the other, each might be exploited by the other. I'll discuss two ways in which a trustee can exploit a truster and one in which a truster can exploit a trustee.

A trustee can exploit a truster, first, by betraying him. She might do so by signalling acceptance of his trust while having no intention of fulfilling it—but because this sort of betrayal violates the authenticity norm (and hence is not a bona fide acceptance of trust), I will not discuss it here. Instead, I will focus on betrayals that are *unintentional*—in which the trustee intends to deliver what she is being trusted for but culpably fails to do so. For example, a contractor might use the cheapest available paint in a house without bothering to look into its chemical composition, inadvertently covering the occupants' walls with toxins. Each element of exploitation is present: the occupants who trusted the contractor for a safe paint job pay a gouging price in the form of their future health (though they may not realize it), while the contractor gains financially as a result (though she may not realize the extent of the price that she has negligently imposed).

The second way in which a trustee can exploit a truster may come as a surprise: she might do so by *fulfilling his trust*. For example, a grown son might trust his parents for financial support, yet feel guilty about doing so; his parents might exploit his guilt at their acceptance of his trust by pushing him to end an engagement with a fiancée who displeases them.[7] The son pays the price of his ruined relationship, while the parents gain by exerting control over the constellation of their extended family.

Exploitation in trust relationships can run in the other direction too, with trusters exploiting trustees—indeed, simply by trusting them. If someone asks you to accept his trust, refusing can be difficult, yet accepting, as we saw, can be burdensome. For example, a CEO trusts an unpaid intern, who needs this step up in his career, to manage her ill-advised love affairs. Or you might trust your friend, who has a hard time saying no, to drop what she is doing and drive you to the airport. You can exploit someone, then, by *imposing your trust on her*.

The three forms of exploitation I will discuss, in summary, are those in which a trustee exploits a truster by betraying him unintentionally or by fulfilling his trust, and in which a truster exploits a trustee by imposing his trust on her.

One might object that the cases of exploitation I have described do not really involve relationships of *trust*. For trust relationships are characterized by cooperative submission to the norms of trust and by responsiveness to the relationship, whereas exploitation, at least of the bad variety, seems to involve *violating* norms for how to treat people and responding only to self-interest.

But our examples show that this objection is mistaken. The contractor authentically intends to perform a safe paint job, even though she does so with culpable incompetence. Moreover, she can do so in response to an aspect of her relationship with the occupants, such as their need for a paint job, or the obligation that she has incurred by accepting their trust. A similar point holds for the parents: they authentically want to financially support their guilt-ridden son, and they do so in response to their relationship with him, whether they are motivated by their goodwill toward him or his future or are simply committed, as his parents, to coming through for him. They might even know (and indeed feel guilty) that they are exploiting him. And the son, even if he is aware that he is being exploited, nonetheless relies on his parents to respond to the relationship in these ways. Finally, consider the CEO. She is authentic about wanting her intern's help, cooperates with him, and is disposed to gratitude when he takes her unfortunate paramours' calls. Moreover, she can rely on him to be responsive to their relationship, which extends its tentacles deeper than his contract—he may pity her, be constitutionally unable to see a need go unmet when he can help, or experience goodwill toward the company with which he has cast his lot.

Exploitation, then, is compatible with relationships in which one person trusts another and the latter accepts his trust. I will turn now to exploitation in relationships of *epistemic* trust.

3. Exploitation in Epistemic-Trust Relationships

I'll assume that epistemic trust is a species of trust generally, as opposed to mere reliance.[8] I'll focus on epistemic trust in testimony, in which a speaker tells something, say *p*, to a hearer. At least in the cases that I am interested in here, this amounts to the speaker's inviting the hearer to trust her for knowledge that *p* (Hinchman 2005) and trusting him, in turn, to accord her epistemic recognition concerning her knowledge that *p*. To avoid confusion, I will refer to speakers of testimony as "she" and to hearers as "he."

Consider first the hearer's trust in the speaker. The epistemic goods that he trusts her for, such as knowledge or evidence, are what we may call *representational*. These either represent the world accurately or indicate that a belief is likely to do so. A hearer who trusts a speaker for representational goods makes himself vulnerable—to misinformation, to practical mishaps, or to a strained relationship with the speaker should her testimony turn out to be false or careless. But the speaker, as trustee, is vulnerable too: having accepted the hearer's trust, she has committed to providing him with knowledge. Should her testimony (to her surprise) turn out false or unfounded, she is vulnerable to the hearer's reactive attitudes or to damage to her epistemic reputation.

It is standard for discussions of testimony, if they thematize trust at all, to focus on the hearer's trust in the speaker (e.g. Faulkner 2007; Hinchman 2005; McMyler 2011), but the speaker too must typically trust the hearer (Dotson 2011, 238; Frost-Arnold 2016, 519–520). The epistemic goods for which she trusts him are what we may call *recognitional* (Hinchman 2005, 565; M. Fricker 2007, 142–46). Recognitional epistemic goods consist in the right response to a person's epistemic agency or to her status as a knower (Dotson 2011, 2014). They come in several forms. One amounts to ascribing a speaker the credibility that she deserves; another is crediting her when appropriate;[9] another involves regarding her as the authority on how her words should be interpreted and on which third parties may be told them. The speaker, in trusting the hearer for these goods, makes herself vulnerable to the hearer (Dotson 2011). His disappointing or betraying her trust may dent her epistemic self-confidence or the confidence of onlookers in her (M. Fricker 2007; Hinchman 2005). It may inhibit her from sharing knowledge in the future, thus compromising epistemic agency (Dotson 2011). She might even risk practical harms from the exposure of her sensitive information.

Yet the hearer too, in his capacity as a trustee for epistemic recognition, may also be vulnerable. If he fails to accord the speaker recognition that she deserves (say, he harbors unconscious prejudicial biases or accidentally lets slip her private information), he risks being targeted by her reactive attitudes; damaging his relationship to her; or gaining a reputation as closed-minded, untrustworthy, or even bigoted.

So epistemic trust in testimony is bidirectional: the hearer trusts the speaker for representational goods, and the speaker trusts the hearer for recognitional goods. Both parties are vulnerable to each other in their capacities as truster and trustee alike.

As we saw with trust in general, so, too, with epistemic trust: its vulnerabilities can arise from the epistemic-trust relationship itself, but need not. They can also precede or motivate it. For example, I trust you for knowledge *because* I am in ignorance, and you trust me for epistemic recognition *because* you need your story told.

Each party to an epistemic-trust relationship may be in a position to exploit the other. Because both speakers and hearers are trusters and trustees, and because exploitation can go both ways between truster and trustee, the following possibilities arise for exploitation in epistemic-trust relationships:

Types of Exploitative Trust in Testimony

The speaker exploiting the hearer:

(1) A speaker exploits a hearer's trust for representational epistemic goods.
(2) A speaker exploitatively trusts a hearer for recognitional epistemic goods.

The hearer exploiting the speaker:

(3) A hearer exploits a speaker's trust for recognitional epistemic goods.
(4) A hearer exploitatively trusts a speaker for representational epistemic goods.

I'll consider (1) and (2) as a unit, envisioning cases in which speakers exploit hearers by accepting their trust for knowledge or by imposing trust for recognition on them (see Section 4).

I will similarly examine (3) and (4) together, focusing on a case in which a hearer exploits a speaker by accepting her trust for recognition and by imposing on her his trust for knowledge (see Section 5).

The exploitation that I will discuss is epistemic. By this I mean that the core, or definitive feature, of the exploitative interaction is one party's acceptance of the other's trust for epistemic goods. *A speaker epistemically exploits a hearer* just in case the hearer's trusting belief in her testimony, and his acceptance of her trust for epistemic recognition, benefits the speaker and costs the hearer in a way that takes advantage of a vulnerability of the hearer's. *A hearer epistemically exploits a speaker* just in case the speaker's trusting the hearer for recognition, and accepting his trust for knowledge, benefits the hearer and costs the speaker in a way that takes advantage of a vulnerability of the speaker's. Finer distinctions can doubtless be drawn, but my present aim is to sketch the broad contours of a phenomenon that further research can fill in more precisely.

4. The Speaker Exploiting the Hearer

We saw two ways in which a speaker can exploit a hearer: in her capacity as a trustee for knowledge and in her capacity as a truster for epistemic recognition. These forms of exploitation are conceptually distinct, but they typically intermingle. In this initial exploration I will consider cases in which they go together. I will consider two types of case: one in which the speaker betrays the hearer by testifying falsely and irresponsibly, thus failing to deserve the epistemic recognition that she trusts him for (Section 4.1), and another in which the speaker testifies truly and responsibly and does deserve his recognition (Section 4.2).

4.1. Betrayal of Trust for Knowledge, Failure to Deserve Epistemic Recognition

A speaker betrays a hearer when she lies to him or testifies a belief that she has formed carelessly. We may automatically exclude a lie from the cases of interest here, because a deceitful speaker violates the authenticity norm and hence is not even trying to do her part in the trust relationship. Testifying a belief that she has formed carelessly, by contrast, is compatible with a measure of trying and so can be an unintentional betrayal. I will focus for simplicity on cases in which this unintentional betrayal is also a *disappointment* of the hearer's trust: here, a failure to give him knowledge.[10] One way in which this might happen is if the speaker holds the belief so carelessly that, even if it is true, she herself does not count as knowing it.[11] Another way is for the belief to be false. In all of the cases I consider, the belief testified by the careless speaker disappoints the hearer's trust by being false.

In the type of example that I will work with, the speaker is in a position of social power and the hearer is in a position of social vulnerability. More specifically, the speaker belongs to a group that is dominantly situated, and the hearer belongs to a group that is nondominantly situated.[12] In the example, this situation is upheld by systemic injustice. What the speaker testifies to the hearer is a false and disempowering narrative about the latter's circumstances. This narrative, or *legitimation myth* (Stanley 2015, 211; cf. Dotson 2012; Collins 2000, 27), whitewashes the injustice of the situation and the responsibility borne by the speaker's own group, instead casting blame on external circumstances, or more typically on the hearer's group. For example, before women's suffrage, democratically empowered men justified denying women the vote on the grounds that women were supposedly constitutionally unsuited to engage in the public sphere—which many female opponents of suffrage accepted. For another example, it is not uncommon for the fantastically wealthy to excuse eye-watering economic disparities by claiming that their society is a pure meritocracy, implying that the economically disadvantaged simply do not work hard enough (Stanley 2015).

Testifying a legitimation myth is not always a matter of stating it in so many words, but can also involve the use of loaded concepts, including stereotypes, in a way that assumes the hearer's agreement. This happens when the speaker talks about something ostensibly different but builds the concept into her assertion in a way that presupposes the hearer's acceptance of it (Collins 2000, 27; Stanley *ibid.*). Think of a well-meaning father talking about his political activities in martial terms that signal the inherent unladylikeness of politics to a daughter raised to aspire to ladylikeness.

A dominantly situated speaker who testifies a legitimation myth to a nondominantly situated hearer epistemically exploits him, at least as long as he believes her (if he does, he suffers from false consciousness). The hearer's belief costs him, because it hides from him the truth about his situation. And it benefits the speaker, because it reduces the likelihood that the hearer will ask uncomfortable questions—and if he won't, then who will? Moreover, the speaker in this case wins the hearer's epistemic recognition, and secures his trust for knowledge, by taking advantage of certain vulnerabilities of the hearer's that arise from his social location. To see this, note that part of what it is to be nondominantly situated is for the vast majority of the knowledge claims prevalent in your society to be generated and passed on by people outside of your own group—by the dominantly situated (Collins 2000, 3–5; Scheman 2001; M. Fricker 2007; Grasswick 2018). Think of wealthy men, however well meaning, who indoctrinated their daughters that the rough-and-tumble of politics is better left to the gallant sex. Or think of an affluent, idealistic young teacher working in an economically deprived school, teaching her students—with the best of intentions—that economic success is theirs for the taking as long as they work hard enough, irrespective of what they or their parents would have to sacrifice to afford college tuition in a culture of scant merit scholarships and rampant gaming of the system on the part of wealthy parents.

Of course, nondominantly situated hearers could, in theory, find contrary views in critical work authored by nondominantly situated thinkers, but—not being part of the mainstream conversation—it may take effort and resourcefulness to get ahold of.[13] This is especially so if your non-dominant position comes with economic challenges, lack of opportunity, or social pressure to conform your thinking, and if the dominantly situated suppress the thought of those like you, for instance by making education hard to access (Collins 2000, 4–13, 33–34).

Nondominantly situated hearers are not always vulnerable in this way, of course. As I will discuss in Section 5.1, being nondominantly situated can sometimes *help* one appreciate social realities in ways not easily available to the dominantly situated (Harding 1993; Wylie 2003, Medina 2013; Dotson 2018; McKinnon 2018). It is when these insights, for structural reasons, are hard to come by that epistemic exploitation of the nondominantly situated is a risk.

In the sort of case I am considering, the speaker exploits the hearer in two ways: first, by acting as a trustee for his knowledge and second, by trusting him to grant her epistemic recognition—which, in the present case, she does not deserve.

Consider the speaker's role as a trustee for knowledge. The speaker's exploitation of the hearer here amounts to a betrayal of his epistemic trust. For her testimony is not only false, it violates the trying-your-best-within-reason norm. The speaker I am envisioning could and should have done better.[14] This is certainly so if her testimony is a lie—that is, if she herself disbelieves it. Of greater relevance here, however, are cases in which the speaker herself *believes* the myth, but could have disbelieved it had she tried harder—had she thought more about it, regarded with suspicion the myth's upholding of her own privilege, or engaged with nondominantly situated thinkers who call the myth into question. Her betrayal is unintentional, but no less a betrayal for that.

One might wonder: if *the speaker* could have avoided believing the legitimation myth simply by trying harder, then so surely could the hearer—especially if intellectual groundwork has already been laid by thinkers from his own nondominantly situated group. Why regard the speaker as blameworthy but not the hearer? In response, it is possible for a hearer to be blameworthy for his own false consciousness—anyone is capable of epistemic irresponsibility. Such cases aside, however, we have seen that in the cases I am considering, there is a structural asymmetry between the epistemic situations of the dominantly and nondominantly situated. The former set the agenda for mainstream research programs and media offerings, whereas the latter must source their information from informal community channels and may face practical barriers to doing so.

Let's turn to the second way in which the speaker exploits the hearer: in her capacity as a truster for epistemic recognition. In their self-appointed role as the disseminators of knowledge claims in their society, the dominantly situated impose this trust on everyone else. The well-meaning father schools his daughters to look to him for guidance about what interests to pursue; the affluent and idealistic teacher uses her influence to instill in her economically disadvantaged students the transformative belief in the power of hard work. Yet both speakers wind up taking advantage of their hearers—to impose trust for epistemic recognition, which, in this case, neither speaker deserves on the topic at hand and from which each benefits by upholding the status quo with their testimony.

In summary, a speaker can exploit a hearer by betraying his trust for knowledge and by imposing on him her trust for epistemic recognition, which, when she is disposed to irresponsibly testify falsehoods, she does not deserve.

4.2. Fulfillment of Trust for Knowledge, Imposition of Trust for Deserved Recognition

A speaker can exploit a hearer without testifying carelessly, or even falsely. She can do so *in fulfillment* of his trust for knowledge, and by imposing on him trust for epistemic recognition *that she also deserves*.

Consider a board meeting, where each person is of equal rank, equally qualified, and supposed to be accorded an equal voice. Yet the creative director, who skillfully wields her off-the-charts charisma, speaks disproportionately often. She happens also to be highly knowledgeable and hence, in this regard, deserving of significant epistemic recognition. But her disproportionate occupation of the conversational space prevents the other group members from asserting their knowledge. The creative director's emotional power thus cultivates in her emotionally vulnerable (because timid) hearers an epistemically vicious habit of cognitive subservience. In this way the speaker epistemically exploits her colleagues. Their acceptance of her trust for epistemic recognition feeds her narcissism, and their belief in her testimony shapes the group's decisions to her interests. It is true that the other group members gain knowledge, but they also pay a steep price in the form of a surrender of their epistemic and practical agency within the group.

Cases like this have consequences for an important idea in the epistemology of testimony. This idea is that a speaker, simply in virtue of testifying, is entitled to expect epistemic recognition from the hearer. More specifically, she is entitled to expect a hearer, not to believe her automatically, but to treat her testimony as a serious candidate for belief (Goldberg, unpublished manuscript). Her testimony exerts "moral pressure" on him to "tailor his doxastic reaction" to her epistemic credentials, "so as to reflect a proper estimate of the epistemic goodness of [her] claimed [epistemic] authority."[15] In other words, the speaker is entitled, simply by virtue of testifying, to expect the hearer to open himself up to the possibility that he ought to believe her, by duly considering her credentials; if they are good, then she is entitled to expect the additional epistemic recognition of being believed. I will call this the *speaker-expectation claim.*

This claim has much going for it. A speaker arguably has a right to be offended if her testimony is ignored or epistemically downgraded without due cause (Faulkner 2011; Goldberg, unpublished manuscript; Moran 2005)—and if a hearer does this because of prejudice, he commits an epistemic injustice to boot (M. Fricker 2007).

But the speaker-expectation claim, as Goldberg himself acknowledges,[16] needs qualification. For competing considerations can sometimes override the moral pressure to meet a speaker's expectation. I will discuss two; both become apparent when we consider ways in which a knowledgeable speaker can exploit a hearer by imposing on him her trust for epistemic recognition and by accepting his trust for knowledge.

The first circumstance in which the speaker-expectation claim can be voided arises when the speaker already commands a disproportionate amount of epistemic airtime. This is illustrated by our narcissistic-speaker case, in which the creative director, though knowledgeable, drowns out other equally deserving voices.[17] In such cases hearers surely have a right or even a duty to disappoint the speaker's expectation to be heard—any teacher who has had confident students stifle class participation can sympathize. The very fact that someone testifies does not suffice to license prioritizing *her* claim to supply knowledge over others'. On the contrary: the epistemic airtime should be more evenly apportioned among those equally deserving of being heard. There are moral reasons for this, but also epistemic ones: a variety of knowledgeable perspectives is likely to be more epistemically enriching than one (Longino 2002; De Cruz and De Smedt 2013; Dormandy forthcoming)

A second circumstance in which the speaker-expectation claim can be voided arises when the hearer has a right not to know what the speaker testifies. The following case of epistemic exploitation brings this out. Imagine two friends, a speaker and a hearer. The speaker is a reservoir of lascivious secrets—about herself, about mutual friends—and her exhilaration in knowing them is incomplete until she gains a feeling of self-importance by sharing them with someone else. Her friend the hearer is caring, but has trouble setting boundaries. Knowing his friend's secrets, let alone keeping them confidential, makes him desperately uncomfortable. What he gains is the feeling of being important to his friend, but he pays the steep price of his peace of mind. The speaker is knowledgeable and fulfills the hearer's reluctant epistemic trust—but in doing so, and in imposing her trust for epistemic recognition on him, she epistemically exploits him.

This scenario generates a second exception to the speaker-expectation claim. The secret-teller is not entitled to expect her friend to hear her testimony at all, let alone attend to her epistemic credentials; the reason is that he has a right not to know the secrets.[18] Asking her to stop testifying would not amount to an epistemically reprehensible silencing, but would rather protect both himself and the dignity of the subjects of the secrets.

The right not to know is not absolute. There are truths that ought to be known and hearers who ought to know them. A criminal hearer arguably lacks the right to be ignorant of how he has harmed a victim, especially if his knowing this can contribute to her healing. There may even be truths, for example about genocides, that there is an intrinsic moral or epistemic impetus for human beings to know. So there is no across-the-board right not to know, but the fact that there is in some contexts is enough to provide a second exception to the speaker-expectation claim.

In summary, there are at least two circumstances in which the speaker-expectation claim does not apply: those in which the speaker occupies a disproportionate amount of conversational space, and those in which the hearer has a right not to know what is being testified.

We have reached this conclusion by exploring cases in which speakers exploit their hearers by testifying knowledgeably. But epistemic exploitation does not always override the speaker-expectation claim. The exploitation might, for instance, be virtuous. Think of a truth and reconciliation commission empowered to hold perpetrators to account, which gives victims the opportunity to testify about their suffering at their hands. The perpetrators, now under arrest, are legally and physically vulnerable. Many would not have decided to use this situation to turn their lives around were they still on the loose, but imprisonment has jolted them to reflect on the direction of their lives, and they are willing, though emotionally conflicted, to try. So even though the speaker's trust for recognition is imposed, the criminal hearers choose optimistically to accept it, taking a positive attitude toward the project of truth and reconciliation, or even (perhaps begrudgingly) toward the speaker herself. And in the same way that one chooses a painful dental procedure, the perpetrators choose to trust her for knowledge about how they harmed her, relying, if not on her goodwill, then at least on her commitment to the common project. This scenario has all the ingredients of epistemic exploitation: the speaker takes advantage of the hearers' vulnerability in order to extract something from them (in this case, the emotional and moral closure supplied by their epistemic recognition and belief)—but at great cost to them (in this case, forcing them to confront their own worst selves). And the speaker-expectation claim holds: the hearers do not have a right to remain in ignorance of her testimony. Epistemic exploitation, then, does not automatically yield exceptions to the speaker-expectation claim—but it certainly can.

In summary, a speaker can epistemically exploit a hearer by fulfilling his trust for knowledge and by imposing on him her trust for epistemic recognition. The stiff price paid by the hearer can take any number of forms, including his knowing things that he does not want to know—though if these are things that he epistemically or morally ought to know, the exploitation can be virtuous. These considerations indicate that speakers are *often* entitled to epistemic recognition from hearers, and thus to their epistemic trust, but not all the time.

This leaves us with two ways in which a speaker can epistemically exploit a hearer: first, by betraying (and disappointing) his trust for knowledge and by imposing on him her trust for epistemic recognition that she does not deserve, and second, by fulfilling his trust for knowledge and imposing on him her trust for epistemic recognition that she does deserve.

This ends my initial exploration of how speakers can epistemically exploit hearers. I'll now turn to the way in which hearers can reciprocate.

5. The Hearer Exploiting the Speaker

A hearer of testimony can also epistemically exploit a speaker. He can do so in his capacity as a trustee for epistemic recognition, as well as in his capacity as a truster for knowledge. I will consider a single example that features both forms of exploitation simultaneously.

The speaker I am thinking of is nondominantly situated, whereas the hearer is dominantly situated.[19] The speaker's testimony concerns what it is like to swim against the current of a legitimation myth and the social insights that she has gained from having to do so. That nondominantly situated people are often in a position to acquire social knowledge of this sort, indeed a better one than dominantly situated people, is a possibility from Section 4.1 that we will now consider more closely. One reason for this is negative: being dominantly situated can prevent one from seeing certain things. One is apt to lack the sorts of experiences that would most strongly call the legitimation myth into question. On top of this, one has an interest in upholding the myth—after all, one's own privilege is precisely what it legitimates—so one might fail to find the time to ask certain questions or entertain certain possibilities (Mills 2007; Spelman 2007). Moreover, the legitimation myth is apt to influence one's very perception, making evidence against it difficult even to see (Srivinasan 2016). A second reason why the nondominantly situated may be in a better position to acquire knowledge of social injustices is positive: their daily lives are affected by legitimation myths. They are confronted with the effects of implicit prejudices, credibility deficits, or knee-jerk suspicion, which the dominantly situated can afford to ignore. Although they too might, as we saw in Section 4.1, perceive the world through the lens of the myth, they are also, arguably, more likely than the dominantly situated to notice ways in which it does not add up—because it is their experiences that it is least likely to match (Collins 2000, 35). A third reason—also positive—is that the nondominantly situated often live in the same communities, excluded from dominantly situated ones by social or economic pressure, providing the opportunity to discourse together (Collins 2000, 9–13).

The nondominantly situated speaker I am considering has social knowledge of this sort, and the dominantly situated hearer lacks it. Because of this, the speaker deserves epistemic recognition from the hearer on the scale of an ascription of epistemic authority. I will discuss how the hearer might exploit the speaker by accepting her trust for recognition (section 5.1) and by imposing on her his trust for the truth (section 5.2).

5.1. Exploiting the Speaker's Trust for Epistemic Recognition

A hearer might exploit a speaker's trust for recognition by betraying it or, perhaps surprisingly, by fulfilling it. I'll consider each possibility in turn. But first we need a word on the recognitional goods for which the speaker trusts the hearer. I'll discuss the following four:

(i) The speaker trusts the hearer *to assess her credibility accurately*. This includes trusting that he will not, due for example to vices such as epistemic laziness (Medina 2013), simply decline to engage with her testimony, but will respond appropriately given her epistemic credentials: believing her if they are good and disbelieving her only if they are substandard. It also includes trusting that he will not perpetrate testimonial injustice against her—that is, that he will not, due to epistemically negative stereotypes, assign her less credibility than she deserves (Fricker 2007; Dotson 2011; Saul 2013; Peet 2017).[20]

(ii) The speaker trusts the hearer *to exercise testimonial competence* (a term coined by Dotson 2011, 245); that is, to do what it takes to hear what she intends to communicate. This includes working to grasp her concepts rather than expecting her to formulate her claims in his—think of the difference between "flirting" and "sexually harassing." It includes recognizing that there may not even be concepts adequate to express her meaning; after all, their common conceptual framework is likely keyed to the experiences and concerns of the dominantly situated, including to sustaining legitimation myths (cf. M. Fricker 2007, ch. 7)—think of someone trying to explain that she was sexually harassed before this term was coined (*ibid.*). A testimonially competent hearer is also open to the possibility that any failure to understand is his doing rather than the speaker's (Dotson 2011; Peet 2017). This is important given that the going epistemic norms, also shaped by and for the dominantly situated, are apt to license "default skeptical responses" to the testimony of the nondominantly situated (Berenstain 2016, 578–581), putting the burden of proof on the speaker to show that her words make sense, rather than on the hearer to understand. Finally, testimonial competence includes the willingness to engage critically within the confines of ascribing the speaker epistemic authority (Narayan 2004).

(iii) The speaker trusts the hearer *to respect her agency regarding the content of her testimony*. This involves, among other things, trusting that he will not spin or "touch up" her story to third parties (even in an attempt to help) and will not take her words out of context (Alcoff 1991/1992, 9). This is important to facilitate the speaker's self-expression, but also because, should the hearer misinterpret her testimony, it is his take and not hers that is apt to gain currency.

(iv) The speaker trusts the hearer *to respect any risks to which her testimony might expose her*. These risks are emotional and may also be practical. It is often emotionally trying to explain experiences of marginalization to someone who is likely to have trouble relating, especially if their shared conceptual framework cannot easily bridge their disparate backgrounds. The emotional risks are greater to the extent that the hearer (even if well meaning) lacks testimonial competence (Berenstain 2016). The speaker may also face practical consequences, such as being seen as a troublemaker and thus treated with suspicion, for example in applying for jobs or for university admission.

So nondominantly situated speakers tend to be vulnerable in testifying about their experiences as nondominant and about the resulting social insights. The situation is ripe for exploitation. I'll start by discussing how the hearer might exploit the speaker by betraying her trust for epistemic recognition. I'll then discuss how he might even exploit her if he fulfills her trust.

One way in which a hearer could betray a speaker is by violating the authenticity norm: accepting her trust for recognition with no intention of delivering. He might solicit it cynically, aiming to discredit her (Berenstain 2016). Or he might aim to come across as socially sensitive to certain third parties without caring to engage with her message. But breaches of authenticity, as we saw, disqualify the relationship from counting as full-fledged trust and hence are not my primary concern. Can a hearer betray a speaker's trust for recognition even if he accepts it in good faith? He can. Let's take each type of recognition in turn: (i) The speaker might, due to carelessness, culpable ignorance, or prejudicial stereotypes, grant the speaker less credibility than she deserves. (ii) He may culpably fail to exhibit the skills and background information required for testimonial competence. (iii) His good intentions might have a paternalistic edge: he may think that recasting the speaker's story (a form of silencing) will help her express or even process it. (iv) He may paternalistically think that the speaker's story is too important not to be heard and, naïvely declining to empathize with her situation, share it with others.[21]

Betrayal of trust for epistemic recognition, even when unintentional, can assume even darker forms if the speaker's testimony surprises the hearer and awakens his baser instincts. He might, for instance, take offense at feedback about his own unintentional yet problematic behavior, perhaps making the incident about his feelings instead of his misdeed (Pohlhaus 2016), or he might gaslight the speaker, claiming (and falsely believing) that she is overreacting (McKinnon 2017).

Betrayal of a speaker's trust for epistemic recognition, even when unintentional, can be exploitative. We have already seen what gouging price the speaker might pay, but what can the hearer gain? If he betrays her in a way that is compatible with understanding and believing her testimony, he gains knowledge on an important matter. If he believes what he takes her to have said but in fact misunderstands it, he does not gain knowledge, but he might still experience self-congratulatory emotions, thinking that he is promoting social understanding. What if the hearer's unintentional betrayal involves disbelieving her, for example by culpably ascribing her too little credibility? Here too there are nonepistemic ways in which he might gain. He may experience the self-satisfaction (or self-righteousness) of feeling that he has done his part vis-à-vis the speaker and her social group. Or he might, by reading his own meaning into her words, feel self-righteously that his exchange with the speaker confirms his favorite legitimation myth.

All of the elements of exploitation can thus arise when even a well-meaning dominantly situated hearer accepts the trust for epistemic recognition of a nondominantly situated speaker.

So far I have discussed only a hearer who *betrays* the speaker's trust for epistemic recognition. But he can exploit her even if he fulfills it—that is, even if he accords her the credibility that she deserves, models testimonial competence, cedes control of her narrative, and honors her risks. He might for example use her trust—even as he fully recognizes her epistemically—to gain access to her bank account. But more interesting are cases in which the mechanism of exploitation is not the hearer's fulfillment of the speaker's trust for recognition, but rather his own trust in her for her knowledge. I'll turn now to cases like this.

5.2. Exploiting the Speaker by Imposing Trust for Knowledge

Recall that accepting someone's trust can be a burden even if you do it willingly. If you are a speaker and you accept a hearer's trust for knowledge, there are cases in which *his trusting you* can be exploitative.

Let's continue our example from Section 5.1, in which a dominantly situated hearer trusts a nondominantly situated speaker for knowledge. I'll focus on the case in which what the hearer gains is knowledge, though (as we have seen) there may be secondary benefits such as the feel-good sense that he is helping to right social wrongs. What the speaker gains is the opportunity to shape views on a topic of importance. But accepting the hearer's trust for knowledge can nonetheless be burdensome, coming with significant opportunity costs to her emotional energy, time, and other life goals (Berenstain 2016, 572–75). She might, for instance, forfeit the opportunity to develop or express other aspects of her identity beyond those in virtue of which she represents a nondominant social group. As a result, hearers might perceive her one-dimensionally, as no more than a representative of her group (Collins 2000). And even well-meaning hearers might treat her patronizingly, expecting her to be grateful for their interest or even to drop other activities for the sake of their social education (Berenstain 2016, 572–75). The speaker may accept these costs in the hope of making a positive epistemic difference, but is no less exploited for that.

If even a well-intentioned hearer can wind up exploiting a willing speaker, it might seem that epistemic exploitation is unavoidable in epistemic-trust relationships of this kind. Are there ways of pursuing such relationships while avoiding it, or at least minimizing its impact?

There are. The hearer might first do his research. There is an array of scholarly and popular resources in which nondominantly situated thinkers from a variety of social locations narrate and systematize their experiences and insights. Rather than expect any given nondominantly situated person to spontaneously condense and recite these results, the hearer can take advantage of this work. Indeed, given (as we saw in Section 5.1) that there may be still evolving forms of expression that many nondominantly situated people do not themselves have access to, a hearer who does this research could shoulder a large amount of the conversational burden should he still opt for a face-to-face discussion. The hearer might also, instead of expecting the speaker to educate him pro bono, offer a more equitable exchange for the opportunity costs that his epistemic trust imposes. On top of this, he might work independently, through political advocacy or talking to his dominantly situated friends, to put an end to the system that leaves speakers like her at a social disadvantage to begin with.

In summary, even a hearer trusting in good faith can epistemically exploit a speaker, but there are measures that he could take to reduce, and perhaps obliterate, the badness of any given case.

6. Conclusion

I have discussed a phenomenon at the intersection of several independently significant forms of human interaction: trust, testimony, and exploitation. Because the aim was a systematic overview of exploitation in epistemic-trust relationships, it was necessary to leave many details undiscussed. But I hope that this initial systematization will motivate further exploration.

To summarize: in epistemic-trust relationships, a hearer trusts a speaker for knowledge and accepts her trust for epistemic recognition, and a speaker trusts a hearer for epistemic recognition and accepts his trust for knowledge. What marks their relationship as one of trust, instead of mere reliance, is that each party has normative expectations of the other and is responsive to some aspect of the relationship. There are many ways in which relationships of epistemic trust can be exploitative. A speaker can exploit a hearer by accepting his trust for knowledge (whether she fulfills or inadvertently betrays it) and by imposing on him her trust for epistemic recognition. And a hearer can exploit a speaker by inadvertently betraying her trust for epistemic recognition or by imposing on her his trust for knowledge.

Our discussion has yielded a few results for social epistemology more generally. One is that it is not only hearers who trust speakers in a testimonial exchange but also speakers who trust hearers. Second, although speakers have a *prima facie* entitlement to have their knowledge claims considered, this entitlement can be canceled if there are other, less vocal, speakers equally deserving of airtime, or if the hearer has a right not to know what is being testified. Third, a hearer can exploit a speaker's trust for recognition in spite of his best intentions not to; this reinforces the idea that testimonial competence is a virtue, or bundle of virtues, that takes work to cultivate. Fourth, epistemic exploitation can take morally virtuous forms. I hope that these results are just the beginning.[22]

Notes

1. Baier (1986), McLeod (2000), Nickel (2007), Faulkner (2011), Ruokonen (2013), and Darwall (2017) take the norms of trust to be moral; Jones (2017) argues that they are not.
2. (Darwall 2017) argues that trust, because it is more like love than obligation, cannot be *betrayed* but only *let down*. I will stick with the notion of betrayal, but the notion of letting down could easily be substituted.
3. One reason is that Wood's account allows for morally neutral or even good cases of exploitation; another is that it captures exploitation in market as well as nonmarket circumstances. Wood makes a few distinctions that for simplicity I omit here. A close relative is the account of Sample (2003), except that she takes exploitation to be necessarily bad, which Wood (and I) deny. One way in which my view might be read as departing from Wood's is that I allow for the possibility that one person can exploit another by accident.
4. This example comes from Zwolinski and Wertheimer (2016).
5. Some argue that exploitation entails that the exploited person is treated *unfairly* (e.g. Wertheimer 1996). But unfairness is hard to cash out and may exclude the possibility, which I discuss later, of morally virtuous exploitation; for discussion see (Wood 1995).
6. Trusting incurs vulnerability by necessity; being trusted standardly does, but I will leave open whether it does so necessarily.
7. This example is inspired by (Origgi 2009).
8. For discussion see the Introduction to this volume and (Frost-Arnold 2013).

9. This is the flipside of Goldberg's observation that the buck stops with the testifier (2006, 134; cf. Hinchman 2005, 568): the testifier does not just *bear responsibility* but also *deserves credit*.

10. Though some argue that the carelessness or irresponsibility of the speaker's belief *itself* excludes it from counting as knowledge (e.g. Baehr 2011; Zagzebski 1996).

11. Some argue that a hearer can count as knowing a truth that he receives from a speaker, even if the speaker herself does not count as knowing it; I won't discuss this possibility, but see Greco (this volume).

12. Talk of dominantly and nondominantly situated social locations is, of course, simplistic. There are many respects in which a given person might be one or the other, and these categories admit of degree. I will ignore these complications here.

13. A situation which in our social-media age is fortunately changing in many parts of the world—though one must still have reliable Internet access and the time to invest, neither of which is a given.

14. We may grant that exceptions are possible: some dominantly situated speakers may simply see the world through the lens of the myth (Srivinasan 2016), so that even their best efforts do not yield evidence against it. Such speakers would disappoint hearers' trust, but do not count as betraying it.

15. This response need not be a conscious evaluation of her epistemic credentials; Goldberg intends this claim to be compatible with any theory of testimonial justification.

16. Personal communication.

17. Frost-Arnold (2014, 794) characterizes the behavior of overly vocal testifiers as "occupying space in [epistemic] trust networks."

18. This right may be moral, insofar as being told things can have practical or emotional consequences. But it might also be epistemic, insofar as a person is entitled to prioritize knowing some things over others. Watson (2018) introduces the notion of an epistemic right, but does not discuss a right *not* to know certain things.

19. See endnote 12 about how this dichotomy is an oversimplification.

20. That a speaker trusts a hearer in these ways does not, however, entail that she is always *entitled* to do so; we saw in Section 4.2 that the speaker-expectation claim, which says that she is, can be voided. If—and only if—there is a case in which it does not apply, the hearer does nothing wrong by declining to assess the speaker's credibility.

21. It is possible for the hearer to merely disappoint the speaker's trust rather than betray it, if he is nonculpably inexperienced. But epistemic culpability can run more deeply than we are inclined to think (Spelman 2007; Mills 2007).

22. Many thanks for helpful comments go to Dominik Fitze, Arnon Keren, Shuting Ling, Fabio Schädler, and the reviewers for Routledge. This work also benefited from discussion with the participants of the workshop "Soziale Erkenntnistheorie: Zeugnis und epistemische (Un)gerechtigkeit" jointly organized by the University of Bern and the University of Zurich and with Michael Dormandy. Thanks for funding this project go to the Austrian Science Fund (FWF).

References

Alcoff, Linda Martin. 1991/92. "The Problem of Speaking for Others." *Cultural Critique* 20 (Winter): 5–32.

Baehr, Jason. 2011. *The Inquiring Mind: On Intellectual Virtue and Virtue Epistemology*. Oxford: Oxford University Press.

Baier, Annette. 1986. "Trust and Antitrust." *Ethics* 96(2): 231–60.

———. 1991. "Trust and Its Vulnerabilities, and Sustaining Trust." In *Tanner Lectures on Human Values*, vol. 3, 107–74. Salt Lake City: University of Utah Press.

Becker, Lawrence C. 1996. "Trust as Noncognitive Security About Motives." *Ethics* 107(1): 43–61.

Berenstain, Nora. 2016. "Epistemic Exploitation." *Ergo* 3(22): 569–90.

Collins, Patricia Hill. 2000. *Black Feminist Thought: Knowledge, Consciousness, and the Politics of Empowerment*, 2nd ed. New York: Routledge.

Cruz, Helen De, and Johan De Smedt. 2013. "The Value of Epistemic Disagreement in Scientific Practice: The Case of Homo Floresiensis." *Studies in History and Philosophy of Science, Part A* 44: 169–77.

Darwall, Stephen. 2017. "Trust as a Second-Personal Attitude of the Heart." In *The Philosophy of Trust*, edited by Paul Faulkner and Thomas Simpson, 35–50. Oxford: Oxford University Press.

Dormandy, Katherine. Forthcoming. "The Epistemic Benefits of Religious Disagreement." *Religious Studies*. Online First https://doi.org/10.1017/s0034412518000847.

Dotson, Kristie. 2011. "Tracking Epistemic Violence, Tracking Practices of Silencing." *Hypatia* 26(2): 236–57.

———. 2012. "A Cautionary Tale: On Limiting Epistemic Oppression." *Frontiers: A Journal of Women Studies* 33(1): 24–47. doi:10.1353/fro.2012.0008.

———. 2014. "Conceptualizing Epistemic Oppression." *Social Epistemology* 28(2): 115–38.

———. 2018. "Distinguishing Knowledge Possession and Knowledge Attribution: The Difference Metaphilosophy Makes." *Philosophy and Phenomenological Research* 96(2): 475–82.

Faulkner, Paul. 2007. "On Telling and Trusting." *Mind* 116(464): 875–902.

———. 2011. *Knowledge on Trust*. Oxford: Oxford University Press.

Fricker, Elizabeth. 2006. "Second-Hand Knowledge." *Philosophy and Phenomenological Research* LXXIII(3): 592–618.

Fricker, Miranda. 2007. *Epistemic Injustice: Power and the Ethics of Knowing*. Oxford: Oxford University Press.

Frost-Arnold, Karen. 2013. "Moral Trust and Scientific Collaboration." *Studies in History and Philosophy of Science Part A* 44(3): 301–10.

———. 2014. "Imposters, Tricksters, and Trustworthiness as an Epistemic Virtue." *Hypatia* 29(4): 790–807.

———. 2016. "Social Media, Trust, and the Epistemology of Prejudice." *Social Epistemology* 30 (5–6): 513–31.

Goldberg, Sandford. Unpublished Manuscript. *Conversational Pressure*.

———. 2006. "Reductionism and the Distinctiveness of Testimonial Knowledge." In *The Epistemology of Testimony*, edited by Jennifer Lackey and Ernest Sosa, 127–44. Oxford: Oxford University Press.

Grasswick, Heidi. 2018. "Understanding Epistemic Trust Injustices and Their Harms." *Royal Institute of Philosophy Supplement* 84: 69–91.

Harding, Sandra. 1993. "Rethinking Standpoint Epistemology: What Is Strong Objectivity?" In *Feminist Epistemologies*, edited by Linda Alcoff and Elizabeth Potter, 218–36. New York and London: Routledge.

Hawley, Katherine. 2014. "Trust, Distrust and Commitment." *Noûs* 48(1): 1–20.

Hinchman, Edward. 2005. "Telling as Inviting to Trust." *Philosophy and Phenomenological Research* 70(3): 562–87.

———. 2017. "On the Risks of Resting Assured: An Assurance Theory of Trust." In *The Philosophy of Trust*, edited by Paul Faulkner and Thomas Simpson, 51–69. Oxford: Oxford University Press.

Holton, Richard. 1994. "Deciding to Trust, Coming to Believe." *Australasian Journal of Philosophy* 72(1): 63–76.

Jones, Karen. 1996. "Trust as an Affective Attitude." *Ethics* 107(1): 4–25.

———. 2004. "Trust and Terror." In *Moral Psychology: Feminist Ethics and Social Theory*, edited by Peggy DesAutels and Margaret Urban Walker, 3–18. Lanham, MD: Rowman and Littlefield.

———. 2017. " 'But I Was Counting on You!' " In *The Philosophy of Trust*, edited by Paul Faulkner and Thomas Simpson, 90–108. Oxford: Oxford University Press.

Longino, Helen. 2002. *The Fate of Knowledge*. Princeton, NY: Princeton University Press.

McKinnon, Rachel. 2017. "Allies Behaving Badly: Gaslighting as Epistemic Injustice." In *Routledge Handbook on Epistemic Injustice*, edited by Ian James Kidd, José Medina, and Gaile Jr. Pohlhaus, 167–74. New York: Routledge.

———. 2018. "The Epistemology of Propaganda." *Philosophy and Phenomenological Research* 96(2): 483–89.

McLeod, Carolyn. 2000. "Our Attitude Towards the Motivation of Those We Trust." *Southern Journal of Philosophy* 38(3): 465–79.

McMyler, Benjamin. 2011. *Testimony, Trust, and Authority*. Oxford: Oxford University Press.

Medina, José. 2013. *The Epistemology of Resistance: Gender and Racial Oppression, Epistemic Injustice, and the Social Imagination*. Oxford: Oxford University Press.

Mills, Charles. 2007. "White Ignorance." In *Race and Epistemologies of Ignorance*, edited by Shannon Sullivan and Nancy Tuana, 13–137. Albany: State University of New York Press.

Moran, Richard. 2005. "Getting Told and Being Believed." *Philosophers' Imprint* 5(5): 1–29.

Narayan, Uma. 2004. "The Project of Feminist Epistemology: Perspectives from a Nonwestern Feminist." In *The Feminist Standpoint Theory Reader: Intellectual and Political Controversies*, edited by Sandra Harding, 213–24. New York and London: Routledge.

Nickel, Philip J. 2007. "Trust and Obligation-Ascription." *Ethical Theory and Moral Practice* 10(3): 309–19.

Origgi, Gloria. 2009. "The Duty to Trust and the Duty to Be Trustful." *Institut Jean-Nicaud*. https://jeannicod.ccsd.cnrs.fr/ijn_00436691. Accessed August 17, 2018.

Peet, Andrew. 2017. "Epistemic Injustice in Utterance Interpretation." *Synthese* 194(9): 3421–43.

Pohlhaus, Gaile. 2016. "Propaganda, Inequality, and Epistemic Movement." *Theoria* 31(3): 345–56.

Ruokonen, Floora. 2013. "Trust, Trustworthiness, and Responsbility." In *Trust: Analytic and Applied Perspectives*, edited by Pekka Makela and Cynthia Townley, 1–14. Amsterdam and New York: Rodopi.

Sample, Ruth J. 2003. *Exploitation: What It Is and Why It's Wrong*. Lanham, MD: Rowman and Littlefield.

Saul, Jennifer. 2013. "Scepticism and Implicit Bias." *Disputatio* 5(37): 243–63.

Scheman, Naomi. 2001. "Epistemology Resuscitated." In *Engendering Rationalities*, edited by Nancy Tuana and Sandra Morgen, 23–52. New York: SUNY Press.

Spelman, Elizabeth. 2007. "Managing Ignorance." In *Race and Epistemologies of Ignorance*, edited by Shannon Sullivan and Nancy Tuana, 119–31. Albany: State University of New York Press.

Srivinasan, Amia. 2016. "Philosophy and Ideology." *Theoria* 26(3): 371–80.

Stanley, Jason. 2015. *How Propaganda Works*. Princeton, NJ: Princeton University Press.

Watson, Lani. 2018. "Systematic Epistemic Rights Violations in the Media: A Brexit Case Study." *Social Epistemology* 32(2): 88–102.

Wertheimer, Alan. 1996. *Exploitation*. Princeton, NJ: Princeton University Press.

Wood, Allen W. 1995. "Exploitation." *Social Philosophy and Policy* 12(2): 136–58.

———. 2014. *The Free Development of Each: Studies on Freedom, Right, and Ethics in Classical German Philosophy*. Oxford: Oxford University Press.

Wylie, Alison. 2003. "Why Standpoint Matters." In *Science and Other Cultures: Issues in Philosophies of Science and Technology*, edited by Robert Figueroa and Sandra Harding, 26–48. New York and London: Routledge.

Zagzebski, Linda. 1996. *Virtues of the Mind*. Oxford: Oxford University Press.

Zwolinski, Matt, and Alan Wertheimer. 2016. "Exploitation." *Stanford Encyclopedia of Philosophy* (Summer 2017 Edition), edited by Edward N. Zalta. https://plato.stanford.edu/archives/sum2017/entries/exploitation/. Accessed August 1, 2018.

11 Self-Trust and Discriminatory Speech

Mari Mikkola

1. Introduction

Over the past few years, and specifically since the publication of Miranda Fricker's (2007) book *Epistemic Injustice*, philosophers have increasingly begun looking at the influence of discriminatory and oppressive practices on our epistemic lives. In her well-known work, Fricker argues that identity prejudices—which typically target marginalized groups with less social power—can create systematic patterns of credibility deficits (testimonial injustice) and render it impossible for subjects to make intelligible their own experiences (hermeneutical injustice). These ideas are closely connected to the idea of epistemic autonomy: a kind of epistemic self-determination that stems from being competent in one's epistemic abilities and hence exhibiting an attitude of epistemic self-trust. Various types of epistemic injustice and epistemic oppression seemingly wrong marginalized subjects precisely in hampering their epistemic autonomy (Dotson 2011, 2014; Fricker 2007).

Despite this initial connection, the literature on epistemic injustice has not closely looked at how intellectual self-trust may be undermined by oppressive practices. In a hefty recent volume on epistemic injustice (see Kidd, Medina, and Pohlhaus 2017), the term "self-trust" appears once and only fleetingly. The articles address some related phenomena like self-knowledge (Hall 2017), gaslighting as epistemic injustice (McKinnon 2017), and the idea of "hermeneutical death:" where one's social experience is so obscured by available hermeneutical resources that the subject "completely loses her voice and standing as a meaning-making subject . . . [and] one's status as a subject of knowledge and understanding is barely recognized" (Medina 2017, 47). How these phenomena are exactly related to intellectual self-trust under conditions of oppression remains, nevertheless, undertheorized. This chapter undertakes to elucidate how self-trust is problematically undermined in ways that seemingly hinder epistemic autonomy. I undertake this task with a specific oppressive mechanism in mind: I will look at ways in which one prevalent type of prejudicial speech—discriminatory speech—seemingly hampers epistemic autonomy insofar as it erodes and perverts self-trust. Focusing on the effects that discriminatory speech can have has received surprisingly little attention from legal philosophers and liberal theorists. This being the case, the chapter aims not only to advance debates in social epistemology by looking at self-trust through the lens of liberal free speech discussions but also to show that liberals have gotten something wrong about discriminatory speech once we understand what it does to intellectual self-trust.

Let me spell out this chapter's task in somewhat more detail. Freedom of speech is typically regarded to be a central liberal value, whereby with "speech" I refer not only to spoken words and utterances but also to signs, public recordings, written word, nonverbal symbols, and other means of expression. Hateful speech is a thorny issue in liberal societies and, if left unchecked, engenders expressions that are deeply morally problematic and socially undesirable. Subsequently, no legal free speech principle *de facto* admits all forms of speech despite liberal commitments to free expression (Fish 1993). Verbal threats are usually *not covered* by legal free speech principles, and outlawing them raises no free speech concerns whatsoever (they constitute crimes). Defamation is *unprotected* and legitimately actionable by tort law: such speech is taken to incur serious material harms to the defamed, and these harms outweigh significant and compelling free speech interests. Hate speech regulations are typically justified in a parallel fashion: such speech incurs significant harms to its immediate recipients (it generates threats of imminent violence) or to the society at large (it disrupts the peace). Therefore, hate speech can be legitimately regulated without compromising liberal commitments to free expression. However, a large bulk of speech (at least in the United States) is afforded *protected* status. Protected speech is judged to advance substantial free speech interests that justify nonrestriction, even if the speech incurs harms. In line with this, a class of prejudicial expressions— discriminatory speech that "reflects group stereotypes and represents groups or their members as inferior by virtue of these stereotypes"—is legally protected (Brink 2001, 133; see also Sunstein 1992). Although this sort of speech is taken to be socially undesirable and harmful in some sense (e.g. in possibly being offensive), liberal philosophers have argued for its legal permissibility on the grounds that its harmfulness is *not* immitigable: discriminatory speech (the argument goes) still advances significant and compelling free speech interests due to which it deserves legal protection, despite being odious. The interests typically appealed to include the pursuit of truth and knowledge, ensuring democratic deliberation and functioning, and fostering personal autonomy and individual progress (Brink 2001; Dworkin 1981; Meiklejohn 1965; Mill 1974; Raz 1991; Scanlon 1972; Sunstein 1992; Yong 2011).

Looking at how discriminatory speech seemingly influences us in deeply covert and hard-to-detect ways, however, undermines liberal arguments that advance a sort of "hands-off" policy to discriminatory speech—or so I will argue here by examining harmful effects that discriminatory speech has on epistemic autonomy. In short: intellectual self-trust is a necessary condition for the pursuit of knowledge and for fostering (personal and epistemic) autonomy; but because discriminatory speech erodes and perverts self-trust, it undermines in subtle, covert, and insidious ways the very grounds supposedly justifying its permissibility. This becomes particularly clear once we appreciate the role that discriminatory expressions conceivably play in shaping and maintaining prejudicial unconscious influences. I will discuss implicit bias, stereotype threat, and essentializing striking generics to make my case. Because these influences have in common with discriminatory speech a crucial connectedness to prevalent, public stereotypes, there is a complex and mutually sustaining relationship between unconscious influences and discriminatory speech. Everyday stereotypes (as I will understand them here) are putative pieces of knowledge that are "associated with a group of people, knowledge that is learned from, and shared with, others in the culture" (Moskowitz and Li 2011, 103; see also Beeghly 2015; Blum 2004). Stereotypes are negatively or positively valenced false, misleading, or exaggerated generalizations that link groups to one or more general traits. They are highly evidence resistant and rigid: we are inclined to see stereotypical behavior where it does not exist and overlook counter-stereotypical behavior when it occurs. This is because one feature of unconscious stereotypical attitudes is that they "bypass autonomous deliberative processes" (Hurley 2004, 176). Because we are not aware of their influences (the attitudes are automatic and unconscious), our subsequent behavioral and epistemic responses can forego norms and attitudes over which we can exercise conscious control. Given what we know about the workings of implicit attitudes, there is reason to think that discriminatory speech is one mechanism keeping such attitudes alive. Hence, I will argue here, discriminatory speech generates perhaps surprising and yet serious ways in which words can also "wound" due to their effects on self-trust. This shows that a laissez-faire attitude to discriminatory speech is problematic, although it does not justify censoring discriminatory speech—nor will I be advocating such legal counter-measures here. Still, the problems that I will highlight demonstrate that a hands-off policy to this sort of speech is misguided and that educational interventions are warranted. In fact, given the prevalence of discriminatory expressions, its corrupting force on epistemic autonomy may well be much more widespread than that of hate speech, though less immediate.

In Section 2, I will clarify the distinction between hate and discriminatory speech and the notion of self-trust. Section 3 introduces the three unconscious influences I will focus on, and Section 4 discusses how discriminatory speech erodes and perverts intellectual self-trust in light of those influences. Section 5 concludes with a discussion of remedies that might undercut the pernicious effects of discriminatory speech without recommending censorship.

2. Self-Trust and Forms of Prejudicial Speech

I contend that discriminatory speech hinders epistemic autonomy: it erodes and perverts intellectual self-trust due to its role in maintaining discriminatory unconscious influences. Self-trust is an attitude that we take toward ourselves in having competence in our epistemic abilities. For instance, Elizabeth Fricker writes:

> Each one of us in one's everyday life relies on one's core package of cognitive faculties—perception, proprioception, memory, intellectual intuition and introspection—reliably to deliver one true beliefs . . . The core phenomenon of epistemic self-trust consists in one's ungrounded reliance on one's cognitive faculties reliably to yield one true beliefs.
>
> (2016, 154)

Karen Jones describes intellectual self-trust as an "attitude of optimism" that one is cognitively competent relative to some domain. Specifically: "[s]elf-trust manifests itself in feelings of confidence, in dispositions willingly to rely on the deliverances of one's methods and to assert what is believed on their basis, and in modulating self-reflection" (Jones 2012, 245). And Linda Zagzebski writes: "[w]hen the trust in question is epistemic trust in myself, I trust my epistemic faculties to get me to the truth" (2012, 37). This is not merely about cognitive states for Zagzebski; rather, she holds that trust involves a hybrid of epistemic, affective, and behavioral components. Hence, in her account, when I trust my epistemic faculties to get me to the truth, (1) I believe my faculties will get me to the truth, (2) I feel trusting towards my epistemic faculties for that purpose, and (3) I treat my epistemic faculties as if they will get me to the truth (Zagzebski 2012, 38). These components are not individually necessary for self-trust, but are ones that Zagzebksi thinks are present "in standard cases" (Zagzebski 2012, 38).

Trusting our own epistemic faculties in these three ways, I hold, is undermined by prejudicial speech. What does such speech amount to? David Brink distinguishes two kinds of prejudicial expressions: discriminatory and hate speech. The following two statements addressed to a black Stanford University student exemplify them, respectively.

1. "LeVon, if you find yourself struggling in your classes here, you should realize it isn't your fault. It's simply that you're the beneficiary of a disruptive policy of affirmative action that places underqualified, underprepared and often undertalented black students in demanding educational environments like this one. The policy's egalitarian

aims may be well-intentioned, but given the fact that aptitude tests place African Americans almost a full standard deviation below the mean . . . [the aims] are also profoundly misguided. The truth is, you probably don't belong here, and your college experience will be a long downhill slide."

2.   "Out of my face, jungle bunny." (Gates Jr. 1993, 45)

For Brink, the latter is racist hate speech, and it can be restricted without compromising free expression. The extant American free speech principle does not absolutely protect all speech, and some speech is legitimately regulable. Hate speech is one type of speech that does not deserve protection, all things considered. An expression qualifies as hate speech if and only if:

(a)   it employs fighting words [like discriminatory epithets] or non-verbal symbols that insult or stigmatize persons on the basis of their [social kind membership];
(b)   it is addressed to a captive audience [it is suitably hard to avoid];
(c)   the insult or stigma would be experienced by a reasonable person in those circumstances; and
(d)   it would be reasonable for the speaker to foresee that his words would have these effects.

(Brink 2001, 134–5; see also Sunstein 1992)

This sort of speech does not deserve legal protection because it hampers our deliberative practices: it limits its recipients' participation in deliberative exchanges, and it prevents its recipients from getting a fair hearing when they try to participate (Brink 2001, 140–1).

The former statement is exemplary of discriminatory speech: it makes use of race-based stereotypes due to which the student is ranked and represented as inferior. The speech does not employ insulting fighting words or require a captive audience, and it neither intends to insult nor to incite violence. In other words, discriminatory speech is different *in kind* in not needing to satisfy the four conditions (a)–(d) earlier—it isn't merely a less extreme form of hate speech, but rather is treated as qualitatively different in law and in liberal philosophical discussions. Discriminatory speech supposedly leaves the door open for further articulate responses, deliberative exchanges, and intellectual challenging. Brink holds that despite making use of insidious stereotypes, discriminatory speech deserves protection: it serves a socially valuable function by contributing to our public debates and by enhancing our deliberative practices and cultures. Hence, although odious and offensive, discriminatory expressions nonetheless supposedly promote substantial democratic and knowledge-advancing values (Brink 2001).

Brink's view is based on J. S. Mill's defense of free expression, and one might immediately wonder how a Millian position justifies discriminatory speech. Mill's harm principle famously holds that the state can legitimately interfere with individuals' freedom of action and expression only if they harm *others*. On the face of it, though, discriminatory speech does just that in seemingly harming its recipients. *Contra* first appearances, however, the harm principle does not proscribe discriminatory speech. First, this type of speech appears to be harmful in the wrong kind of way. It is offensive and odious, but Mill denies that offensiveness constitutes the kind of harm that his principle prescribes against. Second, the harms generated by discriminatory speech can supposedly be mitigated by significant benefits that free speech on the whole is thought to afford. Thus, Brink advances a Millian argument for *protecting* discriminatory speech. As Mill famously claimed, even if the received opinion were wholly true, unless it is "vigorously and earnestly contested, it will . . . be held in the manner of a prejudice, with little comprehension or feeling of its rational grounds" (1974, 115). We must challenge received opinions in order to keep them alive, which requires allowing dissenting opinions. The falsity of some statement, then, is no reason to censor it, and even false statements can be valuable: they can play an important role in advancing our knowledge-seeking practices by challenging accepted opinions and so preventing them from becoming dogmatically accepted.

Both epistemic and moral autonomy require free expression (Meiklejohn 1965; Scanlon 1972; Sunstein 1992). We should not simply follow life plans set by others; rather, being able to choose one's way of life—which requires a free exchange of ideas—is a principal ingredient of human happiness and the "chief ingredient of individual and social progress" (Mill 1974, 120). Individuality, happiness, and social progress demand the exercise of deliberative capacities that for Mill include "observation to see, reasoning and judgment to foresee, activity to gather materials for decision, discrimination to decide, and . . . firmness and self-control to hold his deliberate decision" (1974, 139). Only in free societies can these capacities develop and be exercised. And because expounding falsehoods can contribute to the development of deliberative capacities, falsehoods can have social and epistemic value. Discriminatory speech may get things wrong and be offensive, but it can nonetheless play a crucial role in knowledge-seeking practices. That is, we can gain knowledge and correct mistaken beliefs by challenging the speaker who propounds stereotypes and pointing out that their reasoning or data were flawed. Hate speech, however, supposedly hampers epistemic and moral autonomy by limiting deliberative participation and preventing its recipients from being listened to when they try to participate. Hence, Brink advances a harm-based argument for *regulating* hate speech and democracy- and autonomy-based arguments for *protecting* discriminatory speech.

I contend, however, that liberals like Brink are mistaken about what discriminatory speech does. Epistemically and morally autonomous functioning demands the exercise of deliberative capacities that, following Mill, can only develop in free societies. The sort of autonomy at issue should be understood as procedural: exercising autonomy involves certain competencies, like the ability to act according to one's own interests, which in turn involves "reflecting on one's beliefs, values, and desires; making reasonable decisions in light of them; and acting on those decisions" (McLeod and Sherwin 2000, 262). Due to its connectedness with prejudicial unconscious influences, however, discriminatory speech hampers precisely these sorts of epistemic capacities by undermining self-trust. In so doing, discriminatory speech harms its recipients in serious, albeit more covert, ways. Before discussing this point in Section 4, let me briefly outline the relevant unconscious influences.

3. Unconscious Influences

In order to establish a link between discriminatory speech and the way in which unconscious influences undermine self-trust, I will focus on implicit bias, stereotype threat, and striking generics. Although there are important differences, all three hinge on common, public stereotypes about social kinds like genders, races, ethnic groups, religions, "the disabled," and socio-economic classes. Everyday stereotypes can influence our interactions with others in subtle and hard-to-detect ways. One such influence is *implicit bias*:

> An individual harbors an implicit bias against some stigmatized group (G), when she has automatic cognitive or affective associations between (her concept of) G and some negative property (P) or stereotypical trait (T), which are accessible and can be operative in influencing judgment and behavior without the conscious awareness of the agent.
>
> (Holroyd 2012, 275)[1]

Implicit bias affects the way we perceive, evaluate, and interact with people from stigmatized groups that our biases target. Importantly, even those who explicitly and sincerely express egalitarian views tend to hold implicit biases, and those from targeted groups tend to have implicit biases against others of their group (for instance, women can be implicitly biased against other women). Implicit biases are not subject to rational revision, are not directly under our epistemic control, and are not attitudes that agents can introspectively access. Their existence has been amply documented, and there is nothing *prima facie* mysterious about such bias. Social psychological research on implicit attitudes relies on and is an extension of an established cognitive science principle that "knowledge is organized in memory in the form of semantic associations that are derived from personal experiences as well as normative procedures and roles" (Jost et al. 2009, 43). Implicit bias works via automatic associative links in memory that are rendered meaningful partly, but in an influential manner, by shared cultural stereotypes. That is, the mechanism of implicit bias comes down to automatic associations that fit common stereotypical views—and these associations tend to take place even when the subjects *explicitly* reject the stereotypes and despite their explicit good intentions to avoid acting in prejudicial ways (Jost et al. 2009, 60).[2]

We can measure implicit bias in various ways. The Implicit Association Test (IAT) is one widely used method. Roughly, an IAT measures how quickly we associate individuals as representative exemplars of a social category with evaluative adjectives. A black–white racial IAT measures how fast we associate and pair positive terms ("good," "pleasant," "safe") and negative ones ("bad," "unpleasant," "dangerous") with white and black faces. Those who take longer to associate black faces with positive words than negative ones and are quicker to pair white faces with positive words than negative ones are "theorized to have internalized a stronger preference for whites relative to blacks, compared to people who respond more equivalently across different category-valence pairings (or in the opposite direction)"—they have an implicit anti-black racial bias (Jost et al. 2009, 45).[3] Furthermore, IAT performance is highly predictive of behavior, and harboring implicit biases significantly affects our interactions with others. For instance, those who harbor implicit anti-black biases are more likely to interpret ambiguous actions of a black person negatively. To illustrate the link, Rudman and Ashmore (2007) measured white US college students' willingness to impose budget cuts on ethno-racialized student organizations, which prior IAT scores showed their implicit biases to target. The participants were asked to recommend ways to spread the university budget across different organizations when faced with cuts. These included the marching band; drama club; political action groups; and Jewish, Asian, and black student organizations. The participants' IAT scores were highly predictive of which budgets they disproportionately slashed: namely, those of the Jewish, Asian, and black student organizations. The IAT scores were highly predictive of discriminatory behavior even after being adjusted for explicit discriminatory attitudes. (For more, see Rooth 2007; Kelly and Roedder 2008; Jost et al. 2009; Bertrand and Mullainathan 2004.)

Public stereotypes not only affect our other-directed behavioral and epistemic outputs, they also influence our *own* performance of particular tasks. Importantly, stereotypes can interfere with the performance of certain tasks by those negatively stereotyped relative to the task. Thus, members of stigmatized groups may underperform because they are unconsciously distracted by worries about confirming the negatively valenced group stereotype. This is known as *stereotype threat*: a kind of self-evaluative threat or a self-stigmatizing anxiety that hampers performance (Antony 2012; Steele 1997). For instance, women tend to do worse in math tests when they are primed for gender prior to the test (e.g. when the examiner states that women usually perform worse in math tests than men). When the test participants were not primed for gender, women's test performance significantly improved (Spencer, Steele, and Quinn 2009). Black students have been found to perform worse than white students of comparable intellectual ability (based on the participants' prior standardized test scores) in tests that were explicitly noted to measure the students' intellectual abilities. When the students were told that the test investigates different problem-solving strategies and does not measure intellectual ability, students from different racialized groups performed equally well (Steele and Aronson 1995). Note that stereotype threat differs from internalized racial or gender stereotypes. It is *situationally specific* and experienced when some negative stereotype applies. In threat-provoking situations, those subject to the relevant negative stereotype tend to exhibit distraction, narrowed attention, anxiety, self-consciousness, withdrawal or over-effort, elevated blood pressure, and increased heart rate (Blascovich et al. 2001; Steele and Aronson 1995). Such factors conceivably contribute to the subjects' poor performance by cognitively draining and distracting them.

Finally, stereotype activation may insidiously hinge on our primitive cognitive architecture. To see this, consider *generics*. Paradigm examples of generic statements include "Ducks lay eggs" and "Mosquitoes carry the West Nile virus." These statements exemplify essentializing and striking property generics (Leslie 2008, 2017). The statements express generalizations that we quickly affirm, although only female ducks lay eggs and only less than one percent of mosquitoes carry the virus. Still, we tend to accept the generalizations, and these sorts of generic claims are surprisingly resistant to counterexamples. Moreover, children acquire the ability to use generic statements to a higher degree sooner than they acquire the ability to use sentences with quantifiers like "some" or "all." This is puzzling because the semantics of generics is much trickier than the semantics of the quantifier sentences. To explain these features of generic statements, Sarah-Jane Leslie proposes that our inclination to generalize does not depend on language (though is enabled by it), but seems to be "an early developing, presumably innate, cognitive disposition" (Leslie 2008, 21). As the two example sentences show, generics tend to pertain to kind-relevant characteristics, and Leslie proposes that such characteristic-relevant dimensions of generics play a role in our primitive generalizations. They provide

> an outline of information to be gathered about a new kind . . . When a value is found for a characteristic dimension of a kind, it is thereby generalized to the kind by the basic generalization mechanism, and so the generic that predicates that property of the kind is accepted.
>
> (Leslie 2008, 33)

Our background expectations associated with a kind do much of the cognitive work and lend themselves to essentializing: we form tacit beliefs about some hidden, category-wide properties or underlying "natures" shared by all category members that ground shared properties and dispositions. We tend to think that all members of some kind share a particular nature that is fundamental to the kind and explanatory of manifest properties, due to which broad generalizations are licensed, along with inferences from properties observed in one kind member to other members. The tendency to interpret kind-relevant generics in an essentializing manner conceivably explains their resilience despite numerous counterexamples: for instance, we seem to hold that mosquitoes are naturally *disposed* to carry the West Nile virus because, by default, we tend to think that manifest striking properties are grounded in a shared kind-nature.

Not all generics are politically or morally problematic, and that we assent to mosquitoes carrying the West Nile virus is not the issue here. Rather, striking social generics should give us cause for concern. Leslie's work suggests that we tend quickly to generalize strikingly *negative* information on the basis of a few encounters with some kind-exemplars. And such striking essentialized properties do not merely pertain to natural or biological features; they also pertain to social properties that trade on public stereotypes. For example, think of generalizations like members of some ethno-racialized group are thieves based on a singular encounter with a group member or that all people who follow Islam are jihadist terrorists based on 9/11 (Leslie 2017). Such generalizations are highly resistant to counterexamples, which makes them deeply problematic: after all, pointing at some examples to the contrary will not do if the work is being done by our primitive cognitive generalizing mechanism. This mechanism, along with stereotypes, makes the world intelligible to us. We need some quick and efficient cognitive tools with which to make sense of and understand our surroundings. Stereotyping, then, has an epistemic goal: to attain meanings in quick and efficient ways (Kawakami et al. 2000). Furthermore, stereotypes come to operate without conscious control or transparency because this epistemic goal is chronically and habitually pursued. Striking generics, then, may lend themselves to quick and automatic stereotype activation. It only takes a few strikingly negative actions from out-group members to make us draw essentializing social group-wide generalizations. And so, we are

> especially sensitive to information that is particularly striking, horrific, or appalling. When we learn of individuals engaging in such an act, we are naturally inclined to seek to generalize this action to a kind to which the individuals belong. The correctness conditions of these generalizations require that some members of the kind must indeed have the relevant property and that the other members must be typically disposed to have the property. We do not, however,

normally have good information about unobservable dispositions available to us, so as a proxy we generalize the property to a kind that we perceive to have a highly predictive and distinctive essence.

(Leslie 2017, 410)

This may help explain why generalizations about human social kinds are so resistant to counterexamples: statistically false generalizations are viewed in an essentializing manner.

4. The Effects of Unconscious Influences on Intellectual Self-Trust

Humans are affected in various subtle and nonobvious ways by prevalent cultural stereotypes. Many common stereotypes are negatively valenced, and we know that negatively valenced implicit biases (for instance) are highly predictive of discriminatory behavior—something that is often not detectable based on the subjects' explicit bias measurements. Moreover, implicit attitudes have bypass effects on conscious and rational epistemic processes. They are automatic, nontransparent, and not under our immediate cognitive control. Given what we know about the mechanisms of largely unconscious influences, liberal appeals to free speech interests *simpliciter* may not mitigate the harms of discriminatory speech. My contention is that there is a complex and dynamic relationship between discriminatory speech and unconscious influences that trades on public stereotypes. I aim to elucidate this relationship in the discussion to come. To anticipate, I hold that discriminatory speech is conceivably *influenced by* and *draws on* implicit as well as explicit prejudices. Moreover, discriminatory speech is seemingly also one (albeit not the only!) mechanism that contributes to us *having* and *continuing* to have unconscious stereotypical attitudes. If I am right about this dynamic connection, discriminatory speech is harmful in particularly insidious, covert, and nontransparent ways: as I will shortly argue, such speech erodes and perverts the self-trust necessary for epistemic autonomy, on which the value of free expression is premised. In other words, if I am right that discriminatory speech is one mechanism that keeps prejudicial unconscious attitudes alive *and* if the three phenomena outlined earlier undermine free speech interests, discriminatory speech undermines its own justification, given its effects on intellectual self-trust. Now, it is an empirical issue whether discriminatory speech keeps prejudicial unconscious attitudes alive, and I cannot settle this matter here. But this is not wildly implausible; actually, it would be quite a remarkable and highly unlikely state of affairs if we were *not* influenced in any way by prevalent negatively stereotyped expressions. Be that as it may, how do unconscious influences conceivably undermine intellectual self-trust, thereby undercutting those free speech interests that discriminatory speech supposedly advances? I will turn to this issue next.

Recall Zagzebski's view that when I trust my epistemic faculties, (1) I believe my faculties will get me to the truth, (2) I feel trusting towards my epistemic faculties for that purpose, and (3) I treat my epistemic faculties as if they will get me to the truth. My contention is that discriminatory speech erodes intellectual self-trust: it undermines our belief in and trusting feeling towards our epistemic faculties. (I will say more about the third condition shortly.) Liberals like Brink tend to assume that, because discriminatory speech does not employ personally vilifying fighting words, it leaves open the possibility of further rational exchanges and challenging of the views expressed. In this sense, discriminatory speech should leave the trust in my epistemic faculties untouched. However, I disagree. Rather, those subject to discriminatory speech are marginalized, put off, and silenced by the negative stereotypes expounded even in the absence of hateful personal vilification, and in ways that generate self-doubt and self-distrust.

Empirical literature on the harms of discriminatory speech is meager and tends to focus on the harms of hate speech. Nonetheless, a growing body of work on the apparent workings of implicit bias and stereotype threat in Anglo-American academic philosophy demonstrates how women in philosophy have withdrawn from partaking in academic exchanges and have experienced reduced credibility when they try to participate (Antony 2012; Saul 2012). Although offering a mere glimpse of a broader problem, academic philosophy can offer us an example of how discriminatory messages that do not fit the definition of *hate speech* can lead to epistemic distancing, withdrawal, and poor performance of cognitively challenging tasks:[4]

> In 2000 I [a female] was interviewing for jobs for the first time [. . .] I was sitting at the head of the table looking out at all the men—there was one female graduate student there, that's it. I finished my talk and the questions began. The professor who I would have been replacing raised his hand and said "So . . . we haven't had a woman teach full-time in the department for 40 years, why should we hire one now?" Absolute silence, no one said a word. Rather than saying something clever like, "you clearly shouldn't as you are not ready" and leaving the interview, I stammered something about perhaps this would help their enrolment, as I would have liked to have had a female role model when I was an undergrad. To this he replied "Well, if we want to recruit more female students why shouldn't we just hire some hot, young guy?" I was totally flummoxed by this point and just trying not to a) yell or b) cry as I knew either of these actions would reinforce his ideas about women . . . Again, NO ONE at the table said a word.

> At one of the first [graduate] seminars I went to, I was the only girl. I raise an objection. I'm told that I have misunderstood the point. I hadn't—the professor in charge of the seminar pointed this out

twenty minutes later once all the boys had finally got round to saying what I said initially. I try to speak again later. My point is completely ignored. Two minutes later, a male makes exactly the same point. The objection in his mouth is hailed as decisive. I worry that my being dismissed and ignored is not because of my gender but because I am foolish; I worry that I don't love philosophy because almost every seminar I go to leaves me second guessing my own abilities. I'm jealous of the ease with which men speak, not having to worry that a single silly remark will mean they are never taken seriously again.

[During my first year] I made a concerted effort to participate and make at least one good comment or question in every meeting of the pro-seminar. However, at the end of the semester when we each got a report on how we did from the two (male) professors, this is what they wrote: "[Name] was sometimes a bit quiet, and we wondered whether she was a bit disengaged." All the other people who were in that class who I told about this agree that, on the basis of my actual participation, this was unfair.

These examples show how members of underrepresented groups can be excluded and ignored in deliberative exchanges without anyone employing insulting fighting words. *Contra* Brink, we can see how nonhateful stereotypical attitudes close off further rational exchanges, prevent the challenging of the views expressed, and hamper epistemically deliberative interactions. In these examples, stereotypes about women in philosophy and the subsequent exchanges had the effects of silencing women, rendering their contributions invisible, and generating recurrent self-doubt. These are hallmark results of implicit bias and stereotype threat, and the self-trust of those subjected to nonhateful gender stereotypes is eroded by disbelief and feelings of distrust in one's epistemic faculties.

Relative to these sorts of examples, micro-inequities are particularly worrisome. This is a phenomenon in which apparently insignificant or singular encounters *cumulatively* make a great difference to people's prospects. Micro-inequities are "apparently small events which are often ephemeral and hard-to-prove, events which are covert, often unintentional, frequently unrecognized by the perpetrator, which occur whenever people are perceived to be 'different'" (Rowe 2008, 45). Examples include not being introduced at meetings, being mistakenly left out of meetings or informal networks, failures to consider group-specific needs in catering, group invitations that made some uncomfortable (invitations to bring along one's wife addressed to gay colleagues), cartoons and jokes that make fun of different cultures or of disabilities, and evidence of "a presumption that someone of a certain gender or race or religion could do some task better" (Rowe 2008, 45). Because discriminatory speech trades on common stereotypes, those subjected to such speech may over time be particularly vulnerable to micro-inequities. Moreover, because such speech may be seen as an acceptable part of everyday life, it is conceivably quite frequent. It is mistaken then to think that an individual instance of discriminatory speech is just an isolated incident that we can easily mitigate by pointing out that free speech *on the whole* advances participation and epistemic autonomy. Micro-inequities over time may make individuals' abilities to develop and exercise those dialectical capacities necessary for epistemic autonomy very unequal and thus result in disproportionately eroding the epistemic self-confidence of marginalized subjects.

I contend that discriminatory speech affects the automatic associations underlying implicit prejudicial attitudes. This point needs empirical testing, but it has pre-theoretical appeal. If one is repeatedly told, "Less talented women get to where they are due to skewed affirmative-action policies," it is not hard to imagine how this would contribute to associating *women's work* with *inferior quality* and lead to instances where a situationally specific stereotype threat hampers job performance or cognitive functioning (like those that many women in philosophy report experiencing). Also think back to essentializing generics. Statements expressing views like "Women are unsuited for some-profession-x" may well, *given* our background social expectations, be interpreted in an essentializing manner: that women as a group are naturally disposed to be unsuited for the profession. This can reinforce associative connections between women's work and inferior quality and, if operationalized, erode women's intellectual self-trust.

The phenomenon of confirmation bias conceivably also plays a role: we tend to gather and remember data selectively in ways that confirm our previously held beliefs and views (Nickerson 1998). So, if public speech repeatedly expounds discriminatory views about women's professional qualifications on the basis of which we make generalizations about gender and work *and* these generalizations turn on unconsciously held social essentialist beliefs about women's supposed "natural" abilities, our rational evaluative efforts may simply confirm our prior essentialist attitudes. Our deliberative processes may focus on selectively chosen evidence for those beliefs. In this case, intellectual self-trust would be *perverted* due to prejudicial unconscious attitudes—or so I will argue next. This relates to Zagzebski's third condition: for her, when I trust my epistemic faculties, I treat my epistemic faculties as if they will get me to the truth. But given the workings of unconscious attitudes, this trust is seemingly misplaced, and we should rather *not* treat our faculties in this way. An attitude of optimism in our intellectual self-trust is unwarranted due to prejudicial unconscious influences, and this is something that we may be utterly unaware of. In fact, social psychological research shows that those who view themselves as objective observers and reasoners tend to be particularly influenced by unconscious biases, in that their trust in their own objectivity prevents them from keeping their biases in check (Uhlmann and Cohen 2007). So, facts about human psychology count against Zagzebski's claim that self-trust is the foundation of rationality (2012, 52). This is supposedly due to epistemic conscientiousness, which is "the quality of using our faculties to the best of our ability in order to get the truth" (Zagzebski 2012, 49). A reflective person holds that "her trustworthiness is greater if she summons her powers in a fully conscious and careful way, and exercises them to the best of her ability . . . conscientiousness is the state or disposition to do that" (Zagzebski 2012, 49). Moreover, conscientiousness gives rise to intellectual virtues, which just are qualities that epistemically conscientious persons endorse. Hence Zagzebski concludes:

> If a reason to believe *p* is something in virtue of which a conscientious person thinks some proposition *p* is true, then self-trust is a reason because it is in virtue of self-trust that I conscientiously think that what I take to be reasons for believing *p* are truth-indicators.
> (2012, 51)

Given the facts of human psychology, however, this story is far too simplistic and idealized—if not downright false. Rather, a reflective person may well think that they are exercising their epistemic faculties in conscious and conscientious ways, which gives them putative reason to believe p. But unconscious attitudes influencing the workings of our epistemic faculties, coupled with confirmation bias and undue optimism in one's faculties, may pervert one's faith in one's own conscientiousness in ways that will be epistemically vicious: the beliefs one acquires will be false, and the processes with which one has come to believe something will be unreliable.

Admittedly, we do not know whether discriminatory speech is causally linked to implicit bias and essentializing generics in the ways I have suggested earlier. But we do know that implicit bias and social essentialist beliefs trade on unconscious automatic associations along stereotypical lines, thus bypassing conscious epistemic processes. And we know that discriminatory speech also makes use of common insidious stereotypes, conceivably generating such bypass effects. The harms resulting from discriminatory speech are covert, indirect, and hard to spot. But, I contend, this gives us sufficient grounds seriously to doubt the claim that substantive free speech interests mitigate the harms of discriminatory speech— especially once we take a diachronic perspective on social relations rather than a time-slice approach that simply looks at the influence of individual expressions. In other words, although free expression supposedly fosters the development and exercise of autonomous agency (Dworkin 1981; Mill 1974; Scanlon 1972; Yong 2011), the effects of discriminatory speech on epistemic autonomy render this view highly questionable. To drive the point further, consider one of the most well-known autonomy defenses of free speech from Thomas Scanlon (1972). (The literature on autonomy defenses of free speech is too extensive to review here in full. For a comprehensive outline, see Brison 2008.) Scanlon considers certain acts of expression that generate harms, but where the harms (in his view) do *not* justify restricting those expressions. These are harms to an individual from having acquired false beliefs due to some acts of expression and harms resulting from subsequent actions performed on the basis those expressions (where the expression leads an agent falsely to believe that some action was worth performing). Scanlon defends the protection of such expressions grounded in autonomous, rational agency. The relevant sense of autonomy that Scanlon employs is as follows:

> a person must see himself as sovereign in deciding what to believe and in weighing competing reasons for action. He must apply to these tasks his own canons of rationality, and must recognize the need to defend his beliefs and decisions in accordance with these canons . . . [An autonomous person cannot accept] without independent consideration the judgment of others as to what he should believe or what he should do.
>
> (1972, 215–16)

The basic idea is this: *qua* autonomous agent, I should not accept without due consideration and reflection others' judgments and acts of expression. If I fail to act as autonomy requires of me and consequently come to form false beliefs, the harms that I incur from having such false beliefs do not justify restricting the speech that lead me to form those beliefs. After all, I should not have accepted the judgment and speech of others without rational deliberation.

Scanlon's autonomy conception trades on intellectual self-trust, insofar as subjects should be epistemically sovereign and self-determining. However, Scanlon fails to consider the circumstances of autonomy that are highlighted by relational autonomy conceptions.[5] We can clearly see the role of self-trust in McLeod and Sherwin's characterization of what autonomy involves:

> to be motivated to exercise her own choices, the agent must trust . . . her capacity to choose effectively . . . [which] involves having good decision-making skills and also being situated to choose well . . . [and] her ability to act on the decisions she makes . . . the judgements she makes that underlie her choices . . . Judgements that are relevant to her autonomy are, for example, her judgements about the trustworthiness of her own decision-making skills.
>
> (2000, 263–64)

Pretheoretically, I agree with Scanlon that if some acts of expression cause their hearers to form false beliefs, so much the worse for those hearers—they should have been more epistemically vigilant. But, I also maintain, unconscious influences pervert the capacities noted by McLeod and Sherwin in ways that undermine autonomy defenses of discriminatory speech. For instance, consider newspaper reporting that proclaims: "Romas exploit the welfare system." In Scanlon's story, we should not accept this act of expression without independent consideration of the facts, how the article was written, where it was published, and so on. Nonetheless, if we have the tendency to interpret negative, striking generic statements in essentializing ways, the situation may be much more worrisome than simply forming false beliefs about individual cases. We may come to form false essentializing beliefs about *groups*, like (roughly) Roma people are dishonest benefit cheats by nature. Furthermore, because the operations of unconscious influences are epistemically nontransparent to us and because the formation of essentialist generics tends to bypass rational cognitive processes, false essentialist beliefs are not readily revisable. Think back to the troubling phenomenon of confirmation bias (the tendency to gather and remember data selectively and in ways that confirm our previously held views). Again, if speech expounds discriminatory views about Roma people on the basis of which we draw generalizations about their "natural moral character," and if these generalizations turn on unconsciously held social essentialist beliefs about the Roma as a group, our rational independent reflection may simply confirm our beliefs in a selective manner. We literally find in the world evidence that supports our prior beliefs and fail to uncover evidence to the contrary—critical reflection bypasses counter-evidence and thus hinders epistemic autonomy by perverting intellectual self-trust. In a sense, those capacities needed for epistemic autonomy are rendered dysfunctional, where this does not obviously run counter to Zagzebski's quality of epistemic conscientiousness.

Scanlon later modifies his position in a way that appears to take these worries seriously. He considers subliminal messages from advertisements and concludes that such messages do interfere with autonomy in producing beliefs and desires that audiences have no control over. Subsequently, audiences have a positive autonomy interest in being free from manipulation (Scanlon 1978–9, 527). However, this qualification does not go far enough. After all, social manipulation akin to subliminal advertisement is not the chief cause of implicit bias, stereotype threat, and essentializing generics (although they conceivably hinge on the same cognitive processes). Instead, common public stereotypes that are part of ordinary processes of everyday life are to blame. The worry for liberals should not only be how to deal with intentional manipulation by advertisers or political regimes. Rather, the worry should be how to deal with those deleterious aspects of everyday life that generate insidious automatic associations we unconsciously harbor, that are not under our direct rational control to be revised, and that significantly influence our behavior. If we are to mitigate the harms of discriminatory speech, we need to rethink how the perilous effects of ordinary widespread prejudicial expressions can be undermined in order to avoid bypassing effects that hinder epistemic autonomy.

Finally, consider epistemic conscientiousness again. Discriminatory messages conceivably influence our interpretations of others in ways that hamper virtuous epistemic agency, but they have self-directed effects to this end too. Stereotype threat seemingly undercuts our ability to be epistemically self-determining, conscientious subjects: in interfering with our ability to perform certain cognitive tasks, it undermines our ability to function conscientiously. After all, following McLeod and Sherwin, being able to exercise autonomy requires trust in one's capacity to choose effectively and act on the decisions made. Otherwise, we lose faith in our own decision-making powers—but this is precisely what stereotype threat does. Moreover, stereotype threat can make comprehending our loss of intellectual self-trust impossible: we fail to understand why in some situations we come to experience anxiety, elevated heart rate, and our minds going "blank." We may see those instances as personal failings, rather than as phenomena that trade on broader structural patterns of group-based inequalities. This sort of insecurity erodes intellectual self-trust by undermining confidence in one's "own" reasons and deliberation, which are hallmarks of epistemic autonomy. Just think back to Mill's deliberative capacities that supposedly can only develop and be exercised in free societies "observation to see, reasoning and judgement to foresee, activity to gather materials for decision, discrimination to decide, and . . . firmness and self-control to hold his deliberate decision" (Mill 1974, 139). Coming to develop these abilities and being able to exercise them are precisely undermined by negative stereotypical messages that confirmation bias (as discussed earlier) and stereotype threat trade on. And if I am right that discriminatory speech is one mechanism keeping these phenomena alive, it contributes to unjust situational distrust in our epistemic competencies.

In upholding stereotypes that undergird unconscious influences, discriminatory speech can erode and pervert self-trust. If self-trust is demanded by and necessary for free speech interests typically appealed to, like advancing knowledge-seeking practices and ensuring democratic functioning, discriminatory speech undermines justifications for its permissibility. Let me clarify: free speech surely fosters some people's intellectual self-trust in a healthy manner. So, I am not claiming that free speech has no value whatsoever. But much depends on the position one antecedently occupies in a social structure and how much social power one possesses. Free speech tends not to benefit those who are frequently and persistently negatively stereotyped. So, if my argument here is right, free speech protections that permit discriminatory speech may foster the epistemic *authority* of some at the expense of the epistemic *autonomy* of others—namely, of those who are persistently stereotyped in negative ways. And so, the supposed benefits of discriminatory speech are woefully misconceived in prevalent liberal views.

5. What's a Liberal (or Anyone) to Do?

In this chapter, I have argued that discriminatory speech can "wound" epistemic autonomy in serious ways, given its connection to unconscious attitudes. Consequently, liberal justifications to protect nonhateful and nonvilifying prejudicial expressions must consider such subtle forces much more carefully. I do not disagree with liberals like Brink that hate speech is harmful in generating social exclusion and unduly reduced credibility and that such speech should be legally regulable. Nonetheless, prevalent negatively stereotyping speech may generate much more widespread and covert patterns of epistemic harms that hamper intellectual self-trust than overt hate speech—a situation that we should find deeply worrying.

In response, one might be tempted to recommend the cultivation of some epistemic virtues in order to undercut the vicious manner in which discriminatory speech hampers epistemic autonomy (for more on epistemic virtues and vices, see Battaly 2017; Turri, Alfano, and Greco 2017). Epistemic vices make us bad thinkers, and the epistemic self-distrust generated by discriminatory speech is seemingly one such vice. Heather Battaly distinguishes three types of epistemic vice. First, vices may produce false beliefs, thus involving "effects-vice." Second, certain cognitive character traits (like closed-mindedness or intellectual arrogance) are exemplary of "responsibilist-vice": It is a vice over which agents have cognitive control, and if the agent does not work towards exercising such control, they will be blameworthy. Third, epistemic vice may involve bad epistemic motives like "motives to believe whatever is easiest, or whatever preserves the status quo, or whatever makes one feel good, instead of motives for truth, knowledge, and understanding" (Battaly 2017, 224)—thus involving "personalist-vice." With these in mind, unconscious attitudes generated by discriminatory speech certainly involve effects-vice, but not so obviously the latter two. The unconscious attitudes outlined earlier bypass rational reflection in being automatic and nontransparent to subjects. As discussed, epistemic subjects may genuinely believe themselves to have reflected on some evidence in the right way. But due to social essentialist beliefs and confirmation bias, rational reflection merely confirms their prior biased views. So subjects are not readily able to exercise cognitive control, and their epistemic agency is not simply a reflection of epistemically vicious motivation.

Because effect-vice is clearly present in the ways in which discriminatory speech can hinder epistemic autonomy, what would the requisite corrective virtue look like? For Zagzebski, the relevant virtues seemingly arise out of subjects' epistemic conscientiousness. However, the discussion earlier raised doubts about the viability of this move. The same goes for virtue-reliabilism, the claim that epistemic virtues are reliable epistemic dispositions that produce fewer false beliefs and more true ones. Although this seems to undercut effect-vice, the concerns I have discussed in this chapter raise doubts about whether we have such epistemic virtues at our disposal to begin with (as Zagzebski put it) in standard cases. The ubiquity of unconscious influences suggests instead that precisely in standard cases, epistemic dispositions may be deeply unreliable. What we need then is some form of virtue-responsibilism, whereby epistemic agents work to shape their cognitive traits in ways that render those traits more reliable (Montmarquet 1992). Epistemically autonomous agency involves taking responsibility and working towards undermining the influence of unconscious attitudes. I find this idea attractive, but we should not endorse it too quickly. A subject may genuinely work toward taking epistemic responsibility and shaping their epistemic faculties in virtuous ways but fail to hit the mark given the intransparency of implicit attitudes. Given how difficult it is to mitigate the influence of stereotypes without social structural change, we might after all wish to advance some legal interventions in order to undermine the influence of discriminatory speech. Let me consider this option next.

Sarah Sorial (2015) has recently discussed hate speech that is seen as a legitimate form of political or academic speech—speech that I call "discriminatory." Her diagnosis of what goes wrong with such speech hinges on legal institutions committing category mistakes: some prejudicial speech has an air of respectability due to which such speech is miscategorized as legitimate political or scientific speech, when it should be seen for what it is—vilifying incitement to hatred and discrimination. Sorial hence argues that we should extend the legal notion of *incitement* to cover prejudicial speech that is sophisticated enough to appear political or academic. In this way, we can prevent such speech from being misclassified as permissible, and legally regulating such speech would perform two important functions. First, it would serve "an expressive function in signalling to affected groups that the institutions of the society do not endorse or in any way validate the views that are being expressed" and second, "legal regulation plays an important educative function in signalling to hate speakers that the society finds these speech acts unacceptable" (Sorial 2015, 320). I agree that legal regulations would serve these functions, but I am unconvinced that these are the remedies we should advance with respect to everyday discriminatory speech. As noted, much of such speech comes in the guise of scientific speech (one of Brink's examples is a sociology professor who in print endorses genetic explanations of black male crime rates [2001, 134]). Even though this speech enforces problematic attitudes, outlawing it seems too drastic. After all, Mill claimed (and rightly so) that some suppressed opinions have turned out to be correct, and censoring discriminatory assertions of purported facts problematically assumes infallibility. Moreover, even Sorial admits that only a small subset of discriminatory speech could be legally proscribed in this manner—by way of example, she notes purportedly academic debates that have been widely discredited, like Holocaust denial (2015, 322). Sorial's legal remedy would be ineffective in leaving much of everyday discriminatory speech untouched.[6]

We might instead take action against the influence of implicit attitudes and subsequent behavior. Although it is not enough to be made aware of counter-stereotypical exemplars in the abstract, being exposed to concrete positive counter-stereotypical individuals can act as debiasing agents and offer effective interventions against the influence of implicit attitudes. For instance, looking at a picture of Martin Luther King Jr. before taking a race IAT can reduce implicit racial bias, at least momentarily (Saul 2012, 259; see also Kang and Banaji 2006). Some research also suggests that we can prevent stereotype activation with certain egalitarian goals. Having such goals is not enough; rather, with sufficient practice and over time one can develop and foster a strong associative link between the goal to be egalitarian and a specific target grouping. Having habitually engaged in preventing problematic stereotype activation, one may be able to activate egalitarian goals without needing conscious control and thus inhibiting the stereotype activation. Over time, if one consistently and frequently inhibits the activation of problematic stereotypes, one may also concurrently develop and use new associations that are consistent with one's egalitarian beliefs and may cause one's cognitive representations actually to change. So, one strategy suggested by social psychologists is to "continually and frequently negate specific associations with social categories—to just say 'NO' to stereotyping" (Kawakami et al. 2000, 885). This alone is unlikely to solve the problem. We can further undermine unconscious influences by being more vigilant about our subtle behaviors when interacting with others and by educating people about implicit unconscious influences—we can engage in what social psychologists call "unconsciousness raising" (Jost et al. 2009, 56). These sorts of interventions can conceivably sever the link between discriminatory speech and prejudicial implicit attitudes, if the two sustain one another.

In short, even though we have good grounds to censor vilifying hate speech, countering discriminatory speech is more an issue of social policy and education that helps foster epistemically virtuous agency. Moreover, new social policies and educational programs are consistent with central liberal values. The prevalent liberal remedy against "bad" speech is more of "better" speech. But, as should be clear by now, this proposal can be far too simplistic and naïve, given how speech affects us

(Nielsen 2012). For one thing, facts about human cognition demonstrate that the liberal presumption of a self-regulating "marketplace of ideas" is deeply flawed. This ignores and obscures how social power relations shape intellectual self-trust, which is a central ingredient of epistemic autonomy that determines how well (or badly) we function in "the marketplace." Nonetheless, there is something to this strategy. Leslie (2017) has suggested that one way to undermine our essentializing tendencies is to avoid using labeling nouns: instead of talking about "Muslims," it helps to talk about "people who follow Islam." Hurley also argues that certain harmful bypass effects generated by violence in the media might be mitigated by a certain kind of "good" educational speech. Specifically, the speech must persuade people "on the basis of scientific evidence that their behavior is actually . . . subject to such automatic direct imitative influences, including toward violence, so that they can take steps to guard against such influences" (Hurley 2004, 187–8). This is an attractive idea. It accords with social psychologists' plea for more unconsciousness raising in order to erect safeguards against the influence of implicit attitudes. After all, if stereotype activation serves a cognitive function, so does stereotype control—we just have to tap into the right function in order to further egalitarian goals (Moskowitz and Li 2011). I would think that the strategy of unconsciousness raising is one that liberals would also be happy with. It fits the idea that "better" speech can undermine "bad" speech without buying into a woefully simplistic picture of how epistemically autonomous agency works. And so, this kind of educational approach should help us safeguard self-trust: we can enable the realization of virtue-responsibilism by creating background conditions that provide epistemic subjects better ways to act in epistemically responsible ways, to work towards undermining the influence of unconscious attitudes, and to uphold deeply held liberal convictions.[7]

Notes

1. Although Holroyd defines implicit bias in wholly negative terms, such bias can also be positive. For instance, one might have automatic cognitive or affective associations between the concept of G and some *positive* property P or stereotypical trait T, due to which one overestimates or overvalues the abilities of G-group members.

2. We can also think about implicit bias in terms of schemas (Valian 1999): we use various schemas as cognitive tools to categorize the world around us, which renders our environment and experiences intelligible to us. To illustrate: we have gender and professional schemas that encode common stereotypes about women, men, and practitioners of certain professions. It is conceivable that the male gender schema coincides with the general philosopher schema and that this partly explains why women in professional settings are often automatically assumed to be part of the administrative staff or to occupy junior positions: the woman and philosopher schemas clash (Haslanger 2009). Tamar Gendler's (2008) notion of *alief* provides another way to think about implicit bias. Aliefs are mental states distinct from beliefs and desires. They

are associative, automatic, arational, antecedent to other cognitive attitudes, affect laden, and action generating. Social distancing provides a plausible example of an alief in action. An example would be someone unconsciously holding on to their handbag more tightly when entering an elevator with a black male despite self-proclaimed egalitarian beliefs. Such instinctual behavior seemingly demonstrates an activated associative, automatic, affect-laden mental state ("black male, thief, danger!"), which is action generating (one holds onto the bag more tightly).

3. Of course, subjects with anti-black implicit bias may also be explicitly biased. But I am here focusing on cases where the subjects self-report holding egalitarian views, condemn racial discrimination, and do not show an anti-black bias on explicit bias measures.

4. The examples are from *What Is It Like to Be a Woman in Philosophy Blog*, http://beingawomaninphilosophy.wordpress.com. They are titled "Why Should We Hire a Woman," "On Trying to be Heard," and "Assessment of Participation," respectively.

5. Scanlon's position also conflicts with social psychological evidence about how human cognition works. However, I won't consider this point here. For more, see Hurley (2004).

6. In rejecting Sorial's view, we can further see why hate and discriminatory speech should be distinguished: we have *prima facie* good reasons legally to regulate the former, but these reasons do not extend to the latter. Our effective responses to these types of speech come apart, and running the two together unhelpfully obscures this point.

7. I have presented earlier versions of this chapter at various conferences and seminars at the Universities of Stirling, Sheffield, Oxford, Graz, Manchester, Cologne, Innsbruck, Tübingen, Bielefeld, Amsterdam, and Eindhoven. I am very grateful to all those present for their insightful comments and constructive advice on how to develop the chapter further. A particular thanks goes to Katherine Dormandy for her detailed, interesting, and extremely helpful comments on earlier drafts of this chapter; thanks also to an anonymous referee from Routledge.

References

Antony, Louise. 2012. "Different Voices or Perfect Storm: Why Are There So Few Women in Philosophy?" *Journal of Social Philosophy* 43: 227–55.

Battaly, Heather. 2017 "Testimonial Injustice, Epistemic Vice, and Virtue Epistemology." In *The Routledge Handbook of Epistemic Injustice*, edited by Ian James Kidd, Jose Medina, and Gaile Pohlhaus Jr., New York: Routledge.

Beeghly, Erin. 2015. "What Is a Stereotype? What Is Stereotyping?" *Hypatia*, 30(4): 675–91.

Bertrand, Marianne, and Sendhil Mullainathan. 2004. "Are Emily and Greg More Employable Than Lakisha and Jamal? A Field Experiment on Labor Market Discrimination." *The American Economic Review* 94: 991–1013.

Blascovich, Jim, Steven Spencer, Dianne Quinn, and Claude Steele. 2001 "African Americans and High Blood Pressure: The Role of Stereotype Threat." *Psychological Science* 12: 225–29.

Blum, Lawrence. 2004. "Stereotypes and Stereotyping: A Moral Analysis." *Philosophical Papers* 33: 251–89.

Brink, David. 2001. "Millian Principles, Freedom of Expression, and Hate Speech." *Legal Theory* 7: 119–57.

Brison, Susanne. 2008. "The Autonomy Defence of Free Speech." *Ethics* 108: 312–39.

Dotson, Kristie. 2011. "Tracking Epistemic Violence, Tracking Practices of Silencing." *Hypatia* 26(2, Spring): 236–57.

———. 2014. "Conceptualizing Epistemic Oppression." *Social Epistemology* 28(2): 115–38.

Dworkin, Ronald. 1981. "Is There a Right to Pornography?" *Oxford Journal of Legal Studies* 1: 177–212.

Fish, Stanley. 1993. *There's No Such Thing as Free Speech: And It's a Good Thing, Too: And It's a Good Thing, Too.* New York: Oxford University Press.

Fricker, Elizabeth. 2016. "Doing (Better) What Comes Naturally: Zagzebski on Rationality and Epistemic Self-Trust." *Episteme* 13(2): 151–66.

Fricker, Miranda. 2007. *Epistemic Injustice.* Oxford: Oxford University Press.

Gates Jr, Henry Louis. 1993. "Let Them Talk." *The New Republic* September 20: 37–48.

Gendler, Tamar Szabo. 2008. "Alief and Belief." *Journal of Philosophy* 105: 634–63.

Hall, Kim Q. 2017. "Queer Epistemology and Epistemic Injustice." In *The Routledge Handbook of Epistemic Injustice*, edited by Ian James Kidd, Jose Medina, and Gaile Pohlhaus Jr. New York: Routledge.

Haslanger, Sally. 2009. "Changing the Ideology and Culture of Philosophy: Not by Reason (Alone)." *Hypatia* 23: 210–23.

Holroyd, Jules. 2012. "Responsibility for Implicit Bias." *Journal of Social Philosophy* 43: 274–306.

Hurley, Susan. 2004. "Imitation, Media Violence, and Freedom of Speech." *Philosophical Studies* 117: 165–218.

Jones, Karen. 2012. "The Politics of Intellectual Self-Trust." *Social Epistemology* 26(2): 237–51.

Jost, John, Laurie A. Rudman, Irene V. Blair, Dana R. Carney, Nilanjana Dasgupta, Jack Glaser, and Curtis D. Hardin. 2009. "The Existence of Implicit Bias Is Beyond Reasonable Doubt: A Refutation of Ideological and Methodological Objections and Executive Summary of Ten Studies That No Manager Should Ignore." *Research in Organizational Behavior* 29: 39–69.

Kang, Jerry. and Mahzarin R. Banaji. 2006. "Fair Measures: A Behavioral Realist Revision of 'Affirmative Action.'" *California Law Review* 94: 1063–18.

Kawakami, Kerry, Jasper Moll, Sander Hermsen, John F. Dovidio, and Abby Russin. 2000. "Just Say No (to Stereotyping): Effects of Training in the Negation of Stereotypic Associations on Stereotype Activation." *Journal of Personality and Social Psychology* 78: 871–88.

Kelly, Daniel. and Erica Roedder. 2008. "Racial Cognition and the Ethics of Implicit Bias." *Philosophy Compass* 3: 522–40.

Kidd, Ian James, Jose Medina, and Gaile Pohlhaus Jr. (Eds.) (2017). *The Routledge Handbook of Epistemic Injustice.* New York: Routledge.

Leslie, Sarah-Jane. 2008. "Generics: Cognition and Acquisition." *Philosophical Review* 117: 1–47.

———. 2017. "The Original Sin of Cognition: Fear, Prejudice, and Generalization." *The Journal of Philosophy* 114: 393–421.

McKinnon, Rachel. 2017 "Allies Behaving Badly: Gaslighting as Epistemic Injustice." In *The Routledge Handbook of Epistemic Injustice*, edited by Ian James Kidd, Jose Medina, and Gale Pohlhaus Jr. New York: Routledge.

McLeod, Carolyn, and Susan Sherwin. 2000. "Relational Autonomy, Self-Trust, and Health Care for Patients Who Are Oppressed." In *Relational Autonomy: Feminist Perspectives on Automony, Agency, and the Social Self*, edited by Catriona Mackenzie and Natalie Stoljar, 259–279. New York: Oxford University Press.

Medina, Jose. 2017. "Varieties of Hermeneutical Injustice." In *The Routledge Handbook of Epistemic Injustice*, edited by Ian James Kidd, Jose Medina, and Gaile Pohlhaus Jr., 41–52. New York: Routledge.

Meiklejohn, Alexander. 1965. *Political Freedom: The Constitutional Powers of the People*. Oxford: Oxford University Press.

Mill, John Stuart. 1974. *On Liberty*. London: Penguin.

Montmarquet, James. 1992. Epistemic Virtue and Doxastic Responsibility. *American Philosophical Quarterly* 29(4): 331–41.

Moskowitz, Gordon B., and Peizhong Li. 2011. "Egalitarian Goals Trigger Stereotype Inhibition." *Journal of Experimental Social Psychology* 47: 103–16.

Nickerson, Raymond S. 1998. "Confirmation Bias: A Ubiquitous Phenomenon in Many Guises." *Review of General Psychology* 2: 175–220.

Nielsen, Laura Beth. 2012. "Power in Public: Reactions, Responses, and Resistance to Offensive Public Speech." In *Speech and Harm*, edited by Ishan Maitra and Mary Kate McGowan, 148–73. Oxford: Oxford University Press.

Raz, Joseph. 1991. "Free Expression and Personal Identification." *Oxford Journal of Legal Studies* 11: 303–24.

Rooth, Dan-Olof. 2007. "Implicit Discrimination in Hiring: Real World Evidence." *IZA Discussion Paper No. 2764*, available at SSRN: http://ssrn.com/abstract=984432. Accessed March 24, 2018.

Rowe, Mary. 2008. "Micro-Affirmations and Micro-Inequities." *Journal of the International Ombudsman Association* 1: 45–48.

Rudman, Laurie A., and Richard D. Ashmore. 2007. "Discrimination and the Implicit Association Test." *Group Processes & Intergroup Relations* 10: 359–72.

Saul, Jennifer. 2012. "Ranking Exercises in Philosophy and Implicit Bias." *Journal of Social Philosophy* 43: 256–73.

Scanlon, Thomas. 1972. "A Theory of Freedom of Expression." *Philosophy & Public Affairs* 1: 204–26.

———. 1978–9. "Freedom of Expression and Categories of Expression." *University of Pittsburgh Law Review* 40: 519–27.

Sorial, Sarah. 2015. "Hate Speech and Distorted Communication: Rethinking the Limits of Incitement." *Law and Philosophy* 34: 299–324.

Spencer, Steven J., Claude M. Steele, and Diane M. Quinn. 2009. "Stereotype Threat and Women's Math Performance." *Journal of Experimental Social Psychology* 35: 4–28.

Steele, Claude M. 1997. "A Threat in the Air: How Stereotypes Shape Intellectual Identity and Performance." *American Psychologist* 52: 613–29.

Steele, Claude M. and Joshua Aronson. 1995. "Stereotype Threat and the Intellectual Test Performance of African Americans." *Journal of Personality and Social Psychology* 69: 797–811.

Sunstein, Cass R. 1992. "Free Speech Now." *The University of Chicago Law Review* 59: 255–316.

Turri, John, Mark Alfano, and John Greco. 2017. "Virtue Epistemology." In *The Stanford Encyclopedia of Philosophy* (Winter 2017 Edition), edited by

Edward N. Zalta. URL = <https://plato.stanford.edu/archives/win2017/entries/epistemology-virtue/>.

Uhlmann, Eric Luis, and Geoffrey L. Cohen. 2007. "'I Think It, Therefore It's True': Effects of Self-Perceived Objectivity on Hiring Discrimination." *Organizational Behavior and Human Decision Processes* 104: 207–23.

Valian, Virginia. 1999. *Why So Slow? The Advancement of Women.* Cambridge, MA: MIT Press.

Zagzebski, Linda T. 2012. *Epistemic Authority: A Theory of Trust, Authority, and Autonomy in Belief.* Oxford: Oxford University Press.

Yong, Caleb. 2011. "Does Freedom of Speech Include Hate Speech?" *Res Publica* 17: 385–403.

Contributors

Katherine Dormandy (Institute for Christian Philosophy and Digital Science Center, University of Innsbruck) works on epistemology, the philosophy of trust, and the philosophy of religion.

Elizabeth Fricker (Magdalen College, University of Oxford; and Notre Dame University) works on the philosophy of mind, the philosophy of language, and epistemology, especially the epistemology of testimony.

Heidi Grasswick (Middlebury College) works on feminist philosophy, epistemology, environmental philosophy, and issues of science and society.

John Greco (Georgetown University) works on epistemology, focusing especially on knowledge, skepticism, and virtue epistemology.

Jesper Kallestrup (University of Copenhagen) works on epistemology, particularly social epistemology, the philosophy of mind, and the philosophy of language.

Arnon Keren (University of Haifa) works on epistemology and the philosophy of trust. He focuses especially on social and political epistemology and the epistemology of science.

Benjamin McCraw (University of South Carolina Upstate) works on epistemology, especially virtue epistemology, and the philosophy of religion.

Mari Mikkola (Sommerville College, University of Oxford) works on feminist philosophy, including feminist issues in the philosophy of language and ontology.

Thomas W. Simpson (Blavatnik School of Government and Wadham College, University of Oxford) works on the philosophy of trust and on issues at the intersection of technology and security.

Alessandra Tanesini (Cardiff University) works at the intersection of ethics, the philosophy of language, and epistemology, focusing particularly on epistemic vice, silencing, prejudice, and ignorance.

Index

Printed in the United States
by Baker & Taylor Publisher Services